Prototype to Product

Alan Cohen

Beijing · Boston · Farnham · Sebastopol · Tokyo

Prototype to Product

by Alan Cohen

Printed in the United States of America.

Published by O'Reilly Media, Inc., 1005 Gravenstein Highway North, Sebastopol, CA 95472.

O'Reilly books may be purchased for educational, business, or sales promotional use. Online editions are also available for most titles (*http://safaribooksonline.com*). For more information, contact our corporate/institutional sales department: 800-998-9938 or *corporate@oreilly.com*.

Editors: Mike Loukides and Meghan Blanchette
Production Editor: Melanie Yarbrough
Copyeditor: Gillian McGarvey
Proofreader: James Fraleigh

Indexer: Wendy Catalano
Interior Designer: David Futato
Cover Designer: Karen Montgomery
Illustrator: Rebecca Demarest and Melanie Yarbrough

August 2015:   First Edition

Revision History for the First Edition

2015-08-10:   First Release

See *http://oreilly.com/catalog/errata.csp?isbn=9781449362294* for release details.

978-1-449-36229-4

[LSI]

Dedicated to the men and women who participated in the greatest engineering project in modern times, the US effort to land people on the Moon by 1969, back when I was a tot. It was an enormous project, it was rapid, and it worked; I am in awe. And, in particular, to Dan Hunter, a member of the NASA team from projects Mercury through Apollo, and a fine friend. Dan was the coolest guy I've ever known (http://bit.ly/ 1eSGJfa), and is sorely missed by many.

Table of Contents

Preface

Product development is the magic that turns circuitry, software, and materials into a product. The word *magic* here is not used by accident; for most folks who design and develop technology as a hobby or even professionally, creating new products is unknown territory—or magic—as far as they are concerned.

This book's goal is to help the reader to gain a better understanding of the "stuff" that happens along the way when great *ideas* metamorphose into great products—in particular, intelligent products with embedded electronics and software—and to supply strategies and tactics to make that "stuff" go more smoothly.

Creating an intelligent product is complex. It's much more than developing some circuits and software, plopping 'em into a case, and hanging out a "for sale" sign. Numerous activities must be performed to turn components and cool prototypes into a desirable, usable, reliable, manufacturable, and salable product.

In part because of the complexity, new product development is a risky undertaking. According to Harvard Business School Professor Clay Christensen, 95% of new products fail. A number of factors play into this high rate, but I've experienced firsthand that many or most new product failures stem from failures in the product development process.

For example, notoriously, most product development efforts end up being late and over budget—often by substantial amounts of 25% or more. Even a 100% overrun is not unusual. Sometimes overruns are caused by simply not estimating effort correctly. They often also come from surprise re-development efforts, which become necessary because product needs were not well known early in development. In my experience, these overruns and surprise re-development efforts often stem from flaws in the productization process, not from the fundamental technology involved.

Budget and timeline surprises in the product development process are usually quite avoidable. They normally come from a lack of knowledge about the process, particularly the failure to realistically plan for productization "stuff" early in the process, and a lack of complete and clear requirements.

But proper product development is about more than avoiding overruns; it can also play a key role in refining a great concept into a desirable product. For example, when the Palm Pilot was released in 1996, most folks in the technology biz *knew* that the concept of a computer-in-your-pocket was a dog. A slew of pocketable computers had come and gone, including Apple's Newton, and all had bombed. Couldn't be done.

The Palm Pilot proved the technology biz wrong: it was a raging success. Much of this success came from a smart product development process where the right kinds of testing were done at the right stage of the process to ensure that the technology Palm developed solved real problems and fit into real lives (we'll touch on the Palm's process a bit more in Chapter 5). While Palm failed to stay ahead of its competition, its paradigm for pocket computing lives on in today's smart phones, which look much more like a Palm Pilot than, say, an Apple Newton.

Many books do a great job of covering *parts* of product development, such as electronic design, software development, industrial design, usability, and mechanical engineering. There are a handful of books that cover product development at a *business* level, reviewing topics ranging from market research, to financial forecasting, to team dynamics. But very little has been written that covers, holistically, the nuts and bolts of efficiently moving from good ideas to manufactured product, and that's what I hope to do with this book.

Why I Wrote This Book

Even though my formal education and background is in electronics and software, my role in projects is generally as a *systems engineer*.

Systems engineering is a field that considers how the different parts of complex systems work together to accomplish their purpose. We're commonly the technology people who lead the effort to produce an actual product, rather than circuits and software in an enclosure. In a sense, we could be called *holistic engineers*, because we're responsible for the whole system working together as a product.

At the purely technical level, we systems engineers lead the effort to plan, at a high level, how a desired set of properties (requirements) can be broken down into subsystems that efficiently get the job done, with an eye toward minimizing time, cost, and risk. Once these subsystems and their functionality are defined, we try to make sure that development continues to proceed in a way that enables all of the subsystems to work together in the final product.

On a day-to-day basis, my job normally consists of bringing together groups of people with varying backgrounds, and helping us all to move toward our common goal. I typically work with engineers from various disciplines (electronics, software, mechanical, etc.), industrial designers, management, marketing, sales, regulatory, finance, manufacturing, and others. Successful product development requires all of these folks to work together effectively for months or years, and systems engineers (along with project managers, whose role we sometimes fill) tend to act as the lubricant to keep things running smoothly.

There are two tasks that tend to catalyze these disparate groups of people into a cohesive team:

1. Helping team members to understand a bit about what other members do in their jobs. This helps members work together more efficiently because they have a deeper understanding of one another's needs. It also builds respect: *everyone else's* job seems easy compared to ours until we understand some of the many details of what they do.

2. Helping to ensure that the cracks are filled between the knowledge and skills that various technology folks bring to the party. Technologists tend to know their own field but are much less likely to know how to work with others on "distributed" problems. For example, suppose that we're looking at how to prevent an LCD display from overheating in a product with a small, watertight enclosure. Electronics, mechanical, software, industrial design, and perhaps supply chain will likely all need to work together to find the optimal solution out of the many possible ones.

Ultimately, both of these top-level tasks are about education, and much of what I do in my role is to educate others. And over time, I've found that there are a number of topics that I get to teach about pretty regularly to technologists and non-technologists alike.

The *why* behind this book is simple and selfish: it's a book I've wished I had for years. Something that I can hand to team members, customers, and vendors to review those topics that come up time and time again, and to do it in an orderly and comprehensive way that gets everyone on the same page, and hopefully the *right* page.

Who Should Read This Book?

This book is intended to be useful to a wide range of folks who want (or need) to learn about the product development process:

- Makers thinking about taking the next step and creating a product, perhaps funded by a crowdfunding campaign on Kickstarter, Indiegogo, or similar.

- Members of product development teams who want to understand how they can work better within their team to build better products, have fewer surprises, and have more fun.

- Management types looking to understand the total scope of product development so they can do a better job of planning costs and timelines, and of supporting the technology folks.

Not all chapters will be useful to all of these groups: for example, management types probably won't want to read about the details of power path management in Chapter 9. However, when these folks have questions such as "Why does developing something as simple as the circuitry and firmware to power a device and charge its battery takes months of work?", they can skim that chapter and get a feel for the surprising number of problems to be solved in that seemingly simple task.

Who Might Be Disappointed by This Book?

You might not get much out of this book if:

- You're a technology expert in the category of product development and you're not interested in (or already know) how other technology experts contribute to product development

- You're looking for in-depth information on a particular aspect of product development, particularly mechanical engineering or design (e.g., industrial design, user experience design, etc.)

What's Covered? What's Not?

This book will not teach you how to be an engineer, industrial designer, or project manager. There are plenty of other good sources of information on how to do those things, as evidenced by the many people who do those jobs well. Rather, this book is intended to help people to do their jobs *better* within the context of developing a product.

It's a practical book, based on my own real-world experience and the information that's proven most useful to most people involved in product development. The topics covered address the issues that I see come up in virtually every product development effort, and which are often addressed nonoptimally.

My first goal is to give a sense of the many different activities involved in getting a product to market, and how those activities can be fitted together in a way that optimizes efforts and increases chances of a successful outcome.

My second goal is to fill in the gaps between the information that's easily available from other sources and the knowledge needed to have a smooth journey through development. This gap varies tremendously by activity. For example, there's (more than) plenty of good material available in the world that generally covers Linux as an operating system, so there's no need for me to add to that general knowledge.

But there are little bits of knowledge that are tougher to find about using Linux in an embedded system, or that designers/developers sometimes don't even think to look for until they get stung by problems, and these are the types of things that are covered here. Examples include dealing with boot loaders, and the challenges in keeping device drivers functional with new kernel releases; these are types of details that I cover to fill in the gaps. The book's slant is decidedly toward electronics and software. Mechanical engineering and design (e.g., industrial design and user experience design) are not covered in as much depth in part because I have less background in these fields, and in part because these have tended to not cause big technical headaches in the product development efforts that I've been involved with. That's not to say that these are not important: great design and mechanical engineering can add tremendous value to products.

How This Book Is Organized

The book is organized into three basic sections.

The first section is a single-chapter introduction that hopefully sets the stage by revealing the single most important rule of product development, and discussing the 11 most common pitfalls that derail development efforts.

The second section, Chapter 2 through Chapter 6, discusses the development process for intelligent products from a nifty product idea all the way through to manufacturing.

The third section, Chapter 7 through Chapter 12, contains deeper dives into specific development topics that are of particular importance in the development of intelligent products, and which I've found that other available sources do not cover well, cohesively, or at the right depth.

A Word on Nomenclature

Design, designer, develop, and *developer* are words with ambiguous meanings, yet they're impossible to avoid in a book such as this.

For example, a person who figures out how to create a new circuit to accomplish a task is usually called an electronics *designer.* Yet a person who does the same kind of task, but in software, is usually called a software *developer.* The folks who specify a product's aesthetics are also referred to broadly as *designers.*

The context in which these words are used usually clarifies the intended meaning, but not always. For example, if I pick up a product and ask "Who designed this?", I could be asking for the identity of only the people who created the aesthetics, or the identities of the technical folks as well.

To avoid confusion, we'll try to stick to the following conventions:

- Creating software will be referred to as *software development,* which is performed by *software developers*
- Creating electronics will be referred to as *electronics design,* which is performed by *electronics designers*
- Creating mechanical parts will be referred to as *mechanical design,* which is performed by *mechanical designers*

- Developing aesthetics (look and feel, and usability) will be referred to generically as *industrial design*, which is performed by *industrial designers*

- The totality of the work done prior to development (i.e., creating the recipe that we'll hand to manufacturing) will be referred to as *design/development*, which is performed by *designers/developers*

A WORD ON JARGON

Technology tends to cultivate jargon—words, phrases, and acronyms only understood by a small group of cognoscenti. Because the following are true:

- Product development encompasses several fields of engineering and design, and often multiple specialized technologies

- The jargon itself can be fuzzily defined; i.e., a bit of jargon can mean different things to different people (it happens all the time!)

Things can seem like a Tower of Babel on occasion. For this reason, I've generally tried to stay away from specialized jargon, although I do define commonly used bits (and point out when their meanings are not always agreed upon). In some instances, this might lead to using expressions that are a little different than what an expert in that field might use, in an attempt to keep concepts clear.

As I'll emphasize throughout the book, the most important thing when it comes to jargon is that all team members use the same words in the same way. If you're not sure how to use a word, or hear a word that's unfamiliar, it's best to be up front about it with everyone who's part of the conversation and make sure that everyone's on the same page. I've been doing this stuff for a while, and still rarely have conversations in which I don't ask *"What exactly do you mean by X?"*

Keeping in Touch

One of the wonderful things about publishing these days is that books can be updated fairly regularly. If anything is unclear or there are additional topics that you'd like to see in this book, please let me know via email at proto2product@cobelle.org. Or visit my blog (*http://www.alcohen.com*), which I'll try to keep updated with material relevant to this book.

Safari® Books Online

Safari Books Online (http://safaribooksonline.com) is an on-demand digital library that delivers expert content (*http://www.safaribooksonline.com/content*) in both book and video form from the world's leading authors in technology and business. Technology professionals, software developers, web designers, and business and creative professionals use Safari Books Online as their primary resource for research, problem solving, learning, and certification training.

Safari Books Online offers a range of product mixes (*http://www.safaribooksonline.com/subscriptions*) and pricing programs for organizations (*http://www.safaribooksonline.com/organizations-teams*), government agencies (*http://www.safaribooksonline.com/government*), and individuals (*http://www.safaribooksonline.com/individuals*). Subscribers have access to thousands of books, training videos, and prepublication manuscripts in one fully searchable database from publishers like O'Reilly Media, Prentice Hall Professional, Addison-Wesley Professional, Microsoft Press, Sams, Que, Peachpit Press, Focal Press, Cisco Press, John Wiley & Sons, Syngress, Morgan Kaufmann, IBM Redbooks, Packt, Adobe Press, FT Press, Apress, Manning, New Riders, McGraw-Hill, Jones & Bartlett, Course Technology, and dozens more (*http://www.safaribooksonline.com/publishers*). For more information about Safari Books Online, please visit us online (*http://www.safaribooksonline.com/*).

How to Contact Us

Please address comments and questions concerning this book to the publisher:

O'Reilly Media, Inc.
1005 Gravenstein Highway North
Sebastopol, CA 95472
800-998-9938 (in the United States or Canada)
707-829-0515 (international or local)
707-829-0104 (fax)

We have a web page for this book, where we list errata, examples, and any additional information. You can access this page at http://bit.ly/prototype-to-product.

To comment or ask technical questions about this book, send email to bookquestions@oreilly.com.

For more information about our books, courses, conferences, and news, see our website at *http://www.oreilly.com.*

Find us on Facebook: *http://facebook.com/oreilly*

Follow us on Twitter: *http://twitter.com/oreillymedia*

Watch us on YouTube: *http://www.youtube.com/oreillymedia*

Acknowledgments

Ultimately, I owe a debt of gratitude to the many people who've taught me many things over my years of developing electronic products. The full list might double the size of this book yet still be incomplete, so I'll stick to those directly associated with this tome.

A huge thank you to...

The good people at O'Reilly, particularly to Mike Loukides, Meghan Blanchette, Gillian McGarvey, and Melanie Yarbrough, who gave me the opportunity to write this book and guided my coarse keyboard meanderings into something that looks like something, all with great patience.

My reviewers, who helped keep me honest and technically coherent: Alan Walsh (who also contributed photos), Bill Nett, Chuck Palmer, Johnson Ku (who also helped on MicroPed), Kipp Bradford, Liz Llewellyn, and Pete Scheidler (who also helped on MicroPed).

My MicroPed team: Erik Schofield, Evan Gelfand, and Jon Goldman (who also created the 3D drawings in Chapter 6).

Alec Chevalier at Liberty Engineering and Rich Breault of Lightspeed Manufacturing, for providing the opportunity to take manufacturing photos.

Adafruit, Digi-Key, Paul Boisseau at Pyramid Technical Consultants, SparkFun, SPEA, and WikiMedia for providing or otherwise being a conduit for photos.

And most of all, to Marian and Ben, who've put up with more than two years of my scratching this itch. I love you guys very, very dearly.

## CHAPTER 1

The 11 Deadly Sins of Product Development

THOMAS EDISON FAMOUSLY SAID THAT GENIUS IS "1% INSPIRATION, 99% perspiration," and his observation holds true for product development. Developing "genius-level" (or even mundane) products certainly requires inspiration, but the bulk of the effort is more like perspiration: work that benefits from insight and cleverness but is also largely about not screwing up. Things like ensuring that software doesn't leak memory and that the right capacitors are used to decouple power supplies. Dotting the i's and crossing the t's.

As we noted in the Preface, most product development efforts fail. It's been my observation that after detailed product design and development begins, failures are not usually due to a lack of inspiration (i.e., poor product ideas) but rather from mistakes made during the "perspiration" part. In other words, most product development failures are good product concepts that fail during the process of turning concept into product.

This chapter is a catalog of the most popular ways to wound or kill product development projects. Most efforts that get derailed do so by stumbling into one or more of a small set of fundamental traps that are easy to fall into—but also fairly avoidable. We'll briefly review these traps to give an overall feel for the hazards, but not dive into too much detail yet. As you'll see, much of the rest of this book provides details of strategies and tactics for avoiding them.

> **TIP** A note on organization: my goal is to point out the specific traps that projects run into most often, but these specific traps have base causes that are more fundamental and which should also be avoided. For example, two common traps (*new-feature-itis* and *not knowing when to quit polishing*) stem from the general fault of *perfectionism*. As an organizational construct, in this chapter I refer to the specific traps as *sins* and the more general negative impulses behind the sins as *vices*. And because sins are often fatal, I call them *deadly sins* to remind us of their degree of danger.

Before we get into specific vices and sins, let's start off with the fundamental principle that lies behind all of these, which is a basic truth that largely determines success or failure.

The Fundamental Principle of Product Development

It's often the case that complex subjects come from simple truths. For example, the Golden Rule (treat others the way you want to be treated) underpins much or most of religious law. In Physics, we only know of four fundamental forces, but those four forces appear to govern everything taking place in our universe, and have kept many scientists busy for many years filling an untold number of pages.

Similarly, there is a basic truth that applies to product development—really a Fundamental Principle: *surprises only get more expensive if discovered later.* Putting it another way: *product development is largely an exercise in uncovering surprises as soon as possible.*

My personal observation is that most of what determines product development success or failure springs from this Fundamental Principle, and much of the rest of this book consists of strategies and tactics for respecting it.

Happy surprises can happen, but surprises that arise during product development are almost always bad, generally along the lines of "You know that nifty power supply chip we're using in our design? It's being discontinued." Or, "It turns out that no vendor can actually mold the enclosure we designed."

Surprises usually lead to change; e.g., redesigning to use a new power supply chip or to have a moldable enclosure. And change is always easier at the beginning of the development cycle than it is later on.

Many analyses have been performed to find the cost of implementing a product change (either fixing a problem or adding a new feature) versus the stage of the product's life cycle at which the change is initiated. The results all look something like Figure 1-1, which shows the relative average cost of a fixing an error versus the phase in which the error was caught during development of a major commercial aircraft (taken from a NASA paper (*http://1.usa.gov/1VkPqjN*)). The figure's dashed blue line shows an exponential curve fitted to the data. As you can see, once development starts in earnest, the cost of making a change typically rises exponentially as development proceeds.

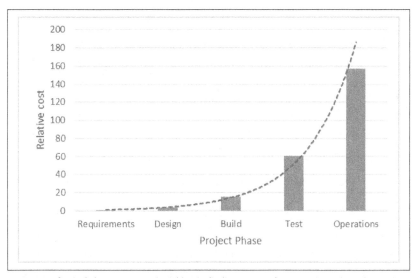

FIGURE 1-1. Cost of changing a product (due to finding an error) versus time when change is made

To illustrate why this happens, let's consider the hypothetical case of a robot that performs surgery. The robot's software will have algorithms that determine the correct ways to drive various actuators (motors) based on the procedure it's performing. But sometimes algorithms or actuators fail; for example, in certain cases, an algorithm might determine the wrong angle for a scalpel to move, or an actuator might malfunction and not move in the way that's expected.

To reduce the possibility of injury if such a failure occurs, it might be good to add an independent system of hardware and software to monitor the robot's actions; in effect, a second set of eyes to make sure that all is working as expected and call for help or halt the procedure if something's going wrong.

Table 1-1 lays out the relative cost of adding this safety monitoring system, depending on where in the product's life cycle we initiate the effort:

TABLE 1-1. Cost of making changes versus time

Scenario #	When Added	Cost Of Adding
1	During initial specification	Just the cost of implementing and testing the feature.
2	While initial development is underway	Scenario #1, plus updating already-existing documentation and revising cost estimates; possible redesign of other hardware and code that interfaces with the new hardware and code
3	After discovering a problem during "final" test, but before product is released.	Scenario #2, plus possibly significant increases in time and cost due to need for an additional cycle of development and testing
4	After product is released and in use	Scenario #3, plus getting new hardware/software into the field (deployment); possible retrofit of existing customer hardware and software; possible revisions to marketing literature; potential customer frustration because device might be unavailable during upgrade. Wounded company reputation. If devices actually failed in the field because of lack of added safety system, then potential injury, anger, and litigation.

It's obvious that the earlier we realize the need for a safety monitor, the less it will ultimately cost to implement. What would have been a relatively modest effort if captured during the specification stage can become very expensive (and make headline news) if realized only after field failures. Discovering surprises late doesn't just make things a little worse—it makes things exponentially worse.

All changes to products follow the same basic pattern of getting much more expensive with time. An electronics component becoming unavailable after design is completed, for example, requires that we redesign and retest circuitry, and possibly some related mechanical and software changes to address differences in component size, heating, communications protocols, and so forth. Rather than getting surprised down the line, it's far better to do some legwork during design/development to ensure that we select components that are likely to be available for a long time.

The conundrum here is that no matter how hard we try, we're unlikely to discover all problems through specification and design—some problems will always rear their heads during build, test, and even (ugh!) once our product is shipping. As we'll discuss throughout the book (and particularly in Chapter 5 and Chapter 6), many of these types of issues can be resolved through thoughtful iteration back and forth between the various development phases, particularly for those parts of our product that are most likely to generate surprises for us.

Now, with the Fundamental Principle for context, let's begin our exploration of specific vices and sins that commonly undermine product development.

The Vice of Laziness

Given the Fundamental Principle, it's pretty obvious that putting off until tomorrow what we can do today is a bad idea, particularly for activities that are likely to uncover surprises. One of the most direct, concrete, and common examples of this vice applies to testing.

DEADLY SIN #1: PUTTING OFF "SERIOUS" TESTING UNTIL THE END OF DEVELOPMENT

An obvious decision that delays unearthing surprises (and making appropriate changes) is holding off on serious testing until after prototypes are largely developed. By serious testing, I mean the higher-level testing that looks at how usable the product is for our customers (sometimes called *product validation*), and at how the hardware, software, and mechanical subsystems work together, often called *integration test* and *system test*. When neophytes think about product development, they tend to think in terms of "first we'll build it, then we'll do all of that high-level testing stuff." This seems reasonable at first glance, particularly since some high-level testing can be difficult to do until all the pieces are put together. However, this approach delays our finding issues and making needed changes, sometimes *big* changes, which can be costly.

For example, suppose that usability testing on our "finished" product determines that our audible alert is too wimpy; when designing it, we didn't realize that users are often in a different room from the product when an important alert sounds, and the audio system we've designed (speaker and associated circuitry) doesn't have enough oomph to get the job done. The fix will likely involve switching to a new speaker and/or updating electronics. Switching to a new speaker might require changing the enclosure size, which can be a substantial effort requiring expensive tooling changes that take weeks. Changing circuitry means new PC boards, which also involve nontrivial costs and lead times. So our "finished" product is (surprise!) not actually very finished, and we find ourselves with weeks or months of unexpected work and delay.

In this instance, much time and expense could have been avoided by early testing of the proposed audio system in real-world settings well before we created enclosure designs, simply to confirm that it can do the job. Or even before going through the exercise of designing our audio system, we could:

- Review competing products to see how loud their audio is; if they all have really loud speakers, there might be a reason
- Visit some sites where our product might be used
- Observe users going about their daily business, perhaps pretending to use our device that doesn't yet exist
- Simulate an audible alert using a smart phone and amplified speaker
- Try some different tones and tone volumes (measured with a decibel meter) to see what's truly needed to catch a user's attention

Usability isn't the only area where early testing helps: early rigorous testing of circuits, software, and mechanicals also ultimately lowers costs and shortens the path through product development.

Note that developing effective tests is not a trivial exercise. More information on this topic can be found in Chapter 5 and Chapter 6.

The Vice of Assumption

When developing a product, we're *assuming* that we know the features needed to achieve market success. Until the product goes on sale and the orders pour in (or don't), we don't know for sure if our assumptions are good or bad.

There are two common deadly sins that fall under the vice of assumption:

1. Assuming that we know what users want

2. Assuming that users know what they want

Let's take a short look at each.

DEADLY SIN #2: ASSUMING THAT WE KNOW WHAT USERS WANT IN A PRODUCT

It's pretty typical for product designers/developers to assume that we know which product features are needed to make the average customer happy. After all, *I* know what *I* want—how could other people want something so much different?

This might not be a surprise, but if you're reading this book, you're pretty unusual. The odds are that you're seriously interested in technology, so much so that you want to learn more about how to develop products. Being enthusiastic about technology is a great thing: without people like you and me, humanity would still be hunting and gathering. But, for better or worse, most people are not technophiles like us. To put this in perspective, as I write this, the best-selling "serious technology" book on Amazon is the *Raspberry Pi User Guide*, ranked at #583 on Amazon. Fully 582 books on Amazon are currently selling better than the best-selling "serious" technology book.

Among other things, we technologists tend to be atypical when it comes to what we want in a product. We like things that have more features and more customizations, and that we can fiddle with for hours. "Normal" folks are mostly interested in getting the job done with a tool that's effective and attractive. Figure 1-2 illustrates the difference between the tools that these two groups might favor.

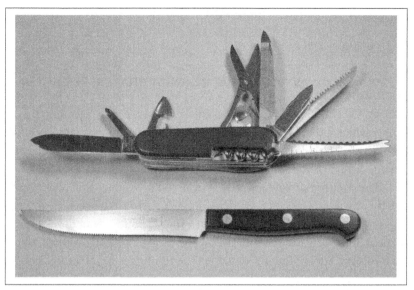

FIGURE 1-2. What technologists typically want (top) versus what "normal" people tend to want (bottom)

So while we have a reasonable shot at knowing what other technologists want in a product, we're rarely very good at knowing what nontechnologists want, because their wiring is a bit different than ours. There are exceptions to this rule, most famously Apple products, which were developed based on what Steve Jobs and those around him thought their customers wanted. This worked, I think, for two reasons. First, their most notable successes were in developing products for categories that basically didn't yet exist. Prior to the iPod, asking customers what they wanted in a new MP3 player would not have yielded great information, because almost nobody had one. Second, Steve Jobs was Steve Jobs—a rare person with a vision for human-centered design and great aesthetics, and who understood engineering and engineers.

Assuming that we don't have a Steve Jobs working for us, there are tactics that we can use that are helpful for discovering what the world's non-techies want, but they're not as simple as one might think. This leads us to our next sin.

DEADLY SIN #3: ASSUMING THAT USERS KNOW WHAT THEY WANT IN A PRODUCT

Well, if we techies don't know what typical users want, surely we can just ask them what they want. They should know, right? Sadly, it turns out that users often don't know what they want. They only know what they *think* they want.

My dad, a retired market researcher, says in his First Law of Market Research: "If you ask consumers what they want, you'll get an answer. That answer might be right or it might be wrong, and you'd better find that out!"

I never understood Dad's First Law until I started developing products. It was then that I found that it's entirely possible to deliver what customers have asked for without satisfying their needs. This leads to nifty conversations like this:

User: "I can't use this!"

Developer: "But it meets all of the requirements we agreed to!"

User: "But now that I'm actually using it, I'm finding that it doesn't really get the job done."

Very frustrating and disappointing to everyone involved!

It turns out that what potential users see in their minds' eyes when envisioning a new product might be very different than the reality once a product is in their hands. Finding out what users really want is largely a function of letting them try things out (features, prototypes, etc.) and seeing if they're happy; it follows that we should start giving them things to try as early as possible instead of waiting until the end and praying that our assumptions (or theirs) were correct.

The Vice of Fuzziness

Fuzziness, or lack of specificity in planning a product and its development effort, is a major source of project failure. There are two big challenges introduced by fuzziness:

1. Stakeholders have differing expectations as to what will be developed.

2. It's rather difficult (OK, fairly impossible) to estimate the resources and time needed to complete development if we don't know the product's details, at least to some degree.

There are three deadly sins that fall under fuzziness:

1. Not having detailed requirements

2. Not having a detailed project plan

3. Not knowing who's responsible for accomplishing what during development

Let's examine these in a little detail.

DEADLY SIN #4: LACK OF COMPREHENSIVE REQUIREMENTS

Product requirements are how we communicate our understanding of what a product will be. They ensure that all stakeholders have the same understanding of a product's important attributes. When creating product requirements, we must work to capture everything that's important to our customers and us; otherwise, the results might be different from what we wanted.

Here's an example of the kind of thing that happens often: Marketing writes requirements along the lines of:

- The product shall have four wheels
- The product shall have a motor
- The product shall be steerable
- The product shall have an engine
- The product's engine shall use gasoline
- The product shall be legally operable on all roads in the US, and in countries A, B, and C
- The product shall be attractive

Being practical sorts who are attracted to quirky designs, the designers/developers go off and build something that they believe will efficiently meet these requirements. Unfortunately, Marketing had a somewhat different product in mind. The difference in the visions of these two groups is captured in Figure 1-3.

FIGURE 1-3. What Marketing wanted, versus the interpretation by designers/developers

Great interdepartmental entertainment ensues, rarely with a happy ending.

While this auto example is obviously an exaggeration, it underscores the basic issue: requirements are how we make sure that everyone's on the same page with regard to what's being produced. We must be careful to include everything that's important to us or we'll end up with (usually unwelcome) surprises. In this car example, some additional requirements from Marketing would have helped create a better outcome; for example, "greater than 80% of Target Market shall agree that the adjective 'sexy' applies to the product's design."

In addition to stakeholders being surprised/disappointed with the final product, a lack of comprehensive requirements also guarantees feature creep, another deadly sin (covered later), since we won't have all the features defined before we develop our product. If we decide on and implement features as we develop, there can be a lot of reengineering of interdependent systems to accommodate our newly discovered needs.

DEADLY SIN #5: LACK OF A GOOD PROJECT PLAN
Project plans! I can hear your groans as I write this.

For most of us, creating a project plan is as much fun as filling out a tax return, and following them is as enjoyable as getting a root canal.

Adding insult to injury, product plans are also inevitably inaccurate at laying out how we'll proceed on a project: things rarely go according to plan for very long. Even on projects that are relatively straightforward, stuff happens, and early assumptions turn out to be wrong. Key people leave the project temporarily or for good. A component vendor decides to withdraw from the US market. Designs turn out to be way trickier than anticipated. Management suddenly decides that the product is needed three months earlier. And so forth.

Project plans are painful and inaccurate. So why bother?

General Dwight Eisenhower got it right: *"Plans are worthless, but planning is everything."* While specific plans are inevitably broken by the end of the first week of work, spending substantial time and effort in the planning process is indispensable. I find project planning to be as un-fun as anyone, yet I'm very uncomfortable working on projects of any significant size without a very detailed project plan, usually with hundreds of defined tasks, including resources (who, what), person-hours (how long), costs, and dependencies assigned to each line item. While I absolutely know that much of the plan will turn out to be wrong, having a detailed plan at least gives me a prayer of being in the right ballpark for estimates of time and effort, and tracking progress (are things going faster or slower than we thought?).

Creating a detailed project plan forces us to think through issues that are easy to miss when we're planning by taking a rough stab. It helps us to remember important details we'd otherwise forget about ("Oh yeah, we should add a week for preliminary FCC certification testing and subsequent design tweaks before final prototype build."), and to understand dependencies ("Looking at the plan, it seems we have a problem! It'll take 10 weeks to have molds made, which pushes production until way after the trade show where Marketing wants to announce we're on sale. We'd better figure out how to get the molds made in a shorter time, or how to be ready to start making the molds earlier.")

 ## TIP Oh, that's why it took so long!

Ever notice that most projects take twice as long and cost twice as much as projected? As compared to quick guesstimates, I've found that detailed initial project plans end up showing that projects will cost twice as much and take twice as long— and are much closer to being accurate. Being off by a factor of two is always big trouble and in a small company or startup with limited resources, it can spell doom.

DEADLY SIN #6: NOT ASSIGNING RESPONSIBILITY

Simply creating a task on a project plan with a due date and a budget doesn't ensure that the task actually gets done by its due date and within budget. One common problem is that when the time comes to start a task, we find that a detail's been missed in the project plan that prevents work from starting on time, and we now have a surprise that impacts budget and timeline. Then once a task begins, there can be confusion around who gets what part done, and how multiple parts come together.

Adding an owner to each task greatly increases the odds of success. The task owner is not necessarily the person who accomplishes the task, but rather is responsible for timeline, budget, communications, and making sure the thing gets done. This helps in a couple of ways, which we'll explore here.

First, it guards against gaps in the project plan. One of the ubiquitous imperfections in project plans is simply missing some tasks and details:

there's a task that needs to get done but we forgot to add it to the project plan. Throughout the project, each task's owner can (and should) keep an eye on that task's prerequisites to make sure that everything's falling into place for things to happen according to schedule and budget. Any issues discovered that could affect either schedule or budget should be communicated and worked out, and the project plan updated as necessary.

Second, there's no confusion over who will make sure that a task gets completed—no "Wait, I thought *you* were going to take care of that!"

For example, when performing testing to gain FCC certification, it's necessary (or at least extremely useful) to have a special test software application running in our product that sequences the hardware into different states, one by one, so the radio frequency (RF) emissions in each state can be measured with little or no futzing around with the product. The task to create this test application is easy to forget about, and is sometimes missing from the initial project plan. If we forget about the test app until we show up to our testing appointment, we might not be able to complete testing in time, and the project will slip a few days or even weeks while an app gets slapped together and we find the next available time slot for testing.

By contrast, if someone owns the FCC testing task, there's a good opportunity to avoid the slip. For example, if Sue knows that she's responsible for that task, she can call the test house months ahead of the scheduled testing, and ask what she needs to do to ensure that testing starts on the right date and proceeds smoothly. Among other things, the test house will tell her that they want a test app. "A-ha! We forgot that on the project plan!", Sue tells the project manager, and the task is added, resources assigned, and the project plan updated.

The Vice of Cluelessness

The vice of cluelessness covers those things we have no inkling of. Since we don't even know what to worry about, we're in a state of blissful unawareness until we smack into a problem late in the game, sometimes even after product release, which can require product changes.

A great mitigation for cluelessness is to rely on people with experience in the technical and nontechnical areas that our product touches, either as employees or advisors. They've walked the walk and know where the potholes are located.

Another mitigation is to read this book: one of my primary goals in writing it is to flag issues that tend to blindside product development efforts.

Of course, there are all manner of things that we can potentially not know about. But there's one area that tends to cause the most trouble, which I'll touch on next: keeping governments happy.

DEADLY SIN #7: NOT ADDRESSING REGULATIONS

The classic and common example of getting stung by cluelessness is smacking into government regulations after design is complete, such as finding out that US Customs is holding up shipments to Europe because our product doesn't meet relevant EU requirements, or merely because our CE mark labeling isn't being displayed correctly.

Generally speaking, for most products sold in significant quantity, there are really two basic classes of requirements that our product must address. There are the "standard" requirements based on business needs, which are driven by what customers want (e.g., functionality, size, color) and by what our business wants (e.g., profitability, design language consistent with other devices we sell).

There's also a second class of requirements (regulations, standards, and certifications) that are imposed upon us by external parties such as governments and sometimes others such as insurers. This second class of requirements, which we'll call *imposed requirements*, generally addresses product safety but can also address product performance (e.g., a measuring cup sold in Europe might need to prove it achieves a certain level of accuracy). We'll cover this class of requirements in some detail in Chapter 10.

These imposed requirements are easily missed during product development as many people aren't even aware they exist. And even if we're generally aware they exist, it can be a challenge to find the ones that apply to our specific product: different governments have different regulations, and different parts of the government have different regulations (hopefully not conflicting ones!). In some industries, products have standards effectively imposed on them by insurers and other groups, and these standards might require some research to identify.

Because unawareness of imposed requirements is so pervasive, and navigating them is not a trivial undertaking, this area gets a chapter of its own later on. But for now, some examples of common imposed requirements include:

- Federal Communications Commission (FCC) regulations that must be met by virtually all electronic devices marketed in the US. In fact, most electronic devices must be tested and certified by a third-party lab prior to being sold in the US. Other countries have similar regulations.

- Underwriters Laboratories (UL) marking. UL is an independent body that tests all sorts of devices to see if they are safe. Many devices that pose potential safety issues carry a UL Mark, earned by having UL test the product and the factory according to specific standards to ensure the product is safe for consumers. UL listing is quasi-voluntary: no law requires it, but some laws might be satisfied by it, and certain customers and insurers might require it.

- Conformité Européenne (CE) marking. CE marking indicates that a product conforms to all relevant European Union (EU) regulations. Different types of products must conform to different sets of regulations. By law, the vast majority of products sold within the EU must have CE marking.

Figure 1-4 shows the product labeling associated with these three imposed requirements. Note, however, that most imposed requirements do not have associated product markings.

FIGURE 1-4. FCC, UL, and CE marks

The Vice of Perfectionism

Beyond the normal impulse that each of us has to do our job well, product development adds an extra incentive that pushes toward perfectionism: our work will be judged by many people, perhaps even millions in the case of successful consumer products. There's the opportunity for much glory and wealth if we get it right, and conversely much embarrassment and the loss of money if our product disappoints. These are high stakes, which can lead to mistakes. Let's take a look at some things that can go wrong when we become too obsessed with making the perfect product.

DEADLY SIN #8: THE SIN OF NEW-FEATURE-ITIS

New-feature-itis is the natural inclination to add cool new features as a project progresses. Obviously, this behavior directly violates the Fundamental Principle of Product Development, but this particular flavor of violation is worth reviewing because it illustrates some of the specific penalties we might pay.

"Hey! Wouldn't it be cool if the product had [fill in cool feature here]?" is probably the most critical—and most dangerous—exclamation in product development. Whether it's a positive or a negative is determined by how and when it's spoken.

At the very beginning of a product development effort, during requirements definition, "Wouldn't it be cool if..." is our best friend. At this stage, we're trying to get as many cool ideas on the table as we can. This is the time when we should talk to prospective users, research similar products, and perform other activities to develop a list of as many potential features as possible. Once we have this list, we'll ruthlessly cut it down to a "final" set of features (i.e., requirements) based on the value that each feature adds to the product versus the cost/risk of implementing that feature.

Once the requirements are locked down, we can create pretty good estimates for development timeline and budget, and get going with the fun part of development: making stuff.

As we know, adding new features once the requirements are locked down will obviously introduce additional time and cost to development. But beyond the obvious cost of "that's a cool idea; I can add that to the firmware in a week" (which often turns into several months), adding features can (and will) cause additional work in ways that aren't always obvious:

- New features can inadvertently break other features.

- New features often require changes to basic architecture, changes that can be kludgy because the new feature was not at all anticipated in the original architecture. As patches are added to support new functionality, the architecture can become brittle and easier to break.

- Test effort usually increases exponentially with the number of features that a product supports due to interrelationships between features. Adding a few little features might result in a lot of extra testing.

All told, feature creep is a major contributor to delays and cost overruns.

Steve Jobs had a great quote that applies:

"People think focus means saying yes to the thing you've got to focus on. But that's not what it means at all. It means saying no to the hundred other good ideas that there are. You have to pick carefully. I'm actually as proud of the things we haven't done as the things I have done. Innovation is saying no to 1,000 things."

It's best to pick a limited feature set at the start of a project, be skeptical about adding new features during development, and focus on making those few features work really, really well. Compared to implementing more features with less polish per feature, we'll get to market faster and cheaper, and most customers will like our product more.

DEADLY SIN #9: NOT KNOWING WHEN TO QUIT POLISHING

The longer we polish a stone, the smoother it will become. There comes a time when we should declare that the stone is smooth enough and move on.

Similarly, we can always make products more polished; it just takes more time and effort. There are always workflows that are a bit awkward, screen layouts that look a bit off, ways to squeeze another few minutes of battery life if we just tweak things a bit, and so forth.

But while we're spending that time and effort, other things are happening. End users are being deprived of a product that could be improving their lives, even if that product could be made a little better with a little more time. Budgets are being depleted, and revenues are not being generated. Competitors might be releasing products that will grab market share. Time is rarely our friend here.

So there comes a time when the product isn't perfect—it never is—but it's ready to release.

What about thoughts about how we can do things better? As long as our product sells well, we'll use those thoughts to make our next-generation product even better for our customers. In the case of software, there can be an opportunity to issue updates to a product that's already in the field.

That's not to say that we should release crummy products as soon as possible, at least not to regular paying customers. A crummy product might help as a stopgap in the short term, but it can also unacceptably damage our reputation or brand in the process. Finding the line between *good enough to ship* and *this might embarrass us* is rarely a trivial task; if it doesn't evoke some passion, anguish, and argument among the folks making this decision, then they're probably not doing it right.

(TIP) A little joke

Two guys are camping in the African Savanna when they spy a lion charging toward them from a distance. Frantically, one of the guys starts taking off his hiking boots and putting on his running shoes.

Surprised, the other man says, "What are you thinking? You can't outrun a lion!"

"I don't have to outrun the lion," said the man lacing up his running shoes, "I just have to outrun *you*."

Similarly, let's remember that we don't have to build the perfect product: just one that's good, that's more attractive to customers than the alternatives, and that supports our big-picture marketing strategy.

The Vice of Hubris

This vice has to do with believing that things will go according to plan.

It's easy (and important) to be confident at the start of the project. We have a detailed project plan in hand that looks reasonable and has been reviewed by a number of smart people; what can go wrong?

Here's my promise to you: we'll find out what can go wrong once development begins. Boy, will we find out. Any bubble of pride that we hold for our ideas and project plans at the start of a project will be punctured quickly once "real" design/development commences. We will fail early, we will fail often, and the measure of a successful effort lies largely in how failures are dealt with.

DEADLY SIN #10: NOT PLANNING TO FAIL

In Deadly Sin #5, I argued the importance of a creating a detailed project plan. Compared to gut feel and rough guesses, a detailed project plan at the start of development is a much better predictor of what our effort will look like. But even a carefully crafted detailed project plan will be wrong, and it will be optimistic, and this should be accommodated realistically.

We must plan to fail.

Since we're planning to deal with surprises, and since surprises are —by definition—unknown, it's impossible to know for sure how much effort they'll take to mitigate. In my experience, even detailed timelines and budgets prepared by highly experienced people should be padded by 20%–30% to account for the inevitable bad surprises. If the folks preparing the initial project plan are not very experienced, or there are seriously new technologies involved, it's easy for a project to end up 100% or more over budget.

Unfortunately, padding a project plan and budget is often easier said than done, particularly when presenting estimates to inexperienced managers: "You want to add 25% for I-don't-know-what?" In these instances, it's good to have a list of significant project risks on hand to demonstrate why we should plan for the unknown. The list will probably not be short, and reviewing the specific concerns is usually more persuasive than padding with a percentage that seems to be pulled out of thin air.

The Vice of Ego

This vice is about valuing customer desires less than our own. Other than "labors of love," successful products, and successful product development efforts, are about what *customers* want. It's not about what we personally want. Doing work in large amounts that we don't enjoy is no good, of course, so the trick is to bring together people who'll enjoy playing the roles that are needed to maximize customer satisfaction. Let's look at a common trade-off that's often made badly when *what we enjoy* competes with *what's best for the product and customer*.

DEADLY SIN #11: DEVELOPING TECHNOLOGY RATHER THAN DEVELOPING PRODUCTS

Most technologists, particularly product developers, love to create new stuff. We tend to think of our jobs in terms of developing new technology. But developing *technology* and developing *products* are different things (although they certainly overlap). In particular, when developing products, developing technology is largely optional. We can choose to create technology for our product, or in many cases we can choose to integrate existing technologies. If the product can be developed quicker/cheaper/ better by integrating existing technology (and it usually can be), then that's the way to go.

Think for a moment about Apple and Microsoft, two companies that have been extraordinarily successful at developing products. It could be argued that neither has developed revolutionary technology; they've only developed revolutionary products. Both Apple and Microsoft snagged from Xerox the concept of an operating system that uses windows and a mouse. Apple's current operating systems, Mac OS X and iOS, are both based on the open source FreeBSD. MS Windows originally ran on top of MS-DOS, which was originally QDOS licensed from Seattle Computer Products. Excel and Word started as knockoffs of Lotus 1-2-3 and Word-Perfect, respectively, to a greater or lesser degree. Apple's vaunted Siri was originally actually purchased from Siri, Inc. And so on.

Certainly, both Apple and Microsoft have plenty of resources to create new technology from scratch, and I'm sure they were tempted to do so in all these cases. What made Microsoft and Apple so successful, in large part, is that they focused on meeting the needs of their customers rather than on developing technology. They're quite content to purchase or otherwise adopt existing technologies if that's what will do the best job of getting great solutions to their customers.

To develop great products with reasonable effort, it's important to adopt the Apple/Microsoft mindset: "What's best for our customers?" And this mindset isn't unique to these two companies; it's ubiquitous across very successful companies that develop new products.

Final Thoughts

As mentioned in the Preface, only 1 in 20 new consumer products are a success. This chapter's been a rogues' gallery of some of the major gotchas, which in my experience can reliably turn fantastic product concepts into members of the failed 19-out-of-20.

The first step in winning the fight is to recognize the enemy, and I hope this chapter has served in this capacity. If you're new to product development, perhaps it's also served as an introduction to some of the higher-level issues that we face: product development is about great hardware and software, of course, but creating this hardware and software requires a good bit of planning, psychology, communications, compliance with regulations, and a host of details that we need to get right.

Of course, just knowing what can go wrong isn't enough: we also need to know how to avoid, fix, or at least mitigate the problems that can arise, which is the goal of most of the rest of this book. In future chapters, we'll be getting pointed and practical about charting the best way through the icebergs, so that our product has a much better shot at being one of the 1-in-20 product development successes.

Resources

This chapter's been about fundamental truths and common ways to fail. Here are a few books on that theme that have been helpful to me—perhaps they'll be useful to you as well:

- *The Lean Startup: How Today's Entrepreneurs Use Continuous Innovation to Create Radically Successful Businesses* by Eric Ries. The premise here is that we never quite know what will work when developing new products, so it's best to fail early and often, learning from each iteration of failure (and success) to move in a better direction.

- *The Mythical Man-Month: Essays on Software Engineering* by Frederick P. Brooks. A classic book published in 1975 but no less relevant today, it covers many of the basic truths of software development, most famously Brooks' Law: adding manpower to a late software project makes it later.

- *Systemantics: How Systems Work and Especially How They Fail* by John Gall. Great tongue-in-cheek coverage of what goes wrong when working with large systems, be they machinery or people. Older and out of print, but can be picked up used for short money.

Here's a fun (and basically-true) illustration (*https://www.webde sign.tm/swing.jpg*) of the misunderstandings that can crop up in product development.

## CHAPTER 2

Development Process Overview

SEVERAL CATEGORIES OF ACTIVITIES TAKE PLACE WHEN CREATING A NEW product, including:

- Dreaming up a cool idea
- Designing
- Building
- Testing
- Purchasing parts

Each of these categories, of course, consists of many tasks and sub-tasks. All of these activities will absolutely be performed between the start of development and the time when we have a successful product on the market. Our job is to see that they can get done in an orderly and efficient way.

For example, we can plan well for FCC Part 15 approval (required of virtually all electronic products sold in the US), testing prototypes as we go along to make sure the final product passes its test. Or we can wait until product development is complete and hope that our product passes its tests; if it doesn't, our product development isn't complete, and we might have to go back and do substantial redesign. Or we can wait until we get a letter from the FCC alleging that we're illegally selling uncerti-fied devices. Obviously, the first of these options has the lowest potential for bad outcomes.

The difference between successful and failed products is largely in knowing, at the project-wide level, what to do and when to it. In this chap-

ter, we'll review the general activities performed during product development and the sequence that often is the most efficient. Note that the
importance of sequencing cannot be overstated: following a reasonable
sequence throughout a project saves time, money, and aggravation, and
creates better odds of success.

Don't Panic!

You might be thinking, "But I'm just working on a small project—do I
really need to do all this stuff?" or "Hey, I've worked on big projects
before, and this is missing some steps!"

For folks who are working on products that are not super complex,
such as something with a button and a few LEDs, it might seem that this
chapter is overkill—and it probably is.

For those working on sophisticated projects, such as a new passenger
aircraft, it might seem a bit light. And it certainly is.

Mark Twain wrote that "History never repeats itself, but it does
rhyme." I think this is also true of successful product development
efforts, which tend to follow a certain basic flow no matter how large or
small they are. (The unsuccessful ones also follow certain patterns, as
presented in Chapter 1.).

There's no single right way to develop products, and every development effort is different for different reasons. Consider this chapter (and
the entire book) as a smorgasbord of ideas, and grab those ideas that
make sense for you and your project. While the basic concepts of *knowing
in advance what needs to get done* and *smart sequencing to minimize risks*
apply in all cases, the specifics of implementing these might vary significantly, particularly for very small or very large projects.

Product Development Life Cycle Overview

The activities that take place in bringing a new product to market naturally fall into four phases:

1. A cool idea

2. Planning

3. Design/Development

4. Manufacturing

Figure 2-1 shows a flowchart of these phases broken into more detail.

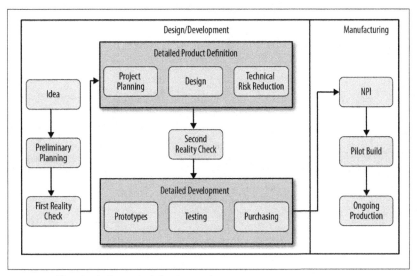

FIGURE 2-1. Flowchart of a product development process

Some of these steps are short, and some are longer. Some might take as little as a few minutes, such as in the case of some friends looking to build something cool to make a few bucks on Tindie (*https:// www.tindie.com/*), or many months or years in the case of large corporations building complex and/or high-risk devices. As mentioned earlier, some steps may be omitted as appropriate—each project (and project team) is different.

The flowchart in Figure 2-1 is used throughout this chapter as a map to remind us of where we are as we step though the process.

A Great Idea

A great idea for a product is the intersection of a *cool idea* and *a need that wants to be fulfilled.* My suspicion is that if you're reading an O'Reilly book, generating *cool ideas* is not a problem. The trickier parts for most of us are:

- Finding a real problem that can be solved by our cool ideas
- Fine-tuning the idea to best solve the problem

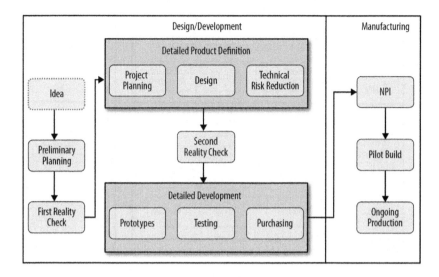

Note that not all successful products start with a cool product idea, at least not an *original* cool product idea. In some instances, successful projects are an exercise in simply copying what someone else has done and using an uncreative advantage to profit from it, such as a larger company using cheaper labor available due to their size so the product can sell for less, or using an existing distribution or sales network to reach more customers than a competitor can. In another scenario, someone else's cool idea that's previously met with commercial failure is repackaged in a new way that might make it successful. Actually, if you spend a little time thinking about the greatest successes in product development of the past few decades, you'll see that most of them fit into this latter category. It turns out that making cool ideas *work well* is even more challenging than coming up with the cool idea.

Preliminary Planning: Does This Make Sense?

Few things feel worse than spending substantial time on an effort that's not enjoyable, goes nowhere, and/or could have been better spent doing something else. As the popular expression goes, "Well, that's [fill in the amount of time] of my life that I'll never get back."

So that we can be smart about how we spend our hours, our first job once we have a cool idea is to do a reality check on whether it's something that we really want to pursue. The fundamental question we want to answer is, "Does this idea make any sense at all?" In other words, "Is there a reasonable possibility that the return will be greater than the effort?"

Return does not necessarily equal cash, but money is usually one important part of the equation. Since time is precious, at this point we'll spend as little time as possible to get a *quick* feel as to whether we're poking in the right direction.

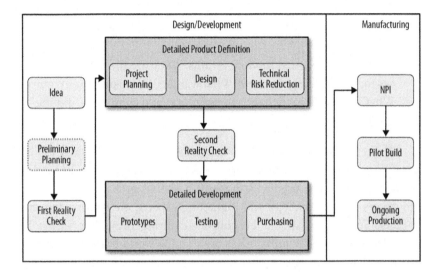

In a sense, the product's details begin to take shape even in the earliest parts of this feasibility planning because it helps to know what the product is (features and functionality) when guesstimating costs, markets, timelines, and so forth.

BALLPARKING

Before we spend a great deal of time with market research, detailed product plans, and other activities that we'll eventually want to do before committing to developing our idea, part of the preliminary planning process is to get some quick, rough answers to basic questions to see if we even have a prayer of success. If chances of success are slim to none, then we can quickly move on without wasting more of our time.

Questions that we'll want rough answers to include:

- What will our product do? What will it look like?

- How many people might want the product? How much might they pay for it?

- How much effort will be required to develop it?

- How much will it cost to manufacture and ship?

- What are some good ways to market and sell it?

- Have others tried to do this? Have they succeeded or failed? Why? Why is our idea or execution different/better?

- Who could participate in design, development, and perhaps also marketing and sales? What will they be looking for in return?

- Will we need external funding for this? What are the potential sources for any funding we need? What will they be looking for in return? What's the likelihood that these sources would commit to funding this effort?

This exercise can be as simple as sitting around a table and tossing ideas on a whiteboard with friends, family, and/or colleagues. But unless we're experts in our product's domain, it should probably involve brief interviews with technology and marketing experts, and prospective customers. Serendipity should be cultivated during these interviews: it's often the case that our initial ideas aren't quite world-beaters, but a little tweaking based on some new information might make a big difference.

While it's natural to focus on our potential product at this point, there's another important aspect that's required for success, which we'll consider next: what are the potential needs of the folks who'll help bring our product to market?

SETTING STAKEHOLDER GROUND RULES

The *ground rules* are the objectives of the project stakeholders, and these should be worked out during this preliminary planning phase so that we know how to keep everyone happy.

In the case of large companies, this includes an understanding of the resources that can be committed (people, money, etc.) and the return expected in exchange for investing resources (money, market share, prestige, experience with a new technology, etc.). There's usually a person or committee that weighs a potential product's costs versus benefits and decides whether to proceed or not.

On the other end of the spectrum, for smaller projects either done "on the side" and/or by companies that don't (yet) exist, there are similar expectations to be met by multiple founders looking to trade their time and/or money for some sort of return. This can be tricky: whereas a larger company typically has a single list of criteria that they expect a new project to meet, within a "seat-of-the-pants" effort each participant might have different expectations, along with different resources (time, money, expertise) they expect to invest. Keeping everyone happy can be a challenge.

In my experience, not understanding what each party is willing to invest and what they expect in return is a leading cause of projects that end in failure and hard feelings. Projects are a journey that usually lasts months or years. If the needs of team members, investors, and other stakeholders are not being met, then stakeholders will tend to become less helpful. And when they do, other stakeholders tend to become grumpy. So before starting any project, it's best to have a good understanding of what each stakeholder is looking to contribute and what they expect in return, and to set up some rules around how to move forward if those contributions need to change (someone has a baby, gets a better job offer, runs out of money, etc.).

Once we understand commitments and expectations, there are two strategies for fitting together the project with the team's needs: we can either adapt the project to the team or adapt the team to the project. In the case of projects that have a single contributor, the way forward is pretty clear: since (to paraphrase Frank Zappa) we are what we is, our best bet is to select a project that motivates us and to plan development so it meets our needs.

In the case of project teams larger than one, things can be more fluid: for example, we could pick a team based to a greater or lesser degree on what the project needs in total, and then plan the project development effort based on the needs and desires of team members.

First Reality Check

Most of our time in product development is spent on carefully growing lovely trees, but once in a while we need to pull back a bit and examine the forest: does the whole thing seem to hang together? At this point, all we have is a group of seedlings, but does it look like these seedlings have a reasonable shot of becoming a lush forest? Or are they already wilting?

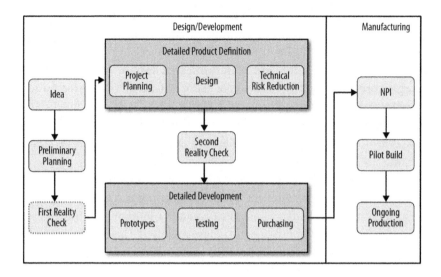

As we'll see in a bit, getting to the point where we're pretty confident in the technical and business success of a new product usually takes a fair bit of planning, certainly more than the surface scratching we've done so far. But before we do even that work, we should make a preliminary assessment as to whether we have a reasonable shot at success.

If the thing's obviously a loser, we can cut bait now and move on to more promising ideas. If we do decide that our concept has a good chance of success, in our next phase we'll go on to spend substantial effort filling in the details required to make a final decision on whether to go for it.

So given our first-order understanding of features, market, expenses, revenue, marketing, sales, and resources, does developing this product seem to make sense? Do the odds of success seem good, nonexistent, or somewhere in between? Does development seem like an adventure or a schlep? Can we keep stakeholders happy?

In many cases, we'll see obvious problems and it will be easy to decide to move on to something else. On the other hand, it's rare that a new product development is a slam-dunk. In fact, if we're positive that our idea is a winner, we're probably being dangerously optimistic. Optimism is best when tempered with a good dose of worry.

In most cases, there'll be a mixture of opportunities and dangers. How to decide? A venture capitalist once told me something that's helpful: "If I declared that every new idea was a loser and passed on investing,

I'd be right 80% or 90% of the time. I'd have an amazing track record of being right! But I'd never make any money, either."

Every new opportunity has a good bit of risk, so my suggestion is to look for big potential upside and risks that seem manageable.

If things look good and we decide to proceed, our next step is to create a detailed set of blueprints for developing our product.

Detailed Product Definition, a.k.a. Surprise Management

Developing a product of any sophistication is a big deal. For projects that go beyond a labor of love, the folks investing resources into the venture would like to have a pretty accurate idea of what they're building, and the time and cost to bring the product to market.

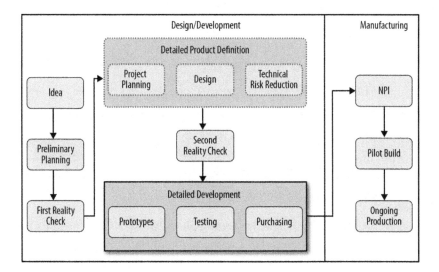

In our preliminary planning phase, we did a basic sniff test: does the product have a reasonable chance of success? In the detailed planning phase, we're looking to sharpen that preliminary planning exercise dramatically in order to cross out the unknowns. The overarching goal here is to make the project reasonably *predictable* so that we're confident of what we're building, and of the time and cost needed to bring it to market.

Boring can be good

In product development, surprises are rarely good. Detailed planning is about making the *product* exciting and the *development effort* as boring as possible.

Stated another way, the goal of detailed product definition is to minimize bad surprises. I sometimes think we should change the phrase *detailed planning* to *surprise management*; it sounds a lot less stuffy.

Whatever we call this phase, here's what we're looking to end up with:

- A fairly detailed definition of our product: how it will look and function.

- An in-depth plan of what needs to be done, when, and by whom. From this information, we can understand:

  — How much development will cost

  — How long development will take

  — The resources/expertise that we'll need to have available

- Solid financial models of how much our product will cost to build and sell.

- An understanding of the major technical and business risks (i.e., what don't we know that can burn us); even better, we'd like to minimize those risks before exiting this phase.

At the end of this detailed planning phase, we should have significant confidence that we know what the product and the project will look like moving forward.

Of course, detailed planning is difficult to do unless we have a pretty good idea of *what* we're building, so at least a substantial piece of the product (particularly specifications/requirements and design) is performed during this phase. We need specific design information before we can reasonably estimate what the job will take; for example, the effort and costs to develop and manufacture a plastic enclosure are a good bit different than that for a sheet-metal enclosure.

And what about the technical unknowns? If our product needs a USB 3.0 port, and nobody on our team has ever designed that circuitry before, we could take a guess at how long the port design and testing will take, but it's *easy* to be off by a factor of 10 or more on off-the-cuff guesses (USB is a particular culprit).

To narrow down the technical unknowns and thus increase predictability, technical risk reduction activities are usually run as part of this detailed planning phase.

Next, let's take a closer look at what goes into the product design and risk reduction activities.

PRODUCT DESIGN

As used in this book, *product design* is the science and art of creating specifications for how users will interact with a product. It includes color, size, ergonomics, screens, workflows, and virtually everything needed to describe how our product presents itself to the world.

> **TIP** *Design* and *development* are sometimes used interchangeably, and sometimes used to mean different things. *Product design* and *product development* are similarly ill-defined in practice. In this book, we'll normally use "design" to refer to the look, feel, and behavior of our product (i.e., what the customer experiences) rather than the creation of the magic inside the product that makes it look, feel, and behave the way it does. *Development* will generally refer to the entire process from idea through manufacturing, and more specifically (as *detailed development*) to the processes that implement the design (i.e., create the magic inside).

At this stage, the design will likely live as:

- 3D models carved from foam or printed on a 3D printer. These are useful for getting feedback from prospective users, and for helping the technology folks think about the mechanical and electrical challenges ahead. However, these usually don't have all the detail we need—or the right colors.

- 2D and 3D renderings on computer monitors that do have the right detail and colors. Less tactile, but great for visualizing what our product will look like.

- Use-case diagrams in flowcharts for each task a user can accomplish and each interaction step between user and device.

- Mockups of software screens that are displayed during the use-case diagram steps, which help the software folks understand and estimate their efforts.

- One or more requirements documents detailing anything important that the product must achieve. For example, "The product must run for one year before requiring a battery change."

Once we've defined the details of how our product appears to the world, we create a boundary around what our product needs to achieve, removing one important category of unknowns that can bite us later on. In reality, there will be design changes as we go along based on new information, but now we have an agreed-upon baseline.

The other big class of unknowns at this stage is typically around the technology needed to turn our design into reality. Next, we'll take a look at knocking these risks down to size.

TECHNICAL RISK REDUCTION

Technical risk reduction is all about turning big technology unknowns into smaller technology unknowns. Big unknowns are usually those things that haven't been done before by our team or (even more scary) haven't been done by anyone, ever. These are the kind of unknowns that can totally derail a project if they turn out to be far more challenging than anticipated or even impossible (e.g., we need to do something that violates the laws of physics as they're currently understood).

The best way to reduce risk related to a big unknown is to implement it, usually on a smaller scale, to demonstrate that it functions. The resulting design, often called a *proof of concept* or *proof of principle*, typically isn't the final design but rather the simplest implementation that gives us confidence around knowing what the final design process will require.

For example, suppose we're designing a battery-powered glass-break sensor for a home alarm system. The sensor communicates its status wirelessly to a base station, which might be several rooms away. Such a product, of course, requires a very reliable RF communications link. Marketing wants our sensors to be the tiniest on the market. Since the battery's the largest part of the circuit, *tiny sensor* means *tiny battery*, and *tiny battery* means *tiny power draw*, and the circuitry that draws the most power will be for RF communications. So for our purposes, *tiny sensor* is synonymous with *tiny-power RF circuit*.

Nobody on our team has ever designed an RF circuit with these characteristics, so how do we estimate the effort to implement such a thing? We could simply guess that a tiny battery will work out because, you know, high tech does amazing things these days so why not? But what if we start design/development using a tiny battery, then find out that this requires us to develop very complex circuitry and software that takes way more time and money than we anticipated (and have available)? Or what if we find out we simply can't use a tiny battery at all because it just can't supply enough energy to run the sensor for very long? Big surprises are what happens.

To gain some confidence that our plans are reasonable, we'll probably want to build an actual RF circuit powered by a tiny battery and test it carefully, either in a bunch of homes (to check RF connectivity in a variety of environments) or in some sort of lab mockup that simulates the worst RF conditions that we want to accommodate.

Instead of building and testing the actual circuit, in theory we could review for RF chip datasheets to find one that offers the low power consumption that we're seeking. That might work, but as philosopher Alfred Korzybski wrote, "The map is not the territory." What works on paper might not work in real life. It happens all the time. It's usually best not to take a chance.

By retiring potentially derailing uncertainties early on, we'll have a lot more confidence around our estimates of the scope of the development effort. At the end of this detailed planning process, if we're smart and diligent at the effort, we'll have about as good a guess as we can get as to what we're creating, and how much it will cost to develop, manufacture, and sell.

Second Reality Check: Go or No Go?

Before we make a commitment to the substantial effort and cost of development, it's time to take another bird's-eye look at the entirety of what we now understand to see if things look good. Do the numbers work? Do we still feel good about the road ahead and the odds of reaching our destination? *Should we do this?*

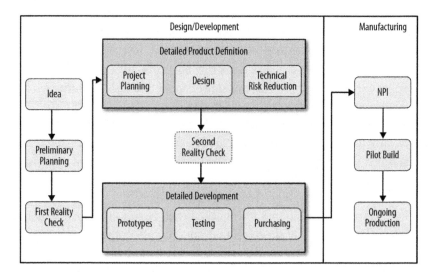

At this point, based on all of our planning, we should now have a pretty good idea of:

- What our product will do
- What it will look like
- What effort will be needed to create it
- What it will cost to manufacture
- How we'll market and sell it
- The potential return for our efforts

These will all be guesses, but they will be far better guesses than we had when the product concept first popped into our heads. In my experience, even these detailed estimates will be low when it comes to cost and time: the real numbers will usually end up 20%–30% worse than even careful estimates by experienced estimators, because surprises happen no matter how hard we try to prevent them. So it's best to pad cost and time estimates up to give ourselves room for error.

Making the decision on whether to move forward should be made with some care. It can be quite useful to pull in some experienced outside people (e.g., advisors or a board of directors) to help us make this decision. Hopefully, they'll have good input, and having to make our case to others is a great incentive to do a thorough job of researching and articulating a good, succinct case. We like our idea and want to convince others, so we anticipate and respond to gaps in our thinking, things we've overlooked, or problems/risks we haven't been willing to acknowledge. In convincing others, we often convince ourselves.

The decision process will look very different in different situations, particularly with regard to the trade-off between certainty and potential upside. In the case of a few friends looking for adventure, certainty will be low (i.e., there's a high chance that things will go substantially differently than planned), but the product's potential upside will (hopefully!) be high to compensate. Large corporations, in most cases, are looking for high certainty with the understanding that potential upside (i.e., revenue) is more limited (although still substantial).

If we decide to move forward, we now have blueprints for what to build (the product design) and how to proceed (the project plan). With these as our guide, we'll next begin the true *development* part of *product development.*

Detailed Development

While development of various types has been taking place prior to this phase, here's where we dig in and turn our detailed product definition into a manufacturable product. We'll create and test iterations of prototypes that increasingly resemble the final product until we have something that we're ready to move into production. Because this is probably the part of the process that most readers of this book are already familiar with, I won't dwell at length on this phase here (but, as with the rest of the info in this chapter, I do provide more details throughout the remainder of this book).

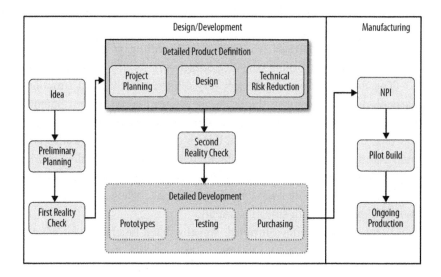

There are three areas of activity during development that warrant some discussion at this high level: prototyping, testing, and purchasing. The first of these is obvious; the latter two are often overlooked when thinking about development so I'm breaking them out to give them a little attention.

PROTOTYPING

When describing prototypes, product developers often refer to them as *works-like* and/or *looks-like prototypes*. Works-like refers to a prototype that functions like the final product. Looks-like refers to (of course) a prototype that looks like the final product. Not surprisingly, a works-like/looks-like prototype both functions and looks like the final product.

Initial looks-like prototypes are usually created as part of a detailed product specification, described earlier. As we develop our product, we might want to change the design because of engineering issues or feedback from further market research, and looks-like models will be updated.

The initial works-like electronics prototype is typically a precarious-looking breadboard of electronics parts and development kits, along the lines of Figure 2-2, which serves several purposes:

1. We can test and debug a great deal of our circuit design before going through the effort of designing and building custom PC boards.

2. Breadboards are typically easier to test and debug than PC boards, because breadboards don't need to be miniaturized. There's lots of room for test points and so forth.

3. Software folks can quickly have something to start development on that incorporates much of the final electronics design; they don't have to wait for PC boards to be designed, manufactured, and populated.

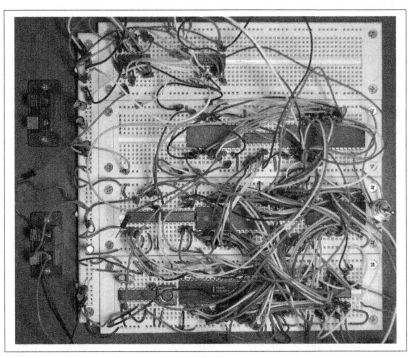

FIGURE 2-2. An electronics breadboard prototype (courtesy Wikimedia Commons)

Breadboards are followed by works-like/looks-like prototypes that increasingly embody the final product. Because breadboards are unwieldy, works-like/looks-like prototypes normally must use custom-printed circuit boards, but initial prototypes might have their enclosures and other mechanical parts created by a 3D printer. Later prototypes will use final (pending testing) materials, typically injection molded, so we can test the product's true mechanical properties and inspect color, fit, finish, and so forth.

Each works-like/looks-like prototype is tested and debugged, and results are fed back into an improved works-like/looks-like prototype. This process is repeated until we have something we decide is ready to move into production. Simple devices might only require one or two works-like/looks-like prototypes, whereas a small and sophisticated device with many parts and tight tolerances like a new cell phone might require dozens of prototypes to get everything right.

TESTING

It's easy to fall into the mistake of thinking of testing as *the thing that comes after development:* develop it, test it, manufacture it. This is a bad way to think. Testing is how we find out about problems, and problems are always cheaper to fix if found early. So testing should occur throughout the development process. As we'll see, it even continues on into manufacturing. There are several broad categories of testing that are somewhat related in practice:

- Design verification
- Certification test
- Design validation
- Manufacturing test

Design verification testing (DVT), sometimes called *engineering testing* or *bench testing,* is the type of testing associated with the development phase. DVT demonstrates that the product's engineering design is correct (i.e., that it meets its requirements). DVT is usually extensive, sometimes incredibly extensive for products that are either complex or which must be highly reliable. On the bright side, full engineering testing is usually only performed once (perhaps on several units) when a design (or an update) is thought to be ready to release to manufacturing.

Certification testing can be thought of as a part of DVT, although I like to break it out separately as it tends to come in one clump at the end of development. Almost all products that contain electronics must be tested to ensure that they meet relevant regulations and standards. Examples of typical regulations and standards include US FCC Part 15 regulations for RF emissions (mandatory), and UL safety standards (optional). For devices that will be sold in other countries or devices that must be highly reliable, many other standards can come into play. For example, most electronic medical devices sold in the US and EU must comply with at least

18 different standards and regulations, and most of these require tests to prove compliance.

Certification testing usually involves handing our finished (or nearly so) device (along with a purchase order) to an impartial test organization that will test against the appropriate regulations and standards for safety and performance. If we pass the tests, we're certified. If we fail any of the tests, we'll need to update the design and try again. Because passing certification testing is so important, we'll later discuss steps that we can take early in the process to reduce the possibility of failure and redesign.

> **TIP** The phrase *design validation testing* is sometimes used for testing that demonstrates that a product's design (look, feel, usability, etc.) is correct and that it meets its intended use in the marketplace. Typical validation testing includes exercises like giving prototypes or finished units to prospective users to see if they can use the product to accomplish the tasks they're intended to perform. Validation is normally done at various points during the product development cycle.

Finally, *manufacturing testing* assumes that the engineering design is correct, but checks to ensure that each device is *manufactured* properly. Testing is performed at one or more points during the manufacturing process to help ensure that we don't ship a defective product.

To better see how DVT and manufacturing testing differ, let's look at an example. During DVT we might try to test every last feature and function of our embedded software to check that the software is written correctly. But during manufacturing test, we assume that the software is written correctly: we only want to make sure that the software image was loaded correctly (e.g., by reading back a checksum after the load).

The good news is that manufacturing testing is usually largely a subset of DVT, so the efforts overlap. But DVT and manufacturing testing are quite different in several respects. *DVT* is performed only once in a while (e.g., when a new prototype is built), and usually by trained, skilled engineers and/or skilled technicians who can figure out what to do if a test doesn't go as planned. *Manufacturing tests*, by contrast, might be performed by factory workers on every single device that's manufactured, perhaps thousands each day, without a design engineer nearby to help if anything unexpected happens. So manufacturing tests must be quick, robust, and easy to run.

For unsophisticated products, a manufacturing test can be as simple as turning on a finished device and punching a few buttons to see if things seem to work. On the other end of the spectrum, for certain sophisticated products (often medical, automotive, defense, and aerospace applications), the cost of developing automated manufacturing test systems can be as high as the cost of developing the product itself!

PURCHASING

Purchasing for *prototypes* and purchasing for *production* are two types of purchasing activities that are different, but linked.

It's pretty obvious that purchasing for production requires a good bit of thought and effort; quantities are typically far larger than for prototypes, and there are many other considerations, such as maintaining a steady pipeline of parts, managing inventory, payment terms, etc.

Purchasing for prototypes is often pretty informal: order a few parts over the Internet, give a credit card number, then parts appear at the door in a day or two. No worries, right?

Well, purchasing for prototypes requires more care than might be obvious, and being too casual about purchasing during the development phase can lead to getting stung pretty good down the road. Two issues are often overlooked:

1. The prototype parts we use should also be acceptable for production, which requires diligence and research. When we order parts for our first production build, we don't want to hear that the nice LCD display used for our prototypes is no longer available; that would likely drive a significant redevelopment effort.

2. Many parts have significant lead times, sometimes months between order placed and arrival, particularly for custom or semi-custom parts. So it's often necessary to order long-lead-time parts as soon as we're reasonably sure that they'll be used rather than waiting until development is complete. Otherwise there might be a delay of weeks or months between the end of the development phase and the start of manufacturing while we wait for parts to arrive.

Once we do have all the parts that we need in hand, we can begin the next adventure in our journey: assembling units that we can sell.

Manufacturing

Folkswho are new to product development tend to think of factories as magic product copiers: we send our final prototype to manufacturing and exact copies start pouring out.

Nope. No magic, just lots of hard work!

As we'll see in Chapter 3, manufacturing is complex, with lots of steps and lots of things that can go wrong, and which *will* go wrong, particularly as we ease into production and find the kinks we need to straighten.

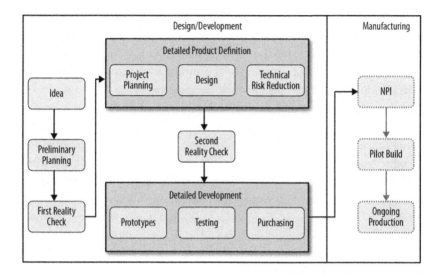

To facilitate kink discovery and straightening, production begins with two activities that we'll discuss next: Factory New Product Introduction and pilot build.

FACTORY NEW PRODUCT INTRODUCTION

Factory New Product Introduction (NPI) is the process of creating and proving processes to ensure that our wonderful final prototype, which was lovingly hand-built and tested by skilled technologists, will be reliably reproduced in the factory at high volumes and reasonable cost, by machines and workers with moderate training, and often halfway around the world.

(What could possibly go wrong?)

In the simplest case of low-volume production, the folks doing the manufacturing are the same folks who developed the product. They know all of the tricks for assembling and testing their product, and can change procedures on-the-fly as they find better ways to do things. NPI in this case is really not very *new*: rather, manufacturing looks more like building prototypes in higher volumes, which is why it's sometimes dubbed *protoduction*.

When manufacturing is outsourced, the game changes, big time. There's lots of *new* in NPI: new people, new processes, perhaps even a new language. This is where things can get pretty interesting, as it can require significant effort to turn all of the things that the designers/developers just kinda know how to do into explicit, clear, and easy-to-follow instructions and processes that work reliably.

Depending on the complexity of a product's assembly and test, NPI can be quite extensive and require a good bit of interaction between designers/developers and factory staff. For example, NPI for a product comprising a single circuit board in a simple snap-together enclosure might take a day. In the case of a complex and critical electromechanical product such as a heart-assist device (which augments a weak heart with a pump), NPI can take weeks or even months; there are lots of ways to make mistakes when fabricating and assembling such intricate systems, and these problems need to be discovered and worked through for obvious reasons. In this case, it's really bad to find out about a process problem through product failures in the field.

Once we've developed a manufacturing process that we're confident will create quality devices with a minimum of effort, we're finally ready to build our first units!

PILOT PRODUCTION

The first manufacturing build of a product is often referred to as the *pilot build*. A pilot build is a "normal" build in that it's performed against the manufacturing process that we expect to be standard, and it (hopefully) produces a salable product. But pilot build is different from other builds in that it's done with extra care and quantification to evaluate the quality of the production process, and the quality of the product it produces.

The production process is closely examined to look for inefficiencies and the potential to produce *nonconforming products* (i.e., products that fail test).

The first products off the line are inspected with meticulous care. Beyond testing for functionality, we'll check all mechanical tolerances, examine the quality of soldering (e.g., any solder flux residue left on the board), and so forth. This process is often called *first article inspection*.

Also, certain types of testing are better performed on production units rather than on prototypes; the two common ones being reliability and certification testing.

Reliability test results from manufactured units might be quite different from results obtained using units assembled in the lab due to subtle differences in assembly, including even little things like differences in the reflow temperature profiles used in soldering.

In the case of certification testing, third-party test houses may insist on doing their final testing on a product that's been produced through our standard manufacturing process. They might also need to inspect the manufacturing process itself.

ONGOING PRODUCTION

At the beginning of production, even after the pilot build, manufacturing is a process of learning and change, and sometimes it's a struggle to just get units out the door.

As the kinks get worked out, manufacturing becomes more predictable—just the way everyone likes it. But it's not time for designers/developers to totally relax. Things can and will happen that warrant our attention.

Parts can go obsolete or supplies might become unreliable for various reasons. In either case, we'll need to redesign our product using new parts.

Also, we might want to redevelop our product's "innards" to reduce cost. This is particularly true when we're producing large quantities, where the achievable savings could be substantial enough to cover the cost of redevelopment. Ways to wring out cost typically include using less expensive components, increasing ease of assembly, and increasing reliability (e.g., decreasing returns under warranty). Changes for reliability are often based on statistical analysis of product issues that have occurred once we've been in production for a while.

Final Thoughts

While the product development process flowchart that we've been using has nice boxes and lines, no project ever has crisp boundaries around activities and clean transitions from one phase to the next (even if the paperwork to management claims otherwise). Things happen, and they need to be dealt with. But by making a solid effort to plan for the right phases and tasks, and trying to sequence these in the most efficient way, we'll reduce effort, expense, and anguish. Process will never eliminate the bad stuff, but it can definitely make the difference between an overall fun experience versus a death march.

Now that we know what the boxes are and how they link together, our next four chapters cover the broad phases of:

- Preliminary planning
- Detailed definition
- Detailed development
- Manufacturing

Rather than moving through these in strict chronological order, we're going to mix them up a bit by starting at the end, with manufacturing; a bit of knowledge of the manufacturing process and the manufacturing world can be tremendously helpful during the rest of the design/development process. After our review of manufacturing, we'll cover the other phases in order.

Resources

The best resource for more information on what's covered in this chapter is ... the rest of this book! This chapter contains a high-level overview, and everything here will be covered in greater detail later. Each of those chapters will also contain, as appropriate, pointers to other helpful resources.

## CHAPTER 3

How Electronic Products Are Manufactured

BACK IN THE 1980S, A FAMILY FRIEND WENT TO WORK AS AN ENGINEER at a major American automaker. Her first assignment was to fix a little problem: an engine part had been designed so that it fit properly in the engine once it was in its correct place. But, unfortunately, there was no way to get the part *into* its correct place during the manufacturing process. So the engine couldn't be built in the factory.

Oops.

It's easy to chalk off this misfire to the general shoddiness that pervaded the American auto industry during those days. In fact, I'd wager that this kind of thing rarely happens at auto companies today, thanks to better CAD tools, rapid prototyping, and smarter processes. But variants of "we can't actually build this" happen all of the time in product development, and the resulting redesign/redevelopment efforts to address the problems can be costly and frustrating.

This chapter presents an overview of the process typically followed during the factory production of devices that contain electronics and have simple mechanical parts, products like computers, smart phones, or wearable sensors. (Products that have more complex mechanicals, such as cars or heart-assist pumps, will follow processes that are broadly similar but far more complex.)

Since manufacturing occurs at the end of the product development cycle, it might seem out of place to have this chapter at the front of this book rather than toward the end. But there's a method to this madness:

not knowing (or paying too little attention to) the manufacturing process is one of the most important root causes of potholes in product development, often resulting in products being developed that:

- Are unbuildable or which cost more to build than they should because excessive effort (time) is needed

- Have reduced reliability (e.g., from cables that tend to not get inserted all of the way and then fall out with use, circuit board features that trap contaminants, etc.)

- Require redesign soon after launch when components become difficult or impossible to obtain

These problems are largely avoidable by practicing *design for manufacturability* and *design for assembly*, DFM/DFA for short. We'll look at some of the formal practices around DFM/DFA in Chapter 6, but to a large degree DFM/DFA is a mindset that designer/developers should embrace throughout development. Successful DFM/DFA, in turn, mandates that product designers/developers have an understanding of how products are manufactured, and that they work together with their manufacturer(s) during development to ensure that there are no surprises when it comes time to start building.

A word of clarification: the phrases *design for manufacturability* and *design for assembly* are used both to denote general activities that improve manufacturability and assembly, and to identify specific optimization practices pioneered by Boothroyd and Dewhurst that we'll touch on in Chapter 6. In this book, these phrases will be used in both senses, and I'll try to make it clear which is meant by the context in which it's used.

My hope is that reviewing the manufacturing process early will help to provide context for the development process described throughout the book.

One more note before we get going: this chapter is heavy on electronics manufacturing, while more information around mechanical manufacturing is found in Chapter 6. The most important reason for this breakdown is that, traditionally, electronic products have had relatively simple mechanical assembly (think smart phones and televisions) and few problems with the mechanical process. In my experience developing products (primarily medical devices with embedded intelligence), electronics manufacturing and "box build" (full system assembly) are typically performed in the same factory using mechanical components manufactured by outside vendors.

Complex electromechanical products (e.g., robots) are becoming more important over time, and these can require extensive and challenging mechanical assembly. But the techniques and processes used for complex electromechanical assemblies can vary significantly from one product to another, whereas electronics manufacturing tends to be more similar from one product to another. While a single chapter can give a pretty good overview of the electronics manufacturing process, a treatment of complex mechanical manufacturing at the same level of detail could easily fill a book of its own. So, if your product is more like a smart phone or television, this chapter should serve as a good overview of the manufacturing process. If your product is more like a robot, this chapter should serve as a starting point, but you should understand that the process will ultimately be substantially more complex.

OK! Enough with the caveats! Let's get started with an overview of the process.

Manufacturing Overview

Prototypes tend to get assembled via a chaotic process, particularly early in the development cycle. By contrast, products are manufactured via a series of discrete and well-identified steps.

Gaining an understanding of manufacturing is largely a matter of understanding the different steps involved. As a baseline, let's start by walking through the process that would be followed (more or less) for medium production volumes, say, 1,000–10,000 units per year. After our walkthrough, I'll describe how things might change when manufacturing in higher and lower volumes.

Figure 3-1 shows a schematic overview of a typical process. Most manufacturing follows a pretty similar process, but as we'll see there can be differences in process between one product and another.

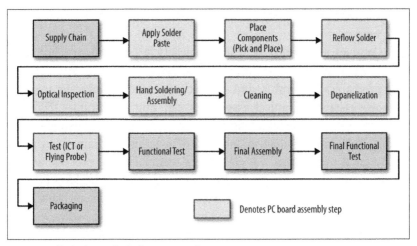

FIGURE 3-1. Typical manufacturing process steps

Note that builds are usually done in batches; for example, if building a batch of 100 units, 100 units would go through step 1, then the 100 would go through step 2, etc.

Now let's review each of these manufacturing steps in a tiny bit of detail. So you won't have to keep flipping back to Figure 3-1 to see where we are in the process, we'll reproduce the process diagram for each step, highlighting the current step.

Supply Chain

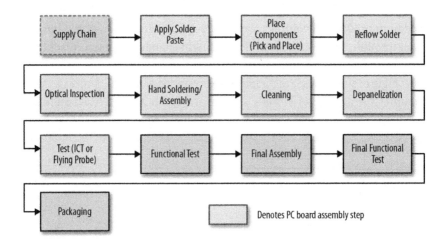

When we think of factories, we think of *building stuff*. But it turns out that the most challenging part of manufacturing is usually not the building part; rather, it's getting all of the needed parts into one place, at the right moment, so that the building can happen. That part is known as the *supply chain*.

We product designers/developers tend to think of the supply chain as simply *the people who order parts*, but obtaining components is actually much, much more challenging than most of us realize. A typical product consists of hundreds or perhaps thousands of components, which all must come together at the right instant for a unit to be built. If even one sub-penny resistor is missing, production typically won't happen.

Not only does everything need to show up on time, it all needs to be obtained as economically as possible. In theory it's just about finding a good price and placing an order, but reality is a lot more complex. Here are some of the challenges faced by supply chain staff:

- Components come from multiple vendors; often dozens of vendors supply parts for a single product.

- Components normally constitute the largest cost of building a product, so buyers need to negotiate good pricing or else the product will cost significantly more than necessary.

- Components can suddenly become unavailable from a source (e.g., a distributor sells its entire inventory to a large customer, an earthquake damages a vendor's factory, etc.), and alternative sources must be found quickly or production pauses.

- Components can go obsolete. Supply chain resources must manage the process of identifying and qualifying alternative sources of identical parts, and/or work with engineering folks on a redesign to accommodate a new part.

- Components have different lead times (the time it takes to receive them once they've been ordered). Common components are available next-day, or even same-day, while some items like custom LCDs might take months. And if the LCDs show up with a defect? It can take months to get replacements without the defect.

- Ensuring that parts are genuine. Counterfeit parts exist, and can compromise safety and reliability. Finding out that a shipping product contains counterfeit parts can lead to a recall and other misery.

Life would actually be pretty easy if, at the start of the project, we could order all of the parts we'd ever need to build all the units we'll ever build, put these parts in inventory, and then draw down that inventory as we built units. We'd never have an interruption in our supply, because all components would always be on hand. The problem is that *inventory* is a bad word among financial and management types: inventory's usually been paid for (or at least we owe money for it), but inventory won't generate revenue until it's built into something. So it represents money that's just sitting on a shelf, being unproductive and taking up space. In an ideal financial/managerial world, parts would show up at the loading dock the day they're used and never need to sit in inventory for more than a few hours.

In the real world, inventory is a complex juggling act. Perhaps only a few days' worth of inventory is kept on hand for parts that are easily available and/or at low risk of having deliveries interrupted, while larger supplies are kept of components that are less common or are otherwise at higher risk of having their supply interrupted. Supply chain folks can work out various deals with component makers and distributors to ensure we have parts to build with while maximizing financial health. In many cases we can negotiate deals that (almost) guarantee a steady supply of components without our having to hold substantial inventories.

Once the supply chain is worked out and we have parts in hand, the building can begin.

Building Circuits: PCB Assembly

Electronics lie at the physical heart of the kinds of products we'll be covering in this book. Since they're so important, let's review a little nomenclature to put us all on the same page, and then we'll delve into some of the details of how electronic assemblies are built.

Electronic circuits are built by soldering components to a *printed circuit board* (a.k.a *PC board* or *PCB*). Once components are soldered to the PCB, the assembly is sometimes referred to as a *PC board assembly* (*PCBA*) or less commonly a *printed circuit assembly* (*PCA*). Figure 3-2 shows a PCB, and the PCBA created by soldering components to that PCB.

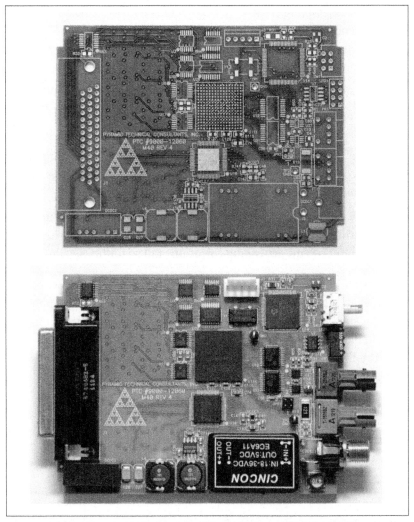

FIGURE 3-2. Bare and assembled printed circuit board (PCB and PCBA) (credit: Pyramid Technical Consultants)

Confusingly, sometimes PCB is also used to refer to a PCBA. The context in which it's used should make it obvious as to whether PCB is referring to the unpopulated board or built assembly. In this book, PCB will always refer to a bare board, while PCBA will always be used for an assembled board. But in real life, it's always good to ask for clarification if an acronym's usage is not totally obvious.

PCBs are custom components ordered from specialized vendors, manufactured based on CAD files supplied by the product developer. The process of assembling electronics components onto these boards is called, boringly enough, *PCB assembly*. The name of this task might be boring, but the actual assembly can be anything but boring if we're unlucky.

The object of PCB assembly is to make sure that:

- All parts are in the correct place, and in the correct orientation.

- All component pins are soundly soldered to the correct pads on the PCB.

- There's no extra solder that can cause trouble, say, by shorting things out (connecting together component pins or other conductors that are not supposed to be connected).

- There's no extra anything else, such as solvents or flux used in manufacturing, which can cause trouble by conducting current where there shouldn't be any, generating corrosion, and so forth.

For all but the smallest quantities, PCB assembly is almost entirely automated. Boards and components go into one end of an assembly line, and finished boards come out of the other end with a minimum of human intervention.

The first step in the assembly process is to apply solder paste to the PCB.

PCB ASSEMBLY: SOLDER PASTE APPLICATION

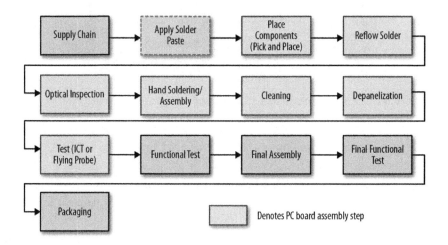

Solder is a metal alloy that's used to electrically and mechanically connect metal parts together. In particular, it's used to form sturdy, highly conductive bonds between component pins and metal pads on the PCB. *Solder paste* is a goopy mix of ultrafine powdered solder mixed with liquid *flux*, the flux's job being to clean any corrosion or contamination from the metal surfaces so that a good solder joint can be made.

The first step in the PCB assembly process is to add the right amount of solder paste to the board in the right spots. This is done using a *solder stencil*, which is custom to each PC board design. The solder stencil is a thin metal sheet with cutouts wherever solder paste should be applied to the board (e.g., on every board pad that will connect to a component lead). Figure 3-3 shows a solder stencil.

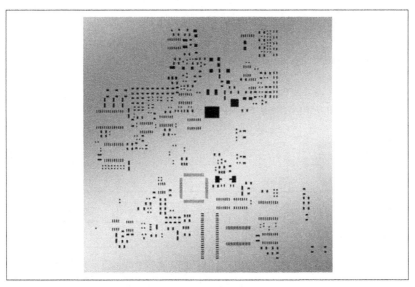

FIGURE 3-3. Solder stencil (credit: Alan Walsh)

The stencil is laid precisely on the board, the paste is smeared evenly across the stencil using a squeegee, and then the stencil is removed and cleaned. The board now has the right amount of solder paste in the right places. Figure 3-4 shows solder paste being applied to a board with an automated squeegee. Because the stencil's silver, it's a little hard to see in the picture that the gray solder paste is filling in the stencil's holes.

FIGURE 3-4. Solder application (credit: Alan Walsh)

Now that the solder paste is down, we can place the board's components.

PCB ASSEMBLY: PLACING COMPONENTS

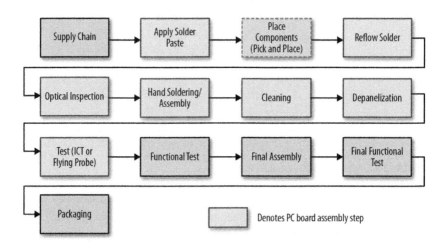

The next step is to place each component in the right spot on the PCB, which is normally accomplished by a *pick-and-place machine*. The components to be placed are typically supplied on reels of tape known as *tape-and-reel packaging*. Figure 3-5 shows some example reels in use on a pick-and-place.

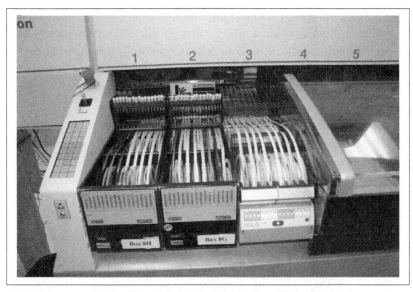

FIGURE 3-5. Component reels in a pick-and-place machine (credit: Alan Walsh)

Figure 3-6 shows a close-up of resistors packaged as tape and reel. Each component is held in an embossed pocket in the carrier tape. Each pocket is sealed with a cover tape (usually clear) that's peeled up just before the part is picked and placed.

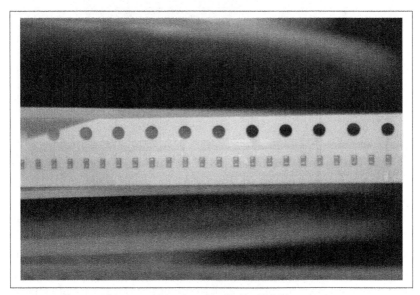

FIGURE 3-6. Close-up of components on tape (credit: Alan Walsh)

Beyond being supplied with the right components, the pick-and-place machine also needs to know which parts go where. This programming is usually accomplished using CAD data automatically generated as part of our Electronics/PCB design application, along with our bill of materials (parts list), which is also usually generated by our Electronics/PCB application.

Tubes and/or trays, shown in Figure 3-7, are sometimes used instead of tape and reel to hold parts for the pick-and-place. Depending on the specific model of pick-and-place, tubes and/or trays typically don't work as smoothly as tape and reel. If using tubes and/or trays is of interest, this should be explored in advance with the folks who'll be doing your manufacturing.

FIGURE 3-7. Tube and tray

Each PC board is positioned in the pick-and-place machine, and then each component is picked up from its tape using a tiny suction cup, placed onto the right spot on the board, and then released. Figure 3-8 shows the suction cup in action. The solder paste under the placed part conveniently serves as adhesive to hold the part in place temporarily until the solder paste is made solid by reflowing it (discussed in a moment). In some cases, if solder paste isn't sufficient to hold a part down (e.g., a large part with few pins), the pick-and-place might put down a bit of adhesive to help out.

FIGURE 3-8. Pick-and-place suction cup holding IC

Pick-and-place machines are fast and accurate, the fastest being able to place hundreds of parts per minute, but there are a few tradeoffs we need to deal with in exchange for this great speed. First off, pick-and-place machines only work with surface-mount devices (SMDs), not the larger through-hole parts that are popular for prototyping. Through-hole parts are usually placed and soldered by hand, which is much more expensive than automated SMD processes. Switching from through-hole parts to their SMD equivalents is usually not a big deal, just something that should be done during PC board design.

The second issue is that all the reels (and tubes/trays if used) must be loaded onto the pick-and-place before it can begin work, which takes some time. This setup time is the same whether we're assembling one board or 1,000, so building fewer large batches tends to make more sense than building many small batches.

A third issue is that pick-and-place machines only accept a finite number of reels, perhaps 20 to 100 or more depending on the model. If we have more unique parts than the number of reels the machine can support, we'll need to run the boards through the machine multiple times to get all the parts placed. To avoid multiple passes, it's a good idea to reduce the number of different parts during design/development by using the same parts as often as possible; for example, we can try to standardize on a few resistor values and sizes, putting several in parallel or serial to create different resistances if needed.

A fourth issue, and often the biggest surprise to people new to this game, is that we sometimes can only purchase full reels of parts even though we might only need a smaller number for our build. By default, parts come on reels in quantities that range from hundreds to thousands of pieces per reel. A full reel of resistors might contain 5,000 pieces, but because resistors cost a fraction of a cent, the entire reel should cost less than $10, which is not a big deal. But a $12 GPS chip that comes in reels of 500 will set us back $6,000 per reel, even if we only need 100 parts. Our $12 GPS chip is now $60, unless our supply chain folks can find a way to resell the parts to someone else.

Fortunately, alternatives to full reels are often (but not always!) available. Component distributors will usually sell a strip of tape cut from a reel in the size we want (called a *cut tape*), or create a smaller reel for us using a cut tape. As mentioned previously, chips can also be supplied in custom quantities in tubes and/or trays, although these will not play nicely with all pick-and-place machines.

We now have PCB, solder, and components. Our ingredients are mixed; next, it's into the oven to bake.

PCB ASSEMBLY: REFLOW

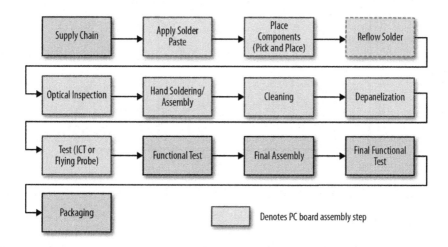

Reflow is the process of converting gloopy solder paste to solid solder joints. In particular, it involves heating the PC board and components in a way that will:

- Activate the flux so it does a better job of cleaning, and then vaporizes away.

- Melt the ground solder in the paste to liquid, then cool it to solidify as a single chunk that binds the component lead to its pad.

In practice, this is bit more complex than simply getting the board to a certain temperature and cooling it down. Heating and cooling should follow a profile that ensures that:

- Components don't heat or cool too quickly, which can cause failure from *thermal shock.*

- The flux has adequate time at an elevated temperature to properly clean and then evaporate.

- The heat has time to soak into the entire board surface; i.e., the entire board gets to the desired temperature. If we don't soak the board sufficiently, some parts of the board might not get hot enough to create a good solder joint.

Figure 3-9 shows a typical graph of temperature versus time during the reflow process.

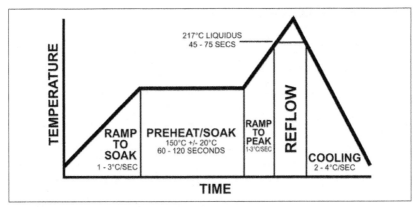

FIGURE 3-9. Typical reflow profile (credit: Wikimedia Commons)

Solder reflow is accomplished using a *reflow oven*. The oven is programmed with the desired temperature profile depending on the type of solder paste being used and other factors. Beyond programmability, reflow ovens must also be designed to ensure that each board is heated evenly. Heating is typically accomplished using hot gas convection (either air or nitrogen), but other methods can be used as well. Reflow ovens come in a wide variety of sizes depending on throughput, from batch units as small as a microwave oven, to large continuous-throughput units like the one shown in Figure 3-10.

Large commercial units that reflow a continuous stream of boards on a conveyor belt (rather than a single batch at once) have multiple zones set to different temperatures, as called out in the reflow temperature profile. If you look carefully under the open top in Figure 3-10, you'll notice the back ends of fans sticking up; these fans move air within each temperature zone to keep temperature even within that zone.

FIGURE 3-10. Large continuous reflow oven with the top propped open (credit: Alan Walsh)

Once out of the oven, our board has hundreds or thousands of newly soldered joints. Are these joints all good? Are the parts still all where they're supposed to be? Sometimes not: better check 'em out, which we'll do next.

PCB ASSEMBLY: OPTICAL INSPECTION

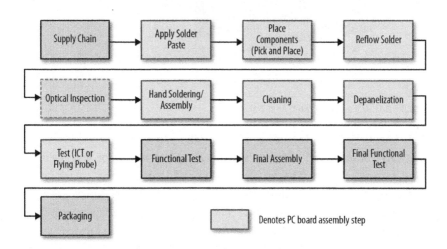

Once components are soldered down, an *automated optical inspection* (AOI) station examines the board to check if our parts ended up looking properly soldered, and in precisely the right places. It will note any parts whose position or orientation is incorrect, so that they can be touched up by hand (called *rework*), or the board scrapped. Figure 3-11 shows an example of AOI output as seen by the machine operator. In this case, the AOI has spotted a part which looks different than it's seen in previous boards, and it's zoomed in on this part and is asking the technician to take a look and enter a verdict: is there a problem with the way the part is assembled to the board, or is this change OK?

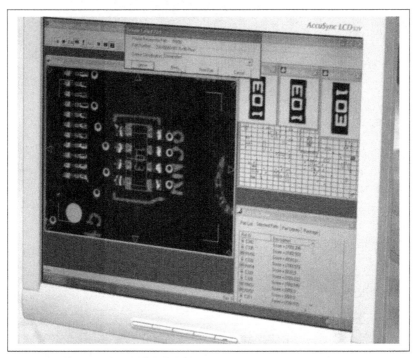

FIGURE 3-11. AOI screen (credit: Alan Walsh)

This time the difference is innocent: the part that's flagged (a resistor network) is produced by many vendors, and a new vendor was used for this particular build. The problem flagged is that the "103" marking on the part is simply in a different font than the AOIs previously seen for this PCBA. If we instruct the AOI machine to memorize this new style of "103," this part won't be flagged for the same reason in the future PCBAs.

Note that while this difference is innocent, little things like this can sometimes halt production until a phone call is made to the right person in design/development to confirm all is OK. In other instances, an AOI operator might decide without checking with someone who knows that an issue is similarly cosmetic when it's truly a serious build issue, and we end up with a batch of bad boards. In manufacturing, every detail counts!

Parts with contacts that are hidden from view can be a challenge to inspect, of course. The classic example of *tough-to-inspect* is chips with *ball grid array* (BGA) packages, which can have more than a thousand soldered contacts all hidden beneath the part; the bottom view of a smaller BGA part is shown in Figure 3-12.

FIGURE 3-12. BGA, bottom view (credit: Wikimedia Commons)

Figure 3-13 shows the PCB footprint of a medium-sized BGA, a few hundred balls. The difficulty in inspecting all of those solder joints once they're lying under a square slab (the BGA package) should be obvious.

FIGURE 3-13. Medium ball grid array footprint (credit: Pyramid Technical Consultants)

Specialized 2D and 3D x-ray systems are used to inspect the invisible. Figure 3-14 shows a portion of an x-rayed reflowed BGA. The red arrows point to solder bridges where two contacts are accidentally soldered together; either this board will be reworked or scrapped.

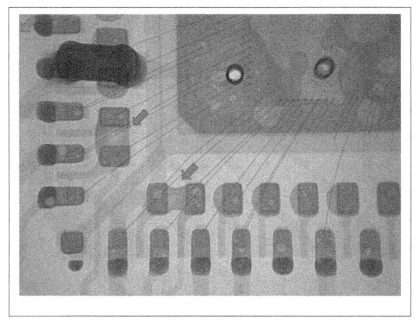

FIGURE 3-14. BGA x-ray (credit: Lightspeed Manufacturing)

Note that not all factories have x-ray systems; that's one item to look into when selecting a contract manufacturer.

At this point, we've assembled what we can on the PCB via automation, and we have a list of any gross defects introduced during that process. Next we'll rely on that most amazing machine of all—humans—to finish off board assembly by doing what the robots couldn't.

PCB ASSEMBLY: HAND SOLDERING AND ASSEMBLY

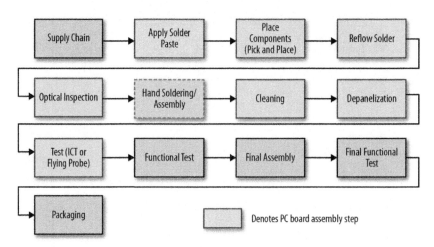

In many instances, a board will require that some work be done by hand, such as:

- Rework of improperly reflowed parts as flagged in AOI.

- Rework due to design changes made after PC boards began fabrication. For example, PC board traces might be cut and wires added (known as *cuts and jumpers*) to change circuit paths. Figure 3-15 shows an example of wiring added as rework.

- Hand soldering of components that are not suitable for reflow. Examples include through-hole parts and temperature-sensitive parts such as batteries.

- Hand assembly of mechanical parts on the PCBA.

FIGURE 3-15. Example PCB rework

As mentioned previously, it's much more expensive to do things by hand than by machine, so designers/developers should take care to reduce the number of parts that require manual work during assembly; but some hand work usually can't be avoided. For example, connectors accessed by end users (e.g., USB connectors) are often through-hole rather than SMD to add strength and reduce the odds of the connector coming off the board through wear and tear.

At this point, our board assembly is complete unless we find a defect during later testing that sends the board back for rework. The next two steps, *cleaning* and *depaneling*, prepare our PCBAs for assembly into the larger product.

PCB ASSEMBLY: CLEANING

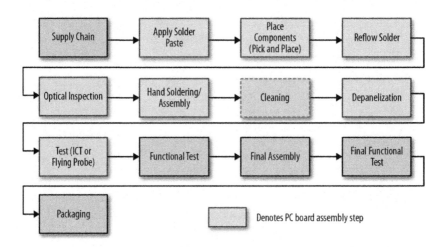

A clean PCBA is a good PCBA. In particular, it's a good practice to wash the PCBA after its assembly to remove any solder flux not burned off during reflow. Flux on the board might cause corrosion and/or unwanted electrical paths, which can affect reliability and performance.

Some fluxes are designated as *no-clean* because they shouldn't corrode if left on a board and do not conduct substantial current; however these are usually cleaned anyway because they might still affect sensitive or high-speed circuitry.

PCB ASSEMBLY: DEPANELING

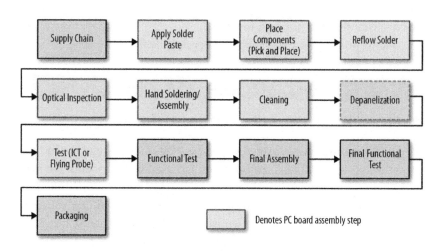

It's typically most economical to fabricate and assemble PCBs as *panels* of multiple boards, the individual boards being cut or broken out sometime after assembly. The number of boards per panel depends on the sizes that the PCB fabricator and assembler can accommodate, the size of each PC board, and sometimes other factors. For example, an 18" × 24" panel can accommodate up to 20 PCBs that are 2.5" × 5" each (with some space to spare).

Figure 3-16 shows a panel of five long, narrow boards. Note that there's a scored line between each board, and a bit of routing (openings cut through the panel) at each board's corner.

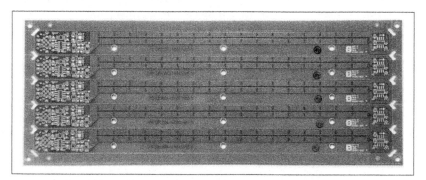

FIGURE 3-16. Five PCBs in a panel (credit: Pyramid Technical Consultants)

Scoring consists of cutting a shallow V-shaped grove across the board, which makes the board easy to snap apart at that line. *Routing* uses a tool to cut a channel clear through the board.

Figure 3-17 shows a single board after depaneling.

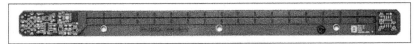

FIGURE 3-17. Single PCB after depaneling (credit: Pyramid Technical Consultants)

PCB assembly is performed while the PCBs are still together in their panel. At some point, often before test (discussed in a moment), the individual boards are cut apart using a *depaneling tool*, or are simply snapped apart by hand (which is more stressful for the board and its components). Depaneling tools employ various means for removing boards, including sawing, routing, cutting with a "pizza cutter" wheel laser, and punching out using special fixtures.

The process of paneling and depaneling has a few important implications for designers/developers pertaining to the edges of the individual boards separated out by the process.

The PCB edges that are cut or broken apart can experience a good bit of stress and strain during the depaneling process, which can cause mechanical deformations close to those edges. It's a good idea to keep a margin of at least 50 mil (0.050 in) between board edges and traces/pads, and at least 100 mil between board edges and components. (Note that PCB measurements are pretty universally called out in mils, which equal thousandths of an inch. Yes, the PCB world still works in inches!)

Other issues have to do with tradeoffs between separating boards via scoring versus routing:

- Routing produces smooth edges versus rough edges for scoring, which is normally only an issue if boards will be seen by the end user, say, if they plug into a connector.

- Routing requires greater spacing between boards (to accommodate the width of the routing tool).

- Routed panels can have significant flex, which can cause issues with PCB assembly.

To avoid problems, it's important to work with your assembler when designing PCB panels. They'll have a good idea of what will work on their equipment.

Our PCBAs are now complete, or at least they *look* really good. Now it's time to see whether they *work* as good as they look.

Test

PCBAs are complex, and normally each will be tested to make sure that the assembly process went according to plan. Note that this *factory testing* is normally quite different than the testing performed in our lab to ensure that our design is correct (*design verification testing*).

The range of effort brought to bear on factory testing can vary tremendously. Factory testing can be as simple as having a technician turn on a product after final assembly to see if things seem to work. On the other end of the spectrum, factory test can probe every nook and cranny of each manufactured unit before it ships to make sure that everything's in good order. The degree of testing largely depends on the likelihood of problems occurring in manufacturing, and the cost of finding these errors once the unit leaves the factory. For example, the occasional failure of an inexpensive toy is probably not a big deal as long as it's not a safety issue, so we probably wouldn't put forth much of a test effort. But even the occasional failure of a computer module that controls automobile braking would be something we'd really want to avoid, and thus a serious factory test effort is in order.

Large factory test efforts can sometimes rival the size (and cost) of the efforts to design/develop the product itself. For these efforts, it's useful to employ the help of specialized *test engineers* who are experienced with the world of factories and factory workers, a much different constituency than most other end users.

There are two basic types of testing, *in-circuit* and *functional*, that can be performed on the PCBA, depending on the product. We explore these in the next sections.

IN-CIRCUIT TEST (ICT)

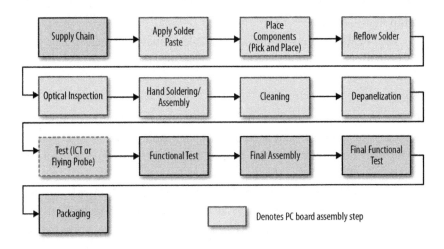

ICT is used to demonstrate that PCBAs are built correctly by analyzing electrical characteristics such as the resistance of each solder joint. High-volume ICT is most commonly performed using a *bed-of-nails tester*, in which a large number of probes are placed on the PCBA simultaneously—up to several thousand in some test setups. Various test signals are introduced into some probes, and responses measured at other probes.

The probes are typically spring-loaded and set into a special board called a *test fixture*, usually custom-made for each PCBA design. Each probe connects to the circuit being tested (sometimes called the *device under test/DUT*, or *unit under test/UUT*) by touching a conductive patch on the board, normally either:

- A *test pad* purposely designed into the board for test, or

- A *via* used by circuit board designers to run a signal from one PCB layer to another, which also happens to serve as nice test point

Figure 3-18 shows a bed-of-nails system in action, and Figure 3-19 shows some test pads and vias which are used for probe contact to the PCB.

FIGURE 3-18. Bed-of-nails tester (credit: SPEA)

FIGURE 3-19. Placeholder for test pads (filled gold circles) and vias (gold circles with a hole through them) (credit: Altzone ($http://bit.ly/1OrVhPw$) licensed under CC BY-SA 3.0 ($http://creativecommons.org/licenses/by-sa/3.0/deed.en$))

The board and test fixture are brought into precise contact with one another and then test software runs through a programmed sequence designed to uncover problems with the board, which can include shorts or opens (e.g., leads lifted from pads), bad component orientation (which sometimes can't be caught in AOI), wrong component values, defective components, and signal integrity issues (i.e., do signals propagate properly to destinations on the board without undue degradation).

Experienced designers/developers try to design product PC boards that permit every electrically unique spot on the board (called a *net* by electronics folks) to be accessible by a probe, but this often cannot be achieved due to various constraints, such as the size of the board ("Sorry, we can't fit another test pad in. We're too cramped for space!").

Since ICT electrically access most or all pins on all components, its connections can also be used to program devices such as flash memory, to perform calibrations and tuning, and to run functional tests (covered next).

FUNCTIONAL TEST

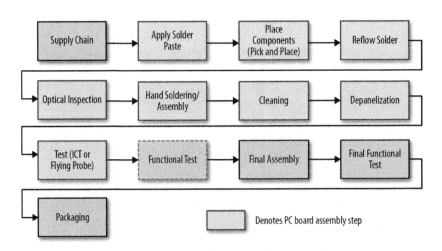

Functional test focuses on the higher-level functionality of the board beyond the direct testing of whether components are properly soldered into place. For example, a functional test might involve loading some test firmware into a processor that's part of the PCBA being tested, having that processor run diagnostics on memory and peripherals, and then outputting the results to a computer via serial port. The PC, in turn, flashes a big green PASS or big red FAIL on its screen, and records the detailed test results to a database for analysis.

Functional test ensures that a range of parts are working together correctly *as a system*. It can also be used to implicitly test circuitry that could not be tested during ICT because of nets that are inaccessible to probes. For example, if a test point is not available to access the net that includes pin X of a certain chip, functional test can implicitly test that pin by running an operation that can only succeed if pin X is soldered to the board and functioning properly.

The downside of functional test is that it tends to not test board connections as thoroughly as ICT does. The safest bet is to perform both ICT and functional test. Later in this chapter when we discuss lower-volume productions we'll look at the tradeoffs of skipping ICT and going exclusively with functional test.

Functional test can be performed as part of ICT, or at a separate station by communicating with the PCBA via serial port, USB, Ethernet, or similar connection. For most products, a final functional test is run after a device is fully assembled. In many cases, functional tests are also performed at interim points during manufacturing. For example, each PCBA in a multiboard system might undergo its own functional test to ensure that it's assembled properly, and then the system is tested again as a whole after final assembly to make sure that the boards are assembled together properly.

BURN-IN TESTING

In some instances, boards are allowed to operate for hours, days, or longer while undergoing functional test, sometimes under stressful conditions (e.g., at hotter temperatures than normally encountered). This might be done for a number of reasons, but most often it's to encourage marginal boards to fail before they leave the factory, which is much better than to fail in a customer's hands.

Well-designed boards rarely require burn-in, but there are exceptions. For example, if a board is going into an application where the cost of failure is tremendous, such as in a satellite, burn-in might be a good idea to reduce an already small possibility of failure in shipped devices.

Final Assembly

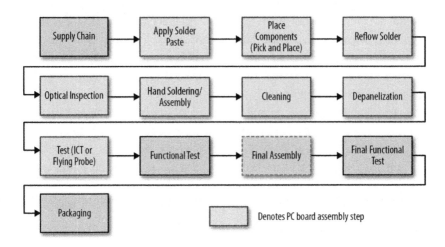

In final assembly. a.k.a. *box build*, PCBAs and mechanical components are assembled into a finished unit, typically by hand. This can take anywhere from a few minutes for simple devices to several person days or longer for sophisticated systems such as scientific instruments.

Through each step, workers carefully follow assembly instructions, diagrams, and/or videos to ensure that each unit is built correctly. This documentation is best produced as a joint effort between designers/developers and factory staff, and time should be budgeted for this activity during project planning.

There are often checks during the process to ensure that things are, in fact, being assembled correctly: for example, we might check a voltage right after attaching an internal cable to ensure that the connection is good, so we don't wait until after our product is fully assembled to find that it's a bad connection (whereupon we'll need to pull it back apart).

It's important to take care during design/development to make the assembly process easy and efficient. First off, final assembly is typically the most labor-intensive step in manufacturing, so anything we can do to shorten the time of this task can yield significant savings. This is where design for assembly comes into play, as discussed earlier in this chapter and in Chapter 1.

Second, a more complex assembly increases the quantity of assembly instructions that we must produce for the factory. It's critical that technicians have unambiguous instructions on how to build the product, and creating these instructions is easier if assembly is simple and straightforward.

Finally, product reliability can be compromised if assembly is tricky. For example, if a technician's hand cannot get direct access to a connector when it comes time to mate with its cable, she might need to place the cable and lock it into place using a small pliers poked through an opening. This can easily lead to a connection that's much less reliable than if it we'd considered this step beforehand and designed the product for good access during assembly.

Final Functional Test

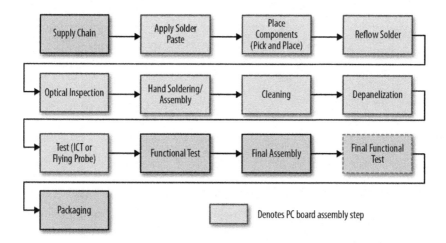

As mentioned earlier, a final test sequence, often called *end-of-line test*, is typically performed after final assembly. While technically this is part of functional test, I've broken it out in our diagram since it tends to be more manual and subjective than other functional tests.

In this step, a technician usually checks the overall fit and finish of the device (e.g., all parts seem to be properly put together—no scratches, and so forth), and then turns the device on and perhaps performs some simple operations to make sure that all seems OK. Normally there's a checklist for the tester to follow, but much of the testing is subjective and therefore tricky to quantify. For example, one tester might notice a faint scratch, whereas another tester might not. Achieving reasonable consistency of pass/fail pronouncements between testers and over time is the challenge here.

Once we're successfully through final functional test, we have a product to ship. Next, we'll box it up to ensure that our unit remains attractive and functional while on its way to its new owner.

Packaging

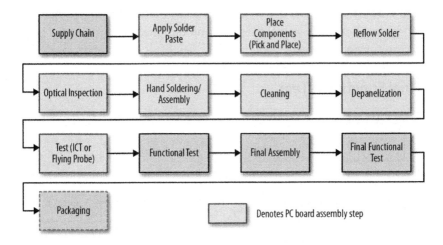

Finished units are made ready for sale by assembling them into a box along with associated parts, manuals, protective foam, bags, etc. These product boxes, in turn, are usually placed into shipping cartons.

Packaging is usually pretty straightforward: bagging, taping, folding, and so forth. It's usually a fully manual step, thus taking a little care to make the job easy can pay good dividends in fewer missteps, (e.g., fewer boxes missing items) and reduced manufacturing costs.

All boxed up, our units are finally ready to turn into revenue!

More, and Less

Now that we've reviewed a general process for manufacturing in medium volumes, let's look at how things might change for higher and lower volumes.

HOW MANY?

While the basic manufacturing tasks are similar no matter what our build quantity is, the way in which these tasks are accomplished can vary quite a bit depending on yearly or lifetime production volumes. As quantities increase, the use of automation tends to increase with it. (PCBA complexity can also impact automation; e.g., building a small number of PCBAs that each contain an unusually large number of components, or components that require particularly careful treatment, might each benefit from substantial automation.)

Suppose that we have a manufacturing task that can be performed, by hand, in one minute. If we expect to only build, say, 100 units of that product over its lifetime, such as in the case of a communications satellite, spending $10,000 to automate this task doesn't make sense. US contract manufacturer labor costs are in the ballpark of $1 a minute, so we'd be spending $10,000 to save $100 over the product's lifetime. However, if we expect to build 1 *million* units over the product's lifetime, such as in the case of a portable disk drive for consumer use, then our $10,000 investment in automation will save $1 million in manufacturing costs, which is a very good bargain.

For purposes of thinking about the relative production volumes, the following categories will be used in this book:

- Very high volume: >100,000 per year

- High volume: 10,000–100,000 per year

- Medium volume production: 1,000–10,000 per year

- Low volumes: 100–1,000 per year

- Protoduction (so called because production techniques are somewhat similar to prototype production): < 100 per year

Note that these are not standardized categories or numbers. For example, when a huge *contract manufacturer* (CM) that builds cell phones hears "low volume," they might think in terms of fewer than 100,000 units per year, whereas a small specialized CM might translate "low volume" into under 100 per year. When communicating with others about manufacturing volume, it's important to provide ballpark numbers to ensure that everyone's on the same page.

HIGHER-VOLUME PRODUCTION

Higher-volume production is substantially similar to the preceding process, but with an increased emphasis on automation and inventory control.

- Supply chain will have more effort devoted to managing inventory, since inventory can become a large investment of perhaps millions of dollars. The supply chain staff at both the company that sells the product and its contract manufacturer will likely include more people. The two organizations will become much more "cozy" with each other, and with component suppliers, in order to ensure that inventory is minimized and supply of components and finished products are not interrupted.

- There will be a greater emphasis on tweaking the design even after manufacturing is running smoothly to cut costs, improve quality, and/or account for component shortages. Supply Chain will have a close ongoing relationship with designers/developers or with a *sustaining engineering* group specifically charged with supporting and improving ongoing production.

- Work performed by hand at lower volumes might be automated. For example, components that are not amenable to reflow soldering in an oven might be soldered using automated selective soldering technologies.

- There will be more emphasis during the design/development process on reducing the need for hand work (i.e., DFA as discussed in this chapter's "Final Assembly" on page 78 and in Chapter 1).

- To reduce the number of assemblies that need repair or are scrapped, greater efforts will be made to collect and analyze statistical quality data. The results will be used to improve the design/development and manufacturing processes.

LOWER-VOLUME PRODUCTION

In lower-volume production, the focus is the opposite of high-volume production; the emphasis is on reducing fixed costs that are difficult to recoup due to the small number of boards that will be built. This typically means more manual work. Here are some tactics that can be suitable for lower-volume production:

Relaxed inventory control

Low-volume products tend to be high-priced products, and the cost of parts is typically a smaller percentage of total product cost as compared to higher-volume products. Also, the effort (i.e., cost) of having professionals carefully manage inventory will end up being fairly high when looked at on a per-unit basis. So the best bet is usually to *not* be in a position where inventory must be carefully managed.

Keeping a relatively large inventory of parts, e.g. always having at least six months' worth on hand, will reduce the risk of an interruption of inventory that becomes an interruption of shipping products. Potential reengineering and retooling costs associated with parts becoming unavailable can be avoided altogether by purchasing enough parts to build as many units as is anticipated for the rest of the product's life; this is called a *lifetime buy*. At the very least, if we ask, manufacturers and distributors will notify us when a part is going obsolete (called an *end-of-life [EOL] notice*) so manufacturers can have the opportunity to plan, including purchasing sufficient inventory.

Substituting flying-probe ICT for bed-of-nails

In flying-probe testing, shown in Figure 3-20, several robotically controlled probes "fly" around the board, making electrical measurements at exposed metal features such as component pins, vias, test points, and so forth.

The advantage of flying probe versus bed-of-nails is that the former does not require an expensive custom test fixture with hundreds or thousands of precisely located probes. Instead, the positions to be touched with the probes are programmed into a computer: the PCB database is pulled into the test system, and a test engineer indicates the points to be probed and the tests to be run. Also, because the per-board customization is only in software, flying-probe tests can be updated with relatively minimal effort when a board design changes, whereas bed-of-nails fixtures require rework (or even a new fixture) when a board design is updated.

FIGURE 3-20. Flying probe (credit: SPEA)

The disadvantages of flying probe versus bed-of-nails include:

- Flying probe is relatively basic compared to bed-of-nails, because fewer points on the circuit are being tested simultaneously, but it can perform a good range of tests including finding open circuits and shorts, verifying resistor and capacitor values, and some more advanced testing.

- Flying probe takes quite a bit more time as probes are moved from test point to test point, rather than contacting all test points at once. This can be a definite bottleneck as manufacturing volumes increase.

Relying on functional test only

There's a growing trend towards eliminating ICT and flying probe altogether and relying only on functional test. The benefits here include:

- Not needing expensive circuit-based test equipment. This is attractive to people who'd like to build in-house rather than using a factory (see "Factoryless board assembly" on page 85).

- Not requiring the specialized services of factory-test engineers. Functional tests are more likely to fall within the expertise of design/development engineers.

The disadvantages include:

- The difficulty in testing 100% of the system. It's generally pretty easy to test most of a system using functional test. In products with embedded processors, just turning on a unit and seeing if it starts/boots properly, while measuring power draw, is often a reasonable confirmation that power supplies, processor, memory, major busses and peripherals are *basically* working. But testing *all* functionality can involve writing a lot of tests.

- Marginal functionality can be missed. For example, suppose that an onboard power supply is designed to produce 2.7V within 5% tolerance, but in fact is only producing 2.5V on one assembled board (a 7% difference). The components powered by the 2.7V supply might actually function at 2.5V, so functional test would look fine. But the out-of-tolerance voltage is likely due to a manufacturing error or a bad part, and subsequently there's a high risk that something bad will occur in that unit over time—circuit failures, shorter battery life, etc. In comparison, this problem would be caught by measuring the voltage directly using ICT or flying probe.

Factoryless board assembly

Feeling adventurous and/or parsimonious? There are a number of techniques for assembling PC boards without expensive factory-grade production equipment. The general theme is to:

1. Manually squeegee solder onto the PCB through a stencil.

2. Place parts by hand using a pair of tweezers or similar (tedious, but not as impossible as you might think).

3. Solder the parts using a soldering iron, hot-air rework station, toaster oven, electric skillet, or inexpensive semi-industrial-grade reflow oven.

Specific instructions for assembling boards "on the cheap" like this can be easily found on the Web. See the Resources section of this chapter for more details.

These techniques can work for smaller boards in smaller quantities, but there can be significant challenges and constraints due to the number of manual steps involved and the nonoptimal equipment that's used. In short, factoryless PCB assembly ain't simple, takes a long time, and there are things that can't really be done by hand (e.g., I'll cough up $100 to the first person who can properly solder a 1,000+ pin BGA package using an electric skillet.) But for short runs and/or simple boards, it's definitely an option.

The People Stuff: Factory Culture

To understand how factories work, it's as important to understand the culture behind the "action" as it is to understand the equipment and processes. While design/development culture is all about nonstop creativity (basically contained chaos at times), manufacturing culture is all about process, precision, and repeatability.

As we've seen in this chapter, there's a lot of stuff that needs to work properly for a product to make it through the factory and out the door to customers. Lots of steps, many bits to be soldered, lots of testing of various sorts, and so forth. Deviations in process, such as setting a reflow oven five degrees too high, almost never make a product better, and almost invariably cause expensive problems like low factory yields or high rates of field failures. In factories, change that's accidental or not carefully thought out is usually a bad thing.

As a result, while designers/developers are mighty engines of continuous change—making changes is what we do for a living—factories are strongly biased towards *stasis*, keeping things the same. Getting a factory to make a quick change is as easy as getting a designer/developer to follow a checklist, which can result in a cultural divide and occasional hard feelings:

Designer/developer: "Why do I need to fill out so much paperwork to get these factory folks to change their process? It's just a capacitor change —what's the big deal?"

Factory: "Another capacitor change? Last time we made a capacitor change, they swore it wouldn't change anything, but we started having failures during ICT because it was a different value and screwed up the test. We had to get test engineers in here on a Sunday to get things running. What's with those design engineers? Will they stop tweaking the product already, it's sucking up way too much of everyone's time, and they'll just yell at us when they get the bill."

For us, that one capacitor change is just a tiny thing, but for the factory that one change might require several machines to be reprogrammed and tests performed to see that the new programming is correct, product test procedures altered, new capacitor inventory ordered, old capacitors scrapped or sold, and so forth.

In addition, as mentioned at this chapter's start, designers and developers tend to not understand how factories work, nor do we naturally tend to think much about the manufacturing effort. We sometimes design things that can barely be assembled in our own office/lab, and we somehow expect that the manufacturing folks will figure out how to do a quick and reliable job of it when the numbers scale up.

In later chapters, we'll discuss some practical ways that design/development and manufacturing can work together to build better products (and have more fun together). For now, it's enough to know that the two worlds are different, but they're different for very good reasons that should be respected.

Final Thoughts

Hopefully this chapter has helped a little to demystify the manufacturing process in order to build a better picture of how disparate parts can be reliably turned into products. In future chapters, we'll talk more about the specifics of designing for manufacturability, and about effectively working with manufacturing folks as a key part of our development process.

In the next chapter, we'll swing back to design and development, diving into the preliminary product planning process that will help us to understand what we're getting ourselves into, and whether it's worth the effort.

Resources

The Web has lots of information about various aspects of manufacturing, but mostly in bits and pieces. There's little that pulls everything together. The way to learn more is to get a tour of a local contract manufacturer (CM) and ask lots of questions. Particularly, if the CM might end up getting some substantial business through you, they can be quite accommodating.

The next best thing to a live tour is to see the various machines and processes in action via videos, so below I've put together a collection of videos available on the Web that do a reasonable job of showing the "good stuff."

FACTORY AUTOMATION

Adafruit has some nice videos (*https://www.youtube.com/playlist? list=PL2D9F7601F958B970*) that show off manufacturing automation in their own factory. While the machinery is pretty typical for a small manufacturing facility, the rest is decidedly more casual and funky than is typical in a manufacturing environment—which clearly works well for Adafruit, probably because of continuous close interaction between designers/developers and manufacturing folks. Two videos in the set are of particular note:

- How it's made - Ladyada and Micah Scott manufacturing Fadecandy at Adafruit (*http://youtu.be/UvWWITJn5UU*) Longer video with some coverage of loading reels into the pick-and-place, solder application, a moment on reflow, and functional test. One interesting bit starts at about 1:50: a discussion of what color LED to have the pick-and-place use on the board. It would be more typical to have a parts list (a.k.a. bill of materials, or BOM) available and for the factory to obtain and load whatever part is specified on the BOM. It's likely in this case that Adafruit has a few standard-sized LEDs in a few colors that stay loaded in the pick-and-place all of the time, and the designer/developer simply picks the color(s) they want in the sizes they've specified, as seen in the video.

- Adafruit pick-and-place machine in action! ADXL335 (*http://youtu.be/ 7BRVY6XNdMo*) A close-up view of the pick-and-place at work.

Shenzhen Tena RK3188 HDMI Stick Factory Tour (*http://youtu.be/ RFHCoLIZ8qQ*) is a video tour of a factory in Shenzheng, China that builds little Android-based computers and TV tuners. This factory is not too different from what we'd expect to see in the US for manufacturing consumer goods. It shows almost the entire build process, including pick-and-place, inspection, programming, functional test, assembly, and burn in. A few notes:

- Inspection after PCB assembly is performed by eye instead of by AOI machine, perhaps because labor is relatively low cost compared to in the US and/or reliability is less critical for this product.

- The blowing air jets at 13:30 are an *air shower*. Air showers are used to blow particulates off before people enter a clean area. In this case, the cleanliness is presumably so dust particles don't land on optical components and cause specks.

- The metal stamping machinery at 18:40 is not typical of a factory; stamped metal is usually ordered from outside vendors.

- At 22:30, the video shows incoming inspection of vendor parts to ensure that the parts meet requirements. This process is not described earlier in this chapter, but should be performed on parts we're not confident will meet necessary specifications.

FACTORYLESS (E.G., DIY) MANUFACTURING

There's no shortage of videos on factoryless PCB assembly videos on YouTube. For hand-soldering and rework, a couple of good sources are:

- David Jones EEVblog (*https://www.youtube.com/playlist? list=PL2862BF3631A5C1AA*) on YouTube has a playlist of videos primarily covering hand-soldering and rework from David Jones' EEVBlog series. Fun, frenetic, and lots of good information.

- SparkFun has a set of tutorials on building SMT boards (*https://www.sparkfun.com/tutorials/category/2*) on their site, including their notorious reflow skillet video. Also available—thanks to SparkFun—on YouTube, is an additional playlist of videos on hand-soldering (*https://www.youtube.com/playlist?list=PL8bhmOjoPT7bX8BctCH5f6-Ec6jlh-cOd*).

For DIY-level PCB assembly automation (i.e., using small machines rather than relying totally on hand assembly), Dangerous Prototypes has a few videos on tools for smaller scale manufacturing:

- TM220A table top pick-and-place overview (*http://youtu.be/yRxcYOonuD8*) Review of an inexpensive table-top pick-and-place.

- Infrared reflow oven Qinsi QS-5100 (*http://youtu.be/GIRLY3VNNVw*) Review of an inexpensive small infrared reflow oven. Has a good discussion of the tradeoffs of using small ovens versus hotplates for reflow.

- 983A/986A Solder Paste Dispenser (*http://youtu.be/s3-y1RjxD1E*) An alternative to stencil and squeegee for applying solder paste to PCBs.

## CHAPTER 4

Preliminary Planning: Can This Be a Success?

FEW THINGS ARE MORE DEFLATING THAN PUTTING FORTH A TON OF effort that ultimately has little or no effect on the world around us. It's like throwing a nice party and having nobody show up. If we develop a product, we want lots of people to use it! We want our product to be successful.

An important part of achieving success is choosing our battles wisely. Digging a tunnel to the Earth's core with a teaspoon would be incredibly cool, but it would also be a fool's errand. It ain't gonna work. There are probably better adventures to set off on that are more likely to succeed.

One of the critical purposes of project planning is to help ensure that we've picked a winnable battle. As discussed previously, there are two fundamental parts to the product planning process that answer related questions:

1. If developed, does this product have a reasonable chance of being a success (however we define success)?

2. If it has a chance of success, what will it *really* take to develop this product (e.g., cost, timeline, people needed, etc.) so we can decide whether the return is worth the effort?

This chapter is about answering question 1. The basic idea is to do a fairly quick reality check to understand whether our product idea is worth pursuing further, or whether it can be ruled out as having an unacceptably low likelihood of ultimately succeeding. In particular, we're looking for obvious showstoppers, but we'll also do a few lightweight "sniff tests" to see if the business concept seems like it will work out.

Before we get going on the planning, I'd like to take a few paragraphs to introduce MicroPed, the product we'll be developing in order to illustrate concepts as we move forward.

Introducing MicroPed

"For the things we have to learn before we can do them, we learn by doing them."

—Aristotle

Both as a student and as a teacher, I've found that learning works best through a mix of theory and reality. For example, $E=mc^2$ is a nice little equation that tells us that a little bit of mass can convert to a lot of energy. But this concept *really* comes to life using examples, for example, that the mass in a single stick of chewing gum (one gram) can convert to as much energy as is needed to drive a car 14 million miles (at 25 mpg).

I'm not sure that there are too many product development concepts that can be illustrated as dramatically as $E=mc^2$, but we'll do what we can. Beginning in this chapter, we'll track an actual project, a tiny wireless pedometer I've named *MicroPed*, to illustrate some of the real-world challenges faced in product development. While the MicroPed project will serve to catalyze the discussion, we'll also expand its specifics into more-general ideas applicable to other products.

Let's take a look at what we're building.

WHY DOES THE WORLD NEED MICROPED?

It's said that *necessity is the mother of invention*. Appropriately, MicroPed was born from the needs of a frustrated pedometer user: me.

Like millions of other people, I enjoy using a pedometer to keep an eye on how much I'm moving around. I've owned several of these devices, but have yet to find one that's ideal. What I really want is a pedometer that I don't have to fuss with or even think about for months on end, but which tracks my walking and running all day, every day. I also want updates on my statistics available via smart phone, web browser, and so forth. I want it to fit easily in my wallet, which—unlike the pedometers

I've owned—I always remember to take with me. And I want it to sit in my wallet for months, perhaps a year, without needing to be removed for battery replacement or recharge.

To my knowledge, no product currently marketed quite fits the usage model I'm looking for. Maybe there's a reason for this: perhaps too few people want such a product, or it's very difficult to develop or will cost too much to manufacture. But maybe there *is* a market for such a thing. I'd like to find out!

Can we build a product that will fulfill my wishes? And if we do, is there reason to believe we can make a profit? We'll try to find first-order answers for these questions in this chapter after we define the product a bit more.

Before we dive in, a few notes about MicroPed are in order. Unlike most products whose goal is to earn a profit, MicroPed's primary motivation is as a pedagogical tool to help illustrate the concepts in this book. I wanted a relatively straightforward development project that helps illustrate key technology points without requiring too much effort from me (hey, I'm writing a book and working at the same time!), and with minimal risk of surprises. It's hoped that at a later date MicroPed will become a commercial product, but that's a secondary (although not trivial) consideration.

Because of MicroPed's goals and their priorities, some parts of the process, primarily on the nontechnical side, are significantly lighter than we'd find in a typical product, in particular:

- Market research (testing the concept with users and getting feedback) is less rigorous than I'd want to see in a typical product. We'll cover the basics, but there should typically be more rigor.

- We won't look for investment at the project's start, nor will we discuss this topic in any detail. Dealing with investors and investment issues is often a big part of starting a new venture, although these days it seems more typical to seek investment after having a pretty good prototype. We'll cover the financial fundamentals, but for startups there are other books to be read that can help. A few are listed in this chapter's Resources section.

Now, let's start creating MicroPed. As promised, we'll start by defining something we think is technically feasible and will be accepted in the marketplace.

MARKETING REQUIREMENTS

Before we can do much planning, it's important to define our product to some degree: less than a full design, but more than a vague concept. This helps us to:

- Think through our product features, which can be important in understanding our potential markets, the costs of manufacturing our product, and some of the challenges that we'll face in development.

- Make sure that we're on the same page with others we're working with such as collaborators, potential customers, etc. In other words, we need to make sure they won't be thinking *Cadillac Escalade* while you're thinking *Nissan Leaf.*

The following wish list is a good start for MicroPed:

1. Small enough that I can comfortably put it in my wallet, or attach it to a shoelace and not have it annoy me.

2. Can operate for a year without needing any servicing, including battery charge or replacement.

3. Syncs data to smart phone, computer, smart watch, and so forth.

4. Waterproof, able to survive swimming and washing machines.

5. Can survive being run over by a car or truck.

6. Stores tracking data on a server (via smart phone or computer), which will be available from any web browser on the Internet.

7. Multiple MicroPeds living in different pieces of clothing and accessories can all be associated with a single user, so I don't need to move a device from, say, wallet to running shorts. The backend system should understand that the data from all of my devices together is the aggregate record of my activity.

8. My data is *my* data. I want to be able to use the data I collect in any way I want without forking over a yearly fee.

9. My data is not *your* data. My data shouldn't be available to advertisers, marketers, health insurers, the NSA, or anyone else unless I want them to have it for some reason.

10. Open source hardware and software. I want interested users to make MicroPed better with improved algorithms. Or they can customize MicroPed for new applications; there are dozens of potential uses for

a device that has a processor, measures acceleration, and supports low-power RF communications, such as a sensing breaking glass, measuring heart beats (ballistocardiography), measuring the force of hits on football helmets, sensing when a baby's fallen asleep, and so forth.

You'll notice that this wish list is oriented toward usage rather than technology. Lists of high-level wants like these are sometimes called *marketing requirements*, because they ultimately encompass the claims that marketing folks will make, claims that can be understood by typical users. Later on, if our research convinces us to develop MicroPed, we'll create another layer of *technical requirements* that get more specific about how these goals translate into unambiguous specifications, so that we all understand exactly what's meant by "small enough that I can comfortably put one in my wallet" (which might translate to "no longer or wider than a standard credit card and no thicker than 4 mm").

Marketing requirements in hand, we have a good idea of what our product will do for our customers. Next, let's think about who those customers might be.

TARGET MARKETS

Since we'd like to profit by selling MicroPeds to customers, we should define who our prospective customers are so we can consider how many of them exist, and think about any other potential needs they might have. Determining the most important markets for a product is usually not too challenging, but it does warrant some thought—obviously, it's best to pick markets that are larger, have a strong demonstrated need for our product, and have money to spend.

For MicroPed, our target markets will be:

1. People with an interest in fitness: athletes, exercisers, and anyone else who wants to keep track of their walking and running.

2. Makers/hobbyists/tinkerers (hereafter referred to simply as *Makers*) looking for an inexpensive programmable platform with an accelerometer and wireless connectivity.

At this point, we've defined our product and target markets at a high level. Now it's time to do some research to see if this product and these markets are indeed a business opportunity.

Can It Make Money?

Before we sink our time and money into a development effort, it would be nice to know whether we'll likely end up making money on the effort. Determining whether a new product is likely to be profitable can be a pretty sophisticated exercise if we examine all of the details and possibilities. It's also a very imperfect art: even companies that spend millions determining whether a new product will be a winner can be well off the mark, sometimes spectacularly so: search the 'net for *Microsoft Bob, New Coke, Clairol "Touch of Yogurt" Shampoo,* and/or *Colgate Kitchen Entrees* if you'd like to peruse some examples.

But while planning the "money stuff" is imperfect, it's still pretty important. Among the things that it's good for are:

- Catching showstoppers like the need to set a prohibitively high price to cover the product's development and manufacturing costs. If you'll need to charge $386,000 per unit for your levitating kiddie car, you might want to think twice.

- Giving us a sense of the potential upside for the product. Even if we do a great job, perhaps only a handful of people might need our product, so unless we can make a great deal of profit on each sale, we'll have a problem.

Before we get to the actual numbers, let's take a moment to define some terms and to map out some financial questions we'll want to answer.

A QUICK LOOK AT THE MONEY STUFF

While this is a book about technology, not accounting, our technology needs to meet financial needs to be a success, so let's take a quick look. At a very basic level, most of us would agree that "making money" means that more money *comes in the door* from selling the product than *goes out the door* in developing and building the product.

Profit is more or less the name we give for *income minus costs*. Normally a product is intended to be profitable on its own. (There are occasional situations where a product is not intended to be profitable itself, but rather will serve a higher purpose that increases overall profits; e.g., a piece of test equipment that's given away for free in order to drive sales of the disposable supplies needed to run the tests.)

Assuming that profit is an important goal, our task at this stage is to forget about development for short while, and to understand whether the product can be profitable once we're manufacturing and selling it. If a product costs more to manufacture than we can likely sell it for, then it can never be a commercial success, and thus it's not worth going through the substantial exercise of estimating development costs.

In this planning phase, we'll identify all of the sources of income and costs directly associated with manufacturing and selling our product, and make some smart guesses as to what their values could be. With this information, we'll construct a model that gives us some idea of whether we can come out ahead.

WAG versus SWAG

While we're on the topic of guesses, there are two acronyms that are often used by product developers: *WAG* and *SWAG*, pronounced like the description of a happy dog's tail and pirate's takings, respectively.

A WAG is a *Wild-Assed Guess*: there's a good possibility that the guess is way off the mark.

A SWAG is a *Scientific Wild-Assed Guess*: a little better, but still liable to be substantially off.

Used in a sentence: "That estimate on manufacturing cost is just my WAG. I'll call some factories and get their SWAGs, but we'll really need some more detailed design info before we get a solid estimate."

Income is pretty straightforward to calculate: it generally equals the number of units sold multiplied by the price of each unit. However, unless we're developing the next generation of a product that's already selling well, determining pricing is a challenge and predicting volume (number of units sold) is always a SWAG at best.

Total costs, on the other hand, has more components to it but is a bit more predictable. Roughly speaking, its components are:

- The direct costs of manufacturing product: materials, cost of contract manufacturing, etc.

- The costs of research and development

- Ongoing costs such as paying salaries, advertising costs, customer support, rent, utilities, equipment, and supplies

- Easy-to-forget-about-stuff like interest on loans, taxes, and depreciation

Doing a full prediction that takes all of these items into account requires a fair bit of work and is best done with the help of experienced accounting help once we know that we want to move forward with marketing our product.

But at this stage of the process, it's not worth sweating all the details. We're simply trying to get a quick feel as to whether the product makes even first-order financial sense once it is ready to sell. So, in this "back of the envelope" planning phase, we'll look at just a few basic items:

Income:

- How many units might we be able to sell?

- How much might we be able to charge per unit?

Costs:

- What will the product cost to manufacture?

- Are there any technologies that will be expensive or impossible to develop or purchase, or any big (i.e., expensive) research projects required before we'll know how to develop and manufacture our product?

Overall:

- What's our estimate for the product's gross margin (percentage of our selling price left after paying for the direct cost of making a unit)? Is this gross margin consistent with gross margins of similar products?

If the answers to these questions look good in this first planning phase, then we'll flesh out predictions for these and other prospective incomes and costs during the detailed planning phase.

Let's start with the fun part: income!

INCOME PROJECTIONS

There are many good reasons to spend some time thinking about the size of our potential markets, i.e., the number of units we can reasonably expect to sell. Beyond the obvious reason (selling more units means the potential for greater income), sales volume will also have a substantial impact on the cost of producing each device: usually the higher our production volumes (estimated annual units, EAU), the lower the unit cost for parts and assembly. So while it might be insanely expensive to build a sophisticated product in small quantities, larger quantities might be far more reasonable.

When gauging market size, it's easy to fool ourselves by thinking about how cool and/or useful we think our product is, and how obvious this will be to everyone else. For example, the inventor of chicken goggles (US patent 730,918, shown in Figure 4-1) was probably dreaming of the many millions of chickens raised in the US each year, but might have failed to properly explore the question of whether any poultry farmer would actually *want* the things.

FIGURE 4-1. Patent 730,918, eye protector for chickens

The best way to do a quick check on the need for a product and the size of its market is to review the performance of *existing* products with similarities, since it will give us a feel for how many people have proven that they'll spend money on something like what we're selling and how much they've actually been willing to spend.

Even though we normally like to think of our product idea as revolutionary, almost all new products are broadly similar to existing products. For example, there's general agreement that the original iPod was revolutionary, but that doesn't mean there weren't broadly similar products. Other personal digital music players existed at the time (albeit not-very-good ones), as did good cassette-based personal analog music players (i.e., the Walkman). In most cases, *revolutionary* can also be described as *an evolution that's so good it changes the playing field.*

In MicroPed's case, there are two prospective markets, and within each somewhat comparable products exist. Let's see what these markets are and what they can tell us about MicroPed's potential.

Activity tracker market

Nowadays, wireless pedometers are called *activity trackers* (even though they still mainly measure footsteps). The activity tracker market isn't tiny, with well-known participants such as FitBit, Jawbone, Nike, Polar, and so on. For perhaps a year or more, my local Target and Best Buy have both had a good bit of aisle space dedicated to these products, so they must be selling a fair number of them.

Turning to the Internet for some more rigorous analysis, a pair of articles in MobiHealthNews, Fitbit shipped the most activity trackers in 2013 (*http://bit.ly/1OrWy9l*) and Fitbit, Jawbone, Nike had 97 percent of fitness tracker retail sales in 2013 (*http://bit.ly/1OrWyWJ*) state that:

- The "digital fitness tracker" market sold $238 million of product in 2013.

- The market is at an early stage and growing rapidly; its size is expected to roughly double in 2014.

The articles' data comes from NPD Group, a respected market research group that tracks sales at retailers, so these numbers are probably reasonably close to reality.

Given that these monitors sell for $50–$100 or so, the $238 million figure indicates that millions of units are being sold each year. So it looks like there's a real market for products in MicroPed's general category, and that market might well be growing rapidly.

So far, so good! There seems to be a significant market that's buying millions of devices that are similar to ours each year, so we have a chance of success.

Note that if we wanted more details on this market, reports are available (known as *market reports* or *market research reports*) that provide more information and analysis. These tend to be pricey (often thousands of dollars) and sometimes of dubious value, but they can be helpful. A few small insights can translate into a lot of money, particularly when sales volumes are high. But in this case, since one of MicroPed's purposes is to have a demonstration project for this book, I'm OK with simply knowing that there's a good potential market (and keeping a few thousand dollars in my pocket).

The next question we should ask is whether, compared to competing products, our product has unique selling points (USPs) and key selling points (KSPs) that will make our product attractive to a substantial group of people. We won't truly know the answer to this question until our product is on the market and selling, but there are several ways to get some pretty good indications.

Large companies tend to do extensive (and expensive) market research, which can be helpful. But one of the best ways to see if our product is attractive to consumers is to simply ask prospective customers whether they'd buy the product as we're envisioning it. We can ask current users of competitive products whether they would purchase our product as an upgrade, or would have purchased our product instead of their current product if it had been available. We can also ask people who don't own a competitive product if our product has features that would persuade them to buy it.

This kind of informal research can be tricky because people's real behaviors might be different than the answers they give. For example, they might say positive things to avoid hurting our feelings. So it's best to look for emphatic answers, such as "I'd buy that in a second. Let me know when it's on the market!" rather than "I'd probably buy that." In these situations, a verbal "probably will buy" usually means "probably won't buy" in real life.

Crowdfunding sites such as Kickstarter and Indiegogo are another way to perform low-cost market research. On the plus side, these give us feedback on new product concepts that's potentially much better than simply asking people if they'd buy our product: crowdfunding participants vote yes by ponying up real dollars so we know that a *yes* is really a *yes*. There's also the obvious benefit of bringing in some money for development and manufacturing.

But crowdfunding isn't a panacea; it also has important limitations. First, product development needs to be well along for a crowdfunding initiative to be successful. As of my writing this, all 10 of the 10 most-funded hardware products on Kickstarter had their industrial design and often much of their functionality in place before their campaign began. It's *much* easier for customers to envision using a product if they can see it. Having something more substantial than a nice idea builds some confidence that the product's development will be completed, and that ordered units will actually be manufactured and shipped.

Another issue with crowdsourcing is that it tests a specific way to sell a product to a specific group of people. Crowdfunding participants are early-adopter types that trend toward young adults, male, childless folks with higher-than-average incomes. This audience is perfect for cool gizmo types of products, but probably not as useful for selling, say, hearing aids.

Crowdfunding sites might also not be great arenas to test sales of items normally sold in standard online or bricks-and-mortar stores: products might sell better or worse when sitting alongside their competition as opposed to being on a crowdfunding site with a video and a page full of marketing copy.

We'll be running a crowdfunding campaign for MicroPed once development is a little farther along, but alas, after this book is on the shelves. But for now, based on informal discussions with potential purchasers, it seems like the idea generates enough enthusiasm that we can have some confidence that a reasonable number of people will want it.

But at what price? How much can we expect consumers to pay? Next, let's take a look at this important question.

Activity tracker selling price

Let's get a feel for the price range that the market can tolerate for activity trackers by looking at what they currently *do* pay. Popping onto Amazon and searching for "wireless activity tracker," I'm presented with devices that range in price from about $25–$150.

Since MicroPed has a unique set of features, it's a little tough to determine with precision which specific activity tracker is most similar.

At the high end, price-wise, are the Jawbone UP 24, FitBit Flex, and Misfit Shine—each at about $100–$125. They are like MicroPed in that they are quite small and don't display actual numbers, but unlike MicroPed they're worn on the wrist, and two of them have some indicators for the user to view (just a few LEDs to track basic progress). The UP 24, Flex, and Shine are rechargeable but must be recharged every week for an hour or so. By contrast, MicroPed will likely use a disposable battery, but that battery need only be replaced once a year, an operation that should cost $2 for the new battery and require a few minutes of effort.

At the lower end of the market at about $50 is the Fitbit Zip. The Zip is a significantly larger (but not huge) device that clips onto a belt, pocket, or similar. The Zip is like MicroPed in that it uses a disposable battery and claims a long battery life (six months). Unlike MicroPed, Zip has an LCD display (albeit of very low quality), but cannot fit in a wallet and is not waterproof.

None of these products are open/hackable like we'd like MicroPed to be, nor as flexible as MicroPed (e.g., fit in wallets, on a shoe, in the tiny watch pocket found on jeans, etc.). Only one, the Jawbone UP 24, is like MicroPed in not directly displaying any activity feedback at all—but the UP 24 is Amazon's bestselling activity tracker as I write this and also the most expensive one that's selling well, so needing a smart phone or computer to see reported information does not seem to deter consumers.

The price we can charge for MicroPed is not entirely clear, but based on our quick perusal of Amazon it seems that the $50–$100 range is reasonable. For reality-check purposes, let's be conservative and go with $50. That way, any surprises on pricing are more likely to be good than bad.

The Maker market

The Maker market is a tougher market to quantify, in part because it's extremely fragmented. One way to gauge potential market size might be to examine unit sales of Arduino and Raspberry Pi, two popular open platforms for DIY experimentation (Arduino is fully open; Raspberry Pi is open source only for software). Some Internet searching indicates that each of these platforms sells somewhere around a million units per year, so this is a nontrivial market.

However, these platforms are much more flexible than MicroPed and they're designed as all-purpose "brains" to be used in conjunction with other circuitry to solve many different types of problems, and also as educational tools. MicroPed, by contrast, will be a specialized platform supporting only acceleration sensing and wireless communication, packaged up in an enclosure, so its Maker market is likely much more limited. It would probably be realistic to discount the Maker market size for MicroPed by 95% compared to these other products, so we're looking at a potential market size of maybe 50,000 or so. Still not tiny, but much smaller than the activity tracker market.

We could do more research here, but it seems pretty likely that the Maker market is a good bit smaller for MicroPed than the activity tracker market. Makers looking for a device to hack could be a profitable market, or MicroPed's hackability might make it attractive to Maker-ish folks who are looking for a tracker. In other words, when they decide to buy a tracker, they might veer toward MicroPed because it's hackable.

Arduinos and Raspberry Pi's sell for $10–$35, but since the activity tracker market will likely be more significant for us, it makes sense to allow the tracker pricing to predominantly drive MicroPed pricing and not go through the exercise of narrowing potential pricing for the Maker market at this point.

We now have some idea of what we should be charging for MicroPed. Next we'll look at the other side of the profit equation and get a feel for how much it will cost to produce each unit.

COST OF GOODS SOLD

The cost to manufacture each copy of our product, technically known as the unit *cost of goods sold*, or *COGS* (pronounced like cogs on a gear), is a make-or-break calculation: obviously, the cost must be well below our selling price. Fortunately, COGS tends to be reasonably predictable compared to the other numbers that we'll estimate at this early stage, but a good estimate will require some effort.

COGS includes just the direct cost to manufacture one unit, and does not include indirect costs such as R&D, salaries for management, sales and marketing, and so forth. Assuming that we use a contract manufacturer, COGS is fundamentally the cost of components plus the price we pay for assembly. Of these two, components are usually the larger cost, particularly for higher volumes and more complex devices.

Making a reasonable estimate of COGS requires having some idea of the components we'll use so we can price those components and the cost of assembling them. And the only way to have an idea of which components we'll use is to do some thinking about the product's design. So this is the time when design/development begins, albeit in a very rough form.

Components, in turn, come in two basic varieties: electronic and mechanical. Software is typically not to be considered as part of COGS unless there is a unit licensing cost for each copy sold; e.g., for a commercial operating system.

In the case of products where mechanical parts merely form an enclosure that holds everything together, COGS is mainly dependent on the cost of electronics components and PCBA assembly. The enclosure will likely be composed of a few plastic injection-molded pieces that might be 10%–20% of the component costs, and will be relatively trivial to assemble. Creating the molds might be more expensive, but that is part of our R&D effort estimates later.

In products where mechanical components go beyond merely serving as an enclosure, particularly if they move with respect to one another during routine use, such as in robotic products, mechanical components become a much more important part of the cost and should be estimated carefully. Parts that move with respect to one another are known generically as *mechanisms*, and estimating the cost of mechanisms tends to be a challenging exercise best left to experts (and beyond the scope of this book).

MicroPed will serve as a good general example for estimating COGS when mechanical parts are only used as an enclosure, so let's dig in.

MicroPed will ultimately consist of a system that includes the wearable unit we think of as the product, as well as related software running on smart phones, servers, and so forth. For the purpose of estimating COGS, we need only concern ourselves with the electronic and mechanical parts of the wearable unit because that's the only bit that will incur a significant cost for each MicroPed unit we sell.

We'll start our COGS estimate by laying out the electronics architecture of MicroPed's hardware piece (the wearable). Then we'll turn that architecture into some circuit building blocks, and estimate the cost of those blocks and of assembling them into a finished unit.

Preliminary electronics architecture

I've been involved in the design/development of many products that are similar to MicroPed, so developing an architecture is a pretty straightforward exercise for me. If it weren't, I'd try hard to find some experts who've designed similar products to help out.

Fundamentally, activity trackers are simple devices: an accelerometer to sense movement, a wireless subsystem to transmit data to a receiver, some smarts to tie things together, and a power source. A block diagram of the MicroPed hardware is shown in Figure 4-2.

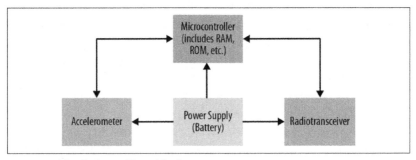

FIGURE 4-2. MicroPed wearable architecture

Materials costs

Since MicroPed looks to be a *reasonably* straightforward device—some electronic parts on a board in a simple enclosure—once we know the electronics architecture, we can get a pretty good estimate of the assembled cost. We simply estimate the cost of each building block within the architecture (which in practice usually translates to a chip or two), and add a little extra for the miscellaneous electronics "stuff" that we'll need (resistors, capacitors, connectors, crystals), along with a battery and enclosure.

Table 4-1 shows a back-of-the-envelope-worthy estimate of the cost to manufacture MicroPed at several smallish quantities. A few notes:

- In this case, each block in our architecture can readily be turned into a single chip (and the battery). As a rule of thumb, if a block requires that more than one or two chips be implemented, that block is probably too broadly defined and should be broken into smaller blocks.

- The cost estimates for parts are based on a (reasonably educated) guess at the parts that we'll be using, and a quick online perusal of pricing from vendors. Most parts vary substantially in cost, depending on the quantities purchased.

- The standard name for a list of parts like this is the *bill of materials*, or BOM (pronounced like "bomb"). You'll definitely want to refer to it this way when you talk to manufacturers and other folks who are "in the business."

TABLE 4-1. MicroPed BOM estimates

Description	Qty 100	Qty 500	Qty 1,000	Qty 5,000
Bluetooth Low-Energy transceiver chip	3.15	2.55	2.15	2.00
Microcontroller	2.90	2.35	2.00	1.95
Accelerometer chip	0.85	0.85	0.85	0.85
Assorted discrete parts, WAG	2.00	2.00	1.50	1.25
PC board (2 layer), WAG	3.00	2.00	1.00	1.00
Disposable lithium battery	0.30	0.25	0.23	0.20
Enclosure, SWAG	10.00	5.00	2.00	1.00
Total BOM cost:	*22.20*	*15.00*	*9.73*	*8.25*

Now let's turn to the second part of the COGS equation, the cost of assembly. For a product like this that's just a PCBA and a simple enclosure, I've found it reasonable and conservative to estimate the total cost of assembly (PCB assembly plus final assembly) as roughly the same as the BOM cost. In other words, doubling the BOM cost gives us the total COGS, as shown in Table 4-2. The contribution of assembly costs to COGS tends to drop in higher volumes and increase a fair bit for complex mechanical assemblies, but for back-of-the-enveloping this rule of thumb will do.

TABLE 4-2. COGS calculation

Description	Qty 100	Qty 500	Qty 1,000	Qty 5,000
Total BOM cost (carried over from Table 4-1)	22.20	15.00	9.73	8.25
Cost of manufacturing	22.20	15.00	9.73	8.25
Unit COGS:	*44.40*	*30.00*	*19.46*	*16.50*

So all told, it looks like the cost of each unit will be $15–$20 per unit in quantities greater than 1k units. To be conservative, we'll use $20 for planning purposes.

We now have some idea of what we can charge for our product, and of how much it will cost to make each one. Fortunately, it seems like we can charge more for MicroPed than they'll cost us, which is necessary for success but perhaps not sufficient. We also need to know whether the spread between cost and price is enough to sustain all of the other aspects of our business beyond manufacturing product, such as salaries, rent, and so forth. That's the next question we'll tackle.

GROSS MARGIN

The percentage difference between a product's selling price and its COGS is known as its *gross margin*. Gross margin represents the money from which we'll need to cover all of our expenses other than COGS, such as salaries for folks not directly involved in manufacturing, rent, utilities, backend IT infrastructure, paying back the cost of research and development, etc. And if we have some margin left over after paying all of our expenses, we'll have our sought-after profit.

How much gross margin is adequate to pay for these things? Because different companies in the same industry tend to have similar types of expenses, products within an industry tend to have similar gross margins. But gross margins between different industries vary quite a bit, because their businesses operate differently.

Typical gross margins for a given industry can be found with a little research. For example, gross margins on software tend to be high—usually 75% to 100%—because the cost of the materials sold is so low (often just a software download or web page click, at a cost of roughly zero), but software makers need plenty of margin to cover their considerable research, development, and maintenance expenses.

On the other end of the spectrum, gross margins at gas stations are way down in the 10% range. Why is a gas station at 10% and not, say, 20%? The reason is that the gas station doesn't need to do very much work (or spend very much money) in order to deliver gas from their storage tank to your car. Almost all of their expense is in buying the gasoline for resale (COGS). If one station raises their prices higher to increase gross margin, then their prices will be higher than the station down the street and they'll lose business. Basically, gas is gas and people won't pay a lot extra for one brand versus another.

Because gross margins tend to run at similar levels for most companies (and thus for their products) in the same industry, estimating the gross margin for a prospective product can be a good "sniff test" to see if a product "smells" like similar products in a financial sense.

In the case of MicroPed, we've estimated a selling price of $50 and a $20 unit COGS, giving us a gross margin of 60% ([$50–$20]/$50).

For consumer electronics, which MicroPed will be nominally a part of, gross margins tend to be in the 30%–50% range. For example, in 2012, Apple Computer's gross margin across the company was 44%. So our guesstimated 60% margin on MicroPed is roughly in the right ballpark. If it were far lower, we'd have to wonder if it could cover all of our expenses. Higher margins are always nice if we can get 'em, although products with margins that are *too* high might well get undercut by lower-priced competitors at some point.

We don't yet know for sure if MicroPed's margins will pay for all of our expenses and recoup R&D costs. That's something we'll look at in our next phase (detailed planning), but so far, so good: we certainly won't *obviously* lose money on each unit we sell, and the numbers seem reasonable for our industry.

Our gross margin calculations so far assume that we're selling directly to a consumer. But what if we sell through distributors and/or retailers, and have to discount our price to them to accommodate their markups? Retailers purchase product at a discount, typically 15% to 33% off the selling price.

So unless we'll only be doing direct sales, our retail price should be high enough to support a reasonable margin after the retailer takes their cut. If we assume a bad case of a 33% discount to retailers, then our wholesale price would need to be $33.50 for the retailer to support a $50 price to the consumer. At a unit COGS of $20 and a wholesale price of $33.50, MicroPed's gross margin is reduced to about 40%. A 40% margin isn't nearly as good as a 60% margin, but still within the 30%-50% common for consumer electronics.

However, if we sell through retailers we'll likely also be selling more product, so COGS will probably drop, restoring some of our margin. Unit COGS can come down *very* substantially if we end up manufacturing in much larger quantities, say 100,000 or more per year. In this scenario, both the BOM and manufacturing costs will likely dive. It would not be shocking if our unit COGS went to $10 in very large quantities. In this case, unit gross margin would go to about 80% (!) if we sell direct, or about 70% if we sell through retailers.

To sum up, it looks like once we start producing MicroPed, we have a pretty good shot at being profitable. But before we produce a product, we need to develop it. Our next step is to do a quick check on the feasibility of developing our product: does development seem straightforward, or do we have a good chance of bumping into trouble?

Can We Develop It?

Fundamentally, development (and research) are long-term investments. We spend time and money to create a product in the hope that we'll eventually earn enough to recoup the investment and earn some profit above that.

In the detailed planning phase of our project (Chapter 5), we'll prepare a development plan with costs that are hopefully in the ballpark of reality. But for now, it's useful to look at one question in particular: does our device require any technologies that we're not likely to be able to develop, buy, or otherwise obtain? This unobtainable content is sometimes called *unobtanium*, and can take various forms:

- Things that violate the laws of physics as we know them. For example, creating a cell phone powered by the body heat in our hands and pockets is pretty unlikely, because the *thermal energy* available is so tiny that even if it were 100% converted to electricity, that electric energy would be insufficient to produce the RF energy needed to make calls, light an LCD screen, etc. Energy can be converted from one form to another, but we can't make more energy from less by wishful thinking.

- Things that exist, but *don't exist for us*. If Acer needs a beautiful custom 15" LCD panel that costs less than $50, they can get it, because they'll buy millions and millions of them. But for the vast majority of us, asking an LCD panel vendor for such a thing will yield little more than a chuckle.

- Things that don't yet exist and don't violate the laws of physics, but which are prohibitively expensive to pursue. For example, a reliable, sturdy, reusable heat shield to protect our personal spacecraft during re-entry into Earth's atmosphere.

Unobtanium is, of course, viral: if a product requires any of it, then the entire product itself becomes unobtanium. We must either work to cleverly remove any need for the stuff, or move on to another product idea. In most cases, I've found that ideas that require unobtanium can be reworked to remove that dependency, usually through some fun, outside-the-box creativity.

So it's obvious that we don't want to rely on unobtanium. But how do we know if our product needs it?

IDENTIFYING UNOBTANIUM

Unobtanium tends to hide in the parts of a project that contain unknowns and risks. Thus, a useful way to identify a lurking need for unobtanium is to list each of the significant technical unknowns and risks in a project, and the reasons we should or shouldn't worry too much about them. For example, for MicroPed, Table 4-3 shows a few of the risks that I've identified:

TABLE 4-3. Some identified MicroPed risks

#	Risk	Unobtanium?	Next steps/mitigation
1	Full year of life from a battery	Probably not, based on widespread marketing claims from chip makers and from personal experience.	Create an energy budget; select parts that accommodate the energy budget; measure power consumption on prototypes in all modes; potential HALT (highly accelerated life-cycle testing); resize battery if needed.
2	Waterproof	No; it's been done, but is easy to mess up.	Consult with mechanical engineers who've developed small waterproof enclosures; testing.
3	Run-over proof	No, from experience.	Develop CAD models of enclosure using a tool that can model stress; testing.

#	Risk	Unobtanium?	Next steps/mitigation
4	Burden of supporting Makers who have difficulty modding the firmware.	Not impossible; companies like MakerShed, Adafruit, SparkFun, and so forth do this. But it still could be a substantial burden.	Use standard Arduino hardware/ firmware/software to take advantage of community support; set up support website before launch.

Again, this is good news. MicroPed is a relatively straightforward product, and it doesn't seem as if there are any features that can't be done, or that are overly risky. But our exercise has caught a few issues that might be problems if not addressed properly, and we've come up with some tasks to reduce the chance of them tripping us up. We'll be sure to build these tasks into our detailed project plan should we decide to move forward on MicroPed.

Now that we've identified any potential for technology showstoppers, we should have a pretty comprehensive first-cut understanding of our product's feasibility. It's time to put our findings together to answer this phase's final question: *should we go for it?*

Go? No Go?

I remember watching the Apollo manned space missions as a little kid. At Mission Control (the folks on the ground who worked with the astronauts) sat a group of people called *flight controllers* who each represented a different system or specialty within the spacecraft or the mission: Booster (the rocket), FIDO (Flight Dynamics Officer, responsible for the rocket's path), Surgeon (medical), Network (the radio networks for communication between capsule and ground), and so forth. Before launch or other major mission milestones, the Flight Director would ask each controller for go/no-go status:

"Booster?" "Go!" "Retro?" "Go!" "FIDO?" "Go!", and so on, all the way down the line.

If all systems were "Go!", they went. A "No-Go" meant that something had to change before proceeding.

Perhaps it's the Walter Mitty in me, but I think of the close of this first planning phase as a miniature version of the Mission Control status check. For MicroPed:

"Do we have evidence that we can sell some?" "Go!" "At a price that might make it profitable?" "Go!" "Gross margin looks reasonable?" "Go!" "Development looks like it's feasible?" "Go!"

All systems Go! We now have some confidence that developing MicroPed isn't obviously a fool's errand and that it's worth moving forward into the detailed development planning phase, which we'll tackle in our next chapter.

## CHAPTER 5

Detailed Product Definition

NOW THAT WE'VE TAKEN A FIRST LOOK AND DETERMINED THAT OUR PRODuct has a chance of being a success, it's time to do some "real development"! We'll split "real development" into two major phases that are pretty typical, particularly for larger hardware products. The first of these phases, covered in this chapter, is about gaining confidence in what we're building and what it will cost. Specifically, we'll do the development that's needed to create:

- A comprehensive definition of what we're building (what our product will look like and act like)

- A realistic estimate of the effort (resources, cost, time) needed to develop the product

- A good understanding of the cost to manufacture our product when we go to market

These items are sometimes called *design outputs* or *phase outputs*, and they become *design* (or *phase*) *inputs* to the next phase.

At the end of this phase, armed with better knowledge than before, we'll revisit the "Is this worth developing?" question. If the answer is still "Yes!", we'll move on to the second phase of development, covered in Chapter 6, which largely consists of iterative *design→prototype→test cycles*, repeated until our product is ready to release to manufacturing.

Phase Overview

The general flow of this first development phase is as follows:

1. **Definition.** Characterize the product in detail from the perspective of the outside world. What will it do? What will it look like? These will end up as requirements that guide designers in developing an attractive and useful enclosure, and guide developers in creating the stuff inside the enclosure (electronics and software) that brings it to life.

2. **Risk reduction.** Identify and reduce key project risks; e.g., anything that we're not pretty certain we can do, or we're not certain of the effort required to do it.

3. **Estimate cost of goods sold (COGS).** Create a sound estimate of the cost to manufacture our product.

4. **Estimate development effort.** Comprehensively plan the product's development. What are the tasks that we anticipate? How long will they take, and how much will they cost? What are the interrelations; e.g., which tasks can't be started or completed until certain others are completed first? This will result in schedules and budgets that can help us decide whether the project is feasible, and will set expectations for stakeholders.

In this chapter, we'll focus on steps 1–3. Estimation of development effort is covered in Chapter 12 because it will make more sense after we describe the entire development process; it's easier to plan if we first know what will be happening.

> **TIP** As a systems engineer, I'd be remiss if I didn't note that most of the activity in this phase is the stuff of systems engineering, particularly guiding the requirements generation and creation of the system and other architectures. While having a systems engineer lead these activities is recommended (and will virtually always be the case in large products like synchrotrons and planes), in all cases it's a really good idea for the technical leaders of these activities to be experienced, curious, paranoid, personable, and somewhat voluble (basically the qualities of a typical systems engineer).

In a moment, we'll break these high-level steps into some smaller bits, but before we dive into the specifics let's take a step back and discuss the importance of *iteration*, a concept that's critical to understanding product development.

Iteration

Folks who aren't experienced at this work tend to expect that product development proceeds in a linear fashion: the product is defined (requirements); the designers and technologists go off and design, develop, and then build it; do some testing and tweaking and then we're ready to manufacture and maintain our product. This is known as the *waterfall* model, as shown in Figure 5-1, because like a waterfall it only moves in one direction.

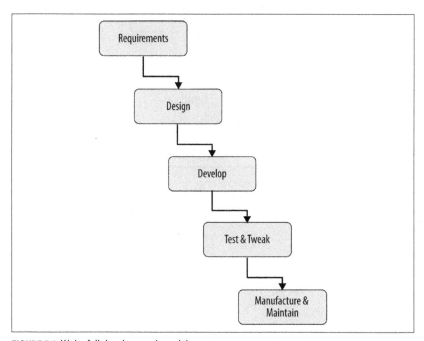

FIGURE 5-1. Waterfall development model

While the waterfall model is tidy, it has little in common with reality because designs don't always achieve the results we expect after they're built: they behave differently than we expected because we forgot some detail, or because the chip or computer language we're using has bugs, or because market research gave us an inaccurate picture of what customers would buy, and so on.

Real product development uses feedback from models and prototypes to create increasingly more mature (i.e., better) iterations of models and prototypes until we arrive at something that's manufacturable and that we're proud to give to customers.

The basic iteration building block is shown in Figure 5-2.

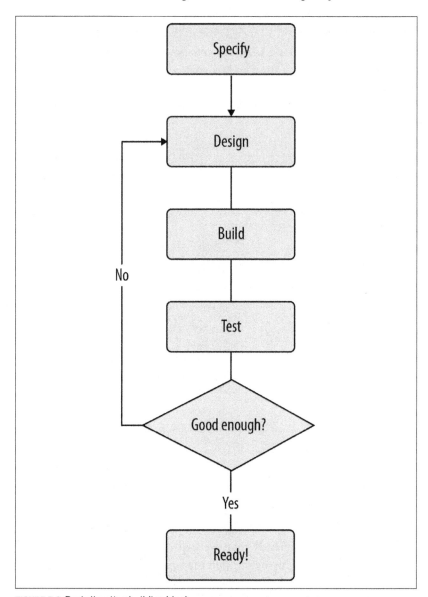

FIGURE 5-2. Basic iteration building block

Iteration happens through all parts of the development process. Each software developer will run through this process perhaps dozens of times per day: think a little, code a little, test a little, repeat. Other technologists and designers follow the same pattern of iterating until their piece of the work is sufficiently developed. For example, a designer will create a drawing or a model made of foam, show it to others for their thoughts, then revise it, show it again, and so forth. An electrical engineer will design a circuit on paper (a schematic), build the circuit on a breadboard, take measurements, then go back and tweak the schematic to improve it, and so on.

Iteration also happens at the higher levels: we build a full-product prototype that (we hope) looks and works like the final product, test it, and if it's not ready for the world we might go back and do some *system*-level redevelopment. Perhaps our tests show the need to change a requirement, such as the product's size, which will impact many elements of the product.

An important distinction between software and hardware is that while software iterations can take as little as a few moments, each hardware iteration can cost tens of thousands or even millions of dollars and require weeks or even months for fabrication and test. Common examples that come to mind are printed circuit boards and certain types of injection molding. As a consequence, engineers who develop hardware tend to be fairly paranoid and careful during development, lest one goofy little problem slip through before fabrication and cause another expensive and long iteration cycle. Software folks tend to be much looser during development because software problems can usually be fixed relatively easily if caught later on.

Another important consequence of this difference in iteration cost is that software development is often a more organic process; e.g., the processes heralded by Agile Development and Lean Startup methodologies. Software can be given to customers early on with only a small subset of functionality, feedback received, and incremental changes made and delivered back to the customer in short order. In the case of software, the fixed cost of an iteration is low, so getting feedback by "trying stuff, seeing what works and what doesn't, then fixing it" is relatively inexpensive. But for hardware? Much more expensive. CAD-based simulations can help to discover more about hardware without building prototypes, but in my experience the simulation doesn't fully replace real prototypes that require significant investments of time and cost. A key to hardware iteration is to be crafty about how we iterate so we get the most bang for the buck (and hour).

As we'll see, much of our process throughout development is about embracing this iteration process and using it to our full advantage.

Now that we've discussed phases and iteration, let's take a high-level look at the development activities that will happen between now and product launch.

The Road Ahead: An Overview

A fair number of tasks lie between where we are now and having a product that's ready to manufacture. And because of iterations and task interdependencies, the map of what lies ahead is a bit complex. But let's give it a try. Figure 5-3 is my attempt to diagram the high-level process of what we'll be doing between now and release to manufacturing.

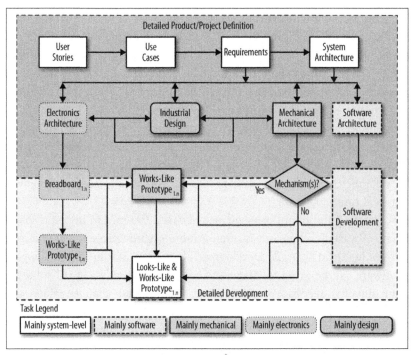

FIGURE 5-3. The road ahead: detailed product specification and development workflow

A few caveats are in order. First, there are probably no two people in the product development world who would quite agree on what this diagram should look like. Others would have some different tasks, different dependencies, and/or different groupings.

And it's also true that each product development effort is somewhat different. An artificial heart is quite a different thing than a talking alarm clock, and projects that have unusual constraints, particularly very tight time constraints (i.e., it must be working by a certain date) or a tremendous amount of new technology (e.g., the Space Shuttle) can look very different.

That being said, the process diagrammed in Figure 5-3 will look fairly familiar to anyone who's in the product development business, so we'll go with it. But keep in mind that this is not a universally accepted process but rather my own take on what normally happens.

Notice that some of the boxes straddle the boundary between the two phases. That's intentional. These tasks might start off as detailed definition exercises, but they tend to continue smoothly into the detailed development phase. For example, a circuit that we breadboard as a proof-of-concept for risk mitigation during the detailed definition phase might continue development in the next phase (and hopefully it does rather than needing to start a new circuit from scratch).

With this diagram as our guide, let's start working our way through the process.

So, What Will It Do? Specifying Our Product

At this point we have some idea of what we'd like to build. We might have a mental picture of our product, and perhaps even some mental videos of it being used in certain ways. In this phase, we'll turn those mental images into a physical design, and those mental videos into requirements that support those ways of using our product (or we'll determine through research that these images need to be fine-tuned).

We might start off by sketching nice drawings of our product-to-be, but as it is said, *form follows function*, and we should be thoughtful about committing to a final form (the way it looks) before we are clear on how it will function. Perhaps a more accurate saying for product development is *form and function must coexist*. Some products are all about the form (e.g., toys and furniture) while others are all about the function (e.g., military aircraft and particle accelerators), and the rest lie on a continuum between these two extremes. Intelligent products with embedded electronics tend to fall into the category of "We know what functionality we want; how can we make this functionality as attractive as possible?". So before expending too much effort in creating a smart product's physical look, we should do some thinking about the details of our product's function. Function, in turn, should flow from how our product will be used. Once we have a good feel for function, we'll use that information to inform the creation of a physical design that supports it.

For example, if we determine that our product will often be carried from place to place, depending on size it might need a built-in handle or another easy way to grip it. A handle, in turn, might mean that the designers will need to work with the mechanical and electronics folks to ensure that the handle's placement and the product's weight distribution don't make things awkward or unbalanced. Already, you can see the kind of interdependencies that happen! Everything depends on everything, which can feel a little overwhelming sometimes: make a little change in one spot and it can affect everything else.

> **TIP** Defining a new product's look and functionality can be a really big deal, particularly for devices that include hardware. It's an endeavor that blends extreme creativity with great rigor, and as mentioned back in Chapter 1 (Deadly Sins 2 and 3), determining what users truly want can be challenging. An entire industry has sprung up to help companies define their products, including well-known firms such as Continuum, Frog Design, and IDEO. We'll look at some useful techniques and processes for defining functionality in this chapter, and the "Resources" section includes pointers to more information, but it's important to realize that this is a large and important area of work.

There are many ways to work through the process of defining functionality in a reasonably methodical way. I have found it most helpful to use tools taken from the software and industrial design worlds, starting with high-level *user stories* and then progressing to more detailed *use cases* and/or *use case diagrams*. Let's take a look at these in a little detail.

> **!** While the definition of *use-case diagram* is reasonably well agreed upon, the definitions of *user story* and *use case* are not. They are always meant in roughly the same way that they're described here, but different folks might mean somewhat different things when they use these words. To avoid confusion, it always pays to discuss their meaning with others when they're used, and to agree on a common definition during the product development process.

USER STORIES

User stories are bits of prose that describe something a person will do that involves the product, such as:

- The user will be notified that the MicroPed battery is low so she will know to change it.

- The user will associate their MicroPed(s) with a database so he can accumulate data for analysis.

- The factory technician will test the MicroPed before shipment to ensure that it is functioning properly.

Each user story calls out a high-level activity, including the person who will perform the activity (user, technician, analyst, etc.) and the reason(s) that they are doing it. By accumulating a solid list of these scenarios, we'll create a good picture of the high-level needs our product must fulfill, which will help us to comprehensively understand what needs to be developed.

Each of these stories is sparse for now. It's tempting to add detail, but there are a couple of good reasons to hold off. First, adding detail begins to put us into design/development territory. Reading the first story, it's clear that MicroPed will need a way to measure battery capacity and a way to notify the user. If we begin to specify these in more detail, such as "The user will be notified *by a popup box* that the MicroPed battery is low so she will know to change it," we'll be making design decisions early which are better left until we have the totality of the user stories and can address the totality of needs.

Second, it's easy to get caught in the design details and forget the big picture, which is a critical part of this exercise. If we're focusing our brainpower on dreaming up a notification mechanism, it's easy to forget about less glamorous stuff like what needs to be done in the factory, what software needs an update process, and so forth.

USE CASES

Once we've compiled the high-level set of interactions that will occur between various people and the product, we can write *use cases* that flesh out our user stories. For example, the "the user will associate their MicroPed(s) with a database so he can accumulate data for analysis" story might convert to a use case that begins like this:

"The user will be presented with a screen that lists the MicroPed devices that can currently be found by his phone (i.e., are within RF comm range), and will ask the user to tap the MicroPed that's to be associated, once per second. The MicroPed that's being tapped will identify itself by RF to the phone, and the user's screen will indicate the selected device. The user will either confirm the selection, request a rescan, or cancel the operation. If the selection is confirmed and the user is not known to be registered with a database, a registration screen will be presented. Otherwise..."

There are a few things to notice here. First, we're starting to make design decisions, such as that the new MicroPed will identify itself via wireless rather than by the user entering a serial number via keypad or scanner. At this point, these decisions are (we hope!) well informed but not fixed in stone. As we iterate through the specification process, we'll likely make some changes to make things easier and better for users, and to reduce cost and increase reliability.

Because these decisions are about how users will interact with our product, the process is typically led by the team members who are champions of the customer experience, such as user interaction designers (abbreviated UxD), marketing, and product management, with the strong support of technologists. As discussed in Chapter 1, we technologists tend to think about technology differently than typical users — that's why we became technologists, after all.

You might have noticed that our example use case is verbose and difficult to read, which is a common issue with use cases. For this reason, use-case *diagrams* are often used rather than use-case *prose*. I happen to prefer plain old flowcharts for this purpose, but there are many other ways to represent the interactions, such as the use-case diagrams defined as part of the well-known (to software folks) Unified Modeling Language (UML).

Figure 5-4 is a flowchart that represents the same use case that we previously began to define in prose. Compared to the prose, I think it's easier to follow, create, and edit.

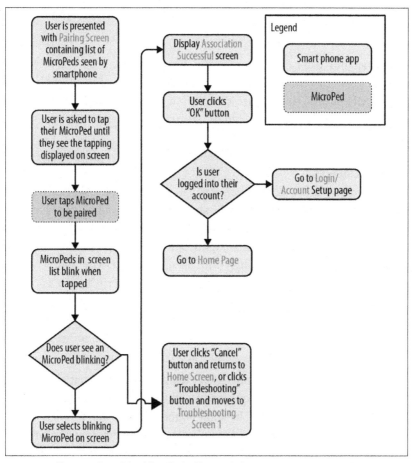

FIGURE 5-4. Use case for pairing MicroPed with smart phone

There are a few things to notice in Figure 5-4 that I find useful but which aren't standard practice:

- Blocks are marked to indicate which entity is performing the action. By maintaining this system across all flowcharts, it's easy to glance at a diagram and pick out the actions for a given entity.

- Names of other screens are called out in a different color than other text, again to make them easy to find for a designer or developer cataloging all the actions a screen must perform, say before beginning construction. If we want to get a little fancy, most diagramming tools will allow us to make each screen name a hyperlink that will take us to another use-case diagram, wireframe sketch, or image of that screen.

Once our use cases are complete, we should now have a very good idea of how our product functions within the context of the world around it. Functional descriptions are critical, but there are other requirements that we'll need for our product to be adequately described; our next step is to pull these together.

REQUIREMENTS

Requirements are a comprehensive list of attributes that describe the product we're building, so that all stakeholders can agree on what we'll end up with. Because I believe that solid requirements are so important to successful products of any significant complexity (or at least that project failures correlate strongly with sketchy or otherwise poorly written requirements), I've given this process its own chapter (Chapter 11). I recommend reading that chapter for a deeper dive, but for the sake of maintaining the pace of this chapter we won't dig into the details now.

By way of example, Table 5-1 contains a subset of MicroPed's requirements. There are a few things to note about these requirements:

- Many of these requirements aren't truly *requirements*, but rather "preferred" features. True requirements (those marked mandatory) are left for things that would be showstoppers if they weren't met. In this case, because MicroPed is a small project being developed in large part as a pedagogical tool for this book (and for my own edification), I get to decide what the showstoppers are (such power!). But in real life, particularly in established companies, these are often determined by the marketing folks, based largely on customer needs, with a lot of support from other groups.

- Some requirements and tests are written a bit looser than they might be written for other products. In particular, products developed by larger organizations, products that are incremental improvements of an existing product (e.g., new model year of a car), and products in the military, medical, and aerospace markets tend to have much more detailed requirements. For example, for step accuracy within 5% of actual on a flat, paved surface, I've called out that there will be testing utilizing a selection of people, but a better requirement would be more along the lines of step accuracy within 5% of actual on a flat, paved surface for 90% of Americans age 15–85 with 95% confidence. This would be a tightly written requirement with little wriggle room, but a challenging one for us to test against. We'd need to do quite a bit of research to understand who should be in the sample of people we test, and we'd likely need a large sample. The requirement as written is an attempt at a reasonable compromise. In a large corporation, this requirement might be written closer to the latter way. Or not. It varies quite a bit from company to company.

Also note that it's quite reasonable to include our user stories as requirements. Use cases and/or use-case diagrams can be included as well, but they do tend to be *hows* rather than *whats,* and as such might be considered *preferred* rather than *mandatory* so as to inform the designers/developers of intent but to not overly constrain their work.

We now know almost everything about what our product will look like to the outside world except how it actually looks! Coming next is a flurry of activity that will result in our creating that look (i.e., our product's enclosure and possibly software screens), along with some of the higher-level decisions about the technology that will live within it. Table 5-1 shows some sample requirements.

TABLE 5-1. Sample MicroPed requirements

#	What we want	Criticality	Rationale	How to test?
1	Bluetooth Smart wireless interface	Mandatory	Bluetooth Smart is the industry standard for communications with low-power (i.e., long-battery-life) sensors. It's supported by the majority of smart phones sold today.	Certification testing or use of certified module
2	Step accuracy within 5% of actual on a flat, paved surface	Preferred	Self-evident	Test for a representative range of users versus manual step counting on a walking course

#	What we want	Criticality	Rationale	How to test?
3	Can operate for seven months or longer on a single battery	Preferred	Seven months is longer than what any other wireless unit is claiming	Measured current consumption of circuit combined with usage model, battery specifications, and circuit design (e.g., shutdown voltage)
4	Programming/ functional test adapter	Mandatory	Need to program each unit at factory; might as well do functional test at the same time	Verification testing
5	Waterproof to nine feet	Preferred	Deepest minimum pool depth specified by ANSI/APSP-ICC-5 2011 standard for in-ground swimming pools	Verification testing to 95% confidence level
6	Waterproof to one meter	Mandatory	IP67 specification	Verification testing
7	Can survive trips through the washing machine	Mandatory	Should be able to remain in clothing indefinitely	Verification testing
8	Can store seven days or more of step counts in one-minute bins	Preferred	That's what some of the competition is doing, although it seems like more granularity than most people need	Analysis and verification testing
9	In regular use, timing on collected data (e.g., bin start time) is accurate to within one minute.	Preferred	If we have one-minute bins, it would be nice if the times were accurate	Analysis and verification testing
10	Meet USPS, UPS, and Fedex requirements for lithium batteries	Mandatory	We want to use these carriers to ship MicroPed	Analysis

#	What we want	Criticality	Rationale	How to test?
11	Meet FCC Class B regulations for unintentional radiation	Mandatory	Required to sell in the US for use in homes	Verification testing
12	Meet FCC regulations for intentional radiation	Mandatory	Required to sell in the US	Verification testing or modular approval

From What, to How and Who

The next sub-phase is my favorite part of the project, a glorious and terrifying blend of engineering, art, and horse trading in which we'll create the product's physical look (enclosure), possibly its software screens (i.e., look but not functionality), and make high-level decisions about the software, electronics, and mechanicals that will live inside the box.

These activities are all highly interdependent, and really should be done collaboratively. For example, an enclosure needs to make sure that all the product's parts can fit inside, but parts can be selected (to some degree) to support a desired enclosure design. Software must be able to run on and work with selected electronics components, but electronics components can also be selected to make life better for software developers. Negotiation skills are important here! Referring back to our workflow diagram for this phase and the next (Figure 5-5), these activities are called out as system architecture, electronics architecture, industrial design, mechanical architecture, and software architecture. That's a lot of architectures—so before we dig in, let's take a quick look at some general architecture definitions and concepts.

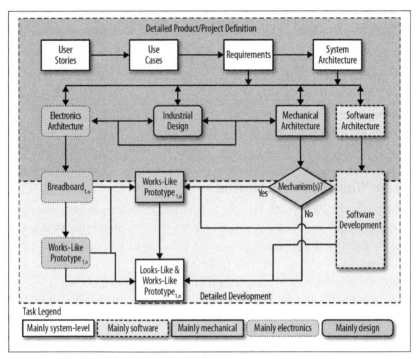

FIGURE 5-5. Detailed product specification and development workflow

ARCHITECTURE BASICS

An *architecture* is a way to break down complex products into smaller, abstracted functional building blocks. These building blocks are at a level higher than individual components, but lower than a single block labeled "product," and they make it easier to discuss and explain high-level functionality.

As an example, Figure 5-6 shows again the preliminary electronics architecture for the MicroPed wearable that we produced back in Chapter 4.

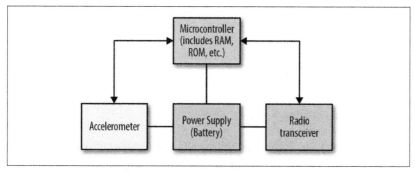

FIGURE 5-6. MicroPed wearable electronics architecture

This is obviously a lot easier to use when describing the functionality of the MicroPed wearable than the schematic it represents, shown in Figure 5-7:

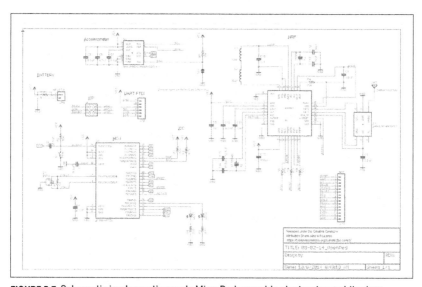

FIGURE 5-7. Schematic implementing early MicroPed wearable electronics architecture

A single product can have multiple architectural *views*, each clarifying different aspects of the system. These can include:

- Electrical

- Software

- Mechanical/physical

- Logical (the partitioning of the system into components and services)

- Information (characterizes key data that flows into, out of, or within the system)

- Operational (defines the runtime operations and interactions among components and services)

- Technology (defines chosen technology platforms including RF chips, web hosting/services, etc.)

Not all of these will be useful for all development efforts. In general, more complex efforts will tend to see a benefit from defining more of these architectural views because of a greater need to abstract complexity.

Architectures can be hierarchical. There can be a top-level architecture, then the blocks in that architecture can devolve into their architectures, then those blocks devolve into their architectures, and so forth. This can get a little confusing in terms of nomenclature, particularly with regard to the phrase *system architecture*, which tends to be applied to any architecture that's somewhat complex. For example, in the case of Micro-Ped, system architecture might be used in several ways, referring to:

1. The entire MicroPed *system* architecture, including the wearable itself, the smart phone(s) it communicates with, the backend architecture that stores and serves up data, etc.

2. The MicroPed *wearable* architecture, which is a system in its own right with hardware, software, and mechanical components.

3. Subsystems within the MicroPed wearable or other entities, such as the software system architecture in the wearable, or on a backend server that has Linux, Apache, PostgreSQL, etc.

To keep things clear, it's good to use specifics that make it clear as to which system architecture we're referring to, such as *top-level MicroPed system architecture, MicroPed wearable software system architecture,* and so forth.

> Nomenclature alert: *Architecture* is yet another term whose definition isn't universally agreed upon. In this book I'm using it generically as defined at the start of this section (blocks that abstract complexity), but other terms are sometimes used for similar abstractions, such as *configuration* and *schematic*. *What* things are called isn't as important as making sure all parties agree that they're all talking about the same things. In practice, it's a good idea to define these terms when using them.

Generally speaking, most experienced designers/developers will agree on the building blocks to be represented in an architecture. But questions sometimes come up on this subject, so let's briefly discuss architecture granularity. Granularity refers to how narrowly we define our blocks, which ultimately determines the number of building blocks we end up with.

My general bias is to minimize the number of blocks in our architecture(s), because blocks add overhead. It's very good practice, particularly in critical systems, to document each block and each interface between blocks in some detail. So extra blocks mean extra documentation. (Similar to when writing, if adding blocks doesn't help, it hurts.)

For example, do we have a single block called "power supplies" or multiple blocks, one for each power supply (e.g., voltage regulator chip and associated circuit), or do we even bother calling out the power supplies at all because their existence is inferred?

One way to tackle this issue is to think about whether an item will likely be referred to individually in higher-level conversations during development. Going back to the power supply example, if our product plugs into the wall and has little or no power management, it might make sense to have only a single power supply block with multiple voltage levels coming from it; nuances of the individual supplies will rarely be discussed by anyone other the electrical engineers directly designing or specifying those supplies. But for a sophisticated battery-operated device where various power supplies will be cleverly switched to save power, there might be lots of conversations between various levels of electronics and software folks about each supply, so it probably makes sense to call each one out, along with a block representing the circuits/software that orchestrates the switching, perhaps all living within a separate power supply architecture.

Now let's move from theory to practice, and see how this architecture discussion applies to MicroPed.

TOP-LEVEL MICROPED SYSTEM ARCHITECTURE

As mentioned, our highest-level system architecture (Figure 5-8) refers to the multiple discrete physical and/or backend service entities such as the MicroPed wearable, smartphone(s), cloud-based functionality, and so forth. It specifies both of these entities and some information about how they interface to one another.

This top-level architecture gives us an explicit list of the top-level deliverables we'll need to create or otherwise obtain: the MicroPed itself, iOS and Android apps, data storage, and so forth. (The "Custodian" app is a placeholder for a backend application that does any necessary housekeeping chores such as emailing reminders of various sorts, running backups, etc.)

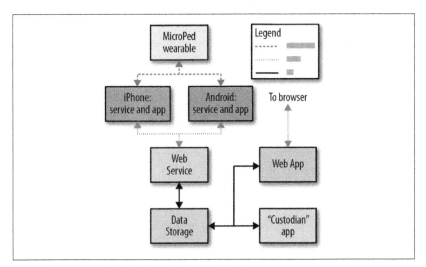

FIGURE 5-8. Initial MicroPed top-level system architecture

A product's architecture will usually become obvious to skilled practitioners as we put together our user stories, use cases, and requirements. This is a first-cut architecture that might change somewhat as we make our way through the rest of this product definition phase, but it should be pretty solid by the phase's end.

As we develop our architecture, we should keep an eye out for off-the-shelf products and services that make our job easier (i.e., reduce development cost and risk). Particularly for backend infrastructure pieces, using off-the-shelf services is usually a better way to go at first than building and running it ourselves. Services of this type include Amazon's AWS and S3, Microsoft Azure, Google's various offerings, and so forth.

For example, after creating the architecture in Figure 5-8, I came across the recently announced Google Fit service for storing and displaying fitness data. Using Google Fit would substantially simplify the system architecture and development effort, and an updated architecture using Google Fit is shown in Figure 5-9. The tradeoff is that we (and our customers) will have to abide by Google's terms. We'll need to decide if that's a good bargain to make.

> **TIP** Particularly in this phase, we should keep a sharp eye out for ways to simplify *everything*. The quickest and easiest (i.e., lowest-risk) path to market is usually the best bet. If the product catches on, then it's relatively easy to reduce costs and make other tweaks later when we have money coming in from sales. A section on technical risk reduction is found later in this chapter.

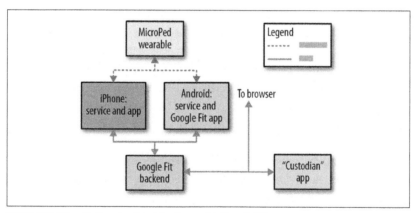

FIGURE 5-9. MicroPed top-level architecture using Google Fit

Alternatively, we could use Apple's Health Kit infrastructure, although (as of this writing) it's a more-limited offering than Google Fit for MicroPed's anticipated usage.

At this level of architecture, each of these blocks is itself a system and should be decomposed into its own architecture if it's something we're developing ourselves (e.g., there's likely no need for us to break down Google Fit's architecture).

For the rest of this book, we'll focus solely on the MicroPed wearable as it's most relevant to our subject, but for the customer to have a good experience, all of the other parts of the MicroPed system need attention, too.

MORE ARCHITECTURES, AND DESIGN

Now that we have requirements and a top-level architecture, a flurry of interrelated development tasks kick off:

- Electronics architecture (and preliminary electronics BOM)

- Software architecture (OS, libraries, software modules, etc.)

- Industrial design (enclosure)

- User experience (UX) and user interface (UI) design (software screens and screen flow)

- Mechanical architecture (the mechanical parts and how they fit together)

UX, UxD, UI, etc. There are a number of terms that are used to describe the different tasks involved in defining how our product interacts with the outside world (as opposed to defining how the technology makes those interactions happen). These terms are used differently by different people, but here's a rough guide:

UI, or User interface: Tends to refer to the layout of individual software screens.

UX or UxD: User experience design. Tends refer to either the overall functionality and flow of the software, or more holistically to software and hardware.

Graphic design: Tends to refer to the pixel-level design of screens.

ID, or Industrial design: Tends to refer to design of a physical enclosure, but sometimes used to encompass all aesthetic design (including UI, UX/UxD, and graphic design).

Each of these will directly support some of our requirements, but as mentioned earlier they must also support each other. For example, the electronics architecture must support the needs of the software architecture (e.g., support Linux if that's what's needed) and be compatible with the mechanical architecture (e.g., the boards must fit in their allotted spaces and not throw off more heat than the mechanicals can get rid of). The mechanical architecture, in turn, must meet the designers' visions (i.e., implement an enclosure that looks like what the designers want it to look like).

Let's take a brief look at each of these activities and then review some of the major interdependencies that must be worked out between them.

Electronics architecture

This task consists of updating the preliminary electronics architecture (Figure 5-8), paying close attention to requirements and the needs of other design/development disciplines (software, mechanical, and design). Our architecture should drill down to the point of calling out particular chips and other components, at least the ones that have an important impact on the parameters we'll need to estimate; processors, sensors, display(s), batteries, and motors are prime examples. At the end of this task, we should have a pretty solid list of the major electronics components we'll be using; the number of PCBAs and their functions, sizes, and interconnections both within the enclosure and to the outside world; estimates of the assembled cost of electronics; power consumption figure; and any information needed for other technologists to do their jobs.

Processors, displays, sensors, radios, and motors tend to use the bulk of the power in embedded electronics and account for the bulk of the cost, so nailing these down is important. We'll also want to get very specific about any physical interfaces with the outside world, specifically connectors (e.g., power, USB) and sensors (e.g., a camera component that needs to peer out from a certain spot and mount a certain way) so that the designers and mechanical engineers can take this into account.

In the case of MicroPed, creating the electronics architecture was a significant challenge due to our desire for long life on a small battery, along with various other requirements and desires. Let's look at the choices that were ultimately made, and why they were made.

After some research, it turned out that the MicroPed electronics architecture envisioned in Chapter 4 wasn't quite the best fit. Rather than using a "simple" RF transceiver chip, it turned out to be significantly less expensive to use a component that contains the RF transceiver *and* its own programmable microcontroller. This led to two candidate electronic architectures for MicroPed, shown in Figure 5-10 and Figure 5-11.

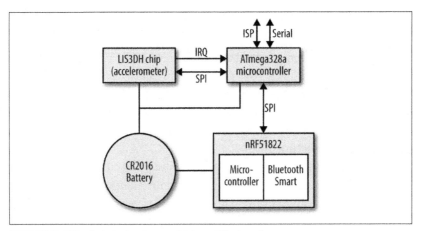

FIGURE 5-10. MicroPed electronics candidate architecture A

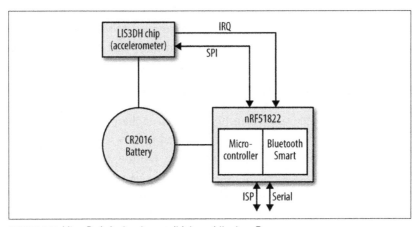

FIGURE 5-11. MicroPed electronics candidate architecture B

The difference is that architecture A includes an ATmega328a microcontroller to ensure Arduino compatibility (a desire identified back in Chapter 4), while architecture B does not. Let's start by briefly discussing the selected components that are common to both candidate architectures, and then we'll look at the differences and their implications.

The CR2016 battery was selected because it's the smallest battery (20 mm × 1.6 mm) that has a capacity that could conceivably power MicroPed for a year: roughly 80 mAh, which means that it can supply an average of 10 µA during that time. The possibility to get down to 10 µA average consumption is a SWAG (Scientific Wild-Assed-Guess) at this point, based on some back-of-the-envelope calculations and experience. SWAG means risk, but this risk is somewhat mitigated because the CR2016 is the smallest-capacity member in a series of batteries of similar size and characteristics. If we can't eventually get our average power consumption down to 10 μA, higher-capacity CR2025 and CR2032 batteries of the same voltage and diameter (but 2.5 mm and 3.2 mm thick, respectively) can be substituted to support an average current draw up to three times higher, although they'll force MicroPed to grow a bit in thickness.

The nRF51822 chip contains Bluetooth Smart radio circuitry and a microcontroller (an ARM Cortex M0). The microcontroller is used by the chip to implement the Bluetooth Smart functionality via control of the radio circuitry, but the manufacturer (Nordic Semiconductor) has kindly allowed designer/developers to use the microcontroller's spare resources and CPU cycles if we buy a special development kit and agree to their licensing. The nRF51822 was selected over other competitive components for a number of reasons:

- Low power and energy consumption
- Relatively powerful built-in microcontroller
- Can run directly from lithium-based disposable batteries like the CR2016
- Inexpensive and well-supported development tools
- Low cost
- On-chip reprogrammable memory

At least as important as any of these considerations is that the nRF51822 is available in tiny pre-assembled modules that significantly reduce development cost and risk as follows:

1. They contain the passive parts (capacitors, resistors, crystal, etc.) required by the nRF51822 to function. RF design can be particularly tricky, so this reduces some nontrivial design/development risk, particularly the risk of a bad PCB design.

2. They are pre-approved for RF use in various countries. Without pre-approval, we'd need to spend tens of thousands of dollars on certification before (legally) selling MicroPeds. More on approvals can be found in Chapter 10.

3. RF performance of each part is guaranteed by the vendor, which reduces our need to develop and execute production tests for Micro-Ped. We'll review production testing in Chapter 6.

The LIS3DH accelerometer was selected primarily for its low power and energy consumption, and low cost.

Now let's turn to the difference between the two candidates, the inclusion (or not) of an ATmega328a microcontroller. The nRF51822's ARM Cortex M0 microcontroller is more powerful the ATmega328a, and can easily handle the processing tasks that MicroPed must perform. So from a performance point of view, we can eliminate the ATMega part to save significant cost and complexity. The downside is that the ATMega gives us out-of-the-box Arduino compatibility. The ATMega-less architecture can still be made Arduino-compatible, but we'd need to develop (and support) a significant bit of software to do this.

As we discussed back in Chapter 4, users who want to reprogram their MicroPeds are likely a much smaller market than those who don't, and thus Arduino compatibility probably should be a lesser priority for us than lower manufactured cost and easier/cheaper development. So it was decided to eliminate the ATMega processor and not be Arduino-compatible at first. If, in the future, we see enough demand for Arduino compatibility, we can develop that feature in a software upgrade.

PHYSICAL ARCHITECTURE (WITH SOME WORDS ON CABLING). MicroPed is just a simple device, with one PCBA sealed within an enclosure and no physical external interfaces. Larger, more sophisticated devices tend to have multiple PCBAs, often one or two main boards with the bulk of the electronics, and several more support boards that have just a bit of electronics each. A typical example is the disassembled notebook computer shown in Figure 5-12, which can serve as an example for us to dig a bit deeper into physical architecture, at least with regard to electronic assemblies. Five PCBAs are visible:

1. The big blue motherboard

2. A blue accessory board on the left, with two USB port connectors and a bit of electronics

3. The green PCBA onto which RAM is soldered

4. A small board with a soldered-on RF module at the bottom

5. A second small board with a soldered-on RF module, with "Anatel" printed on the label, mounted on the motherboard

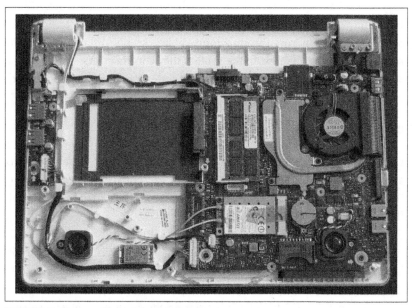

FIGURE 5-12. Disassembled notebook computer

When fully assembled, this computer will contain several more boards—at least one each for the keyboard, hard drive, battery, and power supply. This equals at least eight boards, mated mechanically and electronically by connectors, cables, and/or PCBAs.

There are several reasons to break circuitry into multiple boards. One is modularity. We can swap one board that provides certain functionality for another that provides the same functionality as long as the connectors are the same, they use the same electrical and software protocols, and they fit in the available physical space. For example, computer memory modules (i.e., circuit boards with RAM soldered down as shown in Figure 5-12) are excruciatingly standardized with regard to size, shape, connector, and performance, so it's quite easy to swap one for another if we want to upgrade to a higher-capacity module or replace a defective module.

Another reason to use multiple PCBAs is a need to locate different parts of the electronics in different places within the enclosure. For example, a printer will typically have an LCD display at its top-front, an internal power supply at the bottom-back, and motors and other electromechanical parts scattered around. While most of these parts (e.g., motors) could connect directly to a main PCBA via cable, there are often reasons why they should have a separate PCBA nearby with some needed electronics. For example, the electrical signals used to drive motors tend to emit a lot of RF noise when run through long cables, so it's often better to put motor control circuits next to the motors they control.

Cabling is often an afterthought, but it deserves some attention early on. Let's take a moment for a short discussion of this topic.

Cabling: It's not just wires

Cables and connectors, sometimes referred to together as *interconnects*, aren't magical electron transporters. They are bona fide components of their own with electrical and mechanical properties that require some thought to use them successfully.

Most obviously, they have physical size. Referring back to the RAM module in Figure 5-12, it's obvious that soldering the chips directly to the board would save space. In this particular case, it probably doesn't affect the enclosure size because the enclosure is roughly a rectangular prism and other parts will likely limit size (e.g., the hinges seem to protrude toward the camera more than the RAM module, so the module occupies what would otherwise be empty space).

Cables need routes within the enclosure to get between their endpoints. They also need to not bounce around very much lest they pull their associated connectors apart and/or make unnerving rattling sounds. This means that longer cables will need to be fastened to something solid (typically the enclosure) at one or more points. Several of the cables in Figure 5-12 are held against the enclosure by plastic tabs, or even tape.

Cables and connectors have electrical characteristics that should be considered, particularly for higher-speed circuitry. They can have significant capacitance, inductance, propagation delay, and crosstalk between signals; and they can act as antennas, spewing RF energy that can cause problems when it comes time for regulatory testing.

The assembly of cables, connectors, and boards needs to be thought through; is there a physical way for factory staff to mate connectors and cables together, or will other parts interfere?

Connectors tend to be less reliable than soldered joints. They can be assembled incompletely (not pushed all the way together) during assembly or pull apart due to physical shock and vibration. Locking connectors are available to mitigate these issues, and even applying some tape (as on one connector in Figure 5-12) can help.

And finally, cables and connectors add to both material and assembly costs.

> **TIP** When many signals need to be run over a cable, or even a few run over a long distance, *low-voltage differential signaling* (LVDS) technology should be considered. Designed specifically for transmitting signals over long cables, LVDS can dramatically increase the distance that signals will travel without significant degradation, reduce total power consumption, and reduce radiated RF energy. As a bonus, chips are available that can multiplex six or more signals (i.e., wires) into a single twisted pair of wires for transmission. A second chip on the other end of the twisted pair demultiplexes the signals back to their original format.

Next let's turn from the physical to the ephemeral: the software code that breathes life into intelligent products.

Software architecture

A great deal of material is available elsewhere regarding the development of software architectures, so I'll not delve too deeply here. Fundamentally, it involves the decomposition of the software functionality into relevant building blocks along with the selection of third-party software such as the OS (if any), libraries, and possibly tools (e.g., development environment and debugger), etc.

Since software runs on and controls electronics, software and electronics designers/developers will need to work together closely here to make sure that everything can work together, that the software doesn't require parts that consume excessive power or cost too much, and that the electronics folks select components that are easy to control in software.

Third-party software should be reviewed to ensure that it not only meets technical needs, but that it also meets business needs:

- Licensing review: do the licenses for our selections meet our needs? Will they require us to publish sensitive source code? If there are fees involved, what will those fees be during the product's life cycle? This can be a very nontrivial project, particularly if open source code is used because open source licensing law is still evolving. Getting the help of a lawyer can be helpful, either to do the review or to look over the results of your own review.

- Life cycle support planning: will we be able to obtain or provide support at a level that we need over the course of our product's life cycle, including bug fixes?

In the case of the MicroPed wearable, the software architecture is fairly straightforward. We won't even need an operating system. Figure 5-13 shows a somewhat simplified version.

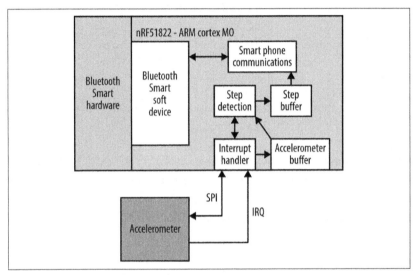

FIGURE 5-13. MicroPed wearable software architecture

The nRF51822's processor will basically go to sleep (in a low-power mode) until the accelerometer indicates it has new samples to send by waking the processor up with a hardware interrupt request (IRQ). The accelerometer interrupt handler reads the new data over the SPI bus, sends it to an internal buffer of raw accelerometer data, and then calls a step detection algorithm to determine if a new step has occurred. Whenever the algorithm detects a new step from the raw data, the time of the step is stored in a step buffer. Other nRF51822 software is responsible for connecting to smart phones and sending step data (and other data, such as battery status) via Bluetooth Smart.

Note that while this description feels like design rather than definition—and it is—we're just doing enough of the design to help us understand that we have a good grasp on the tasks our detailed design will need to cover, in order to help specify our architecture and estimate the effort involved. It will turn out more than occasionally that when we move into detailed design, we'll discover that our preliminary architectures are somewhat wrong. But we'll still be in far better shape than if we hadn't even tried to get it right early on.

The "Bluetooth Smart soft device" in the nRF51822's Cortex M0 is a binary code library supplied by the chip maker. We must load it into the part during assembly, along with our custom firmware. It's the smarts that drives all of the complexity behind coordinating the chip's Bluetooth Smart hardware. Our own code on the Cortex M0 uses Bluetooth Smart by making calls into this soft device. This paradigm of chip makers embedding a processor into peripheral chips and supplying binaries to drive functionality is becoming more common as the price of putting a processor on a chip plunges. It not only gives customers a processor at no extra cost, but it allows chip makers to improve peripherals by releasing new software that can be updated in existing devices.

So, we now know the electronics (and associated software) that will go inside the box. It's finally time to design the box!

Industrial design

> TIP
> In this section, *industrial design* broadly refers to all of the various disciplines (including UxD, UI, etc.) that define the look of the product's mechanicals, software, and packaging.

Industrial design effort, including enclosure, software screens, and other user experience issues (e.g., packaging), is often very substantial during this phase. By phase end, these design activities (particularly as they relate to mechanical design) are usually fundamentally complete, perhaps only needing tweaks during development as events warrant. For example, if technologists find they need to increase an enclosure dimension to accommodate a larger-than-anticipated PCBA, the mechanical engineers will consult with industrial designers to make sure that any changes preserve the design intent.

As with software, the elements of industrial design are amply covered elsewhere so I won't go into detail, but here are some of the activities that designers might engage in:

- Conducting detailed studies with potential users to help understand how they'll use our new product. Hopefully this process was begun at a high level by marketing folks earlier in the process, but this is often the phase where we refine the specifics.

- Developing multiple concept sketches of enclosures and software UIs to show to potential users and other stakeholders so that we can gain agreement on "look and feel."

- Creating models of product concepts using foam or 3D printing so stakeholders can better envision the product.

- Creating mockups of proposed screen designs, again for stakeholder review. This can be done as:

  — Wireframes (simple sketches showing text, text entry boxes, and other elements)

  — Illustrations of the proposed screens that include graphics as they'll be seen by users

  — Interactive mockups that simulate screens and screen flow; users can fill in text, click buttons, proceed to other mocked-up screens, and perform other realistic activities. Mockups of this sort can be created using the tools in the popular Adobe Creative Suite, and with other applications. Even better, if the software folks will be using a platform or framework that supports easy UI design, such as Microsoft .NET or Qt, the mockups can be done within that platform, which gives us a head start on software development.

For the MicroPed wearable, the desire to make it small is of greater importance than how it looks because it will spend most of its life hidden from view. So in this case, we'll first work out the minimal size for the mechanical structure that can contain the electronics and then try to spiff it up a little. But, more typically, shaving every millimeter from a product is not so critical and there's more room for styling.

Mechanical architecture

Mechanical Engineers are in the middle of a lot of negotiations in this phase—their job is to collect information about what the enclosure will look like from the designers and about what needs to fit inside from the electrical engineers, and then to figure out how to use mechanical engineering magic to make everyone happy.

The goal is to create a basic plan that identifies the mechanical parts to be developed and manufactured (although they won't yet have their designs complete), and the configuration by which the circuitry will be accommodated among those parts. As mentioned previously, it's often the case that we'll end up with one or two main PC boards to accommodate the bulk of the circuitry, but there are often a number of small accessory boards identified by the mechanical folks to hold battery clips, LEDs, the display, and so forth. And all PCBs are hooked together by cables. Agreeing on which PCBs will go where, their sizes, how they fasten to the chassis, and cabling paths are all part of the mechanical planning.

MicroPed's mechanical architecture is really quite simple. A preliminary mechanical architecture is shown at the bottom of Figure 5-14. This model consists of a disk the size of a CR2016 battery, a rectangle to its left that represents the guesstimated surface area and height of the circuitry to be used (in turn based on our preliminary electronics architecture), and a circuit board underneath.

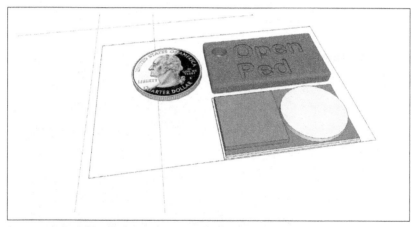

FIGURE 5-14. Early MicroPed mechanical architecture

The object behind the mechanical architecture, marked *OpenPed* (an earlier working name), is a first-cut guess at what the product might look like, basically a box large enough to contain the mechanical architecture with a hole added to attach to a keychain, shoelace, etc. (You might notice that there's no hole in the corresponding circuit board; the circuit board and enclosure were developed together later to accommodate a hole.)

The quarter is in the image simply as a size reference.

MECHANISMS. Mechanisms are mechanical contrivances with parts that move with respect to one another: motors, gears, linkages, that sort of thing. Like enclosures, mechanisms are developed by mechanical engineers. Most smart products (think MicroPed, smart phones, TVs, and similar) don't require significant mechanisms so mechanical engineers on these projects focus on creating enclosures.

But products like printers, robots, and cameras do have mechanisms (as well as enclosures), and designing/developing these mechanisms is a very different thing as compared to designing/developing enclosures. Figure 5-15 shows the paper feed mechanism from a disassembled inkjet printer. As you can see, it's a nontrivial assembly of a motor driving various gears, rubber wheels, and rollers with springs and other bits. This assembly is designed to grab a single sheet of paper from a stack and move it through the printer with great accuracy and repeatability, and without damage to the paper. And to do this tens of thousands of times during its lifetime. And to cost only a few dollars to produce, and be reasonably easy to assemble.

FIGURE 5-15. Paper feed from a disassembled HP Deskjet 940c printer (credit: Snewkirk7953 ($http://bit.ly/1VlFczB$) licensed under CC BY-SA 3.0 ($http://bit.ly/1VlFkPA$))

Enclosures tend to be reasonably predictable, i.e.,

- Manufactured enclosures usually act pretty much as expected based on the CAD models they're produced from.

- Enclosures don't often fail with normal use.

By their nature, mechanisms tend to be more influenced by tiny variations in manufacturing and assembly unless we take nontrivial precautions. For example, a four-thousandth of an inch variance from ideal is pretty typical in injection-molded plastic. This probably won't be noticeable in an enclosure, but it happens to be about the thickness of a sheet of paper. So if a paper feed mechanism is counting on plastic parts being exactly the right size in order to pull a single sheet of paper, that mechanism might simply not work when manufactured. And because parts in mechanisms move against one another in normal use, parts will wear over time, exacerbating any problems due to size variations.

Mechanisms must be specified and developed to account for manufacturing tolerances and wear. This can be done numerically using CAD tools, but there's no substitute for exhaustive testing with prototypes to see how they fare. In practice, multiple prototypes are run through many thousands of cycles to see if functionality and reliability are as expected.

Mechanisms are tricky business. If our product requires any nontrivial mechanisms, it will impact this phase in a couple of ways:

- Because of the need for lengthy testing cycles, mechanisms should be started as early as possible in development, such as during this phase rather than waiting for the detailed design phase.

- In order to specify our product's mechanical architecture, we'll need to predict which mechanisms will achieve the reliability and cost that we require. It's critically important to engage people with serious experience with mechanism development to help make these predictions.

After all of this work and decision-making, our product feels like it's coming alive! We should now have a pretty good idea of what our product will do, how it will do it, and what it will look like.

But before jumping into detailed development, there are a few more steps to take that will increase our chances of success by turning some unknowns into much-better-knowns:

1. Researching and proving out technical unknowns.

2. Updating and refining the estimated cost of manufacturing our product when we're ready for the market.

3. Creating a detailed development project plan so we have a reasonable sense of what resources we'll need (e.g., people, materials, travel, analysis, studies, agency testing and certifications, and vendors), how long it will take, and what it will cost.

We'll start by tackling the technical unknowns because the other two tasks depend on what we find in this exercise. And because it's easier to plan a project after we understand all of its parts, project planning is covered later in the book (Chapter 12) after we discuss all of the development phases.

Technical Risk Reduction

In a sense, risk is a synonym for uncertainty. Reducing uncertainty equals reducing risk. One of this phase's goals is to knock down any substantial uncertainties around our product's technology to the point where we're confident that we can estimate, with some accuracy, the time and cost of development.

> **TIP** In this book, we're examining *program/project risk*—that is, items that can derail a project by increasing cost and/or timeline. Another category of risk involves the possibility of product failure and/or user injury. This category is particularly crucial when developing products that can cause significant harm or expense if they malfunction, such as vehicles (cars, trains, planes), medical devices, and military products. It also impacts any product that must be highly reliable, which can include consumer products that must have very low product return rates. Because of the high cost of returns, a return rate of even 1% can destroy profitability in a competitive (i.e., low-margin) market. This chapter's "Resources" section contains some pointers to information on analyzing and mitigating risks stemming from product failure.

Back in Chapter 4, we discussed the usefulness of capturing a list of all the significant technology and development risks that we think of, as we think of them, such as "Full year of life from a battery." This is sometimes called a *risk register*. In that chapter, we used our risk register to determine if anything looked serious enough to stop us from proceeding with product development. In this phase, we'll look to reduce these risks to a level where we feel they won't come back to seriously surprise us later in development.

In practice, technical risk reduction is accomplished in several ways:

1. Buying our way out; i.e., identifying already existing hardware and/or software that does what we want and which we can obtain at a tolerable price.

2. Developing our way out; i.e., developing technology as experiments designed to increase our confidence that at-risk items can be accomplished within tolerable (and reasonably predictable) time frames and costs.

3. Redefining the product to avoid the risk altogether.

Option 1, buying our way to safety, is fairly straightforward. Beyond doing Internet searches to find an off-the-shelf product that does what we're looking for, it can be instructive to review how other products with the same needs solve them. In some instances, teardowns of those products can be found on the Internet or purchased; otherwise, it's a great idea to buy them off the shelf and pull 'em apart ourselves. One useful feature of third-party teardowns is that they often include estimates of production costs, which can be a reference point for understanding our own cost estimates. For example, if a competitor with a very similar product is using a certain wireless chip and that product has good performance, then that chip might be a good bet for us.

Another option is to approach a company who's already accomplishing what we need and to license or purchase their technology. For example, I was involved in a project that used Windows as its embedded OS, where we needed to check disk integrity every time we started up and have our GUI properly work with the user if an error was found. At the time, Windows had nothing in its public APIs that we could easily use from our own application, so we faced a serious development and test cycle. Instead of tackling this ourselves, we approached the author of a popular shareware disk-checker application and struck a deal where he packaged up the subset of functionality we needed and sold us that source code for our own use. He got a big premium on his time because his code was already developed and working, and we saved a ton of time and money over developing it ourselves.

Experimenting our way to safety is often necessary even if we buy part of the solution, although the effort and risk should be greatly reduced. Each product is unique and there will be risks stemming from that uniqueness. For example, even if we use all off-the-shelf electronics modules, we'll want to test everything as a system to make sure it truly meets our needs. Our enclosure and configuration will likely be unique, which can introduce risks around thermal management, manufacturing and assembly, and other areas. Keeping with the theme of simplifying everything, any risk reduction we can buy—even if only partial—is often money well spent.

On the electronics and software side of things, experiments usually involve breadboards and pre-built PCBAs that implement some portion of what we're doing. These pre-built boards—known by various descriptors like *development kits, evaluation kits,* and *breakout boards*—can range from a single chip soldered down to a board with a connector that makes for an easy breadboard connection to a complex PCBA with dozens of chips. In most cases, these PCBAs are designed to be easily interfaced with other circuitry in a breadboard.

> TIP
> In theory, a breakout board is strictly a board with a single chip, created to break out the chip's pins to connections that are easily accessed for breadboarding. The phrase still *tends* to be used to refer to boards that contain a single chip and perhaps some supporting passive parts, but this is not always the case. For example, consider that Intel's *Edison Breakout Board* contains more than 30 components, including seven chips.
>
> The phrase *development kit* (often shortened to *dev kit*) tends to indicate a more fully featured board with a programmable onboard processor of some sort.

Figure 5-16 shows an early MicroPed breadboard that is a basic proof-of-principle unit built to gain confidence around Bluetooth Smart connectivity and using an accelerometer. It contains off-the-shelf PCBAs:

- An Arduino Pro Mini board from SparkFun Electronics that supplies the microcontroller

- An nRF8001 Bluetooth Smart chip breakout board from Adafruit Industries

- An mma8452q accelerometer breakout board, also from SparkFun

Because MicroPed only requires a few chips, this breadboard happens to implement the entire MicroPed architecture as originally envisioned. Most products are more complex and their breadboards usually contain only a subset of the complete circuitry at this early stage, in particular the bits we're most worried about.

Using this breadboard, we demonstrated that the electronics and software could successfully tie these parts together and implement a basic software algorithm to detect steps from the accelerometer data. The nRF8001 breakout has open source iPhone software available for it, which we also experimented with to get a good feel for how the software works on both sides of the Bluetooth Smart "pipe."

But not everything we gleaned from this breadboard was good news. We were not able to demonstrate that energy consumption could likely be reduced enough for a full year's use on a single coin-cell battery. We moved on to trying a different Bluetooth Smart chip, the nRF51822, which (among other benefits) has features that can reduce energy usage in our application, although it's also more complex to use. This "failure" was disappointing, of course, but we were glad to learn of our bad guess early in development when a chip change was relatively easy to make.

FIGURE 5-16. Early MicroPed electronics breadboard

Several risk reduction experiments for MicroPed revolved around the enclosure. Early on, a 3D print was made (Figure 5-17) based on a best guess at MicroPed's final size and shape. I carried it in my wallet for several months and gave copies to others to try to get feedback on whether or not it was a convenient size.

FIGURE 5-17. Early MicroPed enclosure model

Waterproofing the enclosure is another area that got some scrutiny. Figure 5-18 shows a disassembled prototype enclosure containing water-finder test paper, which turns bright lavender on any contact with water. Running prototypes through the washing machine or dishwasher with this paper inside is a quick way to understand progress with regard to water tightness (one of the MicroPed risks identified back in Chapter 4).

FIGURE 5-18. Test for water ingress

Even in the case of hardware, experimentation is sometimes best done virtually before moving to physical construction and measurement. Software tools such as spreadsheet or modeling software (CAD tools, mathematical tools, simulations, etc.) can be very useful in finding problems early, such as by using finite element analysis CAD software before fabricating mechanical parts to ensure that parts won't be unduly stressed or displaced during use.

Creating virtual models and simulations also gives us benchmarks that we can use to test against our physical results once prototypes are fabricated. Any discrepancies between estimates and measured results might indicate that we've misunderstood something or made a mistake that requires investigation.

For example, it's very helpful to have theoretical power consumption targets for circuits to compare against. If our prototype (and production) circuits draw much more power than we've estimated, then we've probably made a mistake somewhere. Often the mistake is as simple and easy to remedy as not setting a control register properly in software, but it could be a sign of problems with hardware design or manufacturing.

Hopefully, this all gives a sense of the kinds of risk reduction activities that can take place, but they are as varied as our needs and our imagination. The ultimate goal is to be able to iterate through all of the items in our risk register and be able to state for each why we believe that the risk is tolerable.

It's generally true that much of what we develop for risk reduction exercises is recyclable for use in the product itself. In some cases, however, it makes sense to do something that's "throwaway" if the real thing will require too much effort. For example, suppose that we want to demonstrate that an RF chipset and antenna combination can give us a certain data throughput at a certain range. If we plan on using the chipset/antenna with a Linux kernel in our product but only a Windows driver is currently available for it, then it probably makes sense to use Windows for the test. Some effort might be "wasted" in configuring Windows to do what we want, but it's likely to be a lot less effort than writing a Linux driver. It's true that the Linux driver will need to be written at some point, but unless the driver itself is a high-risk item, we should probably wait until the detailed design phase. Suppose we find that the chip set won't give us the throughput and range we want. If we start by writing the Linux driver, we'll have wasted effort on that work. It's best to get the substantial risks out of the way first with near-minimal effort.

In many cases, the results of technical risk-reduction experiments will cause us to change the components our product will use, as it did in the case of MicroPed. Hopefully, by the time this activity is complete, we'll have a nearly final list of components, particularly the big-ticket items that will drive most of the cost. Our next step is to turn that list into a solid estimate of manufactured cost.

Updated COGS Estimate

Back in Chapter 4, we created a rough, preliminary COGS estimate to see if we had a good chance of selling our product at a profit. Now it's time to update and refine that estimate to see if we still look to be profitable.

To review, COGS is comprised of a number of costs, including:

- Electronics component
- PCB costs
- PCB assembly, including test
- Mechanical components
- Product assembly (i.e., box build), including test
- Packaging and shipping

We should now have enough information to get realistic quotes on all of these. But getting quotes is only part of the process. We're also looking for feedback that can help to refine our detailed development efforts. To this end, it's best to approach vendors as collaborators. Our vendors will typically have deep experience at doing what they do and tapping their knowledge can be a gold mine. Rather than asking "How much will it cost for x?", it's better to ask this as "We're thinking of x. Can you help us understand if this is a good way to get what we want and how we can best work together to make this happen, and then give us a quote?"

Vendor feedback can run the gamut from simple suggestions to higher-level design/development suggestions, such as:

- "You'll definitely want ENIG finish instead of HASL to get that BGA soldered down reliably."

- "You might want to reconsider using that particular display. Just between you and me, we're seeing a lot of defective parts. There's something screwy with the cable."

- "I see that you're planning on having a metal part fabricated to hold that mechanism together, but if you switch to glass-filled plastic for the enclosure you might get the stiffness and tolerances you're looking for without the need for a separate metal piece, and you'll save a bundle."

By taking a collaborative approach, we'll typically end up with a product of better quality and lower cost.

 Different manufacturing vendors have different capabilities. Make sure that you check any specific requirements with the vendor who will actually do the work.

Turning to MicroPed, first-pass quotes from vendors based on updated COGS are shown in Table 5-2. Note that they're broken out a bit differently than in Chapter 4, mainly due to my quoting the PCB fabrication and assembly as a single item.

TABLE 5-2. Updated MicroPed unit COGS

Description	Qty 100	Qty 500	Qty 1,000	Qty 5,000
Electronic components cost (less PCB)	10.50	9.00	8.50	8.25
Enclosure	14.75	6.75	5.75	3.25
Cost of PCB plus PCB assembly	10.00	5.00	4.50	4.25
Final assembly, test, packaging	6.00	4.00	3.00	2.00
Unit COGS:	41.25	24.75	21.75	17.85

In the higher quantities (1,000 and 5,000), COGS is looking a little higher than the detailed projections in Chapter 4. The big difference is in the enclosures, which are running more than $2 higher than expected at these quantities. The good news is that back in Chapter 4, I did anticipate that some surprise would happen and rounded up to $20 each for 1k or more units. So as long as we don't get another significant surprise on pricing, our margin calculations are basically unchanged and we're still fine.

Go/No Go: Redux

Our product began this phase as a dream. Now at this phase's end, our dream is well defined and coming to life. Given all of the work that's been done up to this point, it might *seem* that the product development is mostly complete. Heck, it's just the details that are left, right? But in my experience, roughly only 25%–33% of the total development budget will have been spent so far, and the rest will be spent on the "just the details" part.

It's time again to do a reality check before proceeding, much like we did at the end of Chapter 4. This time we have much more information, and a decision to move forward will mean committing more resources (perhaps as much as 75% of the total budget).

Can we do this? Are all stakeholders ready to proceed?

In the case of MicroPed, we're still at *thumbs-up*:

- All worrisome technical challenges have been minimized.

- COGS and margin are still roughly where we expected.

- Development cost and timeline look palatable. (As mentioned earlier, this topic (project planning) is covered in Chapter 12 after we've completed coverage of the rest of development.)

Now we have the confidence to move into detailed development, the final phase before we're ready to manufacture and sell.

Resources

When it comes to specifying functionality and aesthetics, opinions on how to be successful range from "Let's just figure out for ourselves what our users want" (which seems to be what Apple does—at least it did under Steve Jobs), to "Let's do lots of studies with lots of users and use powerful statistical techniques to see what they want." My general experience is that good design comes from a combination of preparation (understanding user needs and studying what similar products do), creative inspiration, and a burning desire to make things easy to use.

There are many books, articles, and sites that focus on different aspects of the process. I can recommend a few:

Design Thinking is a well-known phrase that means somewhat different things to different people, but it's fundamentally about how user-centered form and function should drive technology rather than the converse. Determine what the product should do, and then determine how to do it. Of course, this is a gross oversimplification and there are many more aspects to it. A good place to begin one's schooling in those aspects is with the *Design Thinking* article by IDEO CEO Tim Brown in the Harvard Business Review (reprint can be found at Ideo's website (*http://bit.ly/ 1VlQaVW*)).

My favorite story of innovative design is how the Palm Pilot, the first successful pocket-dwelling Personal Digital Assistant (PDA), the direct progenitor of the smart phone, was developed. At the time, a string of failed pocket computers including the Apple Newton had "proved" to most people in the technology world that this market category could never be successful. Jeff Hawkins set out to prove everyone wrong, and he absolutely got the job done by using what I'd consider to be good and practical Design Thinking, starting with whittling a chunk of wood that could fit in his pocket and pretending to use it as a PDA (*Wired* (*http:// wrd.cm/1gNfhRW*) has an article about this). Palm products are probably more well known today for the stumbles of their later models, but the

Pilot totally broke open a new market thanks to the magic combination of creativity and discipline needed to define great products.

A great down-to-Earth book on creating useable software screens is *Rocket Surgery Made Easy: The Do-It-Yourself Guide to Finding and Fixing Usability Problems* by Steve Krug. Unlike most books of this genre it's unrelentingly practical and specific, and can be used immediately by tiny or large development groups. *Rocket Surgery* is more targeted toward websites, but smart device interfaces are not so different (and thanks to HTML5 and various supporting technologies, they become less different every day).

User Story Mapping by Jeff Patton with Peter Economy is a readable and comprehensive look at creating and working with user stories to define software products. My experience is that the same approach holds, more or less, for hardware/software products.

The Lean Startup by Eric Ries emphasizes that there's a lot of guess-work in developing products. It's a good idea to make little guesses and test them with users quickly in lots of iterative cycles rather than to make a large bunch of guesses and test them all at once (i.e., waiting until our "final" product to run testing). Frequent testing and refinement is also a tenet of Design Thinking, and is emphasized in the other books just mentioned.

Product Design and Development by Ulrich and Eppinger is a good book on product development with a more formal slant than this book, oriented toward academic coursework but still practical. It's a useful book in general, but in particular its sections on development process phases and architecture complement this chapter nicely.

In this phase, we discussed reducing the risk of technology unknowns that might derail our development efforts. There are other risks that can be mitigated, particularly risks of product failure (unreliability) and of harm occurring (e.g., in a medical device or vehicle). These types of risks are often identified, prioritized, and mitigated through processes known as *Failure Modes and Effects Analysis* (FMEA), its sibling *Failure Modes and Effects and Criticality Analysis* (FMECA), and *Fault Tree Analysis* (FTA), each of which has a pretty good write-up in Wikipedia. Weibull.com, an excellent resource for reliability engineering information, also has good discussions of these:

- *http://www.weibull.com/basics/fmea.htm*
- *http://www.weibull.com/basics/fault-tree/*

TIP Expert Tip: If you do undertake FMEA, FMECA, and FTA activities, which I recommend, large quantities of beverages and pastries are absolutely required at all team meetings. *You have been warned.*

## CHAPTER 6

Detailed Development

At this point, we've defined our product's functionality and look, and we have a high-level understanding of the mechanical, electrical, and software systems that will comprise the product. Now we just have to finish developing it, which usually consumes well over half of the product's total development effort.

In principle, we can now just assign bits to individual designer/developers based on the previous phase's outputs (requirements, architecture, use cases, etc.), and then each designer/developer creates their piece of the product. When the pieces are complete, we assemble everything together and *voila!*—we have a finished product.

Of course, the reality is more complex than this. There are many details to get right. Getting each bit to work on its own is challenging, and getting all the bits to work together is still harder.

Revisiting our roadmap from Chapter 5 (reproduced in Figure 6-1), detailed development is an exercise in iteration.

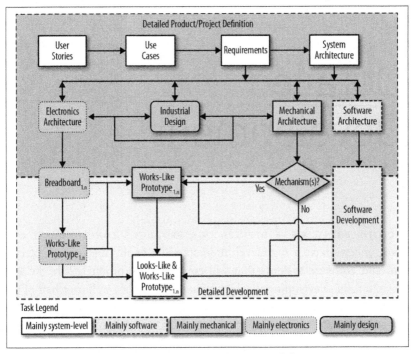

FIGURE 6-1. Detailed product specification and development work flow

Individual designer/developers work on their pieces, developing, testing and iterating until those parts work OK on their own. These individual pieces are integrated into prototypes, and more testing is performed to see if things work together as desired. Feedback from prototype testing is used to update individual pieces, which are reintegrated into updated prototypes. And the process continues until we have a product that we're ready to send out into the market.

The bulk of the day-to-day work in this phase is in designers/developers doing what they've been trained to do: electrical engineers developing circuits, software developers developing code, and mechanical engineers designing mechanical parts. What tends to separate success from failure here is less in the technical abilities of each participant (although this is not an insignificant factor), and more in having a process that ensures that everyone's efforts tie together into a coherent whole.

Think in terms of a symphony orchestra: each player might be excellent, but we don't want everyone excellently playing their own thing. We want each player to work together with their groups and sections, and all of these to work together to produce a single coherent performance of beautiful music. Likewise, in product development, we want each designer/developer's work to come together to create a single coherent product.

In this chapter, we'll be taking a high-level look at the types of activities that take place in this detailed development phase, with slightly deeper dives into areas that are interdisciplinary or otherwise not comprehensively covered well in other sources. We'll first walk through the detailed development process, and then go on to discuss a few major topics of a general nature that are keys to success.

Detailed Development Process

As mentioned in Chapter 2, Mark Twain once quipped that "History doesn't repeat itself, but it does rhyme." Similarly, no two detailed development efforts are the same in the number and nature of their various iterations, but they all follow similar paths and encounter similar issues.

To get a general feel for things, it might be useful to start by reviewing the process followed during MicroPed's detailed development, shown in Figure 6-2:

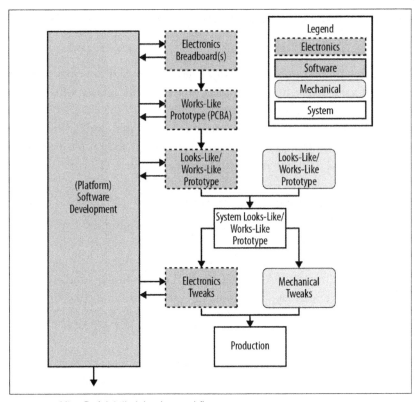

FIGURE 6-2. MicroPed detailed development flow

The MicroPed wearable has fewer parts than most smart products, but this flow is pretty representative of most detailed development efforts. Next, we'll take a walk through the process and discuss some of the details that lie in Figure 6-2's boxes and interactions. Since many products are more complex than MicroPed, or are different in other ways, we'll broaden the discussion when appropriate by pointing out what might be done differently in other situations.

We'll begin with the overall interplay between the electronics and software development efforts because this plays such a critical role in the detailed development of intelligent products.

SOFTWARE AND ELECTRONICS: CHICKEN AND EGG

There are a couple of major considerations that shape the development of software and electronics:

1. Software usually requires hardware to run on.*

2. Most hardware these days also relies on software for even basic functionality, such as setting registers to allow a display to work properly.

It is a chicken-and-egg situation.

One possible approach is to develop all of the electronics as best we can without involving software, then to build PCBAs and hope that the software folks can get everything working. This is, in fact, what often happens, but it's a bad idea. Untested hardware assembled in a PCBA will have usually have major bugs that will be found as soon as we start running software, and then we're stuck with PCBAs that are painful to rework (change). These bugs might even prevent software from running at all, greatly limiting our testing.

Also, it's often the case that executing software on our hardware will teach us important things about how we can do things better, which in turn will result in significant hardware changes.

PCBAs are not designed to easily change (i.e., to be rewired), and change through iteration is crucial throughout this development phase. A better way to proceed through this chicken-and-egg situation is to embrace and cultivate iteration by incrementally building up the electronics, one functional block at a time as one or more breadboards.

In practice, this should start with electronics and software people working with off-the-shelf development kit(s) for the processor(s) and key components we've selected for our product. Next, breadboards are created to add electronic functional blocks, and these blocks are designed to electrically integrate with the processor development kit(s).

You'll recall that we also created breadboards in Chapter 5, but those breadboards were more specifically for exploring high-risk unknowns to determine project feasibility and scope. In my experience, it's a good idea to breadboard not just the "unknown" parts of the system, but also the "that shouldn't be a problem" parts of the circuit. Little goof-ups commonly crop up on our first attempt at the latter; on a breadboard they can be fixed by moving a few wires, whereas once we're on a PCBA they might be difficult or impossible to fix without a new and expensive PCB design/build cycle.

---

* Unless we're running on virtual hardware; i.e., an emulator. But even still, we eventually need to run software on the real hardware.

After a new functional block's electronics are breadboarded and integrated with a processor development kit, software and hardware folks work very closely together—often at the same desk, for days at a time or longer—to either demonstrate that the block is basically working properly and can be controlled by software, or that the electronics folks need to go back and make major changes to their design. The basic iteration process that describes this is shown in Figure 6-3.

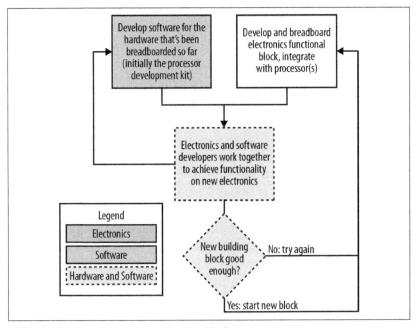

FIGURE 6-3. Electronics and software iteration block

This proceeds until we've done as much as we reasonably can without moving to PCBAs that implement the full design (we'll discuss moving to this phase in a moment).

Now that we have a basic understanding of how electronics and software design/development play together, let's focus in on the specifics of how each technical discipline proceeds individually.

ELECTRONICS

Our major electronics components—chips, displays, and so forth—should have been selected in the detailed definition phase covered in Chapter 5, in part so we can have a good estimate of cost of goods sold

(COGS). The general flow for electronics development in this phase is as follows:

1. Design and develop the circuitry as individual building blocks on breadboards.

2. Integrate these breadboards to demonstrate that the building blocks can work together as a system.

3. Create PCBAs that implement full product functionality but are designed for testing and debugging rather than actual product use.

4. Create final PCBA designs that are ready to move into manufacturing.

Let's look at each of these in more detail.

Breadboarding

We live in an age where much can be simulated using computers and software. Computer simulations of circuitry can be useful but tend to be limited to certain specific situations, such as high-speed connections and analog circuits. More generally, however, electronics design and testing is still accomplished using real components rather than virtual ones. (Links to resources on circuit simulation can be found in this chapter's "Resource" section.)

MicroPed's electronics are reasonably simple in that there are few parts: let's start by reviewing this effort, and then see how things might be different for a more-complex circuitry. For example, all of the chips we've selected are designed to be powered directly from batteries like the one we're using; so unlike most products, we don't even need separate power-supply circuits. With few parts, building a single breadboard to implement full functionality, shown in Figure 6-4, was fairly easy.

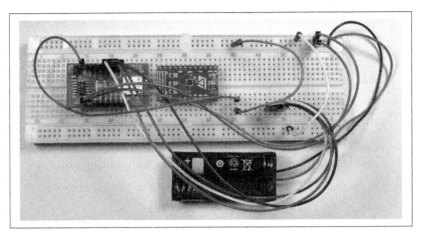

FIGURE 6-4. Fully functional MicroPed electronics

As discussed in Chapter 5, it's easiest to breadboard using development kits and breakout boards as often as possible. In this case, all of the parts selected for MicroPed were available on breakout boards, which made life relatively easy. Otherwise, we'd want to create our own breakout boards, as most parts these days are tiny and have surface-mount pads with no pins to hook to.

Figure 6-5 shows a breakout board of this type that we created to breadboard a Bluetooth Smart *module* based on a Bluetooth Smart *chip* (Nordic nRF51822) that we eventually used. The module itself is highlighted in the red oval. It's smaller than a US dime with more than 40 electrical connections on its bottom.

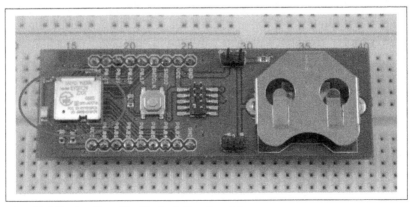

FIGURE 6-5. Breakout board for Bluetooth Smart module

Why pick a Bluetooth Smart module rather than purchasing the chip itself and associated components? While the module is significantly more expensive than the individual components, it has some nice advantages for lower-volume production:

- Modules come built and tested, which reduces our design and production risk, particularly around tuning the RF parts.

- Modules have FCC modular certification, which eliminates our need to do certification for intentional RF radiation (i.e., Bluetooth transmission). This will save thousands of dollars. (Like all electronics products, we'll still need to be certified as an unintentional radiator.)

- Modules are prequalified as Bluetooth-Smart-capable, which enables us to advertise that capability. Otherwise, we'd need to apply to the Bluetooth SIG (Special Interest Group) that holds the rights to the Bluetooth Smart mark and get qualified. Again, this saves us thousands of dollars.

- If production volumes become high enough to warrant moving from module to components, we can use the same chip, thus preserving the radio's major characteristics (range, power consumption, etc.).

Note that some circuits can be difficult or impossible to breadboard: electrical signal paths on PCBAs can be highly optimized, while the signal paths on breadboards are generally quite nonoptimal, e.g., long wires waving in the breeze. For some types of signals, such as low-speed digital signals and power supplies, breadboards are usually OK. Perhaps a few precautions should be taken, such as extra decoupling capacitors. For other types of signals, such as high-speed digital and sensitive analog lines, breadboards can substantially affect the circuitry and thus are unsuitable. In these cases, it can be *very* useful to build small test PCBAs that contain the non-breadboard-friendly parts of our circuits, with provision to bring signals off the board, as appropriate, which are breadboard-friendly.

As mentioned, because of MicroPed's unusually low electronics-parts count, a single physical breadboard can easily accommodate all of its circuitry. But more-typical smart products contain dozens or hundreds of components that fall into a dozen or so subsystems, and the breadboarding process should be segmented and staged. For example, individual electrical engineers can each develop a breadboard with one or perhaps a handful of subsystems, and once these various breadboards are proved out, they are integrated together into one or more "breadboards of bread-boards" (usually a glorious mess of wires) to test the ability of all circuits to work together.

Works-like electronics prototype

Once our breadboards seem to be functioning properly as a system, the next step is to build fully functional works-like PCBA prototypes that we can test. In principle, these PCBAs can be works-like/looks-like (i.e., in the final form factor needed for our product), but in practice this is usually not a good idea. Production boards tend to be cramped and difficult to troubleshoot, whereas our works-like boards should be easy to trouble-shoot and test. Large boards with lots of extra test points and other debugging features are a good way to go.

> **TIP** Reminder: a works-like prototype *functions* (we hope) like it will in the final product. A looks-like prototype *looks* like it will in the final product. And a works-like/looks-like prototype does both.

The works-like prototype for MicroPed is shown in Figure 6-6. The circuitry is the same as the production board, but it's easier to test and troubleshoot. Some of the extra debug and test features incorporated into this board (compared to the product PCBA) include:

1. External power supply connection to permit the use of a power sup-ply whose voltage and current we can adjust, instead of a battery. This is helpful for many reasons. For example, it will let us simulate a battery running out of charge (turn down the voltage and current capacity a bit).

2. The ability to add current-sense circuitry before the power pin of every IC so we can monitor its power consumption. This comes in handy, for example, if the circuit as a whole is drawing more power than expected and we'd like to know which specific part or parts are responsible so we know where to start troubleshooting.

3. Bringing all on-board signals of interest to connectors for off-board observation; e.g., the SPI bus used to communicate between two

chips. In this case, signals were brought out to header pins with 100 mil spacing, allowing the PCBA to be plugged into a standard bread-board, which is very handy for troubleshooting. As mentioned previously, some signals will not be happy about being brought off-board; we have to be careful that the debugging features we add don't break things themselves (the Observer Effect of debugging, if you will).

4. Bringing some extra unused signals off-board. These can be helpful for software folks to test/debug functionality and timing: they can be toggled by software at various points and monitored by a logic analyzer or oscilloscope to understand sequencing, timing, and so forth. You'll often hear developers of real-time software say that an oscilloscope is their favorite debugger—think of these hardware test/debug as part of the software tool chain.

5. A "real" connector for programming and debugging the processor, rather than the test pads used on the production board. The connector type is usually dictated by the debugger that we'll be using; in any case, it will get a good workout during testing and debugging so it should be able to withstand numerous insertion cycles. Production circuit boards sometimes have the same type of connector, but since these units are typically programmed once (or at most infrequently) and processor debugging is not normally wanted in production units, we'll usually make a change to save space and cost. For example, instead of the connector, we can program the processor via PCB test pads or even purchase parts with software preloaded into memory by the distributor (a common and useful value-added service).

FIGURE 6-6. MicroPed works-like prototype

It's often the case that chips are available in several different packages: larger packages with pins that are easier to access directly, and smaller packages with pins that are difficult or impossible to access directly. It's usually good to go with the easy-pin-access packages on these works-like boards because they're easier to troubleshoot and to solder down, and then switch to the smaller parts for production PCBAs when we're trying to minimize size. However, in some cases, we might want to go with the smaller parts on the works-like board; for example, if we want to use this as an opportunity to test an unusual PCB footprint we've created, or to test the ability of a PCB assembly house to properly solder down a part, or when circuit characteristics might be significantly affected when switching packages.

Printed Circuit Boards

Once we've satisfied ourselves with our circuitry's functionality via appropriate testing (more on this later in this chapter), it's time to convert our *works-like* board(s) into *works-like/looks-like* board(s), as shown for MicroPed in Figure 6-7. This is typically a process of:

- Removing the features we've added for debugging.
- Adding features we'll need for manufacturing testing.
- Switching IC packages if needed.

- Scrunching the board size down to what we've been allotted. If necessary, we can use various PCB technologies that permit denser configurations—for a cost (more on this in a moment).

FIGURE 6-7. MicroPed works-like/looks-like PCBA prototype (in prototype enclosure)

The PCB assembly process was covered back in Chapter 3. Being mindful of the assembly process helps us to create boards that work with the process, rather than ones that need to be shoehorned in and fussed with. When designing our production PCB(s), a process called *PCB layout*, it's important to work closely with the folks who'll be fabricating the PCBs and with those who'll be assembling the PCBAs. Happy vendors will result in lower costs, better outcomes, and less stress for everyone.

In the case of PCB fabricators, they'll normally have a myriad of options that can affect board size, noise, layout effort, and other factors. Some of these include the number of conductive layers, board material and thickness, minimum feature sizes and spacing, panel sizes, testing, turn-around times, blind and/or buried vias, microvias, and other High Density Interconnection (HDI) techniques (more information about these features can be found in this chapter's "Resource" section). These options can have a very dramatic effect on cost, timing, and reliability. It's far better to discuss options with potential PCB fabricators before starting layout to find out our options, and determine what makes the most sense for our effort, rather than hoping that what we design can be made and won't break the bank.

On the PCBA assembly side, vendors will typically have design rules that should be followed, including things like the minimum spacing between traces/components and PCB edges, clearance between PCBs in a panel, panel sizes, and so forth. They might make reference to the standards published by IPC (founded as the *Institute for Printed Circuits*), a trade group of organizations involved in manufacturing PCBs and PCBAs. Beyond following design rules, it's very helpful for our assembly (and PCB fabrication) vendors to review our boards during the design process. They're usually very happy to do this, because they know that catching potential issues early will make their job easier.

Once our works-like/looks-like PCBAs are assembled, we'll perform more verification testing to make sure that they meet our needs. We'll test the electronics itself, and we'll also integrate our boards into a full product looks-like/works-like prototype so we can understand how our electronics are working with everything else at the product level. We'll look at these activities later in this chapter, but first let's turn to the development of software, which is the magic that brings our electronics to life.

SOFTWARE

Like electronics, detailed software development is a process of deconstructing high-level functionality into smaller units that can be tackled individually, implementing these units, and finally integrating them together to construct the system-level functionality. There's no shortage of detailed information on how this is done—I've included some references in the "Resources" section at the end of this chapter—so I'll avoid redundancy in this section and stick to a few higher-level topics.

At least in the product development efforts that I've been involved in, software development almost always starts off with the largest budget, and even then is more likely to slip schedule and exceed budget than are other technology efforts. A study published in the September 2011 issue of the Harvard Business Review, *Why Your IT Project May Be Riskier Than You Think*, found that one in six IT projects are disasters; on average, these overrun budget by 200% and time by 70%. While I've not seen a similar study of embedded product software, my experience indicates that it wouldn't be substantially different.

Listing all of the potential causes (and mitigations) for software development becoming derailed could fill a good-sized book, and many good-sized books on the subject exist. Since this is such a large and well-travelled area, we won't review it in detail. However, there is one common structural fault that we should address as it emphasizes a common theme in this book; specifically, this fault lies in not thoughtfully working with the iterative nature of the development process.

In many or most projects that go very wrong, each software developer writes and tests the software modules assigned to them ("yeah, the code I wrote seems to be working properly"), and then all is integrated and formally tested together only at the project's end ("we're almost done; we're just putting all of the pieces together"). "Final" testing finds all sorts of issues, the unfixed-bug list grows, bugs are fixed but break previously working code, the unfixed-bug list grows still longer, and so forth. Months or years after "we're almost done," we're *truly* done—if stakeholders haven't run out of money or patience.

In this software section, we'll look at some practices that embrace iteration throughout the detailed development process to keep projects on track. First, let's start with a short discussion of the software effort's overall structure.

A tale of two software developments

Largely dependent on product and software sophistication, the software effort is often split into two major sub-efforts representing different software layers. The software that deals directly with operating and monitoring the hardware is known by various names such as the *embedded, platform, or operating system* software, whereas the software that runs on top of this layer is usually known as the *application* software, as shown in Figure 6-8.

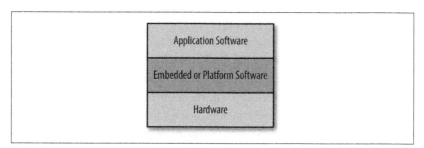

FIGURE 6-8. Software layers

In most instances, the applications software will revolve around end-user interaction (e.g., via a GUI), but non-GUI applications can also be useful.

The MicroPed wearable arguably doesn't have a user interface. It has an API that's not very sophisticated, so splitting software up this way doesn't make sense in this instance. But for sophisticated systems, typically those that are running an OS or platform such as Android, these two efforts are normally split up and can be run fairly separate from each other, integrating together at intervals to ensure that both are working together.

A key to enabling concurrent development of the application and platform is to keep the application's dependency on the platform from becoming a bottleneck; i.e., make sure that application developers aren't stuck waiting on platform work to be completed. For example, if our selected platform is Android, quite a bit of our application might be tested running on an Android emulator that's running on a desktop computer, or on an off-the-shelf Android phone or tablet. The application is moved to the "real" platform and finished up once the hardware and platform developers have gotten device drivers and other "under the hood" parts working and integrated.

If our application is dependent on device drivers and/or libraries that are not yet written, software stubs can be quickly written to broadly simulate functionality of the missing drivers/libraries to be written. These won't have quite the same functionality as the real code, but they can implement the real API.

Now that we have a broad idea of how the software development process proceeds, let's take a closer look at the iteration in the detailed development process so we'll have a better idea of how to work with it.

(Almost) instant iteration

Referring back to the high-level flow diagram of this phase (shown again in Figure 6-9, one thing that sticks out is that the software effort is represented by one long block, whereas hardware efforts are represented by multiple discrete blocks. Software development looks different within most other product development efforts because software development *is* different. As discussed in Chapter 5, in the case of hardware there tends to be significant overhead for each iteration. As a result, there are typically fewer iterations, each carefully planned and sequenced, each normally substantially different from the previous one. Software, on the other hand, almost always has much less obvious overhead cost per iteration (change a little code and rebuild the project), and as a result it tends to iterate rapidly—so rapidly that at the high level it can look and feel more like a single continuous effort rather than a series chunks. As updated electronics become available, updated software is moved over to it for integration testing.

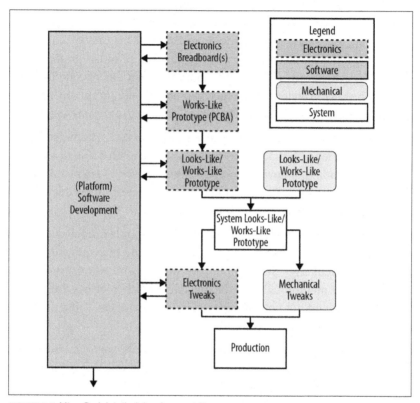

FIGURE 6-9. MicroPed detailed development flow

It can be challenging to maintain a continuous effort for long periods of time, so chunks are sometimes imposed on software efforts. Agile software development breaks development up into sprints with specific objectives to be attempted in a specific period of time, usually 2–4 weeks. Even in projects that don't use Agile tactics, it's a good idea to define waypoints where certain defined goals should be met, such as passing specific tests. These waypoints could coincide with hardware releases but don't have to. But even if we impose chunks on the software effort, it will still have more of a continuous flavor to it as compared to other technical efforts.

I believe that the relative ease with which software can be iterated and updated is both its greatest strength and its Achilles' heel. The ability to change functionality by retyping a few lines of code or installing an app is almost miraculous compared to the effort of changing hardware functionality. However, software's ease of iteration can also seduce us into bad practices if we don't keep an eye on system complexity.

One potential bad decision is to assume that we can get things "pretty close" via a seat-of-the-pants effort, and then test the system and easily smooth off the rough edges at the project's end. This can work for small efforts that involve a developer or two, but as software projects grow larger, the complexity of the interrelations between bits of code can grow rapidly, usually exponentially, which can lead to significant challenges if some discipline is not exercised from the start. Here are some examples:

1. There can be situations where code modules work as intended by their developer, but do not work well with each other due to a poor understanding of how the modules are supposed to interact. Code must be rewritten, which would not have happened if we'd had clearer specifications at the start.

2. Because of the many execution paths that the code can follow, certain execution sequences are rarely experienced, and thus difficult to test at the system level. Some of our code might be inherently bad, but unless we methodically test the individual units (routines, methods, etc.) we might not find a problem during system test — but our customers can find it.

3. If we update (e.g., fix a bug) in one code module, we might introduce new bugs within that module or change the module's functionality in ways that break compatibility with other modules.

As mentioned earlier, many books and articles have been written on software development practices that can mitigate the issues that come with growing complexity, which are the very issues that tend to cause overruns in cost and time. Let's take a look at three of these practices— version control, test-driven development, and continuous integration— that are fairly ubiquitous these days (or should be).

Version control

My first car, a 1965 Ford Mustang, was almost 20 years old and in rough shape when I bought it—both for transportation and as a restoration project. I quickly found out that these two goals conflicted with each other: during restoration, the car was in pieces and not going anywhere.

Software potentially has a similar issue: if developers are updating "the software," then how do we ever have something stable enough to test? That's where version control comes into play. Version control allows each designer/developer to copy their own version of the software to their local computer (called a *check-out*) so they can make changes without affecting the "main" copy (often called the *trunk*). When their changes are completed and believed to be working, the changed files are added back (called a *check-in*) to the trunk, where they can be tested to see if they work properly with the rest of the software.

Version control also keeps track of who made what changes, and why they made those changes if they add that info during check-in (i.e., "Fixed bug 1313"). This can help us to know which developer to contact if we have questions about what's been done.

Version control helps prevent developers from stepping on each other's toes. Suppose two programmers check out the same code, make changes to the same file, and then both check in their changed file. The version control system will warn the second person checking in that their file would overwrite the other changes that were checked in. It can also help them to see what changes were made by the first check in, and help them to add just their new changes without overwriting the first set (a process known as *merging*).

Version control software also lets us do lots of other nifty tricks that have to do with storing versions of program files; for example, once we release a version of software to production, we might want to start working on our next major version to be released in several months. If an important bug crops up in the released production software and we'd like to fix it before the next major version is ready for release, we can use version control to return to exact code that's in the current release, fix just that one bug, and release an interim update with just that fix.

The use of version control software is ubiquitous these days, and plenty of information is available on the subject. The two most common systems in use today, *Subversion* (commonly abbreviated as *SVN*) and *Git*, are free and work very well. SVN uses a single main server for storing shared versions, while the newer Git is distributed: every developer's computer that uses Git is also a Git server. Git tends to be better for larger software projects (like the Linux kernel, for which it was developed), but it has a significant learning curve. SVN is easier to use but not as efficient for larger projects.

Both SVN and Git can be used for any documents (and other files, for that matter), not just for source code; in fact, SVN is a nice solution for general document control, which we'll discuss in Chapter 12. Git, on the other hand, seems to be pretty difficult to comprehend for non-programmers. Links to these packages and more information on how to use them are found in this chapter's "Resources" sectionsection.

Test-driven development

One of the challenges of software changing so rapidly is that it's very easy to break one thing while updating or fixing another. To deal with this, it's best to create suites of automated tests that test each code module, and to run these tests each time we make a change.

We could write all of our product code and then write tests, but that would put off bug-catching until later, when fixing it is more expensive. There's a good case to be made for developing the tests at the same time we develop product code, a process called *test-driven development* (TDD), which refers to testing incrementally as we develop our code.

In TDD, before we write product code, we write a little test code. When our product code passes the test(s) we wrote, we write some more test code. Then we update the product code to pass the new tests. This process is repeated until we have both our code and a full set of tests for it.

There are various test frameworks to streamline this process. Perhaps the most well known are the _Unit frameworks, such as JUNit for Java, CppUnit for C/C++, and NUnit for .NET, but other good frameworks are available, such as Unity and GoogleTest.

TDD is very effective, particularly as projects grow larger and interdependencies become more numerous, which increases the chances of code changes breaking functionality.

Continuous integration

Continuous integration pulls together version control and test-driven development to help ensure that software's continuous iterations move things forward in an orderly way.

The basic idea is that as developers check in updated code to the trunk, the software is automatically rebuilt and tested (i.e., run against the tests developed through test-driven development, and others). This process can be run as often as any new code is checked in, or less often (say, once a day) particularly for large code bases that take a while to build.

The advantage of continuous integration is that it catches errors as soon as they're introduced, when they're easiest and cheapest to fix. This chapter's "Resources" section points to more information on this practice.

This completes our high-level look at detailed software development. Let's now turn to the last (but not least!) of the detailed design technology efforts: mechanical engineering.

MECHANICALS (ENCLOSURES)

During our product's detailed development phase, we (hopefully) worked out the basics of our mechanical configuration. In this phase, we'll refine those basics into fully developed mechanical parts. Like all product development, enclosure design/development is a balancing act—we're trying to satisfy system-level product requirements and the needs of other designers/developers. In particular, in this phase, mechanical engineers must collaborate with electrical engineers and industrial designers to finalize specifics, including the selection and location of knobs, dials, buttons, switches, plugs, connectors, and specific mounting points for PCBAs.

Compared to other designers/developers, the work of mechanical engineers tends to have a larger (or at least a more visible) impact on the cost of manufacturing, for two reasons:

1. Mechanicals typically involve injection molding, and creating injection molds can be a very expensive and time-consuming process.

2. Mechanicals are usually assembled by hand in production, and manual assembly processes can be notoriously difficult to develop, implement, and test.

Let's review these two important issues to get a better understanding of where we want to end up at the end of this process, and then we'll work backward to discuss some of the steps that lead to successful mechanical design/development. Note: as discussed back in Chapter 5, mechanical design/development in smart products is normally limited to enclosures and related items, so we'll limit our discussion to this area (as opposed to mechanisms).

Injection molding

While 3D printing and other rapid mechanical prototyping technologies are a godsend, they are still primarily *prototyping* technologies. They help us to do a better and quicker job of getting to production, but production of plastic mechanical parts in quantity is still usually done by injection molding, much the same as it has been for decades.

As diagrammed in Figure 6-10, injection molding is accomplished by injecting hot plastic into a mold at great pressure. Granules of the selected plastic are poured into the hopper and then pushed by a screw mechanism through a heated barrel and into a mold. The molten plastic fills up all the mold's nooks and crannies, whereupon the mold is cooled, opened, and the plastic extracted and finished (e.g., extra bits caused by the molding process are cut off).

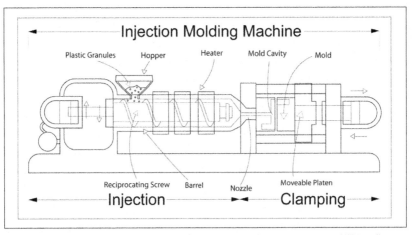

FIGURE 6-10. Injection molding machine, schematic view (Illustration courtesy Wikimedia Commons)

The mold itself is made of two blocks that are fitted together when the molten plastic is being injected, then are pulled apart to allow the molded part to be released after it cools. As an example, the two parts of a mold for Lego pieces are shown in Figure 6-11.

FIGURE 6-11. Two parts of a Lego mold (Photos courtesy Wikimedia Commons)

Designing parts for successful injection molding is a challenge, because we can't just mold anything we dream up—we need to take the molding process into account during the design process.

Most obviously, parts must be ejectable; i.e., they need to successfully pop out of their molds after cooling. One simple (but critical) step to take in this regard is to create enclosure walls at a slight angle from perpendicular (called a *draft angle*), as illustrated in Figure 6-12. The part being molded is sandwiched between the two parts of the mold. Notice how adding a draft angle prevents the parts wall from dragging against the mold walls during separation. Draft angles are typically only a degree or so depending on part sizing and surface finish.

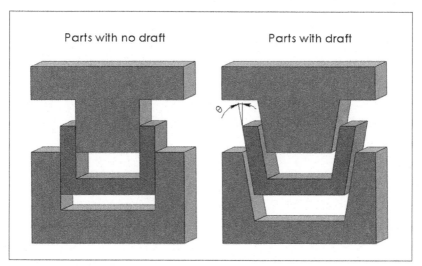

FIGURE 6-12. Draft angle

A more-challenging issue is working with mechanical features that jut out from the main body of an enclosure, which would prevent a mold from opening unless we take special action. These features, called *under-cuts*, are accommodated by various means. The most "notorious" of these, used for undercuts on a molded part's exterior, are side actions. These add a mechanism to the mold that keeps a piece of mold material in place during molding, then pulls the piece out through mold's side after the plastic cools so that the plastic can be removed. For example, suppose we wanted to mold a hole in one of the side walls of the enclosure in Figure 6-12. This could be made possible by a side action, as shown in Figure 6-13. "A" shows a cross-section of the closed mold filled with material, with the side action (a bar) inserted; "B" shows "A" split open so we can see what the side action is doing, specifically keeping plastic out of part of the wall. "C" illustrates the unmolding process: the side action is pulled out, and the unmolded plastic has the desired hole in its wall.

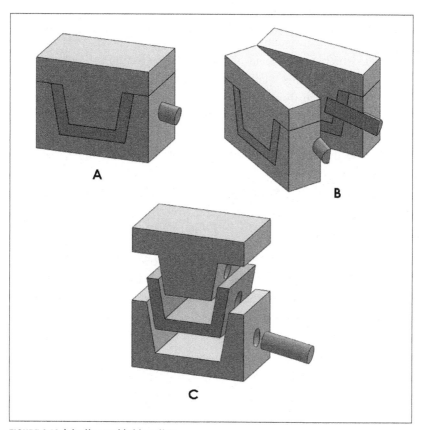

FIGURE 6-13. Injection mold side action

Side actions enable otherwise-unobtainable features, but they add significant cost and risk.

Other clever means of achieving undercuts are also available, including using lifters, collapsing cores, sliding cores, and pickouts. Links to information on these can be found in this chapter's "Resources" section.

Some other injection-mold-related issues that should be accommodated in mechanical design include:

- Plastic must adequately reach all of the parts of the mold. For example, this causes minimum wall thickness to increase for larger parts.

- Plastic shrinks when cooling and thinner parts of a piece will cool faster, which can lead to warping or other defects.

As can be seen, a lot of thought goes into the successful design of molded parts!

Production molds are normally made from steel or aluminum, and the differences between these are significant. Steel is a much harder material, which makes it ideal for high-volume and/or high-precision parts as it will hold its shape well through upwards of a hundred thousand, perhaps even more than a million molding cycles. Various aluminum alloys are used with various properties, but compared to steel, aluminum generally cannot achieve as high of a tolerance and molds wear much more quickly; thus aluminum is typically suited to prototypes and short runs (i.e., low volumes).

The downside of steel is that because it's so hard, it's difficult to cut as compared to aluminum. Creating a steel mold is slow and expensive, typically taking 5–10 weeks and costing upwards of $10,000 per mold. By contrast, aluminum molds can be created in days (even hours in some cases) at a cost that's in the neighborhood of 20%–50% of steel.

Another consideration with molds is that while they are relatively easy to tweak by cutting away more material, adding material is difficult and in some cases impossible. So it's best to start with more material in the mold (i.e., thinner plastic parts) and then cut carefully as needed rather than the other way around.

The simplest types of molding accommodate a single material (i.e., resin). But it can be desirable to mold multiple materials together, most commonly a hard plastic "core" with an added external rubbery texture that provides for a better grip and feel. A classic example is the rubbery patches often molded into the sides of computer mice (such as the light gray patch on the mouse shown in Figure 6-14). These patches could be molded separately and glued on, or molded right onto the rigid plastic beneath it, a process called overmolding which typically produces better and cheaper results. There are two ways to accomplish overmolding: one is to mold the rigid substrate in one mold and then insert the substrate in a second mold where the rubbery parts are molded on. This is known as *insert molding*. A second method is known as *multi-shot molding*, where the process is accomplished by a single sophisticated mold used with sophisticated injection machinery.

FIGURE 6-14. Computer mouse with overmolding

Beyond the obvious increase in tooling and manufacturing costs, overmolding has a profound effect on an enclosure's mechanical engineering. For example, it typically increases part thickness, which can impact enclosure size and/or PCBA geometry, and designs need to accommodate the soft materials' higher draft requirements and minimize excessive flash (extra, unwanted material).

The takeaway on injection molding is that it's an expensive and sophisticated process that requires careful planning. Perhaps even more so than for other detailed design efforts, it's important to work closely with our manufacturing vendors starting early in the process to ensure that what we develop will live up to our vision when it's shipped out to customers; what one vendor routinely does, another vendor might say is impossible.

Now that we have a feel for the most important fabrication process in mechanical component development, let's move on to examine some strategies to help us develop a great set of mechanical parts that come together as inexpensively and easily as possible.

Mechanical design for manufacturability and assembly

Design for manufacturability (DFM) and *design for assembly* (DFA) are different but related endeavors that both seek to maximize mechanical quality and reliability while minimizing cost, although the terms are sometimes used interchangeably. DFM addresses the creation of parts, while DFA addresses the assembly of those parts.

For any given desired mechanical outcome (e.g., an enclosure that looks the way we want it to and that encloses the parts we need), there are many combinations and permutations of mechanical components that we can use, as well as many ways to manufacture and assemble them. Optimizing these is a very creative endeavor, particularly for mechanically sophisticated products.

One of the tenets of DFM and DFA (sometimes contracted together to *DFMA*) is that the best part of all is the part that doesn't exist, because it costs nothing to produce and nothing to assemble. That's a tricky way of saying that a key goal is to minimize parts count as much as is reasonably possible.

Next, we'll dive a little deeper into the areas of DFM and DFA, but before we do I'd like to point out that the discussion here is pretty generic. Specific algorithms exist that can be used to formalize these activities, particularly the well-known work of Boothroyd and Dewhurst referred to in this chapter's "Resources" section.

DFM. It's easy enough to create some virtual parts in our mechanical CAD software that will work together to do what we want on the screen. Virtual parts cost nothing to manufacture, and can be made to behave, but real parts have real costs and imperfect behaviors. DFM's goal is to design "real-world" parts that can be manufactured using existing processes at minimum cost. It's fundamentally an iterative process of thinking up different ways to create a part, trying different materials, processes, and design options to come up with the best parts and strategies for manufacturing them.

Developing moldable parts as we just discussed is a prime example of DFM, and our job here is normally to reduce the cost of a part over its lifetime. A part's cost over its lifetime includes the cost of the mold(s) plus the total cost of the parts produced during the product's lifetime, and all other associated costs. Another example is the need for a frame to firmly hold a hi-torque motor in place. This might be accomplished by molding high-tensile-strength plastic (e.g., a glass-filled resin), with sheet metal, or with machined parts. And each of these material choices will likely have many options as to the specific materials, designs, and processes used to manufacture those designs. The best method will depend on the number of parts we'll be manufacturing over time, and other factors.

One of the costs associated with a part is the cost associated with its assembly into our product. Different designs will incur different assembly costs, which is where DFA (covered more in a moment) becomes important. In mechanical assembly, "inexpensive" is fundamentally synonymous with "easy to do it right." Time is money in the factory. Easier, goof-proof assembly translates into shorter assembly times and lower production costs.

Ease of manufacturing and assembly also leads to higher-quality results by increasing reproducibility. While most electronics manufacturing is automated these days, most mechanical assembly is not. Robots are excellent at doing precisely the same thing over and over virtually forever, while humans are pretty easily confused and sometimes inattentive, which can lead to deviations in manufacturing; a screw of the wrong length gets inserted, or a washer is forgotten, or an almost-symmetrical widget is placed with the finished surface on the wrong side, and so forth.

A few decades ago, shipping products often had these kinds of quality problems. Quality tends to be much better these days, in large part because manufacturers have embraced DFA.

> **TIP** On the bright side, humans are much easier to train than robots. Our minds and bodies are incredibly flexible! This is why robotic assembly tends to be used for simple tasks, very-high volume production, and/or tasks that are difficult or hazardous to do with people (heavy loads, dangerous conditions, etc.).

DFA. There are three basic goals in DFA:

1. Reduce the number of parts needed to assemble each unit.
2. Reduce the number of different part types used; e.g., trying to use a single screw size and length throughout an enclosure.
3. Have assembly steps be optimally quick and reproducible (i.e., goof-proof).

As an example, let's look at something as simple as fastening a PCBA in an enclosure. There are a myriad ways to do this: we could use screws going into standoffs, have threaded posts coming up through board holes fastened down by nuts, or use glue or any manner of clips. Each of these has advantages and disadvantages. To get a feel for the tradeoffs involved, let's compare two options:

- PCBA holes are aligned with threaded bosses, and screws inserted and tightened down (Figure 6-15)

- Clips molded into our enclosure's sides that snap the PCBA into place when pressed down (Figure 6-16)

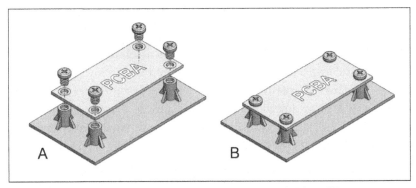

FIGURE 6-15. PCBA holes lined up over bosses (A) and then screwed down (B)

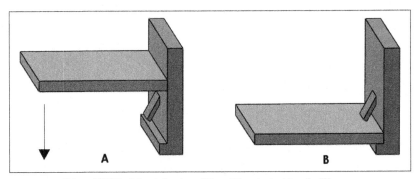

FIGURE 6-16. Edge of PCBA sliding into place (A) and then locked by clip (B)

Figure 6-15 requires the assembler to slide the PCBA around until the holes line up with the bosses, and then to drive each screw in with the right amount of torque. All told, it might take a minute or so to screw down the PCBA. And hopefully the screw doesn't accidentally drop before the worker begins driving it into the hole, or we'll either play a quick game of "find the screw" or a customer will wonder about that rattling sound in their unit (before the screw shorts something out and the unit's returned for repairs). Other potential problems include the screw not grabbing the hole correctly, perhaps at a bad angle, or the operator using the wrong size of screw. These can lead to problems including stripped threads, a split or weakened standoff, and/or incomplete fastening (i.e., screw head isn't firm against the board).

The clip configuration shown in Figure 6-16, by contrast, can be designed to be almost instant and goof-proof. If designed correctly, the PCBA will only fit if placed in the correct orientation, and an audible click will be heard when the clips snap into place. The process should take only a few seconds.

Obviously, Figure 6-16 is much easier to assemble and uses fewer parts: so why would anyone use Figure 6-15? The downsides of Figure 6-16 include:

- We'll likely need a more-sophisticated mold, which will increase our fixed costs.
- Disassembly can be a challenge.
- Positional tolerance of the board might be less than we'll get with screws.

There are also variants of Figure 6-15 that are better in most instances without increasing mold sophistication and cost. One popular variant is heat staking, shown as a cross-section view in Figure 6-17. A plastic stud sticks up through a hole in the PCBA (panel A), and then a tool heats and pushes the stud to soften and flatten it down (panel B), holding the board into place (panel C). Heat staking is an easy, inexpensive, and reasonably goof-proof fastening method that can be used for many types of parts in place, not just PCBAs. The downside, of course, is that it's not quite as simple and goof-proof as clips. Heat staking is also reasonably permanent, which can be a plus or minus depending on the application.

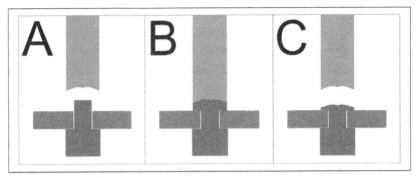

FIGURE 6-17. Heat staking

Screws, clips, heat stakes, and many other assembly techniques are at our disposal and should be evaluated. DFA can be performed in conjunction with DFM by considering the assembly process alongside DFM. It's also very useful for designers/developers to work with factory staff who actually perform these operations day after day—they'll often have great insights into what operations will be painful, and perhaps on better ways to proceed. Even better, we can ask them to assemble a prototype while we watch for problems. Commercial software is also available, notably from Boothroyd Dewhurst, which can greatly help with both DFM and DFA.

DFM and DFA activities tend to continue throughout mechanical development. Like virtually everything else in product development, they iterate until we run out of new ideas to do them better (unlikely) or our new ideas don't improve things enough to add design/development effort and slip schedule.

Up to now, we've described mechanical development as being an exercise in virtual parts being developed in CAD applications. As mentioned in Chapter 2, there's a famous saying that "the map is not the territory." Likewise, CAD models aren't physical parts that we can hold in our hands. As we're developing our mechanical components in CAD, we'll want to generate matching physical parts at various times; in our next section, we'll look at some ways to do this.

Mechanical prototyping

The methods and materials that can be used to create mechanical prototypes are limited only by human imagination. Cardboard, foam, tape, glue, foil... anything and everything. And while these "kitchen cabinet" technologies can be helpful early in development, they obviously won't do for creating models that closely match our product's mechanicals. In particular, they don't support the critical activity of accurately prototyping mechanical components from the CAD models being developed by mechanical engineers.

In this section, we'll focus on technologies used to transform CAD models into physical objects that we can evaluate, specifically the technologies used to create plastic prototypes, because this is the area that causes the most confusion and (in my experience) results in the most bad choices.

A decade ago, creating plastic prototypes was specialized work that normally took days or weeks and cost thousands of dollars. Things have changed, of course, and today we can purchase a pretty nifty 3D printer for a fraction of a thousand dollars and create our own models in minutes or hours.

Prototypes created quickly with inexpensive 3D printers or other rapid prototyping technologies are certainly useful, but they have limitations. There's a reason why injection molding is still the standard for creating plastic parts, despite the high fixed costs for molds: no other technology creates parts with such a wide range of properties (e.g., strength, finish) as quickly, reliably, and inexpensively (on a per-piece basis). While the quality of 3D printing and other rapid-prototyping methods gets quite good, particularly as cost increases, it's not the same quality that we get with injection molding. For example, surfaces rarely achieve the same level of finish, whether smooth or textured, and are of limited use when evaluating mechanical properties (including subtle items like the feel of a snap, which relies on mechanical properties).

More than a dozen rapid prototyping technologies are in use today. While no single technology equals injection molding in all areas, different technologies are as good (or even better) in different ways. The key to picking the right prototyping method for a prototype is to match its attributes to what we'd like the prototype to accomplish. There are a variety of different reasons to print mechanical prototypes during development, including:

- Getting a better idea of what an enclosure looks like while we're iterating its design

- A beautiful model to show prospective customers at trade shows before the product's ready

- Testing how parts fit together before committing to cutting expensive injection molds

- Testing safety and electromagnetic compatibility with regulatory agencies before actual product is being manufactured

- A full enclosure to integrate with electronics into a looks-like and works-like product prototype.

I haven't seen an authoritative list of the most common rapid proto-typing technologies in use today, and this is a fast-moving area that's likely to change rapidly in the next few years. The technologies that *I* normally run into are FDM, SLA, CNC, aluminum-tooling injection molding, and cast-urethane molding. Let's take a quick look at each of these to see how they can help us.

FUSED DEPOSITION MODELING (FDM). *Fused Deposition Modeling* (FDM) printing is the technology that most of us are familiar with, the technology used by all printers that cost less than $2,000 or so and starting at as little as a few hundred bucks. Printing is done in layers; plastic material, usually supplied as a roll of filament, is fed through a heated nozzle that moves in two dimensions, depositing a thin stream of melted plastic that fuses to the plastic it touches. After a layer is printed, the bed on which the model rests moves down, or the head moves up, and the next layer is deposited. Layers are built up until the model is complete.

A variety of materials (filaments) are available. The most popular are ABS and PLA (*Acrylonitrile Butadiene Styrene* and *Polylactic Acid*, if you must know). ABS is a stiff plastic; a petrochemical that's quite solid and durable and is often used commercially as a material for molded rigid parts. PLA is a softer plastic created from plant products, inherently non-toxic and biodegradable (it's even used in medical implants designed to dissolve within the body), although added colorants might alter its toxicity. PLA is rarely used commercially for rigid parts.

Of the two, PLA is generally better behaved during printing because it flows better due to its lower melting point and better viscosity. Models tend to be more dimensionally stable (i.e., they don't warp), look smoother, and are reasonably sturdy but not very rigid. ABS printing is generally fussier and creates a distinct melting plastic smell, but prints are more rigid and strong. Both are available in a wide variety of colors.

Many other filament materials are available with various properties, including flexibility, translucency, electrical conductivity, and extra stiffness. Some of these print well, but some can be persnickety so it's best not to assume that outcomes will be good until a material's been tried.

One issue with FDM and other types of 3D printing is dealing with overhangs. Material needs to be deposited on something, not just squirted into thin air, so some sort of support needs to be printed under any part features that jut out and would otherwise be suspended in air. Some FDM printers have multiple heads and are able to print support "scaffolding" from soluble materials so they can be dissolved once the print is complete. Otherwise, we'll need to cut the support material away, which can cause blemishes.

FDM printing is sort of "a jack of all trades, master of none." It's inexpensive and quite good at many things, but other technologies tend to be better for any specific quality.

STEREOLITHOGRAPHY (SLA). *Stereolithography* (SLA) technology is based around liquid resins that cure when exposed to a laser. In practice, a laser traces one horizontal layer at a time on the surface of a vat of the liquid resin (photopolymer).

Because the minimum feature size printable by an SLA printer is limited to the focus of a laser light, they create models that tend to be more mechanically accurate, support finer/more-complex features, and have a better surface finish as compared to FDM printers. (FDM feature size is limited in feature size by the wider nozzle width needed to extrude melted plastic.) The downsides are that SLA printers are more expensive to buy and operate; photopolymer liquids cost significantly more than typical FDM filament materials. The choice of materials is much more limited—color and translucency are sometimes the only variables—and cured photopolymers tend to be fragile/brittle.

SLA parts are typically used when mechanical accuracy is most important, or as a relatively low-cost and easy way to get a pretty good surface finish without manual steps after printing (e.g., polishing).

MACHINING (CNC). If we want our prototype to be made from the same material as our final product, one option is to machine the parts from a block of the desired material. Our 3D model is fed into a *computer numerical control* (CNC) milling machine that carves it out using end mill (cutting) bits of various sizes.

Machining plastic parts is a good low-cost (usually hundreds of dol-lars per piece) way to generate a small number of prototypes with proper-ties that are quite close to that of our production units. This can be useful for mechanical testing, and often for gaining regulatory approvals prior to having production molded parts. Test houses will often let us use these parts instead of production parts.

There are a few things to know:

- Because material is being milled away by an end mill bit of a finite physical size, there are limitations as to what can be done. In particu-lar, thin walls, deep pockets, and sharp corners can be challenging or impossible.

- While metal can be machined to a mirror finish, my own experience with machined plastic is that finishes are not quite as good, and tool marks are often visible. Check with your vendor to see what's realis-tic.

- Setup costs can vary tremendously depending on factors like the method used to determine the *tool path* (the path traveled by the end mills as they cut material) and the need for specialized fixtures. Tra-ditional methods of specifying the tool path can be time-consuming (i.e., expensive) and require testing to ensure good results; on the other end of the spectrum lies software like that used by Proto Labs' CNC service that instantly determines the tool path from our uploa-ded CAD file. Proto Labs even generates a 3D rendering of the proto-type that will result from the selected tool path, calling out any expected deviations from our uploaded model caused by limitations in the milling process.

- Lead times to get our parts can range from a day or two to several weeks, depending on part complexity and other factors.

ALUMINUM-TOOL MOLDING. Earlier we discussed using aluminum molds for plastic injection molding during production, but aluminum molds can also make sense for prototypes; in exchange for various limitations on what we can achieve, prototype-oriented vendors of injection molding services offer lower costs and quicker availability of molds and parts as compared to production-oriented vendors. It's not super-cheap (figure spending thousands of dollars) or super-fast (at least a few days from submitting CAD drawings to getting parts), but it has the advantage of being the prototyping technique closest to production.

A good variety of materials and finishes are available compared to most other prototyping technologies, but there are fewer options than we'd have for production-grade molds. Other typical limitations for prototype-level services include feature size, and the inability to tune the vendor's process to mitigate cosmetic imperfections and other issues that crop up.

CAST-URETHANE MOLDING. In this method, a model of a part is printed (e.g., using SLA), and then a mold is made around the part using rubbery material (usually silicone). The 3D model is removed, leaving us with a mold to be used with pourable polymers that can be selected/engineered to have properties fairly similar to those we'll use in production. Urethane plastics are typically used for the molded parts, and a fairly wide variety of urethanes are available that can simulate various plastics used in injection molding. Surface textures can be reproduced, and colorants can be added to the urethane so production color can be molded right in—much cooler than paint.

Another plus is that since these molds are flexible (i.e., stretchy), features that would require side actions for ejection in metal-tool molds can normally be accommodated by simply stretching the mold when removing the part.

Cast-urethane molds are inexpensive but have a limited life (somewhere in the 10–100 parts range) and can't do everything that a metal-tool mold can (e.g., fine features and tolerances). But cast-urethane molding can be a very economical way to create quality parts for prototypes that will be handled by prospective customers and for certain types of engineering verification (more on verification shortly). I've even heard of this method being used with success for short run production. Most vendors can turn parts around in a few days after receiving our CAD model files, but the time required to cast each part is relatively long, taking at least some hours.

Once we have *works-like/looks-like* prototypes of electronics and mechanicals, our next step is to integrate these with our *works-like/looks-like* electronics into a full system, a *works-like/looks-like* product prototype. Our product is coming to life now!

System Integration

Integrating electronics and mechanicals into a full *works-like/looks-like* product prototype is a huge milestone in the development of our product: mentally, it marks the moment when we begin to feel like there's an honest-to-goodness product emerging from all of our efforts.

But feelings of triumph are often tempered by a good dose of humility as the parts go together and testing commences. The magnitude of tempering will correspond to the degree of diligence we've put into DFA and other activities that have prepared us for this event. The following types of nonsubtle issues have been known to come up more than occasionally:

- Parts simply don't fit together well—too tight or too loose.

- Cables are too short

- Connectors or other parts cannot be mated because other components prevent fingers from going where they need to go, or eyes from seeing what they need to see

- Circuit boards touch metal mechanical parts (a potential short-circuit hazard)

- Electronic components are taller than expected, preventing a PCBA form fitting in its allocated space

- Anything else that you can imagine, and much more that you can't yet imagine

As a result, our first attempt at integrating everything into a full *works-like/looks-like* system prototype is often accomplished via judicious use of Dremel tools, X-acto knives, wire strippers, dental mirrors, long thin things to poke with, a large selection of adhesives and glues, Kapton tape (a thin insulator), trips to the store, overnight delivery services, incantations, cuss words, sugar, caffeine, and so forth.

This is why we plan to iterate, of course! Getting things right the first time is better than iterating, but we'll never get everything right the first time.

TIP 3D models of PCBAs can be generated from many electronics schematic/layout software applications, such as Eagle CAD, DesignSpark PCB, and Altium—either by the package itself or via third-party tools. These models can be imported into our Mechanical CAD application, or even 3D printed, to help ensure good mechanical compatibility, and to find and fix "gotchas" that would hinder assembly once we have real components.

One thing to be careful of here is that the components used in our electronics application have 3D models that are correct—they often aren't. The best bet is to get 3D models directly from component vendors if available, and to otherwise check all electronic component models against their datasheets for sizing. Also remember to account for alternate parts that you might specify to be allowable; alternative parts might be electrical equivalents of the part they'll replace, but their sizes can be quite different.

Another trick for dealing with connectors, which can be particularly tricky to get just right with regard to mechanical and assembly issues, is to glue real connectors to a board that's been 3D printed or at least cut to the correct PCB size.

Once we do get everything together, thorough verification testing will begin so we can see what's working and what isn't (more on testing in a moment). System-level discussions will take place around what needs to be updated so that everything fits and works together better on the next works-like/looks-like prototype revision, and then the designers/developers will go back and make the needed changes. They'll iterate the parts they're responsible for and that work will be pulled into the next iteration of a *works-like and looks-like* prototype, and so on, until we have a full prototype that passes testing and is ready to be released to the manufacturing folks.

Since the key activity that happens once we have full *works-like and looks-like* prototypes is testing, this is a good time to tackle this topic, and we'll do that next.

Testing

As a person who mainly works in the development of medical devices, testing holds a special place in my heart. Testing is a very, very big deal for medical devices, particularly ones that do dramatic things (e.g., restarting hearts and beaming radiation into tumors). This level of testing can easily warrant a book of its own, but since most readers are not likely to be developing medical or other critical products, we'll only cover the basics here. However, it's good to be aware that total test effort is usually related to the criticality and complexity of the product or subsystem being tested. A $5 toy that flashes LEDs will likely receive minimal testing, whereas commercial aircraft test budgets can reach billions of dollars.

There are two categories of testing to be considered in this phase. *Verification testing*, sometimes called *engineering testing* or *bench testing*, is performed prior to a product moving into manufacturing. It ensures that our product is *designed* properly.

The second category, as introduced back in Chapter 2 and Chapter 3, is *manufacturing testing*. This is performed, usually on each unit, to ensure that units have been *produced* properly. While we're not manufacturing our product yet, except as prototypes, we'll need to develop manufacturing tests to hand off to the factory at the end of this phase.

Let's take a quick look at each of these categories of testing.

> **TIP** *Validation* is another term that's used with regard to testing. While *verification* tests that the product's internal (company-generated) requirements are met, validation is higher-level testing that determines whether the product meets customer needs. A common saying is that "verification tests whether we designed the product correctly, and validation tests whether we designed the correct product." Validation is much more of an open-ended exercise than verification, but it typically involves having prospective users work with a product to see if they can accomplish the goals that we intended. Also, formal validation is much less common than formal verification.

VERIFICATION TESTING

Verification testing is typically performed by demonstrating that our design meets the requirements we developed in Chapter 5. While it's certainly true that some products are tested by the "try-a-bunch-of-stuff-and-see-if-it-seems to work" method, this is not the preferred basis for testing. Intelligent products typically have lots of different functions, modes, and conditions (e.g., battery full versus battery almost dead versus battery dead). Unless we carefully consider and test the many different possible states, we'll likely miss some, our customers will get to test those states before we do, and the test might fail the first time it's tried.

Testing is usually accomplished using comprehensive *test procedures* that walk test personnel through a series of steps that demonstrate that our requirements have been met, and that the product will work as expected when customers use it.

Test results are recorded in *test reports* that correspond to test procedures. The test report can be a separate document, or in many cases is integrated into the test procedure. (My preference is to integrate the two together in most cases. That way, we only need to look at one document rather than looking back and forth between two.) Each test procedure will normally have explicit pass/fail criteria, along with a place for testers to elaborate on any failures or other interesting behaviors.

Table 6-1 shows two steps from a MicroPed verification test procedure that covers power consumption. These are written in a "shorthand" that assumes the tester knows how to set up the device and instruments to measure average current through J1. For larger projects where testing might be performed by less-knowledgeable/skilled staff, or for projects where it's important that there be no ambiguity (e.g., safety-critical equipment) steps might be spelled out in greater detail as in Table 6-2, and illustrations might be added to aid the tester. In this case, most steps won't include a recorded value, but perhaps only a checkmark indicating the step was done.

TABLE 6-1. Example portion of "shorthand" test procedure/report

Step	Action	Record	Pass criteria	Comments
1	With the DUT advertising at a one-second interval, and using the *uCurrent Gold* current adapter set at 1mV/nA, measure the average current through the J1 jumper pins for 10 seconds. Use the oscilloscope's averaging function at 1msps.	Average current over 10 seconds: _____	Pass = less than 15uA Circle one: P/F	
2	With the DUT advertising at a 10-second interval, and using the *uCurrent Gold* current adapter set at 1mV/nA, measure the average current through the J1 jumper pins for 10 seconds. Use the oscilloscope's averaging function at 1msps.	Average current over 10 seconds: _____	Pass = less than 5uA Circle one: P/F	

TABLE 6-2. Example portion of detailed test procedure/report

Step	Action	Record	Pass criteria	Comments
1	Remove jumper J1 from circuit board.	Complete? ☐	n/a	
2	Attach the inputs of the *uCurrent Gold* current adapter to the two J1 pins.	Complete? ☐	n/a	
3	Attach the *uCurrent Gold* outputs to an Oscilloscope probe.	Complete? ☐	n/a	
4	Switch *uCurrent Gold* to 1mV/nA range.	Complete? ☐	n/a	
5	Make sure that *uCurrent Gold* "BATT OK" light is lit. If not, replace battery; record that "BATT OK" light was lit before proceeding.	"BATT OK" light lit (Y/N)	n/a	

In theory, we could have a single large test procedure that steps through all testing, but testing is normally broken into multiple bite-sized procedures that are more manageable. For example, one MicroPed test procedure steps through the different states that the Bluetooth Smart radio can be in, and records power consumption in each state. Other test procedures step through various use cases and record how often the different radio states are entered. By knowing the power consumed in each state, and how often we're in each state, we can determine average power consumption and thus develop a good estimate of battery life without having to test units for a full year.

There are no hard and fast rules on how long a single test procedure should be, but generally it should require no more than a few hours of an operator's time. This makes it easier to go back and re-run procedures as needed, such as when we make updates that might change a procedure's results. If we have very long procedures, any given procedure is more likely to be affected by any given change and thus repeated. Also early failures in long procedures can block testing of much functionality.

In practice, many test procedures involving user interfaces tend to correlate closely to the use cases we developed in Chapter 5, which makes sense: those use cases capture how the product should behave when used and now we're testing that it behaves as we specified.

It's important for test procedures to cover both *positive* and *negative* cases, particularly for user interfaces and anything safety-related. Positive cases (also called *go cases* or *happy cases*) are use cases where things go well: the system functions as expected and the user can accomplish the task at hand. Negative cases (*no-go cases* or *unhappy cases*) test what happens when things go wrong.

For example, perhaps we have a use case whose success requires a WiFi connection of at least a certain bandwidth. The positive case test would verify that the task can be completed when an adequate connection is present, while the negative case tests should be written to cover various scenarios where the connection is inadequate; for example:

1. The user begins the task when no connection is present.

2. The connection starts out OK, but drops while mid-task.

3. The connection stays up, but bandwidth sometimes drops below what's needed.

Note that in this example, we've called out one positive case and three negative cases, and we can probably find a few more negative cases without thinking too hard about it. This is typical: there will normally be more negative cases than positives. Also, negative cases are often more challenging to test. For example, our positive case here is pretty straight-forward: connect with a WiFi access point that has adequate bandwidth, and off we go. Negative cases 1 and 2 are pretty easy to run; just turn off the access point at the proper time. But case 3 is nontrivial: how do we modulate available WiFi bandwidth during a test? It's certainly doable, but it does require some effort.

Negative cases can be particularly challenging to test for electronics. In critical systems, we'll sometimes need to design circuits into our hardware that can force hardware failures just so we can test the outcomes. In an inherently safe consumer product, we might not be too concerned about what happens in the rare event that a circuit goes bad, but we might want to know that information in a life support system and will go the extra mile to find out.

For complex and/or critical products, verification testing can occur at multiple levels, which are sometimes defined as:

System-level verification
Testing the entire system working together as a system

Unit-level testing

> Testing discrete bits of functionality, such as a particular software routine or a circuit. This allows us to test these bits more thoroughly by forcing conditions that they wouldn't often see when configured into a system. For example, we could test a circuit at the upper and lower voltage limits that are guaranteed by the supply that's powering it in order to make sure that the circuit will work properly given the supply variations we expect in manufactured units.

Integration-level testing

> Testing multiple units running together, but not a complete system. As with unit-level testing, this can be done to test modules together before the entire system is ready for testing, or as in the case of unit-level testing it can be used to observe behavior under conditions that would not normally be seen within any given unit.

As mentioned in the start of this section, verification testing is about demonstrating that our product's requirements have been met by our design. The degree of rigor with which we demonstrate this can range from casual to obsessive, tending toward the latter for products that will be produced in high volumes, or whose failure to meet requirements would otherwise be painful when it's in customer hands. This matching of requirements and testing is referred to as *requirements traceability*; let's look at this in a bit more detail.

REQUIREMENTS TRACEABILITY

Fundamentally, the goal of requirements traceability is to ensure that every requirement is implemented as evidenced by tests that prove this is so. There's typically not a one-to-one correspondence between requirements and test procedures. For example, in the example MicroPed test procedures mentioned a few paragraphs back, I mentioned that a single requirement (battery life) is tested by executing multiple test procedures and combining the results.

It's also the case that a single test procedure can help to prove out multiple requirements, as in the case of the MicroPed test procedure that measures current draw also being used to demonstrate that we've met a requirement that the product begin advertising mode when it powers on.

The mapping between requirements and tests is known as the *traceability matrix*. This matrix can be tracked on a spreadsheet for simpler products. Larger product development efforts can have large traceability matrices with thousands of traces to keep track of, and these can benefit from using specialized software as discussed in Chapter 11.

Another issue that comes up in verification testing involves proving performance requirements, such as reliability and accuracy. These tend to rely on testing multiple units through many use cycles, often using robots for repeated mechanical steps (e.g., pressing a physical start button 10,000 times). This type of testing requires some sophisticated statistics and/or mathematical modeling skills that are beyond the scope of this book, but I've included some useful references in the "Resources" section.

By now, hopefully you have an appreciation for the challenges of verification. For simple products verification testing can be fairly straightforward, but test effort tends to grow as the square (i.e., second power) of the number of product features because of the growth in the combinations and permutations of states that the product can be in. (This is yet another argument for keeping products simple: verification test effort is greatly reduced.)

MANUFACTURING TESTING (AND DEVICE PROGRAMMING)

We described manufacturing testing in a little detail back in Chapter 3. If you haven't had the chance to read the "Test" section of that chapter yet or if it's not fresh in your mind, I recommend that you take a (or another) look now.

In this phase, we'll develop that test hardware and software which will move into the factory when we release our product to manufacturing. It will be used by manufacturing staff to ensure that the units they build are made correctly.

Manufacturing tests tend to be a small subset of verification tests, but unlike most verification tests they're developed to be run many times per day, hopefully take just a few moments per test, and require only simple operations by lightly trained workers. Particularly for PCBAs that are large, complex, and/or high-volume, developing manufacturing test plans, software, and equipment is the domain of specialized manufacturing test engineers—it can be very sophisticated stuff. But for smaller products containing just a few chips (other than large FPGAs or application-class processors) in low-to-moderate volumes, DIY manufacturing test development can work out fine.

Since testing usually involves connecting the *device under test* (DUT) to a computer, programming the DUT's memory is often performed at the same time; we'll be doing this with MicroPed. This programming might involve activities other than copying software, such as serial number, security keys, license keys, etc. Some products require calibration during assembly, which nowadays usually means that a unit is tested in some way and calibration constants (e.g., multiplier and offset) are written to memory.

> **TIP** If a device has any network interfaces (e.g., wired or wireless Ethernet, Bluetooth, etc.), each interface is supposed to have an ID associated with it known as a *MAC address* (for *media access control*). This ID is supposed to be unique to that interface; i.e., normally no two Ethernet ports anywhere should have the same MAC address, not even two units of the same product. In some cases, MAC addresses come pre-assigned on network chips and modules, but in other cases we'll need to assign (place into memory) a MAC address and program it in device memory (see the "Resources" section at the end of this chapter for pointers to more information on how addresses are determined).

The first step in developing our manufacturing test systems is to determine what's needed: what are a minimal set of tests that will give us a high degree of confidence that the DUT was manufactured properly?

MicroPed provides a basic but broadly illustrative example. MicroPed has only one PCBA, and we're only concerned that components are soldered down and working properly (e.g., no calibration or MAC address assignment is needed), and there are only two chips. MicroPed's passive components are used to support its chips, so if the chips work properly, the passives should be OK, too.

Let's call out the specific testing that we want to perform, which will determine our hardware and software needs:

1. When first powered on, confirm that:

   a. The DUT is in Bluetooth Smart advertising mode.

   b. The unit is discoverable over Bluetooth Smart by the test system. (Since the microcontroller controls MicroPed's radio, testing the radio implicitly tests the microcontroller.)

   c. Power consumption is as expected for advertising mode; this will test for any gross issues, such as short circuits.

2. Attempt to pair with the DUT over Bluetooth Smart.

    a. Confirm that power consumption is as expected when paired.

3. Moving the DUT in three dimensions.

    a. Confirm that the DUT reports reasonable acceleration numbers in each dimension.

We'll also want to program the system software into the DUT's memory at the start of the test process so we'll add the following steps before the test steps we just listed:

1. Program DUT flash memory.

2. Repower the DUT to ensure a "normal" start up.

Next we'll need to create a hardware system to support these tests; a block diagram of something that should fit the bill is shown in Figure 6-18. Connected to the DUT is a hardware programmer that's compatible with the DUT's microcontroller. The programmer, in turn, is controlled by software running on a Windows-based computer that will program the binary image into DUT memory and test to ensure that it's written properly.

The DUT is also connected to an Arduino controlled by the Windows computer, which serves several functions:

- It can measure current drawn by the DUT. To do this, we'll first need to convert current to a voltage (using a current-to-voltage converter), as the Arduino's analog-to-digital converters (ADCs) measure only voltage.

- Without some help, Arduino ADCs are not very accurate because they compare external voltages to a not-very-accurate onboard reference voltage and report the ratio of the two. To increase accuracy, we'll also feed the Arduino a *precise* voltage from a precision voltage reference.

- The Arduino will also connect to a Bluetooth Smart module, allowing us to communicate with our DUT wirelessly.

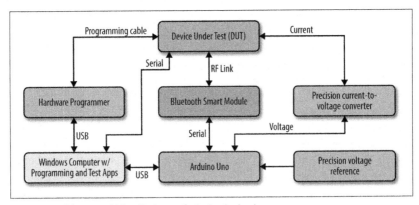

FIGURE 6-18. Diagram of MicroPed manufacturing test setup

So while the manufacturing test tasks here are fairly simple, we'll still need six pieces of equipment (besides the DUT), all integrated correctly and controlled by software.

The operator will use two different applications on the Windows computer, one for programming memory and a second for testing. The first of these is provided by the Bluetooth Smart chip vendor, and the second (UI shown in Figure 6-19) runs testing on the unit after programming. This application happens to be written in C#, but virtually any other language and/or platform can used. National Instruments' LabView graphical programming language is a common choice for high-end test software, paired with test hardware from National Instruments and other vendors.

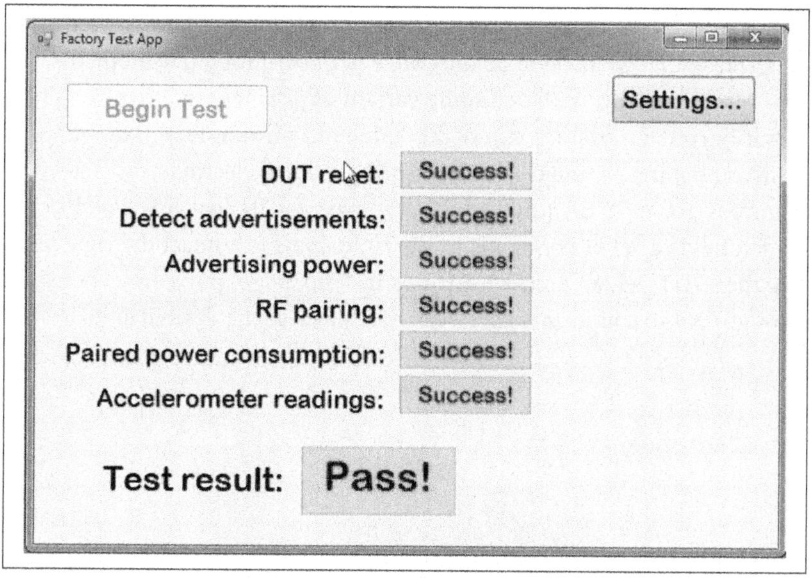

FIGURE 6-19. Manufacturing test Windows application screen

As can be seen in Figure 6-19, manufacturing test software should require a minimum of user interaction, and it's useful to give some feedback as to what steps are taking place and which are successful. This can often help test technicians to debug the process; e.g., "Whenever advertisements and pairing work but power consumption fails, we know that we probably have a batch of boards where the flux wasn't cleaned properly. We'll start by checking for that."

The results can be printed on paper or noted by hand, but the best bet is to store the info, along with serial number, date/time, operator ID and so forth, to a database where it can easily be recalled and analyzed for trends.

Next, let's look at making the *mechanical* interactions between factory staff and DUT as easy as we've made our *software* interactions.

CONNECTIONS AND FIXTURING

The way we connect to the DUT deserves some careful attention. In some cases, we'll get lucky and onboard connectors already bring out the signals we'd like to interface with, so we can attach to those connectors during manufacturing test. Alas, usually we're not that lucky and will need an alternative plan. We could add a new connector to the board that brings out our desired signals, but this adds cost and size to accommodate a task that we hope to do only once per board for a few moments.

More typically, we'll use some variant of *pogo pins* in a fixture to temporarily contact existing exposed conductors on our PCB, such as vias, pads, and pins. A pogo pin is a spring-loaded electrode, as shown in Figure 6-20. A PCBA (dubbed a *bed of nails* for its looks) is constructed, which holds a set of pogo pins in the right spots to contact the right spots on the DUT when pressed against it. The pogo pin connections are brought out to connectors so we can easily access the desired signals.

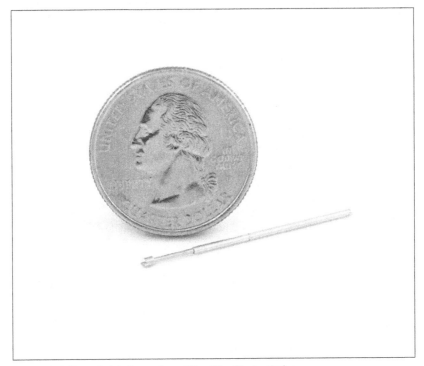

FIGURE 6-20. Pogo pin (photo courtesy of SparkFun Electronics)

As can be imagined, the bed of nails and DUT must be aligned properly when brought together, and so we'll need some sort of fixture to make this happen easily. Figure 6-21 shows a simple fixture for PCBA testing. In it, you can see the tips of 13 pogo pins (six in the top row, seven in the bottom) poking slightly through the PCB under the cutout. The DUT is pressed into the cutout as shown in Figure 6-22, which forces correct alignment, and the part is latched into place so that the touching pogo pins depress slightly to ensure good contact. Now testing can begin.

FIGURE 6-21. Simple bed-of-nails test fixture (photo courtesy of SparkFun Electronics)

FIGURE 6-22. DUT latched in fixture (photo courtesy of SparkFun Electronics)

Testing larger boards can require the application of hundreds or even thousands of pogo pins at once. Specialized commercial equipment is available to help us manage so many connections (e.g., ensuring even pressure over the entire board area), but a custom bed-of-nails board still must be built for each PCBA design that will be tested.

While bed-of-nails testing is probably the most popular technique for manufacturing testing, there are techniques that can be used in place of it or as a complement. As mentioned in Chapter 3, flying-probe testing uses a small set of robotic probes to "fly" around the PCBA and touch the same kinds of exposed conductors accessed in bed-of-nails testing. If flying probe testing will be utilized, a program must be written to specify which points are to be touched, and the tests to be performed.

Another test technology to be aware of is called *boundary scan*, which is often called by the acronym *JTAG* after the group that first defined the standards for it (the *Joint Test Action Group*). In PCBAs that are very dense, many of their signal lines might be "hidden" on inner board layers or beneath components where they're not accessible to pins or probes. Boundary scanning is a facility, built into many sophisticated ICs (e.g., processors and FPGAs), which permits an external device to connect via a few pins on the chip, and then to:

1. Query individual pins as to their state.
2. Set the state of individual pins.

JTAG is the standard for interfacing to chips that implement boundary scanning. We can do a fair bit of production testing via JTAG by setting and reading the states of various pins to see if they respond as expected. Also note that while JTAG was originally developed for exactly this sort of testing, it's also used (perhaps even more commonly) for debugging software on chips that support it. JTAG in this context is used to observe and change the states of all sorts of registers and subsystems on the chip, usually while stepping through code.

Before we wrap up on production test, one more thing to consider is that whatever we build to support a factory must be able to truly work in the factory. For example, we might assume that we'll have access to the Internet, say for storing data on a server that we can access globally, but find that Internet access is not available on the factory floor. It's important to work with our selected (or potential) manufacturing partners when developing production test to ensure that all is smooth.

So far we've discussed PCBA testing, but other testing is also performed during manufacturing. There's usually some sort of final test (known as end-of-line test) after the product is fully assembled, to ensure that the PCBAs and enclosures are assembled together properly, often as simple as turning the device on and checking that a few things work. We might want to run other tests as well to ensure that everything works smoothly, such as exercising mechanisms if our product has any, testing for water tightness if applicable, and so forth.

Sometimes finished products are operated for a period of time prior to shipment to look for early failures. This is known as *burn-in testing*. As shown in Figure 6-23, the rate of product failures tends to start out relatively high due to "infant mortality" issues, and then levels off until failures due to wear out begin to happen late in the product's life. Burn-in can be used to catch a good portion of the infant mortality failures, saving us from shipping products that would end up being returned in a short while.

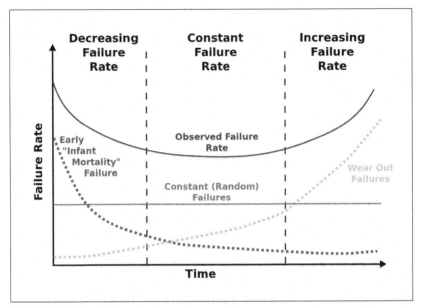

FIGURE 6-23. Product failure rates versus time

A variation of burn-in testing can also be performed on a statistical sample of every lot of our product that's manufactured, to make sure that quality goals are being met. For example, a certain lot might exhibit a higher rate of failures, and we might trace it back to a new worker installing a part slightly incorrectly.

Hopefully, by this point it's clear that manufacturing testing is usually a bit more effort than simply turning a unit on after assembly and seeing if it "kinda seems to be working." As with most parts of product development, the key here is to have different groups of people working together throughout the development process so that the product electronics and software are properly testable, that the appropriate test fixtures and software are developed when we're otherwise ready to begin manufacturing, and that the test system can work properly in our factory. This process of ensuring easy and adequate testing is often referred to as *design for test* (DFT).

> **TIP** Working together on manufacturing test can be challenging because the designer/developers, test engineers, and factory are often housed in different companies, which might be located far from one another. For projects of any significant size, one thing that I've found helpful is to have a weekly sync-up teleconference for these three groups using a screen-sharing tool such as *TeamViewer* or *GotoMeeting*.

All of this talk of production testing makes it feel like we're close to production, and at this point in the process, we should be! Once our full *works-like and looks-like* prototypes are passing through testing, and we can perform production test on the units and their contents, it's time to start the process of moving into manufacturing, which is up next.

Moving into Manufacturing

It's easy to feel like the products we develop are our children. At the start, they're just an idea. A bit later we have something physical, but it doesn't do much at all yet. It probably does only a tiny fraction of what it will need to do before it can find success in the world. We pour our efforts in, and things start to take shape; we start to have moments where we can envision this creation out in the world, on its own, fully functional. Our efforts continue, transitioning from Herculean pushes to subtle corrections. Then the day comes when it's time for our product to head off on its own, to face the world without our day-to-day help, even though we'll stay in the background to help as needed. On the design/development side, this process of moving our product into manufacturing is called by several names including *design transfer* and *release to manufacturing*. On the manufacturing side of things, it's commonly known as manufacturing *new product introduction* (*NPI*). This process was generally covered back in Chapter 3 in its own section, but let's add a little practical detail.

First, we'll need to understand our manufacturer's needs well in advance. Hopefully they'll be participating in design reviews and will have a good feel for our product and its needs. They'll typically want:

- Schematics
- Gerber files: the files that describe the PCBs and component locations for PCB assembly
- Mechanical CAD files, as appropriate: STL, SLDPRT, IGES, STEP, etc.

- Bill of materials (BOM): a list of components

- Assembly drawing(s)

- Assembly instructions (if assembly is nontrivial)

- Test fixtures

- Software binaries

- Forecasts of future production volumes: how many units, and when

Contract manufacturers will usually source and store components for us (for a fee), or we can source and store them ourselves. Many have good resources to help us here, such as savvy buyers and good relationships with vendors.

Manufacturing will begin with one or more *pilot runs* where the process kinks are discovered and worked out. The first units produced will normally be subjected to *first-article inspection*, which is a fancy way of saying that designer/developers and manufacturing staff will check them out in detail to ensure that everything is built as it should be. This process tends to lie somewhere between full verification testing and standard manufacturing testing.

Some products make the transition to manufacturing quickly and successfully. We hand the items previously listed to a contract manufacturer along with a purchase order, and assembled units appear in a few days or weeks. While MicroPed is not yet (as of this writing) being manufactured in quantity, it's the type of product that tends to be in this class: simple PCBA, simple test procedure, and simple assembly. Also, it's not a safety-critical product: if an occasional unit fails prematurely, nobody will get hurt. Thus we can sleep at night if our manufacturing process isn't fully tuned at the start and we get some field failures.

Other products require quite a bit of support when they first leave the nest. For example, let's contemplate a product on the other end of the spectrum from MicroPed in this regard: a *left ventricular assist device* (LVAD), which aids failing hearts by pumping alongside them and taking some of the load off so the heart can rest a little. Modern portable LVADs consist of a small pump implanted into the patient's chest and patched into their circulatory system, with power and controls located outside the body. Small mechanical parts to be assembled, sophisticated electronics, cleanroom environment, and because the consequences of failure are so substantial there'll be lots of testing of components, systems, and the manufacturing process itself—it will take months of designers/developers working alongside manufacturing staff to get the manufacturing process to the point where product can be validated and units produced for sale.

Most smart products fall somewhere between these two extremes. Hopefully we've been working with our manufacturer through development and have paid attention to DFA and supply chain, and we'll soon be churning out product with a minimum of fuss, perhaps after a few rough spots get smoothed over.

Our product is developed.

Final Thoughts

We began this detailed development phase with a good idea of what we wanted to build; now it is being built and shipped to customers. This chapter's covered a lot of ground, as does the real development effort it covers. And as long as this chapter's been, it's just a high-level glimpse intended to pull the many different pieces together. The "Resources" section points the way to material that can facilitate a deeper dive into some of these individual pieces.

Each product development effort is an adventure, and all good adventures have ups and downs: "the thrill of victory and the agony of defeat." There's no avoiding it. The trick is to end up with the thrill of victory, of course.

Toward that end, I want to share a few final thoughts.

As mentioned at this chapter's start, the bulk of the work in this phase is designer/developers doing the designing and developing, and performing the technical work they've trained for and practiced. Certainly, great products won't happen without great designer/developers. But neither do great individual efforts, by themselves, result in a great product. The keys to releasing a great product into the world, I'm convinced, are systems thinking and collaboration. We want a single transcendent performance of Beethoven's *Ninth Symphony*, not seventy-five simultaneous solos.

Systems thinking means always having the system in mind and recognizing that the many bits of hardware and software we develop are never islands unto themselves. Rather, they exist only to contribute to a larger whole. For a user, our product is no more nor less than their experiences with our system. As development moves forward, everything we do should be in support of that system experience, whether it's implementing a gorgeous design, finding a button with just the right click to it, or heading off bad experiences by increasing reliability.

Collaboration is a tricky thing. Everyone agrees on the theoretical need for collaboration, but in practice it's easy for it to fall by the wayside. Managers wonder why they're spending budget on people having discussions instead of "getting work done." Technologists want to stop blabbing and get on with the "real work." But getting things right at the system level requires collaboration, and getting the wrong system developed a little bit faster doesn't help us out in the long run.

Finding the right balance between collaboration and independent work is where things get interesting, and this needs to be approached on a case-by-case basis based on the interdependency of systems. For example, selecting and integrating a camera chip into a product involves our electronics, our operating system (a driver must be written), and probably some deep knowledge of the graphics subsystem on our processor—each of these is individually quite complex. Getting all of these complex tasks aligned into a fully functioning path that makes images accessible to software applications will go a lot faster if designers/developers work closely together. On the other hand, developing code to validate user input might be a solo effort, particularly if the validation criteria are well defined in advance.

This chapter completes our look at the process of product development. While I've dug into some subjects in a little detail, I've tried to stay up at a high level to give a feel for the big picture. Starting in the next chapter, we'll move down to a lower level, looking in a bit of detail at some of the areas that I've found to be the greatest source of unnecessary work, cost, and general aggravation in product development. These include:

- Selection of our product's "smart platform" (i.e., its processor and operating system)

- Powering our product (wall outlet versus batteries, etc.)

- Keeping users safe and governments happy (regulations, standards, and so forth)

- Writing requirements that actually help us do a better job

- Meta-activities: project planning and management, and issue tracking

But before we move on to these topics, here's the promised list of resources to help expand what we've covered in this chapter.

Resources

Since this is a wide-ranging phase with lots of activities, there are many resources that can help us out. Much of what's done is "just" basic engineering covered by standard engineering references, but here are some useful resources that go beyond the standard "stuff" or which are otherwise mentioned in this chapter.

ELECTRONICS

While I've promised not to drop into the basics of any given technical field, I must make one exception with regard to a recommendation: the reference by which all electronic design books are measured is *The Art of Electronics* (*https://en.wikipedia.org/wiki/The_Art_of_Electronics*) by Paul Horowitz and Winfield Hill. Conversational, practical, and rigorous, Horowitz and Hill (as it's usually referred to) covers the basics of electronic design and prototyping with little pain and lots of insight—even bipolar transistors become easy to understand, thanks to Transistor Man (*http://www.adafruit.com/products/867*). The Third Edition will hopefully be out by the time you read this, but even the dated second edition is incredibly useful. If you design electronics and don't read H&H, you will regret it.

Another great resource for "hardcore" EE design/development information is David Jones' EEVBlog (*http://www.eevblog.com*), with great videos and a resource wiki (*http://bit.ly/1gNh5dJ*) that points to many more resources.

In many cases, circuit simulations can be incredibly helpful as a complement to breadboarding as they let us easily see, for example, what happens if component values are a little off but still within tolerance. One helpful resource that's often overlooked these days is Simulation Program with Integrated Circuit Emphasis (SPICE), which is software that simulates the behavior of circuits based on models of components. SPICE has been around for decades and many variants are available, but the one most commonly used (in my experience) is LTSPICE, available as freeware (*http://www.linear.com/solutions/LTspice*) from chip maker Linear

Technology. While chips tend to be well-behaved and basic circuit simulation is less important, SPICE is particularly useful for checking the behavior of circuits that don't depend on ICs, including those that use transistors, diodes, resistors, capacitors, inductors, and so forth. These can often exhibit surprising behavior, which simulation can catch.

A good overview of printed circuit board (PCB) basics (*https://learn.sparkfun.com/tutorials/pcb-basics*) can be found at SparkFun's site. Martin Tarr has some good information on advanced high-density interconnect (HDI) PCB features (*http://bit.ly/1gNh8Ge*) such as blind and buried vias, and microvias.

We tend to think of PCBs as simply a bunch of copper paths between component pads, but they can be the source of all kinds of trouble if we're not careful. LearnEMC.com has a nice tutorial on PCB design issues, including some good rules of thumb. In terms of software packages for doing schematic capture/PCB layout, Eagle CAD (*http://www.cadsoftusa.com*) dominates the low end (a free, limited version is available (*http://www.cadsoftusa.com/download-eagle/freeware/*)), while Allegro, Altium, and PADS seem to be most popular on the high end. High-end software is much more expensive—and much more capable—than the low-end offerings.

The trickiest bits to get right in PCB design involve understanding how fast-moving signals interact with the PCB and component pads, which is an issue known as *signal integrity*. Software such as HyperLynx SI (*http://www.mentor.com/pcb/hyperlynx/*) is recommended for modeling signals with frequency components higher than, say, a few tens of MHz. Other packages in the HyperLynx line and from other vendors can be used to model other aspects of PCBs/PCBAs, such as power and thermal characteristics.

SOFTWARE

As mentioned in this chapter, the two heavy hitters in version control are Subversion (*https://subversion.apache.org*) and Git (*http://www.git-scm.com*), both free and open source. While both use command-line interfaces "out of the box," various GUIs are available for click-and-draggers like me. I particularly like TortoiseSVN (*http://tortoisesvn.net*) (free and open source) for using Subversion in Windows, and Atlassian SourceTree (*http://www.sourcetreeapp.com*) (free) for using Git in Windows and Mac.

Test-Driven Development for Embedded C by James Grenning does a nice job of covering TDD using the language (C) that's still the most common in the embedded world.

The free and open source Jenkins (*http://jenkins-ci.org*) is probably the most popular application for orchestrating continuous integration. Jenkins is quite powerful and flexible thanks to the availability of more than 1,000 plugins. The availability of so many plugins indicates that Jenkins is a popular package, but it's also a clue as to the potential complexity of setting up continuous integration. Particularly for larger projects, setting up a comprehensive system requires a good deal of effort, and most of this effort won't be in setting up Jenkins itself but rather in creating tests and processes. *Jenkins: The Definitive Guide*, written by John Ferguson Smart, is available as a free PDF (*http://bit.ly/1gNhigX*) or from O'Reilly as an ebook or printed copy.

INJECTION MOLDING

Proto Labs (*http://www.protolabs.com*), which specializes in the rapid creation of mechanical prototypes and is particularly well-known for their quick-turn Protomold molding service, is a great source of information on injection molding. Their resources (*http://www.protolabs.com/resources*) page is a good place to start, and some very worthwhile educational products (*http://www.protolabs.com/resources/educators*) are available. I highly recommend all of these educational tools, particularly the "Injection Molding Part Design for Dummies" book. Even Proto Labs' quoting process is educational—once you upload your CAD file for a quote, you'll get specific feedback and recommendations on any issues that might cause difficulty during fabrication. Their recommendations tend to be conservative, but it's always good to know where the risks lie. Their quotes also allow us to try different materials, finishes, quantities, and turn-around times online and immediately see how these effect pricing.

DFM & DFA

While DFM/DFA are (in my opinion) neglected subjects in product development, some great resources are available.

The most-cited reference in this area is Product Design for Manufacture and Assembly (*http://bit.ly/1gNhpJr*) by Boothroyd and Dewhurst, and Knight. Boothroyd and Dewhurst are considered pioneers in creating methodical processes for DFM and DFA. Their eponymously named company has some useful information (*http://www.dfma.com/resources/index.html*) on its website and offers excellent (but not inexpensive!) DFM/DFA software that has proven very useful. This software can accurately estimate product manufacturing and assembly costs given design and process information, which allows us to play with different designs and processes to see how they'll affect cost.

Dragon Innovation has a series of free online DFM course (*http://bit.ly/1gNhuNe*) videos, adopted from a course taught at Olin College of Engineering by Dragon CEO Scott Miller. It's very real-world oriented, and I'd consider it mandatory viewing even if it weren't free.

RAPID MECHANICAL PROTOTYPING

Generally speaking, the best strategy here might be to purchase an FDM (or possibly SLA) printer for day-to-day use (or to get a membership at your local maker space to use theirs), and to use service bureaus for doing very-high-quality prototypes. Very-high-quality work requires very-expensive machinery; we don't need that level of work that often, and service bureaus can turn things around pretty quickly.

3D printing is a rapidly advancing area, and the world of FDM printing in particular seems to change by the day. While there's no shortage of books and articles on the subject, it's still not so simple to compare various printers to see what's best for our intended use. Make's annual *Ultimate Guide to 3D Printing* series provides a good overview of the technology and what's available, and takes a stab at comparing printers and print quality. When purchasing a printer, it's useful to design a part and then have it run on several printers that you're considering. 3DHubs.com (*https://www.3dhubs.com*) is a service for finding and hiring 3D printers (and their owners) to create prints for us from specific models of printers. This is somewhat hit or miss because most vendors are individuals trying to defray the costs of their home printer, and have varying degrees of skill and responsiveness/customer support.

In terms of service bureaus, the previously mentioned Proto Labs (*http://www.protolabs.com*) offers a good variety of "engineering-grade" prototyping technologies with excellent service. ProtoLabs also has great educational material on their website, and will send you demo parts for free, showing different sorts of features they can make and demonstrating features that lead to molding flaws (thick ribs, drastic changes in wall section, etc.)

Many other similar services are available. Two that I've heard great things about but haven't used myself are Redeye (*http://www.redeyeonde mand.com*) (a division of 3D-printer conglomerate Stratasys) and Quick-Parts (*http://www.quickparts.com*).

TESTING

Alas, while verification and manufacturing test are both critical topics, both involve wide-ranging technologies and techniques, and much of what's done in practice seems to be passed down as "tribal knowledge" among test engineers rather than as written material.

Both Adafruit (*http://bit.ly/1Vm4BsT*) and SparkFun (*http://bit.ly/ 1Vm4z4t*) have good articles on manufacturing testing, which are aimed at small, lower-volume boards but cover the basic issues.

As mentioned earlier in the chapter, National Instruments is a major supplier of software and hardware used in manufacturing testing, and their products are often used for verification test, too. The Automated Test (*http://www.ni.com/automatedtest/*) page on their website is a gateway to some useful information, including case studies that give a feel for what's done in various industries.

MOVING INTO MANUFACTURING

The first course (*http://bit.ly/1Vm4EFf*) of the aforementioned Dragon Innovation DFM series has a good overview of some of the considerations in selecting a factory. It tends to be oriented toward consumer products manufactured in Asia (Dragon's expertise) rather than, say, medical devices manufactured in the US, but the basics are the same in most every situation.

## CHAPTER 7

Smart Platforms: Processors

PROCESSORS AND THEIR ATTENDANT SOFTWARE ARE, OF COURSE, WHAT put the *intelligent* into today's constellation of intelligent devices. These days, processors and software support a very wide range of functions and products. On the high end lie sophisticated and reprogrammable products such as smart phones that require powerful processors and sophisticated operating systems. On the other end of the spectrum lie products with simple and fixed functionality implemented in a few lines of code on a tiny processor, such as a flashlight that has different blink modes.

The processor and operating system (or lack thereof) can be thought of as a product's *intelligent platform*. It determines many of the features we can support and the limitations we have to live with. For example, if we select an ARM Cortex processor running Linux, we're not going to run for years on a single disposable coin-cell battery. We'll need a good-sized battery that will be recharged daily. If we pick an MSP430 running without an OS, we might indeed be able to run for years off a coin cell, but we won't have the horsepower for a high-end touchscreen/LCD GUI.

Selecting our intelligent platform is probably the most far-reaching technology decision that we'll make during design, particularly for devices that support significant complexity. Our choices will have a substantial impact on materials cost, power consumption, development complexity, and risk of failure.

In moderate quantities, processor unit costs range from a few dimes to over $100. The difference in processing power, size, and energy consumption between these price points is as extreme as the cost differences. In this chapter, we'll review the vast processor landscape with an eye toward understanding which processors tend to fit which levels of functionality, as well as the relative level of effort needed to integrate these devices into our product.

> Low-end processors tend to be packaged as *microcontrollers*, while higher-end processors tend to be packaged as *microprocessors*. What's the difference?
>
> Microprocessors tend to include only the individual processing units (CPUs), while microcontrollers include the CPU and other components needed for operation, such as memory, timers, counters, clocks, and various interfaces. Microprocessors are more flexible (and usually more powerful), but they require more support circuitry and greater design effort. Microcontrollers normally require less design work and have lower associated costs for development and in production.

Processor types tend to clump together into three categories, roughly low-end, middling, and high-end, depending upon how they're typically used. In this chapter, we'll survey these three clumps and then take a look at some variations and alternative technologies.

Low-End Microcontrollers

These feature 8- or 16-bit processors and sell for up to a few dollars depending on quantity and features. There are approximately one zillion models of low-end microcontrollers available with virtually any combination and permutation of memory (RAM/FLASH/ROM), converters, types of inputs and outputs (I2C, SPI, UART, USB, etc.), simple LCD controllers, and many, many other features.

> **TIP** The very first microcontroller, the TMS1000, had a 4-bit processor, and 4-bit microcontrollers are still available today. They don't have much processing power but are very inexpensive and thus are typically used for products like electric toothbrushes, toaster ovens, and flashlights. Since 4-bitters are used in relatively few new designs as compared to their more-bitted brethren, we won't cover them in detail.

Fortunately, chip makers have parametric selectors on their websites. Select the features you want and they'll pop out a list of parts that meet your requirements.

Low-end microcontrollers are typically used in applications that require unsophisticated processing and display of information. Think appliances (e.g., toasters, dishwashers), pedometers, flashlights, and so forth. However, some can actually do quite a bit if we're a little clever, such as audio processing and home automation.

Besides low price, other important benefits of these devices are small size and very low power consumption. They are relatively simple devices that draw minuscule power when sleeping (sometimes under a micro-Amp) and, when awakened, can quickly accomplish a task before going back to sleep. It's entirely possible to build circuits based on these parts that can run for years on a single coin cell.

Typical speed is between one and 20 million instructions per second, but since their instructions only operate on 8- or 16-bit chunks of memory, operations that deal with more-bitted chunks (such as floating-point operations, sophisticated graphics, and moving large blocks of memory) can require many more instructions than they would on a 32-bit processor. Floating-point math, in particular, is very, very taxing for these processors compared to others.

Low-end microcontrollers are almost always programmed in assembler or C (or a C-like language as on the Arduino platform) and many software tools are available, both open and proprietary. Because of computational and memory constraints, applications are typically run "bare metal" without an OS. Depending on which we use, some minimal operating systems are available (if we'd like to use one), such as FreeRTOS, Nut/OS, and uC/OS. In low-end microcontrollers, these are mainly useful for "hard core" high-reliability applications, such as in medical or aerospace applications. We'll cover the use of OSes in embedded system in the next chapter.

My general experience is that these parts are easy (and even fun) to use. They tend to be a good choice when a project will be manufactured in moderate quantities and can use the less expensive models—say, under 10,000 units—and microcontrollers that cost less than $2. But beware that the more expensive low-end parts can get relatively pricey—sometimes $3 or more—which in many cases is more expensive than low-priced "middling" processors that are much more capable. It always pays to review different processor families when selecting parts.

The product families in this space most commonly used for new designs are 8051 variants, AVRs, PICs, and MSP430s. Let's take a quick look at how these compare with one another.

8051 CLASS

These are 8-bit processors that derive their architecture from the Intel 8051 processor introduced in 1980. As might be expected from a 35-year-old processor design, 8051s aren't as sophisticated as other, newer processor families, but they also tend to be relatively inexpensive. 8051s can be found in standalone microcontrollers, and they're often built into the silicon of special-purpose chips that require some processing power of their own. For example, wireless controller chips (e.g., Bluetooth) often have an 8051 processor built into their silicon that's used by the controller but might also be used by the developer. Thus, in many cases, 8051s cost nothing!

However, in most cases, "free" 8051s don't have enough memory or are missing needed peripherals so adding another processor is necessary. But depending on our application, sometimes we can get lucky and the free limited memory and peripherals are enough for our application.

A variety of stand-alone 8051s are available with various peripherals, supported by common software tools. In the case of 8051s "coming along for the ride" with some other functionality on a chip, we're usually limited to using whatever is supplied by the chip maker.

AVR

AVR normally refers to a line of 8-bit microcontrollers from Atmel that are a fair step up in processing power and sophistication from most 8051s. Of note, the popular Arduino platform is based on the AVR family.

AVRs are very easy to use, and a huge number of inexpensive hardware (programming and debugging) and software tools are available, both open and proprietary.

All AVRs share the same processor, but they are available in many, many variations with different amounts of memory and a broad range of peripherals. Peripherals range from the typical digital/analog converters and timers to USB ports to fancy things like an encryption/decryption module. Low-end parts sell in quantity for 50 cents each or even less in large quantities, while high-end AVRs can cost more than $10 a pop.

To capitalize on the AVR's good reputation, Atmel has also released a 32-bit "AVR32" family of parts. Despite the name, the AVR32 is totally unrelated to the 8-bit AVRs.

PIC

The PIC brand is typically associated with a family of 8-bit microcontrollers from Microchip. In my experience, they're pretty comparable to AVRs in most respects other than having a convoluted memory organization. This only becomes painful if writing in assembler, as C deals with the memory issues "under the hood," abstracted away from the developer.

Like Atmel and its AVR brand, Microchip has created more sophisticated offshoots of its 8-bit PICs, including the 16-bit PIC24, DSP-enhanced dsPIC, and 32-bit PIC32 families, but in my experience these are less commonly used in new designs.

MSP430

The MSP430 is a line of 16-bit microcontrollers from Texas Instruments. Compared to the AVR family, these parts are roughly similar in cost, features, and support. Because they are 16-bit parts, they tend to be higher performance than AVRs, which can be a nice plus in situations where data is often used in chunks bigger than 8 bits. MSP430s are particularly known for supporting extremely low-power operation, although other low-end microcontrollers have been playing catch up in this regard and there might not be a clear advantage of one family over the other anymore.

Again, a wide, wide variety of parts are available that differ in memory types and sizes, and peripherals.

Middling Microcontrollers/Processors

Moving up to the middle space between the low-end microcontrollers and desktop/laptop-class processors, the market is dominated by 32-bit ARM-architecture processors. ARM is a company that designs processor architectures (cores) and licenses them to chip makers who add peripherals, memory, and so forth and actually manufacture the parts. ARM cores are targeted at mobile (battery-powered) applications, and are used within the vast majority of cell phones and tablets, including the iPhone and iPad lines.

The ARM-based offerings are vast, ranging from low-power devices for a buck to high-end parts that power smart phones and cost more than $10, even in significant quantities. There are an extraordinary number of variations available with different memory and peripheral options.

ARM-based devices are a substantial step up from low-end parts in both sophistication and performance. Some of this sophistication happens automatically behind the scenes, but leveraging much of it requires effort on the part of software and hardware developers. Integrating an ARM-based chip into a product is usually a good bit more work as compared to a lower-end part.

In this chapter, we'll review ARM's latest (as of early 2015) generation of ARM cores in general use, known as the Cortex series, as these are likely to be of most interest to readers developing new products. But various families of ARM cores have been around for a couple of decades, and chips based on older families (particularly the ARM7, ARM9, and ARM11) are still readily available. For example, the Raspberry Pi is based on the older ARM11 core (although the newer Raspberry Pi 2 has been updated to use Cortex cores).

ARM's naming conventions can be confusing to the uninitiated, but at the high level, each core in the Cortex series falls into one of three profiles, M, R or A, depending on its intended use.

CORTEX-M: MICROCONTROLLER PROFILE

The Cortex-M architectures emphasize low power and low cost for simpler applications. Compared to 8- and 16-bit parts:

- Pricing is competitive, starting at under $1 in moderate quantities.

- Performance is usually substantially greater, particularly for mathematical operations.

- Power consumption is in the same ballpark, but can be very different for different applications. A Cortex-M device might be the low-power-consumption champion for a device that needs to perform a lot of math-intensive signal processing, but an MSP430 might be much better for a sensor that must run for years on a disposable battery.

Several flavors of Cortex-M's are available, currently the M0, M0+, M2, M3, and M4 in order of increasing capability. Note that these do not all share the same instruction set. This is invisible to the developer if using C or another compiled language, but can be an issue in the event that work is done in assembler.

Because ARM cores are wrapped in clusters of various options that differ by chip maker, development tools are typically specific to each part and are supplied by respective manufacturers. Some third-party tools are also available, but these are mostly proprietary (not open source).

Cortex-M is supported by a fair number of lightweight operating systems. A variant of Linux (uClinux) is theoretically supported on the M3 and M4, but if we *really* want to use Linux, then a beefier processor will normally be a better match.

CORTEX-R: REAL-TIME PROFILE

Cortex-R architectures are specialized and aimed at systems where timing is most critical. In particular, the R's target applications where guarantees are needed that the processor (and the software it's running) can respond within a short time period. This is known as *real-time processing*, which we'll discuss in some more detail later in this chapter. An example of a real-time process might be an electronic shock absorber that adjusts car height as a wheel goes over a bump. If the system doesn't respond to changes in vertical acceleration quickly enough, we'll have a very strange and bumpy ride.

Real-time systems don't *require* specialized processors. However, the R architectures are optimized for these applications and thus make it easier to achieve timing goals. They are aimed at embedded use and are typically found deep within larger systems that use other processors to handle user interfaces, generally in industrial, medical, aerospace, and automotive applications.

CORTEX-A: APPLICATION PROFILE

Cortex-A cores are designed for smart phones and similar portable devices that have a rich graphical touchscreen UI, a large OS such as Android/Linux, iOS or Windows CE, peripherals such as WiFi, and so forth. These are extremely capable processors that require a fair bit of energy to run; think rechargeable battery packs, not coin cells.

Virtually every smart phone sold today uses one (or more) Cortex-A cores at its heart. Multiple 32-bit core architectures are available, ranging today from the A5 to the A12. New to the A series are 64-bit cores: the A53 and A57.

Chips with Cortex-A cores typically support multiple peripherals targeted at smart-phone-like applications, such as graphics acceleration, audio and video subsystems, USB, sophisticated memory management units, and so forth.

These devices are extremely complex: their reference manuals normally run several thousands of pages. Integrating these parts into a sophisticated system is a substantial hardware and software undertaking that should be approached with care and can easily take person-months or person-years of effort. They require complex circuitry and software just to start up properly and to support power saving modes. Special companion chips, called *Power Management ICs* (PMICs) are often used to ease these chores.

Beyond the inherent complexity of the Cortex-A parts, in fact *because* of that complexity, there's another trap waiting for us: even those thousands-of-pages reference manuals often don't have all the information we need! Next, let's look at how we can mitigate this and other support issues that can crop up with these devices.

Support gaps

Chips with Cortex-A cores are typically designed for large customers that will buy hundreds of thousands or millions of units. These customers get fantastic support. It's not unknown for chip makers to even send their designers to spend weeks working alongside their customers' product developers to ensure that the chip gets properly designed into a new product. Hundreds of millions (or even billions) of dollars are at stake.

On the other hand, if we're just buying a few chips or even a few thousand, technical support will typically be sparse or nonexistent. It's simply too expensive for chip makers to support small customers in a comprehensive manner. Reading the reference manuals carefully is a must, but even that doesn't always get the job done. These parts are so complex that details might not be fully and correctly communicated from chip designers to documentation folks, and as a result the manuals might be incomplete, misleading, or incorrect. It's perfectly possible, even common, to follow the reference manual to the letter and have a part not work as expected only to later find out that the manual was simply wrong. In theory, chip makers will publish any errata that they know of, but in reality there's often a gulf between what the vendor's website says and what their applications engineers know.

One way to mitigate support gaps is to select silicon that's used on popular development/prototyping platforms, such as Texas Instruments' BeagleBoard/BeagleBone kits. This puts us in a league with lots of other folks who are using the parts in smaller quantities, and online communities exist for sharing experiences and solutions.

> **TIP** As of this writing, the BCM2835 ARM-based processor chip used in the popular Raspberry Pi is *not* readily available to small manufacturers (unless the rest of the Raspberry Pi is soldered to it).

Power consumption

Even though these Cortex-A parts consume very little power compared to a desktop computer, their power draw is still significant and requires substantial optimization if long battery life is important. They support a staggering number of different low power modes and schemes that software and hardware developers must juggle when developing portable devices. While I don't have definitive numbers, my experience indicates that 25% or even more of the total electronics and software effort for a sophisticated battery-powered device goes into power conservation.

Thermal considerations

The power used by the processor ends up as heat. Even a small bit of heat can cause a big temperature rise in a small, unventilated space. Increased heat can cause the processor or other parts to fail, so thermal management should be.

Big Iron: Desktop- and Server-Class Processors

The "big iron" class of processors is dominated by the Intel x86 and its many 32- and 64-bit variants. They are all about processing power and use a lot of energy even in low power modes: think *big* batteries or wall sockets. They can be used in units that might be easily transported, perhaps as small as a lunch pail, but not for devices that will fit in a pocket. These devices almost always run Linux or Windows to support software applications.

In practice, these processors are rarely designed directly into a device. Rather, an off-the-shelf motherboard is purchased either with a processor

installed or the processor is mated to the motherboard during manufacturing. The procedure is more like the *integration of a PC* into a system
rather than the *integration of a processor* onto a board.

The nice upside to using these parts is that they are essentially desktop PCs, and thus virtually infinite information and tools are available.
Software is a cool summer breeze when developing for big iron (even if
the big iron itself can get pretty warm).

One issue to consider when integrating PC-class parts is continued
availability. Consumer-oriented parts might only be on the market for a
few months and numerous tweaks might occur during that time, such as
component changes. Special long-life versions of motherboard/processor
combinations are available, but their cost is several times higher than
their consumer brethren. These units are often referred to as *single-board
computers* (SBCs) rather than motherboards. Manufacturers of these long-
availability units include Kontron, Advantech, Aeon, and other names
that you're unlikely to run into when shopping for a desktop computer
motherboard.

This concludes our look at the processor platforms that are most
commonly used in products, but there are other oft-overlooked options
that can be a great fit. Let's review these next.

Other Hardware Platforms

While most designs will end up using one of the processor-containing
chips we've discussed, there are a few other alternatives that can be attractive: systems on modules, digital signal processors, and programmable
logic devices.

SYSTEMS ON MODULES (SOMS)

Back in the old days, a microprocessor chip was a processor, period. A
complete computer circuit design also required power supply chips,
peripheral chips, and so forth. As Moore's law marches forward and we
learn how to put more transistors on slivers of silicon, not only are microprocessor chips becoming more powerful, they are also adding functionality that used to require separate parts. Microprocessor chips that have
lots of extra circuitry on board are sometimes called *systems on chip*
(SOCs). SOCs can pack an amazing amount of stuff on a chip: the processor, power supplies, memory, communications busses, RF, USB,

clocks, timers, data converters, video encoders and decoders. The list is almost endless.

However, there's still some amount of "basic" circuitry that's unsuitable or impossible to put on a processor chip, such as capacitors of non-minuscule value, high-power circuits, magnetics (transformers and coils), and so forth. These parts must still be designed into a circuit and soldered down to a board.

Systems on modules (SOMs), a.k.a. *computers on modules* (COMs), provide a processor, peripherals, and other parts all integrated on a small PC board, eliminating the need to design and manufacture the basic circuitry needed to support the processor and common peripherals such as USB and Ethernet. Figure 7-1 shows a Gumstix Overo SOM, based on the Texas Instruments OMAP 4430 system-on-chip running at 1GHz. Taken as a whole, this SOM provides:

- Dual ARM Cortex A9 cores

- 2D and 3D graphics acceleration at up to 1080i resolution

- 2 USB ports

- Video/camera subsystem

- Power and battery-charging management

- 1 GB RAM

- Audio processing

- WiFi and Bluetooth

- DSP, RTC, and much, much more

Almost everything we need for a fairly powerful system is integrated into a single ready-to-go module.

The connections to the SOM are through the two 70-pin rectangular connectors at the board's bottom. To use this SOM, we'd design a custom PC board to use it (typically referred to as a baseboard) that contains any additional circuitry (LCD display, sensors, etc.) and has connectors that mate with the SOM's connectors. The connectors actually do a good job of holding the SOM to the baseboard, but we might want to add some other hold-down hardware that also might incorporate a heat sink for the processor chip (they can throw off some heat).

FIGURE 7-1. Gumstix Overo SOM

There are nice upsides to using this SOM versus developing the same circuit from scratch:

- It saves many hundreds of person-hours of design, debugging, and other related prototyping costs.

- It contains the "tough-to-manufacture" stuff, in particular the processor and memory *ball grid array* (BGA) packages that can require fancy PCB technology and are difficult to solder properly; our custom baseboard will probably be able to use cheaper PC boards and assembly processes.

- The manufacturer provides a complete software *board support package* (BSP) with device drivers. As we'll see later in our next chapter, having an already integrated and supported BSP gives us a big leg up in building our software.

The major drawback is that SOMs are a bit pricey. As of this writing, this particular SOM runs $200 for a single unit with significant discounts at high volumes, but even in volume, it's unlikely to cost less than $100 each. By comparison, the raw cost of building it ourselves in high volumes would be roughly half the SOM cost.

I'm a big fan of using SOMs if one needs to use an application-class processor. Make-versus-buy tradeoff analysis varies by design, but I've generally found that SOMs are very cost-effective until volumes hit 10k units or so. Unless we *know* that volumes will be much higher than 10k units, one good strategy is to start off by using a SOM and then do a cost-reduction redesign using the same parts as the SOM when volumes warrant the effort.

SOMs are also available for less powerful processors, although they're often called something else (like a "module"). Some are as small as a dime and cost as little as around $10 each in quantity. Figure 7-2 shows a SOM in the guise of an Arduino Pro Mini 328 board. For less than $10, we get an Arduino-compatible ATMega328, clock, power supply, and so forth. Just solder it down to a baseboard and off we go! This little board will save dozens of hours rather than hundreds, but it has another nice feature: the circuit design is open source so we can simply transfer the design directly to our baseboard when we start building in quantity (although we should review the terms of its open source license to ensure that it's compatible with our business objectives).

FIGURE 7-2. Arduino Pro Mini 328 board (photo courtesy SparkFun Electronics)

SINGLE-BOARD COMPUTERS (SBCS)

Moving up in size from COMs are *single-board computers* (SBCs). These are basically overgrown COMs with standard connectors. These are fundamentally complete small-form-factor computers lacking only a power supply and a monitor (if one is desired). They are available with lower-power (and lower-capability) x86 chips like the Intel Atom or AMD Fusion, or with application-class ARM cores. As they're designed for industrial use, they're typically kept on the market for several years, sometimes for more than a decade. SBCs sport high price tags of typically $150 and up in small volumes for boards with relatively recent processors.

One way to "cheat" at buying an SBC is to use a platform such as the Raspberry Pi or the similar BeagleBone. The Raspberry Pi Model A features a fairly capable (although previous-generation) ARM11 processor, graphics acceleration, 256MB RAM, SD card slot, a USB port, and all sorts of I/O for $25 each, quantity 1. A "mainstream" SOM with similar capabilities would cost several times that even in large quantities, and the support would not be anywhere close to what the Raspberry Pi community provides. For an extra $10, the Model B doubles the RAM and adds Ethernet and another USB port. An absolute bargain!

Raspberry Pi is now also selling a true SOM, the Raspberry Pi Compute Module, shown in Figure 7-3 next to a Raspberry Pi. The Compute Module is basically a Raspberry Pi on a small board with signals going into an edge card connector instead of USB, Ethernet, and other standard connections.

FIGURE 7-3. Raspberry Pi Compute Module and Raspberry Pi Model B (credit: Raspberry Pi Foundation licensed under CC BY-SA *http://creativecommons.org/licenses/by-sa/4.0/*)

For $45, the BeagleBone Black is similar to the Raspberry Pi but substitutes a more modern (and capable) ARM Cortex-A8 core and adds 2GB of onboard storage (and retains the micro-SD card slot). Unlike the Raspberry Pi, BeagleBone Black schematics and PCB layout are open source, and the processor (AM3359) is not only readily available, but is guaranteed by TI to be available for 10 years from introduction. So if you ever want to reproduce the BeagleBone circuits on your own, most of the work is done. However, you probably won't save much money by building it yourself as the AM3359 processor alone runs $20 or so in moderate quantities.

DSP CHIPS

DSP chips are special-purpose processors that are optimized for *digital signal processing* (DSP). DSP applications involve taking a digitized signal of some sort (e.g., audio, video, or acceleration) and making changes to it. For example, in the case of audio, that might mean boosting or reducing certain frequencies in music (equalization).

DSP algorithms normally involve performing simple fixed- or floating-point math operations very rapidly. So DSP chips are typically designed to do very fast math, including multiplication in particular.

DSP chips were originally pretty specialized, but over time they've started adding other features to make them more microcontroller-like. And at the same time, microcontrollers have gotten faster at math. Add it all up, and we see that microcontrollers and DSPs have become somewhat similar. Certainly, there's a lot of overlap.

DSPs can be useful in special situations but are not typically a first choice for adding intelligence to a product. Microcontrollers such as those based on the Cortex M4 provide substantial DSP capabilities for audio processing and perhaps even low-resolution video, although they still aren't the equal of true DSP cores. For video applications, processor chips tend to be designed around application-class processors but often include a DSP core or two on-chip for video processing alongside the "main attraction" processor(s).

All told, unless you need to do a lot of signal processing, you should not typically need a DSP. But they still have their place in some specialized applications. More-common DSP families include Texas Instruments' TI5000 and TI6000, and Analog Devices' Blackfin and SHARC.

PROGRAMMABLE LOGIC DEVICES (PLDS)

Programmable logic devices (PLDs) can be thought as "software for electrical engineers." Like processors, PLDs must be programmed before they are used. What makes PLDs different than processors is that PLDs are configurable circuits, while processors are fixed circuits that execute instructions.

A number of PLD technologies are available, but two in particular—FPGAs (Field-Programmable Gate Arrays) and CPLDs (Complex Programmable Logic Devices)—are most typically used in new products today.

FPGAs are chips that contain basic circuit building blocks (called *logic cells* or *elements*) that can be configured by electrical engineers into an infinite variety of circuits. The configuration is applied fresh every time the part is powered up, so FPGAs allow us to build hardware that's as malleable as software.

Complex Programmable Logic Devices (CPLDs) are basically smaller, more integrated FPGAs. They contain fewer logic cells but tend to require less in the way of support circuitry. Henceforth I'll just refer to FPGAs, but know that everything that's discussed generally applies to CPLDs, too.

FPGAs are programmable chips, and so are CPUs. How are they different?

CPUs are devices with fixed hardware that execute instructions from a supported list (the instruction set). When a CPU is "doing its thing," it's executing a program written from these instructions.

FPGAs, by contrast, are Lego sets for constructing our own digital circuits. A designer describes how the hardware should be designed, and the FPGA "magically" turns into that hardware. When an FPGA is "doing its thing," it's just hardware built from lots and lots of logic gates. The basic building block of an FPGA is a general-purpose logic cell that can be used to implement simple bits of Boolean logic. Each FPGA contains somewhere between thousands and millions of logic cells, along with a chunk of RAM, which are all connected per our configuration instructions.

These instructions are normally written in one of two languages, *VHDL* or *Verilog*. Because these languages describe hardware, they are a lot different than languages used to write software to run on CPUs. As mentioned earlier, the FPGA is configured every time it's powered on, so the configuration can be updated in the field to fix bugs and improve functionality.

 FPGA designers are Electrical Engineers rather than software folks—it's *real circuit design*.

The typical FPGA use case is in hardware that must perform extremely fast operations through specialized design. To see this a little more clearly, let's consider both CPUs and FPGAs in simple functional terms as black boxes that take in information, do *something*, and then send information back out.

In the case of a CPU, doing something is executing code, usually one instruction at a time. Suppose that we have an array of 100 sensors that we're monitoring to look for a certain pattern. The classical way to attack this with a CPU is to read each sensor's value one at a time until we see the pattern. It requires 100 iterations, a few instructions executed during each, to read the entire array and check for the pattern. In all, several hundred operations must be performed for each read of all 100 sensors.

In the case of an FPGA, we can specify a highly parallel circuit that reads all 100 sensors at once and compares them in one operation or at most a very few operations. If each operation on the CPU and FPGA take similar amounts of time (and they do), the FPGA can scan the sensors way, way faster than the CPU can in a few operations versus a few hundred.

Note that FPGAs usually have many pins, sometimes 1,000 or even more, to support this kind of highly parallel operation.

Pre-built and tested VHDL/Verilog code is available to implement many common hardware functions normally found on special-purpose chips such as Ethernet, USB, and DSP. Opencores.org, a repository for open source FPGA code, has hundreds of projects that implement all kinds of building blocks (called *cores* or *blocks*), and many more can be licensed from various vendors at some cost. Even CPUs are available as FPGA cores in VHDL/Verilog. These are known as *soft processors*, and VHDL/Verilog code is available to specify soft processors that range from low-end (e.g., an AVR clone) to the latest ARM application-class cores.

So FPGAs are a magical piece of silicon that can implement custom circuits of virtually any type, including processors and peripherals, and can do specialized operations much faster than a CPU can. And unlike a circuit board, they can be reconfigured in the field whenever we want. *What's the catch?*

There are three catches, actually: cost, complexity, and power.

FPGAs run the gamut in cost from a few dollars on the low end to thousands of dollars each (!) for parts that come with millions of logic cells. (May you never experience the thrill of hoping that your board with multiple thousand-dollar, thousand-pin FPGAs was soldered correctly.)

Perhaps most importantly, FPGAs typically cost a lot more than processors to accomplish the same task. For example, emulating a simple $2

AVR using an FPGA requires a part that costs several times more than the AVR, and which uses far more power. And we need to go through the schlep of getting the AVR core working on our FPGA. FPGAs don't hold their configuration info when turned off; at boot time we need to have some circuitry, usually a microcontroller, read the configuration from memory into the FPGA.

So FPGAs tend to make sense for specialized tasks where CPUs can't get the job done fast enough, or where on-the-fly hardware configuration is important. And where lots of power is available (e.g., not powered from small batteries). These tasks typically include:

- Specialized video/image processing, including machine vision.
- Cryptography (in particular, *cracking* codes).
- Applications where it's tough to redesign hardware if bugs are found after it's been built (satellites, for example). Just send a configuration update, reboot, and our new hardware is installed.
- High-speed communications interfaces.
- Software-defined radios, such as radios that can be reconfigured to use new protocols on the fly, typically used by the military.

FPGAs configured for special operations are often used alongside CPUs that handle the GUI and other basic "stuff," including FPGA configuration at bootup. There's been a recent trend toward putting FPGAs and CPUs on the same piece of silicon to facilitate this mix of technologies. Prices range from under $20 for a part with a Cortex M3 and moderate FPGA "fabric" to thousands of dollars for parts with dual Cortex A9s and hundreds of thousands of logic cells. Power draw is moderate given the capability. While chips combining CPUs and FPGAs is still a niche market, I believe it has the potential to grow large. Imagine being able to customize a single processor chip to have whatever combination of interfaces (USB, Ethernet, video, etc.) that we want.

Final Thoughts

By this point, it should be clear that we have many options when it comes to selecting the hardware platform to power our device. How to choose?

Every product is different and each deserves a methodical analysis as to what's best. Aside from the advice that I've tried to sprinkle throughout the chapter, I have three pieces of general advice.

First, I recommend going with whatever's simplest among the options that are likely to get the job done. Product development is largely an exercise in risk management, and more complex equals more risk. Complex also equals higher development cost, and higher production costs. The only real downside of favoring simple over complex is that simple tends to limit options. I can't recall a project that I've been involved in where we hit a wall by selecting too simple of a processor, but I can certainly remember projects where complexity created bad surprises around schedule and budget.

My second recommendation is to buy rather than make whenever it's reasonable. Doing things from scratch is inevitably way more difficult than we think it will be and it's usually more important to get a product out the door in order to get market feedback than to spend time reducing cost the first time around. If the market likes our product, we'll be able to redesign for reduced cost and incorporate market feedback.

And finally, try to find out which processors products similar to yours have selected. Sometimes there's a good reason that they chose as they did, and analyzing their choices can be enlightening.

Good luck!

Coming up in our next chapter, we'll explore options around the other component of our smart platform: the operating system.

Resources

There's no shortage of information available regarding processors; the difficulty is in finding information that's concise and comprehensible.

If you'll be working with a low-end or middling microcontroller, you'll need to understand processors at the nuts-and-bolts level. Even if you run an OS on one of these processors, it probably won't be a big comfy OS that abstracts away all of the processor internals from software developers. If you're new to this world, probably the best way to get started is by acquiring and playing with an AVR-based Arduino board like the Arduino Uno. The Arduino platform, including hardware and tool chain (software tools), do abstract away *some* of the pain-in-the-butt parts of developing on microcontrollers, but they still expose the important bits (bad pun). A couple of recommended books are:

Getting Started with Arduino (*http://arduino.cc/en/Guide/HomePage*) by the creators of the Arduino, available free online or as a printed book.

Arduino Cookbook, 2nd Edition does a nice job of bringing the reader up to speed on all manner of topics from getting started to sophisticated topics like operating motors and network communications.

Once one has a good understanding of one low-end microcontroller architecture, understanding the others is not too arduous. Atmel, Microchip, and TI websites have plenty of information and inexpensive development kits for their respective AVR (*http://bit.ly/1OTDHnb*), PIC (*http://bit.ly/1Ox1nhB*), and MSP430 (*http://bit.ly/1Ox1t98*) chips.

For AVR users, a particularly good resource is the AVR Freaks (*http://www.avrfreaks.net/*) site, which lives up to its name.

Once we enter the world of middling micros and the domain of ARM cores, things get quite a bit more complicated (and powerful). ARM architectures are very clever, which is another way of saying "unobvious, but once you understand it you'll approve." ARM has some good training videos (*http://bit.ly/1Ox1zNX*) up on YouTube, including a very useful architecture overview (*https://www.youtube.com/watch?v=7LqPJGnBPMM*) to get started with. Since ARM doesn't make its own chips but rather licenses their architectures for others to put in their own chips, you'll also need the appropriate datasheet(s) from the manufacturer of whichever chip you select. The quality of documentation ranges widely. In fact, before selecting an ARM-core part, it pays to check the part's literature to see how helpful it is.

Since x86 processors run virtually every desktop PC and server on Earth, there's plenty of info available on these processors, but the good news is that you probably won't need it. x86 processors are almost always used with a heavy-duty OS such as Windows or Linux, which nicely abstracts away the details of the processor architecture. We'll look at OSes in our next chapter.

FPGAs are complex but quite fun to play with for anyone with some electronics background. As with low-end microcontrollers, the best way to learn is to pick up a development board and play. Diligent (*http://bit.ly/1OTDIaD*) and Papilio (*http://papilio.cc*) are better-known brands that are well-supported by training material, but many others (*http://bit.ly/1OTDIaD*) exist. A common and entertaining use for FPGA development boards is to recreate early video arcade games (like Pac-Man) by implementing their original microprocessors and supporting logic. This allows the original games' binary code (or something pretty close) to run. Processor emulation can also be done in software on a processor (for example, on a Raspberry Pi), but the FPGA versions typically do a better job.

## CHAPTER 8

Smart Platforms: Operating Systems

IN THE LAST CHAPTER, WE LOOKED AT THE PROCESSOR PIECE OF THE "smart platform" that provides the hardware brains for intelligent products. In this chapter, we'll look at the software piece of the platform: the operating system.

Before we dive in, let's get a short but inevitable dialog of the way:

- Many people developing intelligent devices: "I know! Let's run Linux!"

- Me: "Not so fast!"

Selecting (or deciding to not select) an operating system (OS) is a fundamental decision that we make early in the development cycle, which will have a profound effect on development effort and often on product cost. Sometimes the selection is straightforward. If we're building a smart phone or similar device, it would be folly to not use an existing operating system. Otherwise, we'd need to do an enormous amount of software development from scratch. Android is a very easy operating system to select for such an application.

On the other hand, suppose we're building a fancy home thermostat. Which OS to use, or whether to use one at all, is a question with a less obvious answer.

An OS gives us pre-built functionality in exchange for the potential for increased complexity, greater resource usage, greater expense, and loss of control. At what point does this become a good deal? Each product is different, and each requires a trade-off analysis.

Some of the functionality that tends to favor using an OS includes:

- Sophisticated user interfaces such as those found on smart phones
- Real-time operation: the need to ensure responses to events within a guaranteed time (specialized real-time operating systems make this [relatively] easy to implement)
- Sophisticated file systems
- Support for complex peripherals such as WiFi and USB: operating systems tend to have pre-written drivers for these
- Sophisticated Internet or database capabilities
- Availability of helpful libraries and applications
- Availability of software tools such as IDEs and debuggers

Note that processor and OS selection are intimately related and usually made together. Many operating systems have certain minimum processor requirements, and any given processor family is supported only by certain OSes (if any).

Once we decide to use an OS, there are a number of types to choose from. These tend to cluster into three categories: RTOSes, middleweight OSes, and heavyweight OSes. We'll dive into those in a moment but first let's review the concept of board support packages, which are critical in the world of embedded systems.

Board Support Packages (BSPs)

In the world of PCs, all processors look pretty much the same (architecture-wise): we always have (relatively) lots of disc space and the Internet is always available. To install an OS, we usually don't need to think much about the kind of processor and peripherals we have. A single OS distribution will normally run on any PC-class processor. We just select the 32- or 64-bit version, load our binaries, and go. Drivers and other support software are loaded from the CD-ROM or pulled from the Internet as needed.

In the embedded world, particularly in the space inhabited by ARM cores, the initial installation of an OS and software is not so simple. Besides the OS, we also need a board support package (BSP) that helps configure the OS to support the specific processor and peripherals we're using. The term *BSP* used to apply to an entire board that contained the processor and peripherals, but nowadays processors are typically built into chips that include all manner of peripherals, so BSPs have become common even for the processor chips alone.

> The availability of a high-quality BSP for a processor (or lack thereof) can have a major impact on the amount of effort needed in mating that part with an OS. Creating our own BSP or nursing along a crummy one is a nontrivial and highly technical task so, whenever possible, try to make sure that a good BSP exists for the processor and OS that you select.

RTOSes

RTOSes (*real-time operating systems*) are lightweight OSes whose roots lie in ensuring that applications can respond to requests within a certain time period. However, RTOSes can be very useful even if the timing considerations aren't important to us, as RTOSes typically have some of the other niceties of an OS (e.g., device drivers) that we can use "out of the box."

Most RTOSes are intended to be run on lower-powered processors in applications where memory is at a premium, so they tend to be lean and mean. The good news is that they are relatively small, taking as little as a few kilobytes of ROM/Flash and even less RAM. The flip side is that they are relatively spartan—even the most sophisticated RTOSes are stripped down compared to larger OSes.

The namesake function of RTOSes is guaranteed response characteristics. Let's look at what this means.

PREDICTABILITY

The traditional purpose of an RTOS is to provide *predictability* in two different areas: timing and reliability.

For timing, an RTOS will provide some degree of assurance that it can respond to an event (such as a switch being pressed) within a certain amount of time, say, one millisecond. The generic term for an event in the RTOS world is an *interrupt request* (IRQ). We can set the timing bounds in software, but there are minimums depending on the RTOS and processor. One fundamental difference among RTOSes is whether real-time performance is truly *guaranteed* or only *very likely*. A *hard* RTOS guarantees that operations will occur within a certain time period, whereas a *soft* RTOS simply makes it very likely. Soft RTOS is a bit of a squishy term. For example, even desktop Windows and Linux qualify as

RTOSes (and work fine in that capacity) if the should-not-exceed response time is long enough. But while Linux and Windows almost always respond within a few hundred milliseconds if set correctly, guaranteed response times for "real" RTOSes are typically in the microsecond range.

For applications that need to be ultra-reliable, such as automobile braking systems, we obviously need an OS that's fairly bulletproof—if the software crashes, the car might crash, too. Beyond timing guarantees, some RTOSes, such as Green Hills *Integrity*, *SAFERTOS*, QNX *Neutrino*, and *ThreadX*, provide various mechanisms to help assure us (and others, such as the FDA) that their operating system is highly reliable when used in our product. The mechanisms usually take the form of:

- The compiler and other tools being certified to one or more internationally recognized standards, such as IEC 61508 *Functional Safety of Electrical/Electronic/Programmable Electronic Safety-Related Systems*.

- Validation/verification tools to prove that the OS and attendant software are functioning properly as installed and configured.

- Artifacts (documentation) that demonstrates the manufacturer's development process, and the testing that was performed on the software and tools.

Assurances of reliability are expensive—expect to write a big check. But if you need it, you need it.

Of course, most good stuff comes at a cost, as we're about to see.

RTOS LICENSING

RTOS licensing arrangements are extremely varied and should be researched carefully as part of a selection process. Free/open RTOSes are available, but the licenses sometimes have interesting quirks. for example, application code running on *Free*RTOS does not have to be open sourced *unless* that code competes in functionality with *Open*RTOS. OpenRTOS, in turn, is a commercial offering from the owners of Free-RTOS.

Commercial RTOSes support all manner of licensing schemes. In the old days, licenses were often sold on a per-unit basis; e.g., manufacture 1,000 units and pay for 1,000 licenses. Modern commercial RTOS licensing schemes favor lump-sum licensing instead, with the lump sum being based on various factors. ThreadX alone supports licensing by product, product line, product family, microprocessor, or OEM product.

And if none of these suits us, the ThreadX folks will try to develop a custom license that does.

Since terminology can be confusing, it's a really good idea to include a description of your specific understanding of what's covered in any licensing agreement that's signed. This can prevent disagreements later over issues, such as "Does switching to a different processor with the same architecture constitute a microprocessor change, which triggers a new license fee?"

Middleweight OSes

Middleweight OSes (my own term) are basically lightweight versions of full-blown OSes. To my thinking, the middleweight field includes three contenders: embedded Linux, Android, and Windows CE.

EMBEDDED LINUX

Embedded Linux is, well, *just Linux*, but stripped down to its essentials. We're not talking a gigabyte-ish desktop distribution here—embedded Linux is Linux in as little as a few megabytes of memory. Depending on configuration, embedded Linux can boot in less than a second, although it's best to count on several seconds for most applications. By comparison, a full-blown desktop Linux desktop takes tens of seconds to boot.

There's a lot to like about embedded Linux!

- It's widely supported so documentation and help are relatively easy to come by
- It has all kinds of great functionality built into it
- A zillion device drivers are already written for it; in fact, many chip makers distribute Linux device drivers (some good, some half-baked) with their parts
- Software tools are pretty good and generally free
- Many, many libraries and applications are available
- The basic bits are very well reviewed and tested
- Good security
- Widespread availability of expertise
- Free; both kinds (*gratis* and *libre*)

The goodness of Linux is well known and doesn't need elaboration. But as we're about to see, embedded Linux has its warts, too.

Embedded Linux Gotchas

Using Linux for embedded systems presents significant challenges in the areas of configuration and maintenance. Let's start with configuration.

Configuring Linux for embedded applications is a nontrivial task. A desktop Linux installation can be huge and complex because we have tons of processor power, RAM, and disk. We don't really care if things aren't perfectly optimized. In fact, since a single desktop box is used for so many purposes, it's not even clear *how* it should be optimized.

On the other hand, embedded Linux typically has a very specific task to accomplish with limited CPU, RAM, and Flash/ROM to draw upon, so we usually need to tightly optimize our installation (also called our *image*). We want the bits we need, and nothing more. Creating an adequate but minimal image including OS, libraries, and applications, along with the software tools to support build and debug (called the toolchain) turns out to be a nontrivial task.

Preparing our image and toolchain used to be a truly awful task, often involving weeks of evaluating and cobbling together drivers, libraries, GUI support, and all of the other bits we need. But necessity is the mother of invention, and we now have embedded Linux *build systems* that greatly ease this task. These build systems allow the user to select the support that they want in their Linux image and—*poof!*—an image and/or toolchain are built.

There are currently about a dozen such build systems in use today, but the industry seems to be moving towards *Yocto*, an open project supported by The Linux Foundation. The project's name is cleverly taken from the smallest named SI unit: a yocto, equal to 10^{-24}. Other common build systems include OpenEmbedded (which is now part of Yocto), LTIB, and OpenWRT, the last of these being geared toward use in wireless routers.

A few things to keep in mind with regard to build systems:

- Different build systems require different BSPs; for example, an LTIB BSP for a processor won't work with Yocto.

- If you add hardware peripherals to your processor, as opposed to functionality built into the processor or SOM, you'll likely need to locate (or write!) drivers for those parts and integrate into the build system. But since it's for Linux, there's a good chance that you'll find a pre-built driver, or something close.

- Building an embedded Linux image is a complex process that's performed by a relatively small number of people in the world. Because these build systems are not tested by millions of users, and because your specific configuration of drivers and options might be unique in the world, it's pretty uncommon to build and use an image without interesting (not in a good way) things happening. Plan on a fair bit of work (person-weeks, at least) in dealing with subtle Linux platform and/or toolchain issues somewhere along the line.

Even though Linux is configured the way we want, we can't quite breathe easily yet. Our configuration might need to be maintained over time, and as we'll see, this isn't always a trivial task.

The Linux kernel is a continual work in progress. Things change all over the place, all of the time. Linux is not quite a total free-for-all, but it is something akin to organized anarchy, particularly under the hood where much of embedded work takes place.

A new Linux version is released every three months or so (e.g., going from 3.4 to 3.5), and the overarching goal of each release is the technical excellence of that release. Backwards compatibility is *not* a particularly important goal. Changes might be made to interfaces and subsystem functionality in the name of making better software, and these changes might break other kernel code that's dependent on the changed code. The breakage will (usually) get fixed by the time the release goes out the door, so the release will work *as a whole* but the new *pieces* might not be backward compatible with earlier OS versions.

At first glance, this doesn't seem like a big problem. If we want to upgrade the Linux version in our product, we just need to upgrade the whole thing. The big problem is that any old custom drivers that we've written (those not part of the Linux kernel) might break when used in a new Linux version. In fact, the more complex a driver is, the greater the chance that it will need to be rewritten when upgrading versions. The most-complex drivers, like WiFi and USB, can easily require person-weeks of rewrite and test. Tool chains might also be dependent on specific Linux versions, and thus a Linux update might have tool chain implications.

A perfectly reasonable strategy to avoid the pain of driver rewrites is to simply not upgrade software when a product goes to market, or at least to not update the Linux kernel being used—perhaps only make changes to applications. But this strategy isn't gotcha-free either. As time goes on, bugs are found in Linux that affect functionality, reliability, and security, and these bugs normally get fixed only in later kernel releases. We only get the fix if we move to the later kernel or if someone (often us) *backports* the fix to the kernel that we're using.

For example, suppose our product is draining batteries much faster than it should, and the problem turns out to be a bad USB driver in our Linux kernel. Three months after product release, a new kernel is released that fixes the bad driver—happy day, we can double the battery life our users are seeing! The bad news is that the new driver is incompatible with *our* kernel. We can upgrade to the new kernel and potentially break compatibility with any custom drivers we've written. Or we try to figure out how to backport the USB driver fixes from the new kernel to ours. In many cases, both alternatives are wince-worthy. And in either case, we'll need to test, test, and test the result to make sure our fix hasn't broken something else.

One partial mitigation to the backport issue is that once every year or so, a kernel version marked *long term stable* (LTS) is released. LTS kernels receive backports to fix major issues for two years after release. This is definitely helpful, but the kernel maintainers' definition of *major* might be different than ours so we will likely need to do some backporting of fixes that don't make the maintainers' cut.

Licensing on Linux can be a positive or negative, depending on your point of view. The kernel is licensed under the GPL, which states that any alterations we make to the source must be freely shared. Unless we're going the route of releasing all of our own code under GPL, including applications, we should definitely do a careful analysis of the licensing situation when using Linux or another GPLed work; we should make sure we'll be in compliance, and that complying doesn't cause headaches. Note that because of the potential complexities of licensing, some companies have a policy prohibiting the use of open source software in any situation. For example, use of open source puts us at risk of infringement if somebody slips (intentional or not) infringing code in the open source distribution we use. Particularly if you work in a large company, it's a good idea to check for any open source (or other software licensing) policies before starting a project.

Commercial Embedded Linux

Several vendors, including MontaVista, Wind River, and Mentor Graphics, *sell* Linux (sort of). Actually, what they really sell is services and products that can make embedded Linux easier to use and maintain.

Compared to commercial operating systems, Linux has very little central control. This has benefits and drawbacks. The good part is that anyone with a great idea can make it happen, and add it to the Linux kernel. No need for a product manager to decide that it's a good idea, proceed to get buy-in and sign-off, wait for implementation and test, and so forth. In Linux, change comes from individuals who are motivated to make that change, and there's nothing on Earth more powerful than a motivated person creating the change they want.

The drawbacks of Linux generally also stem from its de-emphasis of central control. Building, using, and supporting an embedded Linux platform is not a tidy exercise. Knowledge tends to live in lots of silos all over the place. Patches, libraries, and other bits of code are often shared when they are still half-baked and undocumented. Tool chains often require tweaking, and it's not rare to spend days or weeks dealing with some obscure issue that could be solved in 15 minutes if the right expert could be located and they had 15 minutes to spare. We need to keep a constant eye on the Web to find issues that might need our attention such as vulnerabilities, changes in subsystem architectures, etc.

Commercial Linux vendors are a soft layer between product developers and Linux's "wild west" — they sell ease and comfort. At least in principle, they make the embedded Linux experience go from that of building a do-it-yourself plane kit to purchasing an off-the-shelf corporate jet or something in between the two. Some folks would never trade building for buying. Some people would never trade buying for building. And many of us are in the middle somewhere.

Commercial vendors provide products and services ranging from tools and support all the way to professional services (i.e., consulting/contracting) that will take on the entire job of building and maintaining Linux and applications for a product.

Here's a partial listing of things that they can help with:

- Stable, tested and supported Linux platforms and/or standard tool-chains that are ready to go.

- Proprietary tools that are easier to use, or provide more features than open source tools.

- A single expert (hopefully!) source to ask questions of, and to "look over our shoulder" (e.g., periodically provide code reviews).

- Providing experts at our site and to work on our project, perhaps only at the project's start, so we can get off on the right foot and learn best practices, particularly if our own team is less experienced.

- Maintaining our Linux platform: keeping an eye out for problems we should be aware of and providing patches, etc.

- Providing documentation on the processes by which they integrated and tested their Linux distribution and other tools. This can be quite important for gaining clearances from the FDA and other regulatory bodies.

Commercial help, of course, doesn't come cheaply. But in some cases, it might be cheaper and/or less aggravating than the alternative.

To sum up, embedded Linux is an extensive and well-tested toolkit that lets us craft the balance we want between features and performance. On the other hand, it commits us to a good bit of effort over the short and long terms.

Now let's turn to the other embedded Linux: Android, a variant of Linux that offers a different set of tradeoffs.

ANDROID

Android, of course, is a software platform that currently powers something like one billion smart phones. Based on Linux, Android attracts the eye of many who are in the market for an embedded OS. The 2013 Embedded Market Study by UBM Tech (*http://bit.ly/1Ox2IFk*) found that 16% of embedded respondents are currently using Android, and 26% were considering its use in the next 12 months.

As one might expect, Linux is a platform that's designed for things that are similar to smart phones—products based on one or more ARM-core processors and have a rich touchscreen interface, good-sized batteries that are recharged daily, and support for varied communications devices and networks which run varied applications that need services such as a lightweight database, and so forth.

Figure 8-1 diagrams Android's architecture. Notice that the Linux kernel is just part of the picture; there's also a large set of libraries, a rich application framework and a Java runtime to support sophisticated applications.

Fundamentally, Android is a package of parts that's extremely optimized for a narrow set of use cases (smart phones and tablets). Even Linux itself has been optimized in a couple of fundamental ways. First, the standard GNU-licensed Linux C library *glibc* has been replaced with *Bionic libc*, which is much lighter in weight (as befits use in a small device), and which sports the more-corporate-friendly BSD license.

In another modification from standard Linux, Android Linux supports *wakelocks*, a mechanism for power management. Being battery-powered devices, smart phones want to sleep as often as possible to cut power consumption—they'll typically go to sleep in a few tens of seconds if it's not obvious that they're being used. Wakelocks allow an application to tell Linux's power management subsystem to hold off on going to sleep so a task can be completed. Android Linux will not go to sleep if any wakelocks are enabled unless forced to sleep by events like pressing the power button. If you have an Android phone, apps are available that display how often your apps have been using wakelocks to keep Android awake, with or without the screen turning on—you can use them to find any ill-behaved apps that are causing a significant drop in battery life.

While these modifications from standard Linux optimize Android's use for certain use cases, we must also be aware that they can break Linux code that's not targeted at Android. For example, grabbing a Linux device driver to use in Android might not be so simple—in fact, it might not work at all or it might exhibit bad behavior.

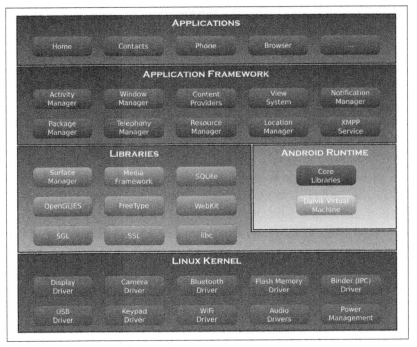

FIGURE 8-1. Android system architecture

The fundamental part of the Android platform is the *Android Open Source Project* (*AOSP*), which is free both as in beer and as in freedom, but tightly controlled by Google. Google does all of the development in private and then releases the sources to the public when they're ready. These sources will build an image that typically only works on Google's *Nexus* reference devices, so phone makers must modify the code for their own devices before making images available, which is a process that usually takes months even for huge companies.

Each Android release is based on a specific Linux kernel release. Android upgrades are generally less painful than for embedded Linux because each release is a complete platform with dependencies worked out. However, there's still the potential pain of porting any device drivers we're using that aren't available for the new kernel, and applications might need updating as well.

Google also supplies optional proprietary Android applications that must be licensed directly from Google if desired. These include Google Maps, the App Store, Gmail, search, and other apps that directly use Google services.

It's entirely reasonable to use only the AOSP part of Android as a software platform for an embedded device, and even to license the proprietary stuff if that's desired. There are many good reasons to do so if our product's functionality overlaps significantly with smart phones and tablets.

Foremost, Android is a complete, optimized platform tuned for embedded mobile use—we get a lot of performance from a package that's already integrated for us. We'll probably need some drivers and an app, but we start off with a lot of things that work really well together.

Android has many useful features, built-in and tested, that we might otherwise not be able to afford to implement or might simply forget about. For example, it has a nice system for doing OS updates over a network, and good frameworks for common sensors, error logging and reporting, and other tasks. A huge amount of effort has gone into building Android and *doing it right* for its target use cases.

Some other substantial benefits to Android are:

- Android's base desktop GUI is familiar to hundreds of millions of users but can be modified if desired.

- Each day, many millions of smart phone users and some huge number of developers are testing Android by using almost the exact same platform that we'll be using. Reliability is *excellent* for such a rich platform.

- Great free tools and support for application development.

- Built on Linux, which is a familiar, open, and well-understood OS.

- Fantastic connectivity options.

Of course, Android is not appropriate for all projects. Most obviously, it has loads of features that most embedded devices don't need, and these features take up memory and suck up CPU. A stripped-down embedded Linux installation can run in a few megabytes of flash and RAM, and boot in a few seconds on a low-end ARM application-class processor. By contrast, an Android image requires flash and RAM that are more in the gigabyte range and a far-more powerful processor in order to boot in many tens of seconds. My own Android phone has a 1.4GHz quad-core ARM Cortex-A9 processor and still requires about a minute to boot Android 4.3.

While it's theoretically possible to start with a full Android release and strip out the unneeded bits, Android was not designed for this use case and does not make the job easy. Expect to wade through code in order to deal with dependencies. This is not something I'd generally recommended.

Another challenge is that while documentation and support for Android applications programming is world class, documentation and support for what's going on under the hood is quite sparse. Certainly, don't count on much support from Google.

And finally, Android's future is largely controlled by Google. If Google decides to take it in a direction that's highly beneficial for them but not for other embedded users, our upgrade path might become less clear. That being said, since so many large entities rely on the fully open AOSP (e.g., Amazon for its Kindle Fire tablets and FirePhone), it's reasonably likely that there will be a highly supported non-Google fork of the AOSP if Google tries any funny business.

WINDOWS EMBEDDED

Once upon a time, say, in 2008, there was *Windows CE*. Win CE was a perfectly good embedded operating system with good features, good tools, and a modest licensing cost (a few bucks per copy). It was a middleweight OS: bigger and more full-featured than an RTOS but lighter than a desktop OS, which made it similar to Android in its scope. Windows CE was quite popular for embedded use, running neck-and-neck with Linux. In the 2008 UBM/TechInsights Embedded Market Study, 19% of respondents reported that they were using Windows CE versus about 22% for all the different flavors of Linux combined.

Then *something* happened—frankly, I'm not sure what—and the whole embedded world got Linux Fever. Windows CE usage started to plummet and Linux exploded. Just five years later, in the 2013 Embedded Market Study, Windows CE (now named *Windows Embedded Compact*) was only being used by 8% of users versus more than 50% who were using some flavor of Linux.

Presumably in an attempt to regain market share, Microsoft has been going through all sorts of gyrations with Windows CE/Windows Embedded Compact, splintering it into many editions and changing its name(s) on a regular basis.

Back in 2008, Windows CE (in my opinion) was a good bit easier to work with than embedded Linux. But embedded Linux support has gotten so much better since then, and market acceptance of Windows Embedded Compact has dropped so precipitously, that ease of use is no longer strongly in Windows' favor. And because Linux is free, it's kind of hard to see a strong reason to favor Windows Embedded Compact for new product development these days. I hope that changes—I happen to like a number of things about Microsoft's OSes, particularly their development tools, which are nicely integrated into the Windows Embedded world.

This completes our tour of commonly used middleweight operating systems. But before we move to the next weight class, let's review a topic that's of importance to developers using any middleweight OS: boot loading.

BOOT LOADERS

For various reasons, operating systems of any significant complexity (e.g., Linux) tend to not start up by themselves. They usually need one or more *boot loaders* to load them into RAM and start them off.

In the embedded Linux world, there are typically three boot loaders that run, one after the other, before the OS is loaded and running.

First, a tiny boot loader internal to the processor (and fixed in hardware) starts off the process by reading a second somewhat-larger boot loader into RAM and executing it. This second boot loader is installed by the user, and its location (SD card, UART, eMMC, etc.) is specified to the first boot loader by setting hardware configuration pins on the processor.

The second boot loader then loads and starts a still-larger third (and final) bootloader, which moves the OS from nonvolatile memory into RAM, and then launches it. This final, larger bootloader requires some thought and configuration during development. The PDF user manual for *U-Boot* (officially *Das U-Boot*), the most popular bootloader of this type for Linux, runs more than 200 pages. Reading the entire manual usually isn't necessary, but a quick perusal is worthwhile. There are a fair number of options that can trip us up or which can be leveraged for better performance.

For example, in systems with a graphical UI, splash screens (the images that we toss on the screen during booting so users know something's happening) require a particular bit of thought and effort. U-Boot can write a custom bitmap to the screen, but this bitmap might only last a fleeting moment until Linux initializes its own display subsystem during boot, at which point we might see a blank screen again for some time until Linux completes its startup. Fortunately, the Linux kernel now supports a configuration option (CONFIG_FB_PRE_INIT_FB), which preserves the U-Boot-displayed splash screen during boot until we are ready to consciously replace it with something else. This saves a *lot* of hassle. Even though it's a Linux option, you're most likely to find out about it by reading the U-Boot manual.

Heavyweight OSes

The heavyweights of the embedded OS world are the desktop and server versions of Windows and Linux. They're big (gigabyte-ish) and they run on big processors with lots of memory.

In Windows-land, what I'm referring to here is called an OS (e.g., Windows 7), whereas in Linux-land it's called a distribution (e.g., Ubuntu 14.04 Trusty Tahr). These are roughly equivalent in terms of the scope of what they provide. There are versions targeted at desktops and somewhat-leaner versions targeted at servers. To keep things simple, for the rest of this chapter I'll use the generic term *heavyweight OS* to refer to Linux or Windows, which target either a desktop or server.

ADVANTAGES

The first obvious advantage of running a heavyweight OS is that out-of-the-box it has tremendous functionality, a sophisticated user interface, and support for a myriad of peripherals and modes of network communications. We can plug almost any random peripheral in and it's likely that the OS will either have a built-in driver for it or a driver can be downloaded.

Development on a heavyweight OS is a relative breeze. We can develop applications on the same computer that we test on so we can update code, rebuild software, and start testing in moments. We can run big, full-featured frameworks and libraries like .NET, JavaSE, Swing, QT, Gnome, KDE, and so on. And because we have so much power and memory, we don't necessarily have to go through the painstaking process of stripping out everything we don't need.

Another advantage is that it's really easy to find developers with experience in creating applications for heavyweight OSes. There are millions of folks out there with many years of experience writing desktop applications.

Similar to Android, common heavyweight OSes have been tested extensively by their manufacturer/packager and by a huge pool of users. We can be confident that things will work fairly reliably.

DISADVANTAGES

As you might expect, there are also some pretty considerable drawbacks to using heavyweight OSes. First, they require considerable and expensive hardware. The cost for the raw components needed to run these OSes will normally run $100 or more, and these parts are complex, use high-speed signals, and are challenging to design with. To avoid the pain, most heavyweight-OS products utilize off-the-shelf x86-based single-board computers as described in Chapter 7 rather than designing from scratch.

The electronics required to support heavyweight OSes are relatively large and draw a lot of power, so we're limited to products the size of a notebook computer or larger. In the case of battery-powered devices, operational time between recharges is usually measured in hours, rather than the days or years that are possible for other types of hardware. And high power draw also means high heat, so we'll need to accommodate ventilation or heat sinking.

Because of their complexity, heavyweight OSes might have more issues around reliability and security versus their lighter-weight brethren. Dozens, sometimes even hundreds, of binaries (applications, services, etc.) might be running in different combinations and permutations at different times, which makes things effectively non-deterministic and thus difficult to test exhaustively. For example, heavyweight OSes can be made reliable enough that they are sometimes used in moderately critical applications, such as in an electrocardiogram used to monitor patients in a hospital—an infrequent and brief crash in this application is not good, but it's unlikely to cause great harm. But I can pretty well guarantee that a heavyweight OS won't be used to control the wing flaps on an airplane any time soon.

Great complexity also presents security challenges. OSes are designed to give users flexibility, but in most product uses we want to limit how an OS is used. For example, we normally don't want our users to do things like install games, surf the Web, and edit configuration files, all things that heavyweight OSes are designed to make easy. Locking down a system designed to be flexible takes thought and effort.

Another aspect of security involves protection from the outside world, such as viruses on USB sticks, and hackers on the network. The more stuff that's running, the larger the potential pool of exploitable code. This is somewhat offset by the easy-to-use security (e.g., firewalling) that's included, preconfigured, and automatically enabled (or at least easy to enable) in most heavyweight OSes.

Heavyweight OSes can be pared down in size to some degree. Linux distributions are infinitely tweakable. For example, we can rebuild the kernel to our liking and strip out unneeded packages. But getting something *really* small requires a great deal of effort. It's normally much less work to start small with embedded Linux and add what we want.

Desktop x86 Windows is available as a special embedded version, currently labeled *Windows Embedded Standard*. Windows Embedded Standard allows product developers to develop a custom Windows image by selecting the modules of functionality they want. The result is smaller than full-blown Windows, but still heavyweight. Of course, like all versions of Windows, Windows Embedded Standard carries a significant cost per unit sold.

Note that there are also various versions of Windows Embedded based on a variant of desktop Windows called Windows RT that are targeted at ARM processors rather than x86 devices. This is pretty new and specialized stuff, and its future is unclear. I'd hold off for now.

To sum up, heavyweight OSes have a place in products that require great flexibility and a sophisticated user interface without needing significant configuration by developers but at a cost of expensive and large hardware that consumes a lot of power. In real-world scenarios, this typically translates into low-volume products where development costs are difficult to amortize. For moderate volumes or higher, Android can provide much of the flexibility, ease-of-development, and user-interface goodness of a heavyweight OS while requiring a fraction of the hardware, but often at the price of significant configuration and integration effort.

We've now explored the gamut of OSes, from little RTOSes that can run on $2 microcontrollers to massive binaries that need gigabytes of memory and gigahertz of processor. Next, let's see how we can turn this all into making a good decision on which direction will work best for us.

Final Thoughts

As is the case with processors, we have many options when it comes to selecting the hardware/software platform to power our device. To help guide selection a bit, Table 8-1 contains my (biased by experience) opinion of how the different options compare. I have not included embedded versions of Windows in this table as it seems to be a quickly changing target and I don't have recent experience with what's currently on the market.

In some cases, the rating for an OS is given as a range, either because it depends on the specifics of what's selected within the category (e.g., RTOS maker or embedded Linux build system) or because the rating tends to vary significantly depending on the application.

This is a somewhat subjective rating intended to give a reasonable idea of what to expect for each OS type. In some specific cases, it can be way off. For example, Android typically requires a substantial effort to configure it for an embedded system, but if we're using a System on Module (see previous chapter) that has all of the peripherals we need, and the vendor has a well-supported Android BSP that happens to include the drivers for our specific LCD and touchscreen, configuration should be pretty easy. It's always important to do a good bit of research before making a selection.

TABLE 8-1. Embedded OS comparison

	No OS	RTOSes	Embedded Linux	Android	Desktop/Server Linux	Desktop/Server Windows
Reliability (resistance to crashing)	Depends on code	Good to Excellent	Fair-Good	Fair	Fair	Fair
Interrupt response time	Depends on code	Good to Excellent	Fair	Fair	Poor	Poor
Flexible or sophisticated communications	Difficult to implement	Poor to Fair	Excellent	Good	Excellent	Excellent
Support other vendor peripherals	Difficult to implement	Poor	Fair	Fair	Fair	Excellent

	No OS	RTOSes	Embedded Linux	Android	Desktop/ Server Linux	Desktop/ Server Windows
Network security	Depends on code; usually good	Fair to Excellent	Fair to Good	Good	Fair-Good	Fair-Good
User security	Depends on code; usually excellent	Excellent	Fair to Excellent	Medium	Poor-Fair	Poor-Fair
Hardware cost (per unit manufactured)	Low	Low to High	Medium to High	Medium-High	High to Very High	High to Very High
Software cost (purchase)	Low	Low to High	Zero-Low	Zero	Zero to Low	Very High
Configuration effort	Low to High	Moderate-High	High	High	Low-High	Low-Moderate
Application development support	Poor to Good	Poor to Fair	Good	Good	Excellent	Excellent
GUI/ touchscreen support	Poor	Poor to Good	Good	Excellent	Good to Excellent	Good to Excellent

With OSes, as in most things, my bias is to go with the simplest option that reasonably supports what we need to do. Software tends to be the most unpredictable and cantankerous part of product development, and a reasonable reduction of OS complexity will pay dividends in reducing development time and effort.

It's easy to hear the siren's call of embedded Linux and Android: "Look at all of the great functionality, applications, drivers, and libraries we get for free! Infinite flexibility, and no royalties!" And if our product requires a sophisticated GUI, Android might be an obvious choice. If we only need a simple GUI, or none at all, but do need to support a range of peripherals and types of communications (USB, WiFi, Bluetooth, etc.), then embedded Linux is a good contender. But either of these options are likely to require a good bit more effort and pain than you'd imagine if you haven't been through the process before.

RTOSes are the obvious choice for critical applications where reliability and predictability are key, like in medical, aerospace, automotive, and industrial uses. But even in these applications, they're not always mandatory. I've been involved in developing medical devices that appropriately used every OS type listed in Table 8-1, including no OS.

One trick to reduce the need for a complex OS (or the need for any OS) is to use more-sophisticated chips in the electronics design. For example, we traditionally think of communications peripherals like WiFi and Bluetooth as requiring substantial software drivers and/or communications stacks to handle their higher-level protocols, and this is relatively necessary for higher-complexity OSes such as Linux/Android and Windows. But if we can stand to spend a little more per part, chips and/or modules are available that implement both the hardware *and* the higher-level protocol stacks for these peripherals, communicating with their host processor via a simple API over some sort of serial bus. These parts can make it possible to stick with simpler OSes (or no OS) while supporting sophisticated communications without great hassle. This can make our lives much, much easier by reducing software effort and risk substantially, though at a higher per-unit cost. Particularly if we know our product will be sold in low volumes or if we aren't sure of volumes, these more-capable parts are often the way to go. As discussed before, getting to market with faster and cheaper development is usually a big positive. If we start selling product in high volumes, we can do a redesign to reduce cost, switching to less-expensive parts and spending effort implementing/integrating the drivers and protocol stacks in our OS.

One final tip is to try to find out what OSes are being used by products similar to yours. This can sometimes be tough to find out, but knowing and analyzing what others are using can be enlightening.

Good luck!

Resources

EE Times conducts an annual survey (*http://ubm.io/1Ox5Wsq*) that provides a good overview of trends in embedded OS usage. This is well worth reviewing when selecting an OS because an OS that's widely used is more likely to be widely supported.

Wikipedia has a comprehensive list of real-time operating systems (*http://bit.ly/1OTDNeC*) that's good for getting a quick feel for the licensing and supported processors for most RTOSes, but digging into feature sets requires significant research on vendor sites—unfortunately, I don't know of any short cuts.

Applications requiring an RTOS often need to be fault-tolerant as well. A good overview of how these play together is *An Overview of Fault Tolerance Techniques for Real-Time Operating Systems* (*http://bit.ly/1Ox5PNx*).

Turning to Linux, whether going the roll-your-own embedded route, or the mostly pre-rolled Android route, getting Linux to play nicely in an embedded application will require a good understanding of how Linux works. The Linux From Scratch project (*http://www.linuxfromscratch.org*) is a step-by-step tutorial that walks you through the process of building a usable Linux configuration from scratch, a good hands-on way to get your "sea legs." The standard LFS project (*http://www.linuxfromscratch.org*) covers Linux on the PC but for more of an embedded flavor, a variant targeting the Raspberry Pi is also available (*http://www.intestinate.com/pilfs/*).

Understanding the Linux Kernel, 3rd Edition, is a thorough (if dated) reference for those times when you need to dig into the innards of the Linux Kernel.

The Free Electrons site (*http://free-electrons.com*) contains a wealth of information about embedded Linux, including some in-depth videos (*http://free-electrons.com/blog/elc2014-videos/*) on selected topics.

Embedded Android by Karim Yaghmour is a good place to start for information on adapting Android for embedded use.

## CHAPTER 9

Powering Our Product

ELECTRONIC DEVICES NEED POWER, OF COURSE. SPECIFICALLY, VIRTUALLY all modern circuits are based around semiconductor chips (integrated circuits) and displays, and these parts each require one or more stable DC voltages, typically in the 1–5V range. In most intelligent products and particularly in the case of products that use rechargeable batteries, a fair bit of effort goes into the design, debugging, and testing of power supplies.

Much literature exists on the details of power supply design, but less is available on the system-level issues. Casual decisions are often made about which batteries, chargers, power supply chips, and other power components to use. Then, months later, design engineers find themselves caught in a rat hole when a major problem crops up that requires a significant redesign, such as finding out that a system's circuitry simply cannot recharge a deeply discharged battery and a new battery with at least a little charge needs to be swapped in. More knowledge and thinking at the front end of a project can help us avoid many of these rat holes.

To better understand this chapter's material, let's begin with a high-level look at the fundamentals, and at some of the challenges we face.

There are two basic categories of design decisions that must be made when designing an electronic product:

1. What are our sources of power: battery, electrical outlet, car power plug, etc.?

2. How will we convert the voltage(s) supplied by the source(s) into voltages that will keep our chips happy?

> **TIP** A refresher: as shown in Figure 9-1, AC voltage (which usually refers to the voltage available at a wall socket) purposely varies with time, while DC tries to remain at the same voltage all the time.

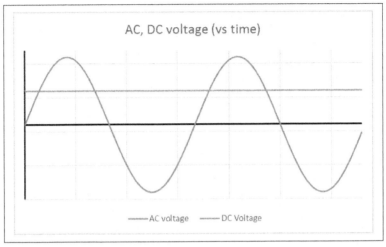

FIGURE 9-1. AC versus DC voltage

Figure 9-2 shows a generic power supply circuit decomposed into its "building blocks." This circuit accommodates both wall socket and battery power; accommodating only one of these would obviously result in removing some of the building blocks. An *AC to DC converter* transforms wall socket power to a safe DC voltage that's easily adjusted to what our circuits need, and then this voltage is used in several ways:

1. Some circuits can use it directly.

2. One or more DC-to-DC converters adjust it to other DC voltages that other circuits require.

3. A charging chip converts it as necessary to charge our battery.

The battery itself will also feed into DC-to-DC converters to convert its voltage to those needed by our circuits.

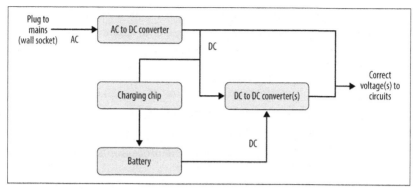

FIGURE 9-2. Generic power supply building blocks

At first glance, this might not seem too difficult—and to be sure, there's nothing super-complex about it. But real power supply circuits need to consider a surprisingly large number of easy-to-overlook details that are missing in this diagram and description beyond the straightforward issues of turning voltages into other voltages.

To illustrate, let's consider the case of powering a smart phone's circuits. A smart phone will typically use several sources of power: 5V from a USB adapter plugged into the wall or a computer port, and/or an internal lithium ion battery that varies between 4.2 and 3.0V as it discharges and charges. These two sources must be converted to perhaps four or more different DC voltages needed by the phone's chips and display. Here are some of the complications we face:

- Since the battery must also charge from the USB port, we need enough energy to simultaneously charge the battery and operate the phone.

- The battery must not charge if conditions aren't right. For example, batteries can easily become too hot to safely charge when left in a car in the hot sun. We could potentially start a fire in the car if we don't address this issue.

- We need a way to tell the user how much capacity is left in the battery so they can decide when to use a recharger.

- We might want to power down some chips, such as the GPS, when they're not in use to save some energy.

- Circuits should seamlessly switch from using USB power to using battery power when we pull the USB cable.

- When starting up the phone, some parts might need to turn on before others, and even within the same chip, some power lines might need to become energized before others.

- Selecting the wrong power supply scheme can reduce runtime on a battery charge because we might run out of juice in only an hour or two, even when the device is sitting unused.

- Some processors can save energy by running at a lower speed and at a lower voltage during periods when the processor isn't doing anything taxing.

- And much, much more.

Throughout the rest of this chapter, we'll review each of Figure 9-2's building blocks in enough detail to (hopefully) help designer/developers avoid common pitfalls:

Batteries
What's available, what makes sense and why, and charging basics.

AC-to-DC conversion
How to minimize cost and stay safe, in the US and all over the world.

DC-to-DC conversion
When to select linear versus switching power supplies.

We'll then dig into the system-level issues that can crop up when integrating these building blocks, including electrical noise, power sequencing, and low-power design.

It might seem curious that this chapter gets into technical details somewhat more than other chapters. The reason is that I've found power systems to be a very important source of unforced errors; i.e., things that would have gone far better if designer/developers just had a bit more information up front. Further, these errors tend to stem from a lack of information sources that tie the different parts together. My goal in writing this chapter (as it is for the rest of this book) is to pull these parts together to make the job easier in order to have fewer issues fall between the cracks.

Note that because this chapter does get a little further into technical details, it will be easier to understand if you have a little background in electronics, but I'll try to keep it to basic circuit "stuff" typically taught in high school physics.

Let's get started with batteries: why *are* there so many types? Let's find out why, and which make sense for our product.

Batteries

We tend to think of batteries as pretty simple devices: voltage sources that supply current for a while and then die. But think about it: if batteries were so simple, then why would so many different chemistries and configurations be available? The reason for so much diversity is that batteries are not as simple as they seem, and each chemistry and configuration has characteristics that make it better for some applications and worse for others.

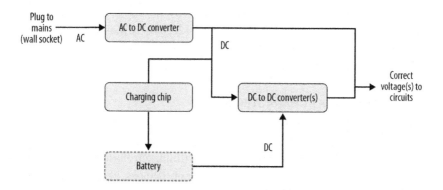

In this section, we'll take a tour of the different chemistries and configurations in use with an eye towards making informed choices during development. Let's start with some basics.

The electricity supplied by common batteries is a byproduct of a chemical reaction involving two metals and an electrolyte. Different metal combinations, such as Zn/MnO_2 or $Li/FePO_4$, yield batteries with different characteristics.

After a battery discharges for some amount of time, the reacting chemicals no longer have enough "oomph" to continue the reaction with sufficient vigor to produce adequate power. At that point, there are two alternatives for getting more power: we can discard the battery and insert a fresh one or we can recharge the battery by pushing electricity back into it, which reverses the chemical reaction. Disposable batteries are sometimes called *primary cells*, and rechargeables are sometimes called *secondary cells*. (More on cells versus batteries will follow shortly.)

Of course, many different batteries are available, from tiny button cells to big rectangular affairs that weigh a number of pounds, and most batteries utilize one of a handful of different chemistries. Batteries based on lithium chemistry are probably the most interesting batteries for product development these days, particularly the rechargeable lithium ion (Li-ion) variants. This is both because of Li-ion's *positive* characteristics which lead to their ubiquity (they're used in virtually every rechargeable device these days, from smart phones to laptops), and because of their *negative* characteristics (they're a bit fussy and can even catch fire, so some care needs to be taken when using them to power our circuits). Because of their importance, rechargeable lithium ions get their own somewhat-detailed subsection at the end of this battery section.

But before tackling Li-ions in depth, we'll look at the general characteristics of batteries that we should consider when making a selection, and how those characteristics compare among the battery chemistries in common use today.

GENERAL BATTERY CHARACTERISTICS

We tend to think of a battery in terms of simple parameters: for example, right now I'm looking at a AA battery from a well-known manufacturer, which claims that it provides 2300 mAh (milliamp hours) at 1.5V. However, when I turn to the battery's datasheet, it looks like it will provide 1.5V when *fresh*, but will actually spend most of its life closer to 1.2V depending on how it's used. The claimed 2300 mAh capacity is really more of an average: according to the datasheet, we can expect 2800 mAh to 1500 mAh—or even far less—again depending on how it's used.

Batteries are based on chemistry, and chemistry is complicated and subtle. For any given battery, parameters such as voltage, capacity, instantaneous power draw, lifetime discharge/charge cycles, time in service, and shelf life will vary greatly depending on how we use them.

> **TIP** Battery datasheets are often overlooked, but they're great sources of information. We should always carefully check datasheets to help understand how a battery is likely to work in our application, and to find any potential gotchas.

Let's review some basic characteristics of batteries that tend to be documented in battery datasheets.

Energy capacity

A good alkaline AA cell might be advertised as having a capacity of 2300 mAh. Can we draw 2.3 mA for 1,000 hours? 100 mA for 23 hours? 2300 mA for five hours? Advertised capacity tells us how much total *energy* the battery can provide when used in a certain way (usually with a reasonably light load and at room temperature), but this capacity might be quite different under different conditions. The 2300 mAh figure might be true, say, when discharging at 23 mA at 21°C, but capacity might drop fully in half (or more) at high discharge rates and at low temperatures (e.g., 0°C or lower).

Power

Power, the amount of energy that can be supplied at any instant in time (i.e, voltage times current), is limited by a battery's *internal resistance.* Internal resistance varies by battery type, charge remaining, temperature, and other factors. Small batteries tend to have high internal resistance. For example, a typical fresh CR2032 (a coin cell roughly the size of two stacked US quarters) might have an internal resistance of 50 ohms, versus an alkaline AA battery at about 0.2 ohm.

Suppose we want to draw 50mA from a fresh CR2032. Its internal resistance will cause the supplied voltage to drop by 0.05A × 50 ohms = 2.5V. Given that a CR2032 has a cell voltage of only about 3V, drawing 50mA isn't going to work well: 2.5 V will be used within the battery and only a half-volt or so will be measured across the battery's electrodes. In fact, due to its high internal resistance, any continuous draw of more than a few milliamps will substantially reduce the CR2032's supplied voltage.

Turning to the fresh alkaline AA cell, things look much better when drawing 50mA. The drop in this case is 0.05A × 0.2ohm = 0.01V; a minimal drop. However, internal resistance tends to rise as batteries lose charge, and it might rise in our AA cell to an ohm or more as the battery nears depletion. 500mA through 1 ohm of internal resistance gives us a voltage drop of (0.5A × 1.0 ohm = 0.5V), which is quite significant. Since nominal battery voltage (the voltage before accounting for internal resistance) also goes down as we discharge, to maybe 1.1V, we'd end up with well under a volt across the AA's electrodes. In this application, we'd likely need to change out our battery well before internal resistance hits an ohm, which might waste capacity. In other words, we'd have usable charge left in the battery, but it won't be usable at the current we need.

Note that battery aging also tends to increase internal resistance, as does the number of discharge/recharge cycles in rechargeables.

Temperature

Since chemical reactions tend to speed up as temperature rises, temperature has an important effect on batteries. Increasing temperature (within a battery's specified operational range) tends to increase its ability to provide current (i.e., effectively lowers internal resistance), which is a good thing. However, increased temperature also increases a battery's self-discharge rate, which can reduce battery life. Later in this chapter, we'll discuss self-discharge a bit more.

Conversely, lower temperatures can lower the self-discharge rate but increase internal resistance, which effectively reduces battery capacity because we'll reach a given discharge cutoff voltage more quickly.

Keep in mind that batteries can self-heat when discharging (or charging), some more than others. This heating can be significant at high currents or in small, unventilated spaces (e.g., in an unvented enclosure).

Pulsed operation

Real circuits draw different amounts of current from moment to moment, depending on what bits are powered on and what those bits are doing. Sometimes this difference can be fairly extreme, particularly with devices that use actuators (e.g., motors), lights (e.g., an LED flash on a camera), or wireless communications. The average current draw by a device might be much lower than the occasional pulse currents it needs. Batteries that maintain a low internal resistance throughout their lifetimes are better at supporting these types of applications.

Battery Size

With one big exception (lithium polymers) that we'll discuss later in this section, batteries come in standard sizes. Sizes are specified via two conventions, which can be roughly categorized as old school and new school.

Old school sizing is what most of us are familiar with. These sizes are mostly assigned a letter, such as AA, AAA, C, and D. The common rectangular 9-volt battery falls under this old-school convention, but it's an anomaly named for its voltage rather than being assigned a letter value.

⚠ It's a good idea to steer clear of selecting 9-volt batteries for products. First off, because of the way they're made, they tend to have very low capacity for their size. Second, their terminal configuration (next to each other on the same side) is a bona fide danger. The terminals can easily be shorted by a stray bit of metal (keys in a pocket, aluminum foil in the trash, etc.) resulting in fire (*http://bit.ly/1OTEHaQ*). If you happen to be storing or disposing any 9V batteries, it's a really good idea to put some tape across the terminals to electrically isolate them.

Beyond the well-known old-school sizes, there are some oddball sizes that can occasionally be useful, such as the small AAAA, A23, and A27 sizes.

TIP "New school" battery sizes are specified using a convention spelled out in the IEC 60086 standard, which includes the battery size, chemistry, shape, and number of cells. The convention is a bit complex and is available online in some depth at *http://en.wikipedia.org/wiki/Battery_nomenclature*. As an example, from its name we know that the common CR2032 battery is based on $LiMnO_2$ (the C), and is round (R), 20mm wide, and 3.2mm tall.

Now that we've reviewed the battery characteristics that are commonly of interest to engineers, let's look at the different chemistries that are in common use today to see how they compare to one another.

BATTERY CHEMISTRIES

A battery's characteristics lie mainly in the chemistry it uses to create electricity. Many battery chemistries are available, but only a dozen or so are common. Table 9-1 lists some of these, along with key characteristics for each. Note that the numbers in Table 9-1 are ballpark, supplied for relative comparisons. Each model (and, to some degree, make) of battery is different because of different chemicals and construction: again, we should always consult a battery's datasheet for actual numbers.

Before we delve into Table 9-1, a quick word on the usage of *cell* versus *battery*: when we put two metals together with an electrolyte, we create a *cell* with a certain voltage that depends on the metals being used. A fresh alkaline (Zn/MnO_2) cell will always create a potential of about 1.5V, which will decrease as the Zn and MnO_2 react and gradually turn to other substances. If we need more than 1.5V from an alkaline battery, we'll have to put more than one cell in series.

Multiple cells, particularly within a single package, are *technically* called batteries. So in principle, an AAA alkaline device (at 1.5V) should be called a *cell*, while a 9V alkaline device (usually made from 6 alkaline cells in series) should be called a *battery*. But in real life, all are normally just called batteries.

TABLE 9-1. Common battery chemistries

Chemistry	Max voltage	Typical voltage	Discharge cutoff voltage	Specific energy (Wh/kg)	Rechargeable?	Shelf life	Safety
Zinc-carbon (dry cell)	1.5v	1.2v	0.9v	40	N	2 years	OK
Alkaline	1.5v	1.25v	0.9v	100	N	5 years	OK
Lithium, consumer disposable (LiMn)	3v	3v	2v	250	N	10 years	OK
Lead-acid	2.1v	2v	1.5v	20	Y	1 year	OK
Lithium ion (Li-ion)	4.2v	3.7v	3v	160	Y	1 year	Use extra caution
Nickel cadmium (NiCd)	1.5v	1.2v	1v	40	Y	A few months	Use extra caution
Nickel metal hydride (NiMH), standard	1.5v	1.2v	1v	75	Y	A few months	OK
Nickel metal hydride (NiMH), low self-discharge	1.5v	1.2v	1v	75	Y	5 years	OK
Zinc-air	1.4v	1.25v	0.9v	400	N	See text	OK

There are three voltage figures listed in Table 9-1. The *maximum voltage* of a cell is the most voltage that a cell is likely to put out, often called the nominal voltage. In most cases, this is somewhat higher than the voltage that we'll see in real use. The *typical voltage* is the voltage that we'll more likely see from a cell during its midlife when it's used in the types of applications that suit it. The *discharge cutoff voltage* is the point at which batteries using that chemistry are typically declared to be dead. In the old days, we ran products until they stopped working or got flaky, which is how we knew the batteries were dead or dying. Today it's common to use voltage regulators that compensate for declining voltage due to discharge, but batteries can be damaged if we let them run *too* low: we need to know when enough's enough and shut things down, usually at roughly the discharge cutoff voltage.

Specific energy is a measure of how much energy a battery can hold per unit mass. We can see that for different chemistries, the amount of "oomph" a battery packs for a given mass can vary quite a bit! Contemporary battery chemistries hold several times more energy per unit mass compared to the (nasty, leaky) dry-cell batteries that were common when I was a young child (and which are still widely used in some parts of the world today).

Shelf life represents my rough stab at a battery's ability to hold its charge while not in use. All battery types tend to generate electricity at a slower rate even when disconnected from circuits, a property known as *self-discharge*. If they sit around for a long-enough time, their charge will be diminished or they'll go dead. This is another area where different chemistries can vary greatly. In datasheets, this parameter is usually specified as percentage change in charge per month, or similar. As mentioned earlier, this rate can vary dramatically with temperature: lower temperatures mean longer shelf life.

Zinc-Air batteries are an unusual case, and actually have two shelf-life ratings: they last for years until activated by exposure to air (e.g., pulling off a tab that exposes the chemistry to air), and then they self-discharge to cut off in a short time (usually days).

Safety pertains to thermal hazards (overheating, explosion, fire) or poisoning the environment. Lithium-based rechargeable batteries can pose significant thermal/venting/explosion hazards if defective or treated improperly. And while most batteries contain substances that are not exactly health foods, the cadmium in NiCd batteries is extremely toxic.

NiCds are now unwelcome in many countries because of their disposal hazard, a topic discussed in more depth in Chapter 10.

Also, like all small parts, batteries can also present a choking hazard to children, but this is not considered in Table 9-1's safety column.

Let's now take a tour of each of these chemistries to get a feel for what we can expect from batteries that utilize them.

Disposable (primary cell) chemistries

While disposable cells produce more waste than rechargeables, until recently they were the clear choice for certain applications due to a combination of high energy density, low self-discharge rate, and convenience: we can find disposables at every drug and convenience store, and they're fully charged (or nearly so) when taken from the package. Pop 'em in and we're ready to go. When they die, there's no waiting hours for a recharge: we just replace them and we're up and running again in a minute.

Next, let's take a quick look at the salient characteristics of disposable-battery chemistries currently in widespread use.

ZINC CARBON. These are old-school disposable batteries sometimes called *dry cells*, the kind of batteries that were popular in the US until the 1980s or so and are still relatively common in other parts of the world. They are cheap and have generally poor characteristics to match their price. They also have a tendency to leak.

These are available in the "standard" sizes from AAAA to 9V. Try to avoid them.

ALKALINE. *Alkaline* is the popular name for Zn/MnO_2 chemistry, which is used in most contemporary disposable cells. Years of tweaking this technology has yielded batteries that pack a good punch and have a good shelf life, with no bad surprises other than occasional leakage. They are available in the standard sizes from AAAA to 9V, as well as in button/coin cells. Great batteries, other than not being rechargeable.[*]

LITHIUM DISPOSABLES. Lithium-based batteries, both disposables and rechargeables, hold a good bit of energy for their size. A fair number of

---

[*] Specialized alkaline rechargeables were available at one time, but never caught on due to various quirks.

disposable lithium battery types are available with different form factors (sizes/shapes) and chemistries (Li/MnO$_2$, Li/FeS$_2$, etc.).

Lithium manganese oxide (Li/MnO$_2$) is the most popular disposable lithium chemistry. It typically runs at 3V in use, holds a lot of energy for its size, can supply a lot of current (power) when needed (depending on the size of the cell it's in), and has very low self-discharge—it can sit on a shelf for decades. In other words, it's an awesome chemistry for disposable batteries.

Most lithium-based coin cells, such as the popular CR2032, use LiMnO$_2$. CR2032s (and the even-thinner CR2025s and CR-2016s) are commonly used for a range of applications that require low current and long life (because of their small size, CR2032s cannot supply high currents). Typical uses include battery backup for real-time clocks and small devices such as activity trackers.

Disposable CR123As, which are a bit smaller and wider than AA batteries (Figure 9-3), are also made from LiMnO$_2$. These can supply pretty significant current, making them suitable for cameras and small flashlights.

FIGURE 9-3. Rechargeable 18650, flanked by disposable CR123A (left) and AA (right) batteries

One issue with Li/MnO_2 batteries is that they cannot directly replace alkaline cells due to the difference in voltage. If we try hard, we *can* actually find $LiMnO_2$ batteries in standard alkaline sizes like AA and so forth, but due to the substantial voltage difference between the chemistries, this can cause big problems if users substitute them for same-sized alkalines. Another lithium chemistry, lithium iron disulfide (Li/FeS_2), provides a voltage that's about the same as alkaline cells; it is available in standard alkaline cell sizes, and can usually serve as a higher-quality substitute for alkalines. Li/FeS_2 batteries provide about the same total charge as alkalines at a higher price, but they have a lower internal resistance that does not change appreciably as the battery discharges, leading to much better performance in high-current and pulsed applications. They also have very low self-discharge, with an impressive shelf life of 20 years or so, making them a good choice for emergency lighting and other standby applications.

If we move into oddball and custom battery types, a large number of other disposable lithium chemistries are available. For example, most cardiac pacemakers use lithium-iodide batteries that are extremely reliable with very low self-discharge. It's important that they operate reliably for years, since a pacemaker failure can mean a very bad day for a patient, and replacing batteries involves the use of a scalpel.

Lithium/Carbon monofluoride (Li/CF) batteries operate at temperatures somewhat lower and higher than lithium manganese oxides, albeit with slightly reduced capacity and voltage. For example, BR2032s using LiCFs are available as substitutes for CR2032s in more extreme temperatures.

ZINC AIR. Zinc air batteries can provide tremendous energy for their size, but that energy must be used quickly. Cells come sealed against the air and are thus inactive, but when exposed to air they provide power within seconds, and lots of it. However, once activated they also self-discharge rapidly, and are spent in a few days. Figure 9-4 shows a common zinc-air cell, without and with the factory tab that covers the air holes. Zinc airs are commonly used for hearing aids, and nothing else to my knowledge. (I've been hoping to find another good use for them for years because they're so interesting, but have not hit on something yet.)

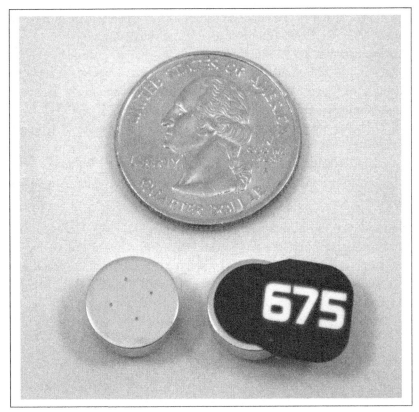

FIGURE 9-4. 675 zinc-air cell, without and with tab covering holes

Rechargeable (secondary cell) chemistries

Some battery chemical reactions are reversible: if we inject current back into the cell, the reaction reverses, turning a spent cell back into a charged cell. This, of course, is the process of recharging.

Recharging can be a somewhat tricky operation, more than just applying a voltage across the battery terminals. It would be great if batteries recharged instantly, but experience tells us that this doesn't happen. Just how quickly we *can* charge is governed by a battery's chemistry and other factors, such as how well we can get rid of heat generated by the battery and charging circuits during the process—charging is not 100% efficient (although it's pretty close for some chemistries), and wasted energy ends up as heat. Also, we need to know when to stop charging a battery or we risk battery damage or other bad consequences (e.g., heat and fire).

Rechargeables can also exhibit "interesting" behaviors depending on how deeply they tend to be discharged before being recharged. Some chemistries exhibit a *memory effect*, whereby if we normally only partially discharge a battery before recharging, the battery will begin to permanently lose capacity. Other chemistries can become very unhappy if allowed to discharge too much, which can lead to shortened lifespan or heating/fire depending on the depth of discharge. Be careful!

NICKEL CADMIUM (NICD). NiCds were the first popular rechargeable batteries, but they have fallen out of favor for a number of reasons. Compared to newer technologies, NiCds hold much less charge for a given size and have high self-discharge. They are also more prone to the memory effect than other rechargeables. The nail in their coffin is that cadmium is a highly toxic metal, and its use is very limited or banned outright in EU countries (for more information, see Chapter 10). Not recommended for new designs.

NICKEL METAL HYDRIDE (NIMH). NiMH batteries are the most popular rechargeable replacements for disposable batteries in the standard AAA–9V sizes. Capacity is a *bit* lower than alkalines for a given size, but internal resistance is also lower and remains fairly constant during discharge, giving better performance in higher-drain and pulsed applications.

Standard NiMH batteries have very high self-discharge, with a shelf life of only months. NiMHs using newer technologies, known as *low self-discharge* (LSD) devices, can maintain an appreciable charge for years. Eneloops by Sanyo are perhaps the best known of the LSDs, but most other major battery manufacturers have begun making them, too.

NiMHs are mainly used as replacements for disposable batteries, recharged in an external charger purchased by the user rather than within the product they power. However, if we did want to charge cells within our product, battery management and gas gauge chips are available (more on gas gauges later) that accommodate NiMHs. In fact, NiMHs power most hybrid electric cars (those that run on gasoline and electricity) today.

All in all, NiMH batteries are capable and well behaved, particularly the LSD devices.

One other note on NiMH batteries: because NiMHs are particularly good at heavier loads, it's tempting to design NiMH C or D cells into high-current applications. *Beware! NiMH Cs and Ds are typically just NiMH AA batteries with a fat jacket on them, and thus have only a fraction of true C or D capacity.* This is true of all the familiar brands that I've dealt with, although other lesser-known brands like Tenergy do provide true NiMH cells in these larger sizes. Always check capacity in the datasheet of the specific battery you're purchasing. And beware that while your product might ship with true NiMH Cs or Ds, customers buying spare batteries might get the "wimpy" versions and have a bad experience.

LEAD ACID. Invented more than 160 years ago, lead acid batteries are the oldest type of rechargeable. They're still ubiquitous, found in virtually every fossil-fuel-burning vehicle and *uninterruptible power supply* (UPS). Lead acids have a few characteristics that make them particularly suitable for these applications, and others such as solar grid storage:

- Inexpensive given the amount of charge they hold
- Can deliver a lot of energy quickly
- Comparatively good performance at cold temperatures
- Low self-discharge
- Easy to recharge
- Can stay topped-off indefinitely through trickle charging
- Very tolerant of abuse

They also weigh a lot and are filled with lead, although it's said that 98% of all battery lead in the US ends up being recycled.

Because of these characteristics, lead acids are best suited to high-current applications where they might sit idle (or trickle charging) for long periods of time, and where weight is not a critical factor.

LITHIUM ION (LI-ION AND LIPO)

Lithium ion (Li-ion) batteries, which actually comprise a family of rechargeable lithium chemistries, provide the greatest rechargeable capacity for a given weight. Their great capacity and the ability to manufacture them in thin space-saving forms make them the predominant choice to power most cell phones, tablets, and laptop computers. Lithium ions are also preferred over NiMHs for "pure" electric (as opposed to electric-gas hybrid) vehicles. Lithium ions cost twice as much to store the same amount of energy, but are comparatively much lighter.

Lithium ions are also fussy and expensive. Most notably, compared to other rechargeables, they're relatively easy to damage through improper use, and have the potential to get quite hot, burn, or even explode when they fail. Grab some popcorn and search the Web for "lithium ion explode" to find some videos of what can happen, and think about selling a product that does *those things* every once in a while. And it really can happen—even to Boeing, whose 787 aircraft were grounded for months due to burning lithium ion batteries. Boeing's Li-ions save 40 pounds per aircraft but also ended up costing hundreds of millions of dollars in repair costs and lost revenue.

To be fair, burning Li-ions are a rarity, but it does happen on occasion and caution is very important. Unless we have the ability to use them properly and safely—which includes issues of technology, supply chain, and manufacturing—we should consider other battery technologies.

Another issue of some concern is that Li-ions can supply a lot of current in a short time. Sometimes this is a good thing, such as when we want our Tesla to beat a Corvette in a drag race. But it also can supply lots of current to circuits that fail, which can cause *those* circuits to do bad thermal things. Designing to limit current to reasonable rates can mitigate this potential hazard.

The most common lithium ion chemistry is *lithium cobalt* (LCO) because it has the greatest specific energy. Lithium cobalt is used in most cell phones, tablets, and laptops. As luck would have it, lithium cobalt is also the chemistry that's most sensitive to mishandling.

Other common lithium ion chemistries include *lithium iron phosphate* (LiFe or LFP), *lithium nickel manganese cobalt* (NMC), and *lithium nickel cobalt aluminum* (NCA). These trade some capacity in exchange for safety, and are primarily used for electric vehicles and other high-power applications.

The vast bulk of lithium ion batteries available today for nonvehicle applications are LCOs, so that's what we'll focus on here. But know that other chemistries exist, and they have different characteristics that need to be handled differently by circuitry, and that blindly swapping one chemistry for another is a *serious* no-no.

Physically, lithium ion batteries come in two basic flavors: "standard" and lithium polymer (LiPo). The two use the same chemistry and are pretty similar in performance, with the basic difference being that LiPos can be made into thinner and more-irregular shapes. Standard Li-ions are normally used for higher-current applications—think motors and flashlights—while LiPos dominate in low-current uses such as cell phones and tablets.

> **TIP** For the remainder of this chapter, we'll refer to "standard" lithium ion batteries as *standard Li-ions*, Lithium polymer batteries as *LiPos*, and simply use *Li-ion* to mean either of these two types interchangeably.

Standard Li-ions are cylindrical, the most common size being the *x*R18650 (shown in Figure 9-5), where x is the letter that represents the battery chemistry per the IEC 60086 standard. As the name indicates, 18650s are 18 mm wide by 65 mm high and look like oversized AA cells. 18650s pack a nice little punch: the Panasonic NCR18650B, for example, is a CR18650 with a capacity of 3350 mAh at 3.6V. 3.35A × 3.6V = 12.1 watt hours, which is more than three times the energy stored in an alkaline AA battery, in a package that's only twice an AA's volume. So we get roughly 50% more power for its size compared to an alkaline AA, with the added benefit of being rechargeable.

FIGURE 9-5. "Protected CR18650" (center) flanked by two unprotected cells

18650s are commonly used for higher-current applications, and usually in packs. Most laptop computer battery packs are composed of between four and nine 18650s. Plug-in electric cars also use 18650s—thousands per car.

18650s are available as single cells and in battery packs. Since 18650 refers to the cell's size and not the chemistry, all 18650s are most certainly not interchangeable. All of the common Li-ion chemistries just described are available as 18650s, and each has a different voltage range, capacity, and charging requirements. 18650s are also available with built-in protection circuitry (see again Figure 9-5), which elongates and fattens them a bit so they *technically* become 19670s, but will still usually be called *protected 18650s*. Using protected cells is an easy way to ensure safety, and I highly recommend them in most situations rather than designing your own protection.

In contrast to standard Li-ions, LiPos (see Figure 9-6) are typically quite thin and roughly rectangular. Rather than being enclosed in a hard shell, the LiPo's "guts" are enclosed in a thin plastic pouch with two or three wires coming off the battery into a small connector, as shown in Figure 9-6. These plastic pouches are not particularly puncture- or water-resistant, but are sufficient if the battery is sealed within the product enclosure (as in the iPhone, for example). Just glue, tape, or wedge the battery into place and close the lid.

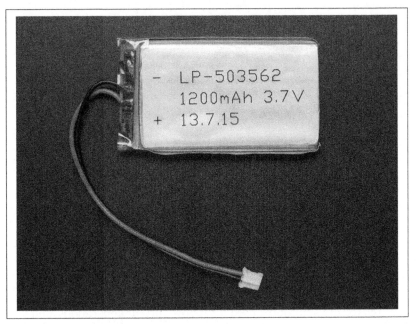

FIGURE 9-6. Typical LiPo battery (photo courtesy of Adafruit)

If a LiPo battery is user-replaceable, as in many models of smart phones, then it normally needs a hard shell around it for protection, with built-in connector contacts that mate with the device, as shown in Figure 9-7 and Figure 9-8.

FIGURE 9-7. LiPo in hard-shell case, showing connector

FIGURE 9-8. Detail of LiPo mating connector (battery not fully inserted)

As far as I know, there's no standardization in LiPo sizes. Basically we find one from a reliable manufacturer that fits in the space we'd like or order a custom unit. The good news is that hundreds of off-the-shelf sizes are available so it's usually easy to find something that fits. The bad news is that most off-the-shelf LiPos are manufactured by a slew of smaller companies so finding one we can be confident in can be a challenge. In larger volumes, custom sizes from an established manufacturer are the way to go.

Perhaps the most interesting aspect of dealing with Li-ions is in charging them, which we'll look at next.

Charging lithium ions

Assuming that the batteries we select are designed and manufactured correctly, the charging process determines quite a bit about how our battery performs—the time it takes to charge, the run time of our product on a charge, the life expectancy of the battery (before it needs replacement), the environment in which it can be charged (e.g., can it charge in a car sitting in the sun?), and potentially whether our battery is safe or not.

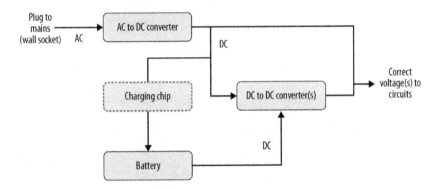

To make things both easier and more realistic, we'll assume in this section that we're using a specialized battery-charge chip to control charging. While it's possible (and tempting) to design charging circuitry and charging algorithms ourselves, in practice I've never seen it done successfully in a product. Even high-volume products such as smart phones use off-the-shelf battery-charge chips in all cases that I know of.

Also, a little jargon that's useful to know:

- C is a current value related to a battery's capacity, stated in mA or A. If a battery is rated at 1000 mAh, C=1000 mA, i.e., we just drop the "h" from "mAh" (or from "Ah"). 1C is used to denote charge current relative to a battery's capacity, as in "we found that, compared to charging at 0.5C, charging at 0.6C reduced charge time by 15 minutes." In this way, we know how to scale the current for batteries of different capacities that are otherwise similar.

- *State of charge* (SoC) is a battery's remaining capacity, in %. A fully charged battery's SoC is 100%, and a battery that's fully discharged is at 0%.

Li-ions are charged in several distinct phases, as shown in Figure 9-9. If a Li-ion's charge is below 3.0V, the cell is either deeply discharged or no longer usable. In either case, charging at full current won't work and can even cause problems. Instead, a small trickle charge of about 10% of the full charge current (*Ic* in Figure 9-9) is applied. This current is applied until either the cell reaches 3.0V, or the charger chip determines that the cell is bad because voltage is not increasing (at which point it will turn off the current and indicate an error).

Between 3.0V and 4.2V, a constant current of Ic is pushed through the battery and the applied voltage exceeds 4.2V to maintain that current. State of charge rises rapidly at this stage, and the voltage across the battery rises until it hits 4.2V, which is the cell's peak safe voltage. If charging goes beyond 4.2V, damage can ensue, so we switch to a new charging phase where we provide a constant 4.2V. SoC continues to increase although more slowly. Current drawn by the battery drops as SoC increases until it drops beneath a threshold of perhaps 5% of Ic, at which point charging stops.

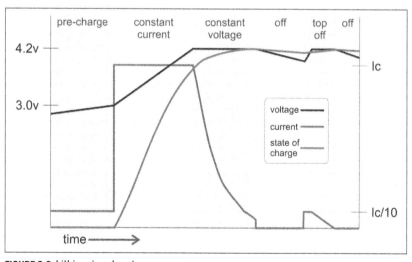

FIGURE 9-9. Lithium ion charging process

Li-ions have appreciable self-discharge, so if we simply stop charging and some time passes before the battery's needed, state of charge might be significantly below 100%. Unlike some other chemistries, lithium ions don't respond well to a simple constant trickle charge to keep them at 100%. Instead, battery voltage is monitored until it falls beneath some threshold, and the recharge process is restarted. This process is known as a *topping charge*.

We've been describing an abstract charging current of Ic, but how large should Ic be? The proper Ic is typically in the range of 0.5–1.0 C. So for a battery rated at 1000 mAh, Ic should be in the 500–1000 mA range. It turns out that the higher the Ic, the faster the battery will reach 4.2V. However, there's a gotcha: batteries charged at a higher Ic have a relatively lower charge when they hit 4.2V, so the constant voltage phase lasts somewhat longer. The total charge time will still be lower than at a lower Ic, but not as low as we might expect due to the longer constant voltage phase. Rapid charging also reduces battery life, sometimes substantially, so it's best to charge at closer to 0.5C unless you really need the shorter charge time.

All told, Li-ion batteries will typically charge from 0%–100% state of charge in 2–3 hours if we have enough power available. Longer times can happen if we cannot supply all of the current we'd like, such as if we're charging a large Li-ion battery using a low-current USB charger as the power source. Shorter charge times come from charging to a lower voltage (good reasons to do this are discussed shortly), or charging at a higher current.

Interestingly, self-heating of charging Li-ions is typically not a problem. Lithium ion batteries are very efficient at charging, and the chemical process actually cools the cell a bit, which offsets any heat from inefficiencies in the cell. Cell heating really only becomes notable when a battery is discharging, particularly when it's almost fully discharged.

While heat from the *battery* isn't a big issue, heat from *charger circuitry* can be a significant problem if we're not careful because a lot of energy moves into the battery during charging, and any inefficiency in the charging circuit (say, by using a linear voltage regulator) can create significant heat. Later in this chapter, we'll take a look at ways to keep power sources efficient to keep the heat down.

Increasing Li-ion life

Lithium ion batteries wear over time and eventually need replacement. There are a number of actions we can take to greatly prolong a battery's service life. Depending on certain tradeoffs around charging and discharging, lifespan can range from several hundred to several thousand discharge/charge cycles. Since these batteries are often sealed in devices, dead batteries can be a significant in terms of cost and/or customer satisfaction, so longevity is definitely worth considering.

Specifications for battery capacity usually assume that charging is to maximum capacity so that manufacturers can claim the biggest number possible. Unfortunately, longevity suffers when we charge to this maximum capacity. Let's look at some tradeoffs between lifespan versus other performance parameters that we can control via our design.

Discharging

Lithium ion cells don't like to discharge all the way. Shutting off batteries, say, when they're at 25% of capacity rather than 0% of capacity can increase battery cycle life by 50% or so. Of course we're getting 25% less energy from the cell during each cycle, but there's still a net benefit in terms of total energy discharged over the cell's lifetime.

Charging

Lithium ion cells also don't like to charge all the way. While 4.2V is the safe limit for charging, cells are actually a good deal happier at 4.1V or below. By limiting charge to 4.1V rather than 4.2V, we can double cycle life while dropping capacity by only 15% or so—an even better bargain than limiting depth of discharge. Limiting voltage to 4.0V doubles cycle life again while dropping capacity a total of 25%.

Rates

Charge and discharge rates also affect longevity. Charging above 1C will significantly diminish cycle life, with 0.7C normally being preferred. Discharge above 1C will also diminish cycle life. In some cases, it pays to move to a slightly higher-capacity battery to reduce the C values for a given charge time and discharge rate, and thus increase cycle life.

Temperature

Lithium ion batteries are specified to charge in the temperature range of 0 to 45°C, and operate in the range of –20 to 60°C. Many batteries, particularly LiPos, have an embedded thermistor (temperature sensor) coming out to a third connector pin that charge chips and other battery management chips use to enforce this range (i.e., they shut off if things get too hot). These seem like pretty reasonable ranges until we consider situations such as a GPS in a parked car—on a warm, sunny day, the interior of a parked car can go well above 45°C in the US, and above 60°C in some other countries.

It also turns out that the 45°C upper limit for charging is tolerable for batteries but fairly stressful. Their lives are prolonged by staying under 30°C. Unfortunately, we don't usually have much control over charging temperature.

Evaluating whether these tradeoffs are worthwhile is highly dependent on our application. For example, smart phone owners might prefer an extra 25% of usage per charge in exchange for needing to buy a new battery in one year instead of two, particularly if the batteries are user-replaceable and inexpensive. On the other hand, if our product is a remote sensing station that recharges daily by solar energy, we'll likely want to increase service life by using a somewhat larger battery that doesn't need to charge to maximum capacity.

How we implement these tradeoffs depends on the specifics of our circuits and application. For example, charging cutoff voltage is a fixed value within some charging chips, while in others it's programmed in one of the chip's registers. Or we might monitor and control the chip from a processor. The important thing is to understand what we want to do, and then to select an architecture that will do it.

Have you ever noticed that most smart phones come with their battery charged halfway? Next we'll look at why that is, and answer some other questions about battery storage.

Storage

A common and sometimes-nasty surprise for first-time uses of lithium ion cells is that they lose capacity, not just charge, if they sit unused in storage. The situation is worse for batteries stored at a higher state of charge and at higher temperatures. For example, a fully charged cell stored in a hot 60°C warehouse can permanently lose 40% of its capacity in just three months. Our 2600 mAh 18650 magically turned into a 1600 mAh model in just three months—it will never again store more than 1600 mAh of energy.

By contrast, storing a half-charged battery at a little above 0°C yields a capacity drop of only 2% over the same three months—still a little depressing, but much better. Best bet for storage is to charge batteries to a 50% state of charge, and store at just 0°C. Since batteries self-discharge, if the batteries remain in storage it's a good idea to follow up by recharging back to 50% every six months or so.

Even better, buy fresh cells from a quality manufacturer just before they're needed.

Most smart devices these days can be adequately powered with a single Li-ion cell, which is what we've been considering up to now. But higher-powered devices, such as laptop computers and robotic vacuum cleaners, tend to be powered by multiple cells. Like most things involving Li-ions, there are some tricks around putting multiple cells together, which we'll cover next.

Multiple-cell batteries

It's common for standard lithium ion batteries to come in packs with multiple cells in parallel and/or serial. Putting cells in parallel is a pretty trivial exercise—they are happy charging and discharging together in this configuration. The one thing to be thoughtful of is that if a discharged cell is put in parallel with a charged cell, their voltages might be different by more than a volt. This can cause a large current draw over a short period of time, with the potential for various sorts of mayhem. Best bet is to buy battery packs with the cells already connected in parallel. Next-best option is to charge cells individually so that they're at the same voltage, and then pair them together.

Cells in serial are a bit trickier. To work properly, they must be *balanced* before assembly, which is a fancy way of saying that they need to all be at the same state of charge. A discussion of balancing and some of the other subtleties of using serial cells is beyond the scope of this book, but there are some good references on the subject; one of these is Elithion's site at Li-ionbms.com.

So how do we measure state of charge if we want to balance batteries (infrequently) or even just to know how much charge is left? Let's take a look.

Measuring state of charge

It's useful for a product to have an indication of battery charge remaining, and users have come to expect this. The indication can be as sophisticated as a percentage value on a screen and an estimate of remaining time until discharge, or as simple as an LED that turns yellow when there's about 30 minutes of runtime left.

Measuring state of charge is nontrivial in Li-ions. The first instinct of many design engineers is to attempt it by measuring voltage, but this is not a good way to go: battery voltage isn't linear with SoC, and it changes based on load, temperature, and battery age.

The most common way to measure SoC is a method known as *coulomb counting*, which consists of tracking how many electrons go into a battery and how many come out.

> **TIP** A coulomb is a quantity of electrons, roughly 6.24×10^{18}. One amp delivers one coulomb of electrons each second, so the way we measure coulombs is to actually measure current going in and out.

The basic principle is as follows: we start with a battery that's at a known SoC, typically the point at which it's just been discharged down to its cutoff voltage. SoC at this point is 0. We then charge the battery, counting coulombs as we go, until it reaches the full-charge cutoff current, by definition a 100% SoC. We now know how many coulombs the battery holds: the amount we pushed into it to go from 0% to 100%. If we continue counting coulombs flowing in and out of the battery, in principle we'll always know SoC.

Coulomb counting is normally accomplished using specialized chips known as battery *gas gauges* or *fuel gauges*. Coulomb counting is a pretty good technique for monitoring state of charge, but it's not perfect. The reality is that batteries change with time and usage, so coulomb counting can only provide us with an estimate of SoC. The only time we absolutely *know* a battery's SoC is when we hit either our discharge cutoff voltage (0%) or charge cutoff current (100%). Gas gauge chips simply contain some smarts to help do a better job of estimating SoC based on their internal models of battery behavior.

One downside of coulomb counting is that we need a full discharge/charge cycle to know the coulombs needed to go from 0% to 100%; running each manufactured unit through a full cycle at the factory takes time and money. The good news is that while even batteries of the same make and model will vary in capacity, the variation usually won't be large. So, as an alternative to determining the capacity of each battery, many gas gauges can be programmed during the product manufacturing process with an average capacity, eliminating the need for a full cycle for each device. The scheme is generally:

- Discharge the batteries until battery-discharge cutoff on several sample units of our product.

- Charge these units until full-charge cutoff. At this point, each gas gauge will have calculated several constants (e.g., coulombs contained by a fully charged battery, offset voltages, etc.), which it will use to determine state of charge in the future.

- Read the calculated constants from each gas gauge (usually as registers via the processor in our product which connects to the gauge), and average together the instances of each parameter. We now have the average constants for our device.

- During manufacturing, we program these average constants into each gas gauge.

As it comes off the manufacturing line, each unit now has a set of constants that are more-or-less correct, and will get even better as the purchaser charges and discharges the unit. As mentioned earlier, every device is *somewhat* different (which is why we average several devices), but for the same product they're all typically pretty similar to one another unless we make a product change, such as using different batteries.

Once we've programmed our gas gauge during manufacturing, we're still not quite all set: when the gas gauge is mated with the battery, the gauge still needs to know the battery's true state of charge at a single point in time, and then it can start estimating charge as it counts coulombs going in and out. There are a couple of ways to handle this.

Since we know that the battery's SoC is 100% when we're at the full-charge cutoff current, we can charge the battery until it's at 100% SoC and then start counting coulombs from that point. A clever way to do this is to ask purchasers to charge their new unit for some period of time (say, four hours) before its first use, which ensures that we'll hit 100% SoC. This isn't ideal, but it's much more palatable than asking a user to fully charge and then also fully discharge the device before they can have an accurate battery reading, which we'd need to do if our gas gauge didn't have programmed constants. There's also another good reason for asking consumers to do an initial full charge. As discussed before, batteries should be stored at about roughly half-charge, so filling the battery prior to first use will give a better first impression of battery life.

A second way to determine SoC from a newly mated battery and programmed gas gauge is to use the battery's *no-load* voltage to get an estimate. We can get a pretty reasonable estimate if we know that the battery is fresh and unloaded. This has the advantage of being ready to use without further charging and/or discharging to a known SoC. Texas Instruments' impedance track devices use this technique.

Since the gas gauges learn (update their saved constants) over time, they can make corrections to their constants as batteries change with use, to account for variations in our circuitry and usage. Corrections are usually made when the battery becomes fully charged or discharged based on cutoff voltages.

Coulomb counting gets us much of the way toward accurate SoC prediction, but there are a few other "gotchas" that can throw it off track. First, battery capacity changes with temperature. Some gas gauges measure temperature either at the gauge or at the battery, and correct their estimates as warranted.

Self-discharge presents a trickier issue. If a battery-powered device isn't used for a few weeks, its SoC will drop by some amount, but since this charge didn't flow out of the battery through its terminals, coulomb counting won't pick it up. If our gauge has the ability to makes reasonable estimates based on open-circuit voltage as discussed earlier, that can help. For devices that are typically charged daily, such as smart phones, this is not an important issue. But is worth considering for devices that might sit idle for longer periods of time or which need very accurate estimates.

Beyond creating a good circuit, there are a few process issues that stem from the need to program constants into each gas gauge chip:

- We need a way to program the parts during manufacturing, or to have them programmed by the gas gauge manufacturer or distributor. Seems obvious, but sometimes this is forgotten until late in the game. Two possibilities are programming while doing in-circuit testing (ICT, discussed back in Chapter 6) or putting constants into FLASH or ROM to be programmed by an onboard processor at first bootup.

- We must account for battery replacements unless units will simply be disposed of when batteries fail. As a battery ages, its constants will change and be updated on its gas gauge. If we suddenly mate a fresh battery to an "old" gas gauge chip, SoC readings can be significantly wrong, at least until we do charge/discharge cycle. The solution could be as simple as having the repair depot or customer run through a procedure after battery replacement. Another possibility is to package the gas gauge in the replaceable battery pack, thus replacing the battery also replaces the gas gauge.

- If we start using a new model of battery or the model we're using gets updated by the manufacturer, the constants that we're programming will need to change as well. Possibilities for avoiding surprises include change notification from the battery's manufacturer and sampling batteries from each new lot that's purchased.

To sum up SoC monitoring:

1. Don't use battery voltage alone. Use a gas gauge chip.
2. Coulomb counting works well for most applications.
3. More sophisticated (and expensive) technologies such as TI's impedance track are available for applications that need it.
4. More so than with most other parts of a design, it's important to account for manufacturing and maintenance issues.

We're getting close to the end of our exploration of batteries, but there's one more topic that's particularly interesting: supply chain.

Safety and supply chain

Given the capability of Li-ion batteries to cause mayhem, they often receive close scrutiny when products are tested for safety by third-party test and certification houses (e.g., UL as discussed in Chapter 1 and more fully in Chapter 10). The easiest way to deal with this is to use cells that contain internal protection and are UL-approved. This gets our own circuitry off the hook, as no matter what we do with the battery (other than accidentally baking it), we should stay safe. The alternative is to use an unprotected battery and demonstrate that our system always keeps it safe during charging and discharging at different currents over the battery's life cycle, which is a nontrivial thing to do.

More than for most other parts, it's important to be careful of the supply chain for batteries. Counterfeits abound, usually with compromised quality and safety compared to name brands. A quick search on the Internet will find all sorts of amusing stuff, like 18650s that are actually a teeny LiPo and a lot of white powder in an 18650-sized tube, and more. Be careful.

This marks the end of our look at the selection, care, and feeding of batteries. Next we'll take a look at using power from wall outlets, the other major source of power for products.

Wall Outlets: AC-to-DC Power Conversion

Compared to batteries, wall outlets offer a stable source of virtually limitless power for most applications, but they do present a few new challenges right off the bat:

- Wall power is alternating current (AC), but our circuits want direct current (DC), and usually at several different voltages.

- Wall power differs between countries with regard to its voltage, frequency, and the physical wall plug needed for access.

- Wall power packs sufficient energy to cause fire and/or injury in normal operation.

There are usually two major bits of circuitry that are used to convert from wall power to the DC power needed by each chip. First we convert from wall AC to a single DC voltage. Next, we convert that DC voltage to the other various DC voltages we need. In this section, we'll focus on the first step, and then we'll tackle DC-DC conversion in our next section.

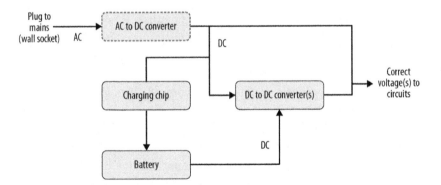

Designing circuitry and physical hardware to convert wall power to DC is a bit of a schlep. The good news is that nowadays it's pretty easy and inexpensive to purchase off-the-shelf solutions that handle this task for us, so in this section we'll concentrate on going this route rather than designing from scratch. Unless our volumes are very high or our needs are unusual (e.g., high current), off-the-shelf solutions are the way to go.

The most ubiquitous off-the-shelf solutions today are USB chargers (a.k.a adapters or power supplies). As seen in Figure 9-10, these consist of a little plastic box with power prongs (known as a *wall wart*) that plugs into an outlet. The wall wart exposes DC power either through a permanently attached cord that terminates in some variety of USB micro- or mini-B connector, or else has a USB A jack so we can add a cable with whatever USB B connector type and cable length that we'd like.

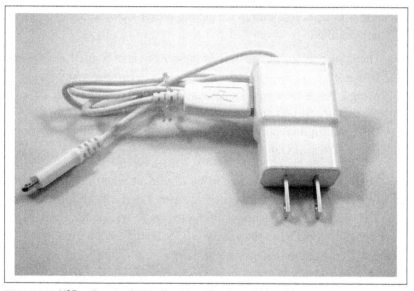

FIGURE 9-10. USB wall wart, which is the (almost) universal AC to DC converter

The USB 2.0 standard that's currently in widespread use calls for ports and chargers to supply 5V DC. 500 mA is pretty typical current capacity for USB chargers, but capacities close to 2 A are readily available. The USB 3.1 standard, which is announced but not yet in use, supports higher currents and voltages up to 5 A at 20V, or 10 times the power of USB 2.0.

> TIP Just a reminder: ampere (A, or amp) is a unit that represents a certain rate of electricity (current), defined as 1 A = 1 coulomb/s = 6.24×10^{18} electrons per second. 1 milliamp (mA) is one one-thousandth of an amp.

The advantages of using USB chargers are many:

- Almost every cell phone powers from USB as do many, many other devices. Most people already have one or more USB chargers, and users can buy a new one from virtually any store that carries technology products should they need a replacement or spare.

- Because of their ubiquity, USB chargers are available from innumerable manufacturers and competitive pressures lead to low prices.

- USB power adapters are also available for standard car power outlets, which instantly makes a new power source available to our customers. Non-USB possibilities for getting power from car outlets are fairly limited.

- The USB port our device uses for power can also be used as an actual USB port. If we need to communicate with a computer anyway, using a single USB port for both charging and communications saves the cost of adding a second connector. But beware that using the USB port for dual purposes can also lead to some design complexity that we'll discuss later in this chapter.

There are also a few issues to be careful of when going with USB power. Foremost is that USB chargers are not perfectly simple to design for. The USB standard defines different ways to use power from a USB port depending on what the source is. Three different source types are defined, all using the same connector:

- *Standard downstream ports* (SDPs) typically found in older computers and hubs

- *Charging downstream ports* (CDPs) found in newer computers and hubs that can support higher-current devices

- *Dedicated charging ports* (DCPs), which are dumb wall warts

The official rules for determining the type of device we're plugged into and how to draw power from it are found in the USB Battery Charging Specification (*http://www.usb.org/developers/powerdelivery/*). An easier-to-read description with some good real-world advice can be found on Maxim (*http://bit.ly/1OTF4lI*). As discussed in the Maxim white paper, the USB standard is often violated by makers of computers, peripherals, and power supplies. Make sure to do your homework, and test your device against a range of wall warts and computers during development.

The other important limitation of USB power is that micro B connectors, which are in common use today (e.g., the USB connector in all smart phones other than Apple's), are only specified to pass 1800 mA (9 watts) of power. Wall warts are available that supply more than this but it's not a good idea to tempt fate—it's always best to stay within the specs.

Moving beyond USB power, many other external AC-to-DC power supplies are available. DigiKey alone lists thousands, in all sorts of output voltages, current capacities, and plug configurations. Devices are available that supply multiple DC voltages, which seems like a good idea because we usually ultimately *need* multiple DC voltages. In my experience, these are not often used for devices built in significant volumes—the devices and connectors tend to be large and unwieldy, and it can be difficult to find a unit that supplies the right combination of voltages at the right currents. For low-volume projects that don't need to look beautiful, these can sometimes work out quite well.

If a lot of power is needed and the product is relatively large, we might want to move to an internal AC-to-DC converter (a converter that lives inside our product enclosure) rather than use a big and clunky external supply. Internal supplies are available in open-frame (unenclosed; see Figure 9-11) and enclosed configurations, and in a wide range of output voltages and currents. One disadvantage of going with an internal converter is that we have to work with potentially dangerous line voltage within our product, rather than only having inherently safer isolated DC from an external converter.

FIGURE 9-11. Commercial open-frame AC-DC power supply module (credit: CUI Inc.)

When selecting an external (or internal) power supply, it's important to plan for the localities into which our product will be sold. With regard to voltage and frequency differences, some power supplies will only work in one locality, some have a switch for selecting the type of power they'll be plugged in to, and some automatically adapt.

Several options exist to accommodate the different wall plugs used in different localities. Most typically, devices support only a single plug type or have a standard socket to support power cords with different plugs. Some wall warts use an ingenious system with different plugs that snap or slide in to support different localities, which is useful: we can place several options in our product's box and users select the one they need. This adds cost to the power supplies but reduces costs due to needing different product models (with different plugs) for different localities.

Another important benefit of using off-the-shelf AC-DC supplies is that most come with a variety of certifications that fulfill safety and *electromagnetic compatibility* (EMC) regulations; Figure 9-12 shows the label on a typical laptop computer power brick with more than a dozen such certifications. Without these certifications, we'll have to go through the effort of meeting standards and getting certifications ourselves. We should still make sure to know the safety and EMC requirements for each locality we'll be selling our product into, and review potential power solutions to make sure that we're covered to the biggest extent possible.

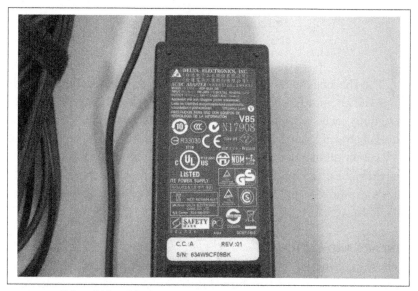

FIGURE 9-12. External AC-to-DC converter showing certifications

As mentioned earlier, once we've converted AC to DC, we'll likely need to convert DC to several DC voltages. Let's now take a look at some ways that's done.

DC-DC Power Conversion

Whether our power source is a battery or an AC-DC converter to a plug in the wall, we'll inevitably need to convert between our source DC voltage(s) and the DC voltages needed by our circuits, and to make sure that these voltages can be supplied cleanly and with sufficient current. It's not unusual to design products comprised of components that require four or more DC voltages to operate correctly. Each of these voltages will be derived from the source DC voltage using a DC-DC converter.

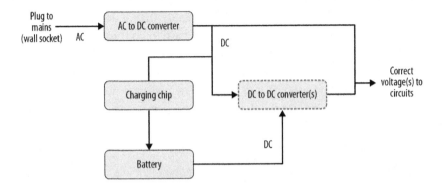

The challenge in DC-DC conversion lies mainly in selecting the right chips and circuits. Once we decide on the conversion chips we'll be using, designing each individual DC-DC converter is straightforward: each is normally based around a chip, and chip makers want us to be successful: they supply all manner of sample schematics, online calculators for component values, and other aids. As long as design engineers read the datasheets carefully—very carefully—and follow their recommendations, all should be well.

LINEARS AND SWITCHERS

Converting between voltages is never a perfectly efficient process — some power is always wasted (i.e., turned into heat). There are two basic types of DC-DC converters (also called *DC-DC regulators*): linears and switchers, which vary substantially in their efficiencies.

Linear power converters can be thought of as "smart resistors" that sit between some input voltage and the lower output voltage we desire. In essence, they always "magically" provide the correct resistance to drop the voltage needed to maintain a setpoint voltage at their output. Since linear converters act as smart resistors, they can only reduce voltage, not increase it.

 A converter's output is often called a *voltage rail*.

For example, if we are converting from 5V to 3V, a linear regulator will vary its resistance so that it always drops 2V. If our 3V rail requires 25mA, the regulator will waste 2V x 25mA = 50mW of energy, and that energy does nothing but heat the air. At least 40% of the energy drawn by our 3V rail from the 5V rail is wasted (i.e., the conversion is less than 60% efficient).

However, if we're decreasing voltage by a small bit, say from 3.3V to 3.0V, things get much better. In this case we'll only waste 0.3V x 25 mA = 7.5 mW of energy at a current of 25 mA, yielding an efficiency of around 90%. So linear regulators work out pretty well for reducing voltages by a small amount, but not as well for large reductions.

Continuous DC voltages can only be converted directly to other DC voltages by reducing them through this sometimes-inefficient linear topology. Changing voltages—in particular DC voltage switched on and off repeatedly—can be converted to lower or higher voltages using energy-storage elements (inductors and capacitors) in a process that wastes no power at all in theory (and very little in practice). Switch-mode converters, usually just called switchers, do exactly this. First a DC input voltage is switched on and off at high frequencies. This amplitude of the switched voltage is increased or decreased, then converted back to steady DC with very little power loss, using inductors and capacitors. The efficiency of this process in practice can reach the 90%–95% range, regardless of the desired change in voltage.

As mentioned, another nice thing about switchers is that they can decrease or increase voltage, while linear converters can only decrease voltage. Switchers that decrease voltage are called *buck* converters, while those that increase voltage are called *boost* converters. Buck and boost converters are different (but similar) circuits.

In many instances, our input voltage to a converter is fixed (for example, 5V from a USB port) so we know whether to use a buck or a boost. But sometimes—particularly when we're dealing with a battery—our input voltage can vary quite a bit. A common scenario is that we have parts that require 3.3V, and we're powering our system from a Li-ion battery that can vary between 4.1 to 3.0 volts during its charge/discharge cycle. Depending on battery voltage, we'll sometimes need a buck, and sometimes a boost. Combination buck/boost converters are available to address these situations, which switch between modes as needed while maintaining high efficiency.

Switchers have tradeoffs, however: they're significantly more complex and expensive than linears, and switching electricity at high frequencies can cause various side effects. In particular, switching tends to cause high-frequency noise in power supplies and signals, and this noise will also radiate into the air (i.e., become a miniature radio station), which might present trouble when we try to pass FCC certification. Careful circuit and PCB design, discussed later in this chapter with references in the Resources section, can mitigate these noise issues.

Table 9-2 summarizes the tradeoffs between linears and switchers.

TABLE 9-2. Linears versus switchers

Linears	Switchers
Less efficient, depending on voltage drop; might need to deal with generated heat	More efficient
Simpler	More complex
Less expensive	More expensive
Can only reduce voltage	Can reduce or increase voltage
Electrically quiet	Electrically noisy

Generally speaking, linear converters tend to be used in situations that require lower supply currents and/or lower voltage drops, and in applications that are sensitive to switching noise or are highly cost-sensitive. Switchers are used in applications that require higher currents and/or higher voltage changes, and are particularly useful in battery-operated devices due to their high efficiency and ability to reduce or boost voltages.

> Switching supplies can be finicky in operation. Datasheets for switchers often include an example circuit including a BOM (components list) that includes specific brand/models, and a PCB layout. It's a good idea to follow these suggestions *to the letter* unless there's a really good reason not to.

Now that we have some grounding in the parts that provide power to our circuits, let's take a look at how we integrate these parts into a holistic, well-behaved system.

System-Level Power Design

Designing each individual power conversion circuit is pretty straightforward; the greater complexity comes at the system level with the tradeoffs that must be made to arrive at a functioning and optimized combination of power converters and the components they power. Getting everything right can require a good bit of disciplined effort, particularly for systems that are large (e.g., lots of chips), systems that run off of batteries, and/or systems that have high-speed signals (say, more than a few tens of megahertz, with clear challenges above 100 megahertz).

There are three main goals in designing a product's power scheme: making sure that we supply the juice our parts actually require, minimizing power consumption, and minimizing cost/complexity. In this section, we'll tackle all three in that order.

SUPPLYING THE NECESSARY JUICE

One of the things that I enjoy about software is that 99.99+% of the time, a 1 is a 1 and a 0 is a 0. Unless our hardware has problems, or a memory bit gets clobbered (e.g., by radiation or a stray cosmic ray) or some ill-behaved code overwrites it, we can count on it staying at exactly 1 or 0 until we decide to change it. In the world of electronics, however, 5V is never 5V—at least it isn't for more than an instant. Voltages at any chip's power supply pin will constantly bounce around for a number of reasons. Bounces of .01% are probably OK; 50% bounces are probably not OK.

Chips have power requirements, and not meeting those requirements because of power supplies that "bounce around" can cause all manner of grief. In particular, power issues often cause subtle problems that we might not catch until late in the game or even after we start shipping, like increased power consumption under certain conditions, substantially reduced reliability, etc. These problems can often be caught in testing, but it's usually much better to design things correctly in the first place. So one of our important jobs is to ensure that power rail bounces are within a range that's tolerable for the parts they power. Let's look at how this is done.

Bounce prevention

Where does the bounce come from? DC-DC converters themselves aren't perfect, but they're very good. If our circuit is designed per a converter chip's datasheet, the voltage *at the converter's output pin* will typically be within 1% or so of the target, which is rarely a cause for concern. On the other hand, if we're drawing more current than a circuit is designed to handle (or less—switchers often have a minimum load that they want to see), or we're otherwise mistreating a converter (i.e., not following the rules in its datasheet), we might see rail voltage sagging or misbehaving in other ways. So rule number one is to do our homework to make sure that:

- We know how much current our circuits need from their rails
- We know how much current our rails can supply
- We know that the supplies we use can give our circuits what they need

Be particularly careful to consider what happens when a product is first turned on, or when large currents are switched on or off such as with motor controller H-bridge circuits and higher-power lighting. Peak current requirements in these situations can be multiples of average current requirements.

It's a good idea (and standard practice) to add *bulk capacitors* to our circuits, which add a little boost of current for a few moments during switching. These sit between the voltage rail and ground, often placed right at a powered part's supply pin. These capacitors store charge when lower currents are being drawn by their associated components. Then when the associated components draw a slug of current during switching, the capacitor will start dumping its charge out as additional current to help keep the power pin up. Bulk capacitors tend to be sized in the 1 µF (microfarad) and up range.

When circuits switch, they tend to radiate energy, as mentioned earlier in the section on switching converters. This noise occurs as quick spikes that can have amplitude high enough to violate chip specifications, or can get conducted into the chip through the power supply pin and cause issues such as noise in analog sections (audio, video, sensors, etc.). *Bypass capacitors* between each susceptible chip's power supply pin and ground can reduce this noise. These are typically of much-lower capacitance than bulk capacitors, and work by shunting high-frequency (i.e., short-duration) spikes to ground.

Component datasheets will often have useful suggestions and guidelines on bulk and bypass capacitance. If a design group doesn't have expertise in this area, it definitely pays to beg or hire someone who does have expertise to review schematics and make suggestions.

Power sequencing

It's often the case that the sequence in which parts are powered up is quite important. Many chips require several power supply voltages, and these voltages sometimes need to be turned on in a specific sequence with proper timing between them and proper ramp times. It's often also important to sequence the order in which *different parts* are turned on: for example, some chips won't tolerate appreciable voltage on their data input pins until their power pin has been powered for a specified time. When designing a circuit, it's important to think through potential use cases and to make sure that all component requirements are met in all cases.

MINIMIZING POWER CONSUMPTION

Truly minimizing a product's power consumption can require a substantial effort, requiring close cooperation between electronics and software developers. There are a few basic strategies employed:

1. Using low-power components

2. Reducing digital switching

3. Reducing voltage

4. Turning off things that are not needed

Let's take a brief look at each of these.

Low-power components

Using low-power components to save power seems like a no-brainer, but it does require some care. Many chips are complex these days, and run in multiple modes that draw different amounts of power. When reviewing components, we should keep in mind the power modes that we'll actually be using and the effort required to take advantage of them.

This is particularly true of sophisticated applications processors designed for smart phones, tablets, and other devices running sophisticated GUIs. The number of modes and options on these parts is staggering: many have dozens of different *domains* that can be turned on and off by software, each of which controls (powers/depowers) different sets of functionality on the part. Tuning the use of domains can eat many person-months of software and electronics effort, so a low-power processor might only be *capable* of low power but will draw a substantial amount of juice unless we work to take advantage of its capabilities.

We should also think about interconnects between components that might draw power. For example, the pull-up resistors on an I2C bus can draw a few milliamps of current, which could be saved, say, by moving to a part that uses a SPI bus instead.

Reducing digital switching

Modern digital chips draw virtually no current when sitting truly idle; no clocks are running in the background, inputs and outputs are stationary, etc. The only power they draw is a momentary "blip" whenever transistors on a chip switch from one logic state to another. Only a minuscule blip per transistor, but chips can have millions or billions of transistors so it all adds up. The more often transistors switch, the more current they draw.

By turning processor clocks to lower frequencies or by turning them off altogether if the processor is not being used, we can often drop power consumption quite substantially. Processor power consumption is usually directly proportional to the system clock frequency, so halving clock frequency also roughly halves power consumption. Since the speed at which code is executed is normally directly proportional to clock frequency, reducing frequency is a good strategy only if we can withstand the drop in performance (and if the processor supports it).

Turning the system clock off altogether can drop power consumption down to almost nothing. Most processors have power-savings modes (e.g., sleep mode) that turn off the system clock, leaving a small bit of the chip turned on to monitor the outside world and restart the clock when the processor is needed again. This scheme provides the basis for powering smart devices for years on a single coin cell: if the system clock remained on all the time, we'd only get a few weeks of life in the best case.

Reducing voltage

The size of each energy blip when a transistor switches depends in large part on the voltage that the transistor is switching: higher voltages mean bigger blips. Halving voltage roughly halves the current spent during each switch, but since voltage is also half, power usage (e.g., wattage) is reduced by about three-quarters, which is obviously a huge savings.

Many chips (but certainly not all) can use a variety of voltages, and significant power savings can be wrested by cutting voltage. For example, the AVR ATMEGA328P used in the Arduino Uno can handle a supply voltage of between 1.8 and 5.5V. According to the datasheet, current when running at 1.8V is about one-quarter the current at 5.5V for a part that's running an idle loop in firmware. Adding the savings from the voltage reduction, we end up with a total power savings of more than 90%. That's some serious savings!

One downside of lower voltage is that transistor switching speed also slows, which usually translates into a lower limit on how fast a part will run. For example, the ATMEGA328P can support a 20MHz system clock at 5.5V but only a 4MHz clock at 1.8V.

Of course, if we lower clock speed *and* voltage, our power savings are even more dramatic; for example, an ATMEGA328P at 1.8V and 4MHz uses about 98% less power than at 5.5V and 20MHz.

Putting it all together: by using lower voltages, lower clock frequencies, and almost-zero-power sleep modes, processors and other digital circuits can cut power consumption by orders of magnitude. This is why most smart devices rarely actually power off when we hit the off button. Instead, they go into an extremely low-power "sleep" mode, then awake in moments when we hit the "power" button. This eliminates the need for a time-consuming boot-up each time we want to perform a task on our cell phone.

Turning off what we aren't using

Like turning off a light switch in an empty room, it makes intuitive sense to turn off circuitry that we don't need while it's not being used. The ability to power blocks of electronics on and off is usually supported by hardware and initiated by software. For example, in software we can set an output pin low to turn off a certain power supply, or send a command to a GPS chip over an I2C bus asking it to go into sleep mode.

This is an effective way to reduce power consumption, but in practice it usually turns out to be a good bit more complex than flipping a light switch. The complexity lies in the many interdependencies between software and hardware, and between various bits of hardware.

On the software/hardware interaction side, there are a few issues. Two obvious ones are:

- The added complexity of software needing to turn things on and off at the right times.

- The need to keep track of interdependencies—for example, software might need to know that turning on Chip A might require us to also turn on Chip B in some circumstances—but not others.

A second, less-obvious issue has to do with software (particularly operating systems) that are not expecting bits of hardware to appear and disappear as they are powered on and off. For example, suppose that we decide to reduce power consumption by turning a USB port chip on only while needed by toggling its power supply. While software operating systems are OK with USB devices being plugged in and out from a local port on the fly, they are not designed to have the local USB ports *themselves* appear and disappear. If a USB port chip is powered off at boot time, then its driver might not get loaded by the OS and even if it is later powered up, it won't be usable by an application. We could force the driver to load, say by turning on the port at boot time and then turning it off again. But then the OS might check up on the USB port at different times even when our application doesn't need the port, and things might hang if the port has disappeared—it's an unexpected occurrence, a use case that the OS might not be designed for.

The best solution to this problem is to use chips with low-power modes that are specifically designed to support our intended usage, ones that have low-power modes designed to support software interactions. For example, to keep the OS happy, a chip might keep the interface to the OS powered up while putting the rest of the part to sleep, waking up fully as needed. These parts are often not trivial to use—hardware and software folks should plan on spending some quality time with each other, and perhaps with the chip-maker's support staff. Efforts can be particularly substantial if an off-the-shelf device driver is not available for a chip which matches the version of the OS we're using—a good thing to keep in mind when selecting components.

These parts are also not trivial to find: the phrase *low-power* in marketing literature doesn't mean it will be low-power in our application. We need to know how the part will be used, and scour data sheets to make sure that low-power features and our application fit one-another.

Hardware-hardware interactions can also crop up. Generally speaking, chips are designed to be powered up when a system is turned on, and then stay on: being powered off while surrounding circuitry's running isn't a use case that's typically considered by chipmakers. Depowered chips aren't simply circuits that disappear. Rather, they're circuits that happen to not have power being fed to their supply pin(s), which can be quite a different thing. When a chip is powered off, there will often still be various paths for current to take to/from any connected "live" pins on connected parts, which can cause trouble unless we always honor a part's datasheet.

For example, suppose that Chip A has outputs that feed into Chip B, and Chip B's datasheet tells us that its supply pin must be powered before voltage can be applied to its data inputs. If we turn Chip B off to save power, we also need to do something about its inputs from Chip A. Perhaps we can turn off Chip A too, or set its output lines to a high-impedance state (which might require additional hardware unless we plan for this), or force its outputs to ground. These solutions require extra effort and cost.

Again, the ideal solution to this problem usually lies in selecting parts that explicitly support low-power modes rather than simply depowering parts when not needed.

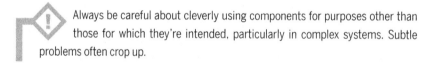

Always be careful about cleverly using components for purposes other than those for which they're intended, particularly in complex systems. Subtle problems often crop up.

MINIMIZING COST AND COMPLEXITY

There are a few basic strategies for reducing the cost and complexity of our power circuitry by cutting the number of components. One simple measure is to select circuit components that use the same voltages, thus cutting down on the number of DC-DC converters.

A second simple measure is to use linear regulators rather than more-complex switchers to make small voltage reductions. For example, if we need both 3.3 and 3.0 volts supplied from a battery, it's usually preferable to use a single switcher to derive 3.3V from the battery and then use a linear part to drop 3.3 to 3.0V, rather than using two switchers to supply the two different voltages.

The larger challenge has to do with taming the complexities that come with saving power by switching parts of circuits on and off, and from varying power sources (i.e., the ability to run from battery or USB charger). This level of complexity is normally tamed by using specialized chips known as *power management ICs* (PMICs) and/or *power path managers*. Let's take a look at how these can help.

Power path management

A common power usage paradigm for products with lithium-ion batteries is to use a USB port for both power and data. Sounds simple enough at first blush, but there are a fair number of different use cases that need to work properly, and we need to switch smoothly between them. For example, we must support charging from dumb chargers and true USB ports when the system is turned either on or off, switch from USB to battery power when the cable gets pulled out and vice versa, and umpteen other scenarios.

There are a number of corner cases that are easy to overlook and a pain to deal with, such as deeply discharged batteries, which must be trickle-charged for a while before they have enough juice to support system boot-up. If we don't do this properly, the system starts to boot, battery voltage drops, system shuts down, charges a few minutes, starts to boot, shuts down again, etc. In some cases, USB ports won't supply enough current to fully power a device, so we'd like to add battery power as needed to keep the system up while maximizing battery life. And we want to stop charging or discharging the battery when temperature is out of spec.

And there's more—much more! For example, as discussed earlier, most smart devices go to sleep when we press the power button rather than powering off. But what happens if a device freezes, and needs a reboot? Does the user have to wait for the battery to die? Or do we have a special "power" switch that sleeps the system on a short press, but actually *does* kill the power if depressed for long enough (e.g., 3 seconds)?

There is great potential for unintended behavior.

As is usually the case when complex tasks need to be implemented often, chip makers have come to our rescue, in this case with magic *power path management* chips that make our lives easy by handling all of the use cases we're likely to slip up on. For a dollar or two they take care of battery charging, juggling multiple power inputs, dual-purpose power buttons, temperature cutoffs, and so forth, and often throw in a regulated power supply and other goodies. These parts are highly recommended—I've never seen anyone design this functionality correctly from simpler components.

PMICs

PMICs are chips that integrate various power functionality, such as multiple DC-DC converters, charging, and power path, into a single chip. PMICs often also contain a slew of other functionality unrelated to power but which can be useful in reducing the need for other chips, such as USB ports, audio codec and amplifier, a real-time clock, and almost any other peripheral you might imagine. In short, PMICs have become "everything-but-the-kitchen-sink" chips.

Some PMICs are general purpose, but in many cases a PMIC is designed to work hand-in-hand with a specific processor chip, usually a sophisticated application processor. In some cases, processor and PMIC are so tightly coupled to each other that using a certain processor chip almost requires the use of its associated PMIC.

PMICs often play an important role in reducing processor energy consumption. One neat trick that's supported by a number of PMICs and processors is the ability for the PMIC to reduce the voltage and clock frequency to the processor when the PMIC detects (or is told) that the processor isn't doing a whole lot and can slow down to save power. This is generically known as *dynamic voltage and frequency scaling* (DVFS).

When selecting a PMIC that's targeted at a specific processor, it's easy to get lazy and assume that the circuits and peripherals on the PMIC are right for our application. While they will very likely be right for the processor, functionality that touches circuitry outside of the processor might not be what we need. For example, if a PMIC has a battery charge circuit that supplies 700mA, it might not be able to charge a large Li-ion battery in a reasonable time frame. So even if we go with the PMIC, we'd need to buy a dedicated charger chip to augment PMIC functionality. But since PMICs are usually pretty inexpensive for the functionality they provide, they're usually still a good deal even if we can't use some of their functionality.

TIP PMICs and power path management chips usually don't make all of our problems go away. We must ensure that they're configured properly and that they play nicely with other electronics and software. However, these parts do greatly reduce the odds that we'll find a serious hardware issue that requires a significant redesign either late in the development cycle or after our product is on the market. As always, it's important to be very diligent about understanding each chip's datasheet and other documentation, and to keep a high-level systems perspective (i.e., "let's make sure all of these components will work together to do what we want") during development.

Final Thoughts

By this point, hopefully it's clear that "and we'll just add some power supplies" is not a phrase that puts experienced product developers at ease. Powering products, particularly those that use batteries, is usually challenging and methodical work.

The most important takeaways here are:

- Most important: Always read the fine print. Make a careful study of datasheets and white papers before selecting parts and implementing circuits. Even experienced design engineers need to spend a lot of time with product literature for each new design. In fact, the most experienced design engineers tend to spend the *most* time reviewing documentation because they know that a wrong assumption made during design can lead to big headaches later on. Spending days reading datasheets might not be fun, but it will absolutely save weeks or months in the long run.

- Electronics and software folks should work closely together to carefully plan all power modes and states, and all transitions between them. Make sure that the chips we select can play nicely with software in implementing these power modes, states, and transitions.

- Respect what we don't know. Buying functionality instead of designing from scratch is almost always the way to go, because our scratch design will inevitably miss usage scenarios.

- Once we think our electrical schematics are complete, it's a good idea to take one last thorough pass through the circuitry to make sure that every chip's power specifications is being respected, at power up, during operation, and at power down.

- As always, breadboards and prototypes make everything better. The more similar these are to our final design (including PCB layout, particularly for switching power supplies), the more useful the information we'll get from our efforts here.

As always in product development, healthy doses of creativity, discipline, and iteration will yield the best results.

Resources

While the basic specifications used to describe battery performance are defined in this chapter, there are other specifications that get used and which can cause confusion. A good glossary of these specifications (*http://bit.ly/battery-spec*) is available from the MIT Electric Vehicle Team.

Texas Instruments has a number of good resources around powering circuits, which are TI-centric but have a lot of useful general information. Videos covering battery management (*http://bit.ly/1OTF1X9*), portable power (*http://bit.ly/1OTF2dN*), and Line power (*http://bit.ly/1OTFolX*) are available on YouTube, and others are available at TI's site (*http://bit.ly/1OTEYLo*). TI also produced a white paper (*http://www.ti.com/lit/wp/swra349/swra349.pdf*) on high-current, low-duty-cycle power draw from CR2032 cells that I've found to be very helpful.

Thoughtful PCB layout is important when dealing with switching noise and other switching power supply eccentricities. The first rule is to follow the datasheet, but a couple of additional references on the topic are available from TI (*http://www.ti.com.cn/cn/lit/an/snva021c/snva021c.pdf*) and Maxim (*http://bit.ly/1OTFith*). As mentioned in the chapter, using USB for power is ubiquitous but challenging because many USB chargers eschew the USB power standards (*http://www.usb.org/developers/power delivery/*). Maxim has a pretty good white paper that discusses USB charging in the real world (*http://bit.ly/1OTF4lI*).

## CHAPTER 10

Staying Safe: Regulations, Standards, Etc.

WE WANT OUR PRODUCTS TO BE SAFE, OF COURSE. WE DON'T WANT OTHers to be injured by what we make, and we don't want to face lawsuits or worse.

However, nothing we make is perfectly safe, no matter how hard we work at it. Given virtually any object, users can figure out *some* clever way to cause harm. Some products, like cars and firearms, are obviously capable of great unintentional mayhem. If not designed properly, anything we plug into a wall outlet can cause electric shock, possibly fatal, under certain conditions. And even a bottle cap can cause a child to choke.

So how do we balance *safe* with *reasonable*? We can always expend more effort making products incrementally safer, but at what point do we say "good enough"? Because this is literally a life-and-death question, governments and various other organizations have spent a lot of time thinking about the answers. The answers show up in the form of regulations, standards, and other rules that we'll review in this chapter. By defining "safe" at the government level, a level playing field is set where all manufacturers abide by the same rules.

Regulations have (generally) made the products that we use safer. Auto regulations are a great example of this. When I was my son's age, there were approximately 3.3 deaths per million vehicle miles travelled in the US. Today that's down to about 1.1 deaths, a two-thirds drop. Better seat belts, air bags, safety glass, the addition of a center brake light, and crush standards are some of the more visible safety features that were introduced into all new cars due to regulations.

While safety is the focus of most product regulations, other regulations also exist that affect marketing and product performance. For example, the US government mandates that fuel efficiency be measured for all cars in a standardized way so that consumers can make better buying choices, which encourages manufacturers to compete with one another on efficiency. It also mandates that each auto manufacturer's cars, in aggregate, must achieve a minimum fuel efficiency.

The downside is that regulations cost money and can sometimes slow innovation, and they don't generally make our product "cooler," or help to sell more of it. Rather, they are merely something we *need* to do in exchange for the privilege of being able to sell our product in a given location.

Like most things in the game of product development, following regulations usually isn't so difficult. The trickier part is in knowing which ones to follow during development so we don't get surprised later on, and that's what this chapter's about. Regulations are different in different countries, but the fundamentals are the same almost everywhere. We'll begin by outlining those universal fundamentals. Then we'll walk through some of the specifics of identifying and meeting regulations appropriate to selling smart products in the US and EU. Together, these two markets account for more than half of the world's entire consumer spending so they're usually the most important markets to be addressed during product development. Finally, we'll consider the interesting case of batteries, which are covered by international transport regulations.

Regulatory Fundamentals

In my experience, the biggest problems caused by regulations ultimately stem from confusion around some pretty basic issues, such as "Which regulations do we follow? What about all of these things called standards —do we need to follow them, too? And what's this certification stuff? Do we need someone to certify us?"

Regulations can be complex and aren't always a do-it-yourself proposition; particularly if our product is primarily intended for children, or if it has a significant potential to cause harm if anything goes wrong, there are enough regulations and details to warrant our retaining a regulatory consultant or lawyer to help guide the process.

TIP Of course, this chapter is not a substitute for a law degree or for reading the actual regulations. Rather, the intention is to give an overview of the process so that you'll know what to expect. Even if you do end up using a consultant or lawyer to help, you'll be able to use your expert's time most efficiently if you understand the process.

That being said, most products that aren't primarily intended for children and aren't easily capable of great mayhem have fairly light regulation. If you're patient and don't mind reading a good bit of legalese, it can be feasible to deal with regulations for these products without outside help. In this section, we'll cover the fundamentals of navigating regulations and regulatory processes to help with this. Let's start with a high-level overview, and then we'll dig into the details.

PROCESS OVERVIEW

No matter *which* regulations we must follow or *where* we need to follow them (e.g., which country), the basic interactions between product development and regulations are normally as follows:

1. *Identify* all regulations that apply to our product.
2. *Add* identified regulations to our product requirements to ensure that we develop our product to meet them.
3. *Test* our completed product to ensure that requirements are met.
4. *Declare* that our product meets requirements.
5. *Label* our product correctly.
6. *Sell* our product.
7. *Alert* the proper authorities if our product falls short on safety when it's marketed, and work to correct the problem.

Before we flesh out the details of each of these steps, let's answer a question that I suspect many readers are asking at this point:

DO THESE APPLY TO LITTLE MANUFACTURERS LIKE ME?

"Surely, small manufacturers can't be held to all of these regulations!"

For better or worse, they *can*. While there are occasional exemptions for small manufacturers and for small batches of products, product regulations generally apply to *everyone*, large and small—the argument being that safety shouldn't be compromised. (Whether they're *enforced* for small manufacturers by overworked government agencies might be another story, but consider what could happen to a small manufacturer's owners if their product causes some big problems and is found to not meet regulations.)

The best bet for small manufacturers is to stick with products that have little regulation. Later in this chapter, we'll see how to figure out if a product we intend to develop is one of these. And the good news is that the regulations around most smart products are fairly lightweight.

LAWS, REGULATIONS, STANDARDS, AND OTHER REGULATORY WORDS

Laws, regulations, standards, certifications, guidances, and marks are words that get used a lot when discussing regulatory "stuff." Each has a different and important meaning.

Laws

Laws (a.k.a. statutes) are rules passed by government legislatures (e.g., the US Congress) that set high-level goals along the lines of "Consumer products must be safe." Product designer/developers don't normally deal with laws directly. Rather, we work with regulations that derive from laws.

Regulations

Regulations get down into the nitty-gritty of *how* laws should be followed and the tests used to *ensure* that they're being followed. To illustrate, here's a sample from the US regulations that govern children's products that covers choking hazards:

§ 1501.4 Size requirements and test procedure.

- (a) No toy or other children's article subject to § 1500.18(a)(9) and to this part 1501 shall be small enough to fit entirely within a cylinder with the dimensions shown in Figure 10-1, when tested in accordance with the procedure in paragraph (b) of this section. In testing to ensure compliance with this regulation, the dimensions of the Commission's test cylinder will be no greater than those shown in Figure 10-1. (In addition, for compliance purposes, the English dimensions shall be used. The metric approximations are included only for convenience.)
- (b)(1) Place the article, without compressing it, into the cylinder. If the article fits entirely within the cylinder, in any orientation, it fails to comply with the test procedure. (Test any detached components of the article the same way.)

- (2) If the article does not fit entirely within the cylinder, subject it to the appropriate "use and abuse" tests of 16 CFR 1500.51 and 1500.52 (excluding the bite tests of §§ 1500.51(c) and 1500.52(c)). Any components or pieces (excluding paper, fabric, yarn, fuzz, elastic, and string) which have become detached from the article as a result of the use and abuse testing shall be placed into the cylinder, one at a time. If any such components or pieces fit entirely within the cylinder, in any orientation and without being compressed, the article fails to comply with the test procedure.

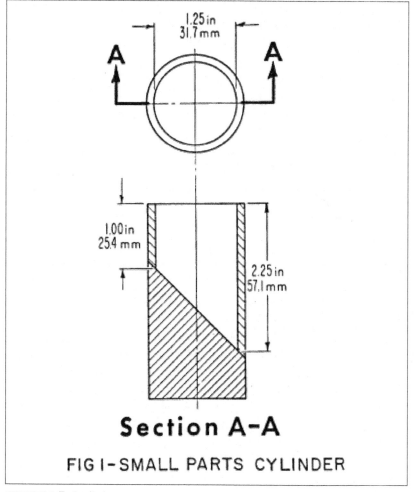

FIGURE 10-1. Test cylinder

While regulations aren't technically laws, they have the *force* of law: if we violate a regulation, we violate the underlying law(s) it interprets.

Regulations are developed and enforced by government agencies such as the Consumer Product Safety Commission (CPSC), the Food and Drug Administration (FDA), and others. In the US, all regulations are conveniently found in one place: the Code of Federal Regulations (CFR). The CFR is broken into *Titles*, each addressing a different area. *Title 16, Commercial Practices*, is one that's of interest to product developers: it covers the regulations enforced by the CPSC. Multiple titles often apply to a single product. For example, if a consumer product contains electronics, then it must comply with *Title 16, Commercial Practices*, as well as the FCC's regulations that are found in *Title 47, Telecommunication*, and perhaps other Titles depending on its function.

Titles are further segmented into *chapters, subchapters, parts,* and *sections*. For example, the choking regulation we just saw comes from CFR Title 16, Chapter 2, subchapter C, Part 1501, titled *Method For Identifying Toys And Other Articles Intended For Use By Children Under 3 Years Of Age Which Present Choking, Aspiration, Or Ingestion Hazards Because Of Small Parts*. This is typically shortened to *16 CFR 1501*; the CFR is constructed so that once we know the Title and the Part, we have enough information to uniquely identify the regulation.

Standards

Standards are rules (of sorts), normally created by non-government committees under the auspices of standards organizations such as the International Electrotechnical Commission (IEC), the American National Standards Institute (ANSI), the International Organization for Standardization (ISO), Underwriters Laboratories (UL), ASTM (formerly known as the American Society for Testing and Materials) ·and others. Multiple standards organizations sometimes share a single standard, such as *ANSI/IEC 60529 Degrees of Protection Provided by Enclosures*.

On their own, standards don't carry the force of law unless laws or regulations are created that mandate their use, which often happens.

For example, IEC's 60601-1 standard defines a large group of design rules that help ensure that an electrical medical device is safe, along with tests that demonstrate that the device's design truly follows these rules. Section 8.4.3 of this standard, titled *Medical Electrical Equipment Intended to be Connected to a Power Source by a Plug*, starts off with a rule:

"Medical electrical equipment or its parts intended to be connected to a power source by means of a plug shall be so designed that 1 second after disconnection of the plug the voltage between the pins of the plug and between either supply pin and the enclosure does not exceed 60 V or, if this value is exceeded, the stored charge does not exceed 45 μC."

The text then goes on to describe how a device is tested to ensure that it actually meets this rule.

You've probably noticed that the wording of this *standard* has a similar feel to that of the choking *regulation* we just reviewed. In fact, regulations and standards are very similar, and it's often the case that regulations simply point to standards. In other words, we can or must meet a standard in order to comply with a regulation. For example, CPSC *regulations* state that all cribs sold in the US must meet ASTM *standards* F406 and F1169. In the US and the EU, electrical medical devices aren't strictly obliged to meet the aforementioned IEC 60601-1, but all electrical medical devices do need to somehow demonstrate that they're safe and demonstrating conformance to 60601-1 is called out by the regulations as one way to do this. (And as a practical matter, *every* electrical medical device that I know of conforms to 60601-1; devising an alternative plan to demonstrate safety is a huge task, and very risky as it might not be acceptable to the relevant agencies.)

Most standards allow manufacturers to skip any parts that don't make sense for a given product. However, if we skip a part, we should carefully document our reasons so everyone knows that we're being smart and not just lazy.

While product makers typically meet standards in order to satisfy relevant regulations, there are some other good reasons why we might want (or need) to meet standards even though we're not legally obligated:

1. Standards can be useful for marketing our device. Suppose we're selling an expensive industrial video camera that can be used under water. Savvy customers might not be happy with us simply telling them they can use it under water: they'll probably want to know the product's IP (ingress protection) rating as defined by the aforementioned ANSI/IEC 60529.

2. Standards can help to protect us in the event of legal troubles. Suppose that a disgruntled customer sues us, claiming that the underwater video camera we sold them wasn't tested properly to prove its water resistance. Which defense will sound better to a jury: "Yes, we

did test it to work underwater!" or "The camera was tested to meet level IP7 of ANSI/IEC 6059, the internationally recognized standard that specifically defines testing for protection against water ingress?"

3. Customers might require that certain standards be met. For example, if our product will be used in a potentially explosive atmosphere, such as for inspecting aircraft or other equipment where fuel vapor might be present, customers will likely insist that our product meet a relevant standard such as IEC 60079, which covers safety in electrical equipment used in explosive atmospheres.

4. Insurers might require conformance to certain standards as a condition of coverage, in which case our customers might be obliged to purchase equipment that meets certain standards or we might need to meet certain standards to obtain our own liability insurance.

Certifications

It's often not enough to vouch for ourselves that we meet one or more regulations or standards. Sometimes we're required to hire independent third parties to perform testing and certify our claims so that it's harder to cheat—this is typically true for safety-critical items. Certifications can be costly and there are some tricks to it, so we'll cover this in more detail later in its own subsection, "Conformance Testing and Certification."

Guidances

Guidances are documents published by government agencies that describe their current thoughts on various regulations under their jurisdiction. For example, a guidance might suggest (but not mandate) various ways to meet regulations for a type of product. In theory, complying with guidance documents is not mandatory. Even more interesting is that agencies aren't even required to follow their own guidance documents in their enforcement of their regulations. However, in practice, it's a really good idea to pay attention to any guidance documents that pertain to the regulations we must meet. It's also pretty unlikely that an agency will do something that clearly disagrees with their own guidance document even if they theoretically can.

Marks

A mark is basically just a label on a product that has some established meaning. Some of the best-known marks (all shown previously in Figure 1-4 in Chapter 1) include:

- The UL mark, which normally indicates that the product has been tested for conformance to the standards that UL believes to be appropriate for that type of product, and that UL conducts periodic inspections to ensure that manufacturing is being performed properly. Obtaining a UL mark is voluntary, but it demonstrates to customers that a product achieves a level of safety beyond what's mandated by regulations.

- The CE mark, which indicates that a product meets the necessary regulations to be sold in the EU. Companies actually assign the CE mark to their products themselves, but in many cases they require third parties to certify that they meet some of those requirements.

- The FCC mark, which indicates that a product has been certified to meet US FCC regulations.

The CE and FCC marks are covered in more detail later in this chapter, and resources for UL mark information are listed in the Resources section.

LOCATION

Regulations, of course, vary from government to government. In any given location where a product is sold and/or used, it can theoretically be subject to several different governments (e.g., federal, state, and city) and thus different sets of regulations. The differences between different countries are usually the biggest potential headache.

Here's a little good news: the obvious pain of complying with different sets of regulations in order to sell a product in different countries has spurred a process known as *harmonization*. Harmonization is the process of countries working together to make their regulations more similar to one another in order to promote easier trade. A great example of harmonization is the European Union (EU), whose 28 member countries have (for the most part) agreed to accept the same product regulations. So once we've met regulations for one EU country, we're normally good in all the others with little or no extra effort.

Harmonization is one reason that regulations sometimes point to standards as discussed earlier: for example, the IEC60601-1 standard is used to assess the safety of electrical medical devices in almost every country in the world. One independent group creates a standard, and then many countries can simply point to it. Everyone wins: countries don't have to duplicate the effort of developing detailed regulations, and makers can meet one set of rules and sell their product in many markets.

But while harmonization helps, there are still some differences between countries. Even within the EU, for example, regulations can sometimes differ from one country to the next. Thus the first step in the regulatory compliance process is to decide on the localities in which we'll be selling our product, so we can determine the specific regulations that will apply to us. We can then develop our product to meet those regulations.

Countries aren't the only entities that have product regulations: even states occasionally do, too, although they typically don't apply to products of the type discussed in this book. The only state regulation that I know of that affects development of smart products is California's Proposition 65. If our product contains any chemicals on this list (*http://bit.ly/1Dxk7wm*), then we'll need to affix a label that states the following:

"WARNING: This product contains chemicals known to the State of California to cause cancer and birth defects or other reproductive harm."

Best bet is to avoid the label by checking any materials against the list as we make our selections.

Particularly if our product is intended for children, explodes on purpose, uses unusual chemicals, or does other dramatic things that can readily result in bodily harm or annoyed neighbors, it's worth checking for regulations in California and other states that might apply.

CATEGORIES OF REGULATIONS

As befitting a book on product development, we're concentrating on product regulations. But note that there are also regulations around how products are manufactured, particularly with regard to workplace safety and any waste created in manufacturing. In the US at the federal level, these are regulated by the Occupational Safety and Health Administration (OSHA) and the Environmental Protection Agency (EPA), respectively. Both have websites that serve as good starting points for more information. It's also important to look into state regulations wherever we'll be manufacturing because, while product regulations most often just follow federal regulations, it's much more common for workplace safety and particularly environmental compliance regulations to be tighter at the state level than at the federal level.

 Regulations can never be looser at the state level than at the federal level unless a state is looking for a fight with the feds, which is rare.

We won't be reviewing manufacturing-oriented regulations because most manufacturing is contracted out, but if you do manufacture yourself, be aware that they exist and must be followed.

AMBIGUITY IN REGULATIONS

One of the frustrations of working with regulations is their *ambiguity*: in many cases, decisions must be made based on inexact information. For example, we must make a determination for ourselves, based on CPSC guidelines, as to whether our product is intended for children. This decision will have a big impact on total project effort, and might introduce significant design constraints. Suppose that we decide that our product is not intended for children (thus avoiding a lot of regulation), but our product later injures a child and a complaint is filed with the CPSC. If CPSC determines that our decision was wrong and that our product really is intended for children, we could be facing one or both of the following:

- A product recall if our product doesn't meet the regulations CPSC thinks it should

- Criminal charges if CPSC decides that we purposely misclassified our product to avoid the effort of meeting more regulations

The possibility of being second-guessed isn't something to panic about—it rarely happens—but it is something to be aware of.

The best way to handle ambiguity is to make an honest effort to do the right thing, and to build a paper trail that documents this. The documentation trail will help to show that we made a good-faith effort should someone, in the future, suggest that we made the wrong decision callously in order to reduce our regulatory burden.

It's a good idea to document, in writing, any regulatory decisions that are not totally obvious. Include references to regulations, guidance documents, and any other material as appropriate. If a decision lies in a gray area, it can be useful to have the opinion of outside parties to support us. A statement from an unbiased third party can be helpful, particularly if they have expertise in the field. For example, if we have a regulatory lawyer write a short letter stating her opinion that a certain decision is correct, it will have a lot of weight if we're ever questioned.

CONFORMANCE TESTING AND CERTIFICATION

As mentioned earlier, many products require testing by an impartial third party to certify that they meet relevant regulations.

There are a variety of companies that provide certification services. Some of the better-known ones include *Underwriters Laboratories (UL)*, *Bureau Veritas*, *Intertek*, the *TÜVs* (there are four of them), and *CSA*. All major providers are international, which is important if we need to certify to regulations in more than one country. Some providers are not-for-profit (e.g., UL, CSA), and some are for-profits (e.g., Intertek, Bureau Veritas).

Unfortunately, certification is not a cheap process. Nobody gets away for less than $1,000, and certifying specialized products (e.g., medical devices) for multiple countries can easily run tens of thousands of dollars.

A few things to keep in mind when selecting and using third-party certification services:

1. Certification services will typically not decide which regulations must be met. We tell them the regulation(s), and they test for conformance.

2. Note that the certifiers must, themselves, be empowered to actually certify whatever it is they are certifying. The testing lab must be listed as qualified to certify to any given regulation we're looking to meet, by the agency that "owns" that regulation. CPSC and others have lists of qualified services on their websites.

3. Services generally charge by the hour, not by the certification. If we fail certification and need to try again, we will pay for the extra effort. Thus, if reasonable, it's a good idea to run the certification tests *ourselves* and work out any problems before going to third-party testing.

4. Certification houses will be happy to tell us why we failed a test, but might not be so eager to suggest fixes. Sometimes they feel it is a conflict of interest to suggest solutions because if we follow their sug-

gestions they will then (in a sense) be testing their own work, which is a no-no. This stance tends to vary among providers, different tests, and different staff at the same provider.

5. If a device will need complex testing in order to be certified, it's a really good idea to meet with the certification service regularly during the design process to discuss potential pitfalls, review the design, and so forth. They can point out design issues that could cause problems during certification, and possibly suggest solutions. This will cost some money, but it will likely be less expensive than making the mistake, failing the test, doing another rev of the development, and so forth.

There's a lot more than can be written about regulations, particularly for highly regulated products like medical devices (my specialty), but at this point we've covered the basics that generally apply to most smart products. Next, let's dig into the specific regulatory frameworks in a couple of real geographical markets: the US and the EU. Again, we'll stick to smart consumer products as opposed to industrial, medical, aerospace, military, and other specialized products based on the assumption that most readers will be developing consumer items. These other products have different regulations that are usually similar, but more comprehensive and often quite specialized.

> If your product claims to diagnose or treat disease, the FDA might believe it's a medical device. For example, if MicroPed's advertising claims that it counts steps or monitors activity level, it won't be considered a medical device. But if it claims to, say, treat halitosis (bad breath) by encouraging users to be more active, it might be considered a medical device, which puts it into a whole new world of regulations. It's a really good idea to get expert advice when developing anything that's health-related to make sure lines aren't accidentally overstepped. Also note that regulations are changing rapidly in this area as the FDA tries to balance the desire to use new technologies with the need to keep users safe from quackery or worse.

Navigating US Regulations

The US is the largest single consumer market in the world, so it's fitting that we begin by reviewing the regulatory situation here.

When we know where our product will be sold, we need to determine which regulations apply and how they apply. Governments are composed of various agencies, departments, commissions, and other entities that are responsible for creating regulations. We must find the agencies that are relevant to our product, and interpret their respective regulations.

US regulations tend to be somewhat tougher to pin down than those of other countries. It would be nice if we could go to a single government entity, describe our product, and then be presented with a comprehensive list of all the regulations that apply to us, but no such luck. We'll need to root around a little bit to find the agencies that have jurisdiction over our product, and then do some research to find out which (if any) of their regulations specifically apply to us.

Most products that contain electronics are regulated by two agencies: the CPSC and the FCC. Any product that contains electronics comes under FCC jurisdiction. Some "consumer" products, like automobiles, medical products, cosmetics, tobacco, and firearms, are regulated by agencies other than CPSC, but unless our product is obviously not for "typical" consumers (e.g., we're developing a medical device or a jetpack), it's best to start with the assumption that the CPSC has jurisdiction over us.

CPSC

One benefit of starting with the CPSC in our search for relevant regulations is that they have a very helpful web page of products (*http://1.usa.gov/1Ktvzvu*) they don't regulate. The page lists several dozen exceptions and points to the agencies that have responsibility for each. In many cases, we'll find that products are regulated by multiple agencies. For example, drugs are regulated by the FDA, but drug packaging also comes under the jurisdiction of the CPSC.

Assuming that our product falls under CPSC jurisdiction, their site has a very helpful page (*http://1.usa.gov/1KtvuI8*) that walks the reader through all of the steps of identifying and meeting regulations.

The most important criterion in determining a consumer product's regulatory burden is whether it's classified as a children's product. All children's products must:

- Comply with a number of general regulations to ensure that they are safe. These are listed and linked to at the second *cpsc.gov* link just listed.

- Be certified to comply with these regulations by an independent third-party testing service prior to being sold.

- Continue to be tested periodically by an independent third-party testing service to demonstrate ongoing compliance.

A children's product is defined as one that's intended to be used *primarily* by children 12 or under. Products that are intended to be used by people of all ages but just happen to be also used by children, are considered *general use products* and don't have to meet the special regulations for children's products. CPSC's site has a great deal of info on making this determination.

If our product is for children, then the intended age range is also important in determining which regulations apply. CPSC has a thorough (313-page!) document (*http://www.cpsc.gov/PageFiles/113962/adg.pdf*) on how to do that for a variety of products.

Once we've made a determination as to whether or not we're a children's product, the next step is to find any CPSC regulations that are specific to our type of product. The table at the CPSC website (*http://1.usa.gov/1CVbIT9*) is our resource here. It lists several hundred types of products—mostly chemicals, materials, and children's products—with links to the relevant product-specific regulations. It's a good idea to peruse the entire list in case the CPSC has different thoughts than we do on what to call our product, and to see if any *components* of our product might be regulated.

Specific product requirements can become quite detailed, particularly in the case of products that have a history of causing mayhem, such as clacker balls and metal-tipped lawn darts. If you really want to make and sell clacker balls with LEDs that light with each *clack*, you probably can: but you'll need to conform to several pages of exacting clacker-ball regulations.

Some general-use products require third-party testing, as described earlier. The product-specific requirements will advise us on whether it's needed; otherwise, we can assume that our own testing is sufficient.

If we don't see any regulations that are specific to our product, then we're in luck: CPSC does not require specific testing and/or design considerations. However, if there *are* product-specific regulations that apply to us, then there's an additional task for us beyond compliance: manufacturers of non-children's products that *are* specifically regulated must create a *General Certificate of Conformity* (GCC), which should be provided to our retailers and distributors (and to the CPSC if they ever ask for it). The GCC describes the regulations that the product conforms with, testing that was done, and other information that can be helpful to anyone who wants to make sure that our product is OK with the government.

Also, all manufacturers of consumer products—regulated or not—have an obligation to notify the CSPC if their product turns out to have safety issues:

"If you are a manufacturer, importer, distributor, and/or retailer of consumer products, you have a legal obligation to immediately report a defective product that could create a substantial risk of injury to consumers or a product that is otherwise unreasonably hazardous or dangerous for consumers."

Such a report can lead to a product recall. Details are at the CPSC site (*http://1.usa.gov/1Jy2Xvg*).

That wraps up our overview of the CPSC, who's responsible for ensuring safe interactions between consumers and physical products. Next let's look at the FCC, whose job is to regulate how products affect other products over the airwaves.

FCC

Like the CPSC, the FCC is an agency that developers of smart products should have some knowledge of. Whether or not we intend for our product to broadcast over the radio spectrum, all electronic products must comply with the FCC's regulations in 47 CFR Part 15, *Radio Frequency Devices* (*http://fcc.us/1CVmKYq*).

Radio Frequency (RF) communication is like shouting across a room to talk to a friend—our friend will hear us, but so will others in the room. If we shout loud enough, those others won't be able to hear their own (separate) conversations.

One of the FCC's jobs is to play traffic cop to radio conversations, making sure that nobody shouts too loud and drowns out other conversations. This job is covered in the Part 15 regulations. It turns out that regulating RF in a way that makes everyone happy is pretty complex. Different types of communications have very different needs. For example, while FM radio stations *need* to shout really loud in order to reach a large audience, WiFi needs to talk in hushed tones so each wireless network doesn't interfere with neighbors down the street. So FM radio and WiFi are given different parts of the radio spectrum to use (i.e., different frequency bands) so as to not interrupt one another; otherwise, FM radio would drown out WiFi. And WiFi is only permitted to transmit at low power to avoid drowning out other WiFi networks in the neighborhood.

If our product uses WiFi, Bluetooth, or any other RF communications method, it must meet the rules for the part of the radio spectrum it uses, and this needs to be tested and certified by a third party. Unless we're clever about addressing these rules (more on this in a minute), this testing and certification will normally run more than $10,000. RF is tricky stuff, so there's also a real possibility that our design won't pass the first time we try, and we might need one or more redesign cycles of the electronics (and subsequent testing) to get things right.

The good news is that this testing can be waived if we use a wireless module that's precertified to meet FCC rules (technically known as having *modular certification*). Modules that are precertified to meet FCC and similar international regulations are available from a wide range of manufacturers, and will be proudly advertised as such. As always, we must check carefully to make sure a module carries the right certifications for our needs.

If the module includes its own antenna, we simply design the module into our product and as long as we're not violating any parameters imposed by the manufacturer, such as the voltage it's powered at, we're good to go. If it doesn't include an antenna then we must add one, but this antenna must be the same basic type as, and no more efficient than, the antenna that was used when the module was certified. The manufacturer should supply info on the antenna(s) they used for gaining modular certification in this instance, but sometimes we'll need to ask for this.

But what if we don't support wireless communications? Well, we might not *intentionally* radiate RF, but it turns out that all circuits emit RF whether we want them to or not—it's a matter of physics. And some circuits, notably those that involve DC motors or that switch high currents, can unintentionally spew a *lot* of RF. For this reason, all electronic devices must be tested and certified as *unintentional radiators* to make sure they're not emitting more RF than the FCC allows. This process typically costs $2,000 for a day's worth of testing. Even intentional RF radiators need to undergo unintentional radiator testing and certification to make sure they behave properly in the frequency bands they're not using for communications.

Unintentional radiators are tested to one of two specifications as defined under 47 CFR Part 15, depending on where they're used:

- Devices that are only used in business environments must meet the Class A specifications.

- Devices that have a reasonable chance of being used in homes have to meet the more stringent Class B specifications.

Once our certifications are in order, we need to file paperwork with the FCC and label our product with the FCC ID number that they'll assign to us.

More information can be found on the FCC's website (*http:// www.fcc.gov*), although it's a bit scattered. Linx Technologies has a good guide to the FCC regulatory process (*http://bit.ly/1OTFZ5P*). Linx also has other good white papers on the legal aspects of RF, as does LS Research (*http://www.lsr.com*).

This concludes our review of the parts of the US regulatory apparatus that most readers of this book will come in contact with. Let's now move on to see how things are done in Europe, the world's second-largest market for consumer goods.

European Regulations

The European Union (EU) is a group of 28 countries that have formed political and economic links that make them look, in many ways, like one giant country with more than 500 million residents. On the economic (and regulatory) side of things, the grouping is more properly called the *European Economic Area* (EEA), which includes all EU members plus Iceland, Norway, and Liechtenstein—although most folks still refer to it as the EU, as will we.

The EU is a good thing for product developers: instead of dealing with 31 separate entities with different regulations to reach 500 million potential customers, we can deal with what is effectively one set of regulations. There are some differences between countries, but these are usually minor.

In order for most products to be legally sold in the EU, they must have a *CE mark* as shown in Figure 10-2. Let's take a look at what this means.

CE MARKING

The CE mark is an assurance from the manufacturer that the product meets all relevant EU regulations. Having a single mark that shows up on most products makes it easy for European consumers, retailers, distributors, and customs officials to easily check if a product at least *claims* to conform to EU regulations.

FIGURE 10-2. CE mark

The European Commission has a very succinct overview of CE marking (*http://bit.ly/1H6bJ1R*). I've reproduced it below, underlining some parts that are particularly interesting and that we'll follow up on in a little more detail:

"The CE marking indicates a product's compliance with EU legislation and so <u>enables the free movement of products within the European market</u>. By affixing the CE marking to a product, <u>a manufacturer declares, on his sole responsibility</u>, that the product meets all the legal requirements for the CE marking, which means that the product can be sold throughout the European Economic Area (EEA, the 28 Member States of the EU and European Free Trade Association (EFTA) countries Iceland, Norway, Liechtenstein). This also applies to products made in other countries which are sold in the EEA.

However, <u>not all products must bear the CE marking, only product categories mentioned in specific EU directives on the CE marking</u>.

CE marking does not indicate that a product was made in the EEA, but merely states that the product has been assessed before being placed on the market and thus satisfies the applicable legislative requirements (e.g., <u>a harmonised level of safety</u>) enabling it to be sold there. It means that the manufacturer has:

- *verified that the product complies with all relevant essential requirements (e.g. health and safety or environmental requirements) <u>laid down in the applicable directive(s)</u> and*

- *if stipulated in the directive(s), had it examined by an independent conformity assessment body.*

It is the manufacturer's responsibility to carry out the conformity assessment, to set up the technical file, to issue the declaration of conformity and to affix the CE marking to a product. Distributors must check that the product bears the CE marking and that the requisite supporting documentation is in order. If the product is being imported from outside the EEA, the importer has to verify that the manufacturer has undertaken the necessary steps and that the documentation is available upon request."

Let's take a look at each of the bolded bits from the preceding quote:

"enables the free movement of products within the European market"
Once our product is CE marked, it is generally good-to-go throughout the European Economic Area.

"a manufacturer declares, on his sole responsibility"
As is generally the case in the US, it's the manufacturer's responsibility to declare that a product meets regulations. Governments do not directly approve products.

"Not all products must bear the CE marking, only product categories mentioned in specific EU directives on the CE marking."
Unless our product is specifically mentioned, it doesn't have to be CE marked. In practice, most products including all electronics require CE marking.

"a harmonised level of safety"
While the requirements for CE marking might vary a bit from country to country in Europe, they are sufficiently harmonized so that CE marking under one country's regulations allows sales in any other member of the European Market. Note that in the case of differences in rules between countries, we can sometimes be smart by picking the country with easier rules.

"laid down in the applicable directive(s)"
This is a bit subtle, but the rules that manufacturers follow in the EU are technically directives, not regulations. Directives are created at the EU-level, and set out the objectives that must be met via each member-country's own laws. For most types of products, this is academic, and directives are the rules we'll need to focus on.

"if stipulated in the directive(s), had it examined by an independent conformity assessment body"

In the US, some products must be tested for conformance by a third party.

"to set up the technical file"

The technical file is the manufacturer's file of documents that demonstrate conformance to regulations. The technical file should always be kept up to date and ready to be shown off because governments (or sometimes other parties) might, on occasion, want to take a look. This usually happens if a product has a high-risk function (e.g., a medical device) or if a product has caused some sort of trouble such as injuring users. The "file" documents don't have to literally be kept in a single physical file, but there should be a document that points to the specific locations where they reside.

"to issue the declaration of conformity"

Similar to regulated non-children's products in the US, the manufacturer must write a declaration of conformity (usually a few paragraphs on a single page), stating the EU directives that it conforms to, along with some other basic information. This document is signed by someone in the company who has enough knowledge to make the statement, typically a senior person.

"affix the CE marking to a product"

Unless it's not practical (or not necessary), a CE mark needs to be visible on the product so that consumers can see it.

"Distributors must check that the product bears the CE marking and that the requisite supporting documentation is in order."

European distributors have a responsibility to ensure that the products they distribute are legitimately CE marked. This helps to prevent sales of products that have no (or bogus) CE marking.

"The importer has to verify that the manufacturer has undertaken the necessary steps and that the documentation is available upon request."

Again, this is to prevent the sale of products that are not properly CE marked.

US VERSUS EU

The above process probably seems like a lot of work—and to be sure, it's not trivial. But in practice, it's typically a more straightforward process in the EU than in the US, because the EU's regulations are more organized and consistent (at least in my experience). For example, notice how we just walked through a single write-up of the process that covers *all* goods in *all* countries in the EU, ranging from floor tiles to medical devices. The details are different for each specific product, but the basic theme of information being reasonably easy to find remains. In the US, the process tends to vary more from one agency to another.

On the other hand, EU regulations do pose a few challenges compared to those in the US, starting with the number of product types that are regulated: more items are regulated in the EU than in the US, so we're more likely to be regulated.

Second, EU regulations have a greater tendency to extend beyond safety and into *performance*—many types of products are required to show both that they're safe and that they do what they're supposed to do. By contrast, US regulations tend to stick only to product safety.

For example, suppose that we're developing an electronic beer mug that flashes an LED when the beer is filled to a certain volume. Once a mug claims to measure volume, in the EU it becomes a *measuring instrument* and might need to follow regulations that ensure that this claim is valid. Even a plain old beer mug with a line showing volume (say, a 500 ml mark) might have to reckon with the Measuring Instruments Directive (2004/22/EC): Common Application—Capacity Serving Measures (CSM). Whether it needs to meet this directive depends on the country that we're selling it in: many directives include options that each individual country can enforce differently. So while the EU is harmonized to a large degree, it's not perfect, and differences can arise between countries. *Enforcement* also varies from country to country. Germany, in particular, is pretty tough (as several well-known Kickstarter projects found out when they tried to get product through customs to their German backers).

A third "gotcha" compared to the US is that the EU makes greater use of third-party standards, and these standards aren't freely available. They typically cost $100–$200 per standard, and some products might need to comply with several. Standards are available from several vendors online as PDFs. Just search for the standards you need—they're called out in the relevant regulations—and you'll find them. Prices vary somewhat so it pays to shop around a little.

When shopping for standards, make sure to get the correct versions (i.e., edition and/or year). New versions appear from time to time, and it can take several years between the time a standard is published and the time it's adopted by government agencies. For example, while the latest *available* version of a standard might be the *third* edition, agencies might still be using (and asking for conformance to) the *second* edition. Regulations will call out the specific versions they reference.

FINDING THE EU REGULATIONS THAT APPLY TO US

The best way to get started with EU regulations is to use the "wizard." (*http://bit.ly/1CVlIMf*) The first step is to find the directives (groups of regulations) that apply to us, by choosing the relevant "product groups" from the drop-down list. Each product group listed maps to a particular EU Directive (group of regulations), which will be displayed. Although we'll need to comply with directives from all product groups that apply to our product, we can only go through the wizard for one product group at a time. If no product groups fit our product, then CE marking is not required.

There are three directives of particular interest for devices that contain electronics:

Electromagnetic compatibility
This is roughly similar to the US FCC regulations for electronic products that don't intentionally radiate RF energy.

Low voltage
This ensures that devices that have input or output voltages between 50 and 1000 V AC and/or between 75 and 1500V DC are safe for consumers. In practice, this applies to products that plug into the wall for power, not to those that run solely on batteries.

Radio and telecommunications terminal equipment
This covers any product that intentionally uses radio frequency energy to communicate, such as WiFi. This is roughly similar to US FCC's regulations for intentional radiators.

Once we select a directive that applies, the wizard walks us through the steps needed to qualify for our CE Mark.

> **TIP** Notified body is a term that crops up with regard to CE marking. As in the US, certain regulations require certification from a third party. A notified body is an organization that is authorized by an EU government to certify conformance to regulations. In practice, the same organizations that are authorized to certify to US regulations are also authorized to certify to EU regulations (and typically authorized for other countries as well). One-stop shopping for all of our regulatory needs.

CRADLE TO GRAVE: SAFE DISPOSAL

The EU is also different than the US in that product regulations emphasize safety even after consumers have disposed of a product. The *Restriction of Hazardous Substances Directive* (RoHS, pronounced row-haas) is the best known of these regulations. Targeted at electronic products, RoHS limits the use of six toxic substances:

- Lead

- Mercury

- Cadmium

- Hexavalent chromium (used in chrome plating)

- Polybrominated biphenyls (flame retardant used in plastic)

- Polybrominated diphenyl ether (flame retardant used in plastic)

Interestingly, the limits on the amount of each hazardous material are *per-component*, not *per-product*. So the key to meeting RoHS is to ensure that all components and raw materials (e.g., plastic for injection molding) meet RoHS individually, which is not too difficult to do these days. It's a good idea to have a "RoHS" checkbox next to each component on our bill of materials spreadsheet to remind us to check each part for RoHS conformance before ordering.

Less well known than RoHS is the *Waste Electrical and Electronic Equipment Directive* (WEEE), which is an overarching plan to maximize recycling of electronic waste. Under WEEE, manufacturers of electrical and electronic equipment must provide a means for their products to be recycled. In practice, this is done by these manufacturers banding together into groups called *producer compliance schemes*, which handle collections and recycling. The bottom line is that manufacturers of electronic products in the EU should expect to join a producer compliance scheme in each country in which their product is sold. The fees to join these schemes are dependent on the amount of a manufacturer's waste that is collected each year.

WEEE compliance also includes adding appropriate labeling, as shown in Figure 10-3, so that consumers know to recycle electronic devices rather than to throw them in the trash.

FIGURE 10-3. WEEE mark

The EU also has a *Battery Directive,* which limits the hazardous materials that can be used in batteries. This directive sets out a couple of interesting tasks for manufacturers beyond simply ensuring that that the batteries they use meet the directive's requirements.

- Batteries must either be externally removable from devices or have instructions for removal if they're embedded, unless "for safety, performance, medical or data integrity reasons, continuity of power supply is necessary and requires a permanent connection between the appliance and the battery."

- As with WEEE, producers must provide a way for consumers to recycle batteries. Usually this is done through the same producer compliance schemes as are used for WEEE.

While the Battery Directive is EU-wide, each member country enacts its own statutes to meet it. This has led to laws in some countries that dramatically limit the use of nickel cadmium (NiCd) batteries, or even ban them altogether. These countries include Austria, Belgium, Denmark, Sweden, Finland, France, Germany, the Netherlands, and the UK. Fortunately, the world of rechargeable batteries is moving away from

NiCds anyway, toward lithium ion (Li-ion) batteries which store more energy for a given size and weight. But these Li-ions lead to another regulatory issue, as we're about to see.

Batteries at 35,000 Feet

There is one other set of product regulations that often applies to makers of electronic products, which is unusual in that it's *international* in scope: regulations around shipping batteries and devices that contain batteries.

The ability for small batteries to store a lot of energy enables us to run our smart phones and laptop computers for many hours. The flip side is that holding a lot of energy in a small space is not only the hallmark of a good *battery*, it's the hallmark of a good *bomb*. And it turns out that batteries can make pretty good little firebombs if they are mistreated, improperly manufactured, or defective. Li-ion batteries are of greatest concern by far because they store the most energy in the smallest space, and because lithium burns really well. (To see what Li-ion batteries can do when things go wrong, search the Web for "lithium battery explode" and check out the videos.)

Li-ion batteries are shipped around the world in very large quantities these days, and of course there's a possibility that these batteries can do bad things in transit. Li-ion batteries doing bad things while in flight is a particularly scary scenario: if a plane contained a large shipment of Li-ions, and they were to explode in a chain reaction (i.e., exploding batteries causing nearby batteries to *also* explode), the result would obviously be ugly.

To avoid in-flight tragedies, the International Air Transport Association (IATA) has created regulations around the shipment of Lithium-based batteries by air that manufacturers should be aware of. Information is available from IATA (*http://bit.ly/1CVmlVW*).

ITAR

The International Traffic in Arms Regulations (ITAR), enforced by the Department of Homeland Security, is aimed at ensuring that military and defense materials and information aren't shared with potential adversaries without proper permission. This brings up a few questions:

- What qualifies as military and defense materials and information?
- Who are potential adversaries?

- What counts as sharing?
- How do we get permission to share?

The products covered by ITAR are those on the US Munitions List (USML), found in CFR 22 Part 121. The USML contains the obvious sorts of things one would expect, such as tanks, planes, and bombs, along with some subtle items, such as information and algorithms that are critical defense functions. The latter category of subtle items is covered in this chapter, as it's more applicable to intelligent products.

In ITAR-speak, the world consists of two categories of people:

- *US Persons*, which basically includes US citizens and any other legal permanent US residents, along with US corporations and government entities.

- *Foreign Persons*, which includes people and entities that are not US Persons.

Under ITAR, it's OK for US Persons to share USML information and materials amongst themselves, but sharing with a Foreign Person is prohibited without permission (or under certain exemptions). The technical term for sharing is *exporting*, and includes purposeful sharing, accidental sharing, and even situations where accidental sharing could take place. For example, if we leave a page face-up on our desk that contains source code covered by the USML, and a Foreign Person walks near our desk and could have looked at it (we weren't keeping an eye on them), that counts as an export. Sometimes the phrase *deemed export* is used rather than the word *export* because we might not know if an export truly occurred; but for the purpose of the regulations, it's been deemed to have occurred.

The most dramatic time that ITAR rears its head is if we're developing a product for military use. Working with ITAR requires a good deal of effort, including:

- We can only have US Persons working on the project.

- We need to make sure that foreign persons can't get access to the work being done. Visitor IDs should be checked, foreign persons assigned an escort, and so forth.

- Vendors, including data storage services, PCB fab houses, and so forth, must be ITAR-compliant.

There are many details that crop up and must be dealt with. For example, if we can't ensure that our building's after-hours cleaning crew only consists of US Persons and is otherwise ITAR-compliant, we must make sure that all work is safely locked up each evening when people leave for the day. Taking our laptop to a foreign country with ITAR material on the hard drive can be a problem.

ITAR-related issues can also crop up when we sell product and purchase components. If our product is covered under ITAR, we might need a license to sell it abroad. Because other regulations besides ITAR can require permission for foreign sales, the US government has set up a central site (*http://www.export.gov*) to help us to navigate through the various agencies and regulations that can affect us.

ITAR (and other export regulations) can also impact us when we order components. Even if we're located within the US, vendors might need some documentation from us before delivering certain parts; they'll normally want to know that we're not associated with one of the nefarious entities identified on various government lists, nor are we purchasing the parts for potential exportation to these nefarious entities. In my experience, this has not been a rigorous vetting (roughly 10 minutes filling out a form), but it can add a day or more of time to component procurement.

For our final topic, let's move to ISO 9001, a standard that applies to whole companies, not just products.

Quality Systems and ISO 9001

When we work with vendors, a key question we should be asking is "Do these folks actually do what they claim to do?" Suppose we buy 10,000 330-ohm resistors specified to have certain specifications such as tolerance, size, power rating, and temperature coefficient. We'd like to believe that each resistor meets its specifications, but how can we be confident of this? We can test each resistor (or a statistically smart sample) to check that they're OK, but that's extra work. Wouldn't it be better if we had a rational basis for being confident that the resistors meet their specifications without needing to test?

The degree to which a product (or service) fulfills its requirements is an objective measure of *quality*. *Quality management systems* (QMSs) are policies, processes, and procedures—essentially "recipes"—that businesses (and other organizations) develop and follow to ensure that their products and services meet customer expectations; resistors meeting their advertised specifications is one example of quality.

Having a quality system is sometimes a legal requirement, such as when building medical devices and for CE marking in many cases. Any set of recipes can serve as a QMS, but there are internationally recognized *quality management standards* that QMSs can adhere to, ISO 9001 being the best-known and most popular; more than one million organizations worldwide currently have QMSs that are certified to conform to this standard.

As a point of clarification, ISO 9001 is a quality management *standard*, not a quality management *system*. Each company is unique and thus each needs its own unique quality system. ISO 9001 simply lays out a general framework that quality systems can conform to—general enough that it can apply to virtually any business, from law firms to resistor manufacturers to food makers.

There are a couple of nice benefits to using ISO 9001 as a guide for a quality system:

1. It's been carefully thought through by many smart people, and thus is recognized throughout the world as being a good way to go. If a QMS conforms to ISO 9001, then it's probably a reasonable set of recipes for delivering products and services that meet customer requirements, and (depending on industry) many or most customers know its value.

2. Adherence to ISO 9001 can be certified by third parties if we want or need them. Audits are regularly conducted to ensure that the quality system conform to ISO 9001 and (just as important!) that the organization is truly following their QMS.

The takeaways here are:

- ISO 9001 certification isn't a guarantee that a vendor's products perform as advertised, but it should give us reasonable confidence. For components that can cause significant havoc if they don't perform as advertised, extra testing to confirm performance can be a good idea.

- Depending on the product(s) we develop, we might want or need ISO 9001 certification for our company. Since ISO 9001 includes product development activities, it's a good idea to implement our quality system before we're too deep into development so we'll be able to follow the right recipes and have our product developed according to the standard.

There are plenty of good resources that describe ISO 9001 (see the Resources section), and the standard itself is very readable (but, alas, it costs about $150) so I won't dive further into the details. However, I've worked with ISO 9001 (and its medical device equivalent, ISO 13485) for a fair number of years and have helped developed conformant quality systems on several occasions, so I have a few thoughts based on my experiences:

- ISO 9001 (and ISO 13485) can be very useful if implemented well. If not implemented well, they're just excess baggage causing extra paperwork.

- Quality systems should be as easy to use as possible. It's much better to have simple but imperfect recipes that people will actually follow than to have perfect recipes that everyone rolls their eyes at. Start simple and improve slowly (but surely).

- Documenting that we comply with our quality system is one of the major challenges here. If we can't provide objective evidence that we've complied, then it doesn't count if and when we get audited. Since few people enjoy documenting what we do ("we're just creating paperwork!"), it's important to make documenting as invisible as possible. For example, it's normally much better to have a computer application guide a user through a process and automatically create a time-stamped audit trail of events than it is to ask the user to fill out a form when they've completed a task.

- Just claiming conformance to ISO 9001 is a much different thing than third-party certification. If a vendor claims conformance without certification, it's difficult to know how good their quality system really is without auditing them, and even then most of us don't know the right questions to ask.

One final note: as of this writing (early 2015), a new version of ISO 9001 is being readied. As discussed previously in this chapter, always keep an eye out for which version of a standard is current and/or needed to comply with any regulations that apply to us.

This wraps up our very short overview of ISO 9001 and our larger tour of the various regulations, standards, certifications, and marks we might encounter. Before moving on to our next chapter, let's close with some final observations.

Final Thoughts

Few designer/developers relish their encounters with regulations, but most of us understand that they're useful for raising the bar on product safety (and in some cases, performance). And whether or not we appreciate their utility, we need to follow regulations because they're the law.

The biggest blunder in regulatory matters is in ignoring them until the end of development (or even later!). It's important to identify and understand the regulations we'll need to follow so that we can develop our product to meet them, and so we can plan schedule and budget appropriately. As with most other areas of product development, it's mainly about avoiding surprises that only increase in cost the later we find them.

Resources

Since regulations tend to be pretty specific, most of this chapter's resources are found in the text where their related topic is discussed.

VOLUNTARY CERTIFICATIONS

The subject of voluntary certifications is somewhat open-ended, and worth looking at particularly for products that plug directly into wall power, use a lot of energy (electricity, heat), or otherwise have a high potential to be unsafe if something goes wrong. For more information on the types of voluntary certifications available and why they can be useful, UL's site has a good and comprehensive FAQ (*http://ul.com/corporate/faq/*).

It can be instructive to look at products similar to what we're developing to see what markings they have, because we might want to get the same markings and certifications. The TechNick website (*http://bit.ly/1CVmw3z*) has as extensive a listing of international marks as I've seen, although there are still plenty of marks "in the wild" that aren't listed and will require an Internet search.

EU REGULATORY FRAMEWORK

In this chapter, I presented what's essentially a "Reader's Digest" version of the EU regulatory framework—enough information for manufacturers to have a pretty good idea of how regulations in the EU work, but certainly not a comprehensive treatment.

If you'd like to really dig in and get the full picture of the EU world of directives, regulations, authorized bodies, notified bodies, and so forth, the 100+ page *Blue Guide* (*http://ec.europa.eu/DocsRoom/documents/4942*) on the implementation of EU product rules is the place to go.

ISO 9001

Because ISO 9001 is so ubiquitous, there are many good resources on the Internet, but here are a couple that I find particularly good. Praxiom produces a series of commercial titles on ISO standards translated into "plain English," such as *ISO DIS 9001 2015 Translated into Plain English*. Praxiom's website (*http://www.praxiom.com/iso-90012008-intro.htm*) also contains a good overview of ISO 9001, at no charge (and in plain English).

The ISO site (*http://www.iso.org/iso/iso_9000*) itself is also worth a look, as well as their free and helpful pamphlet (*http://bit.ly/1CVmFnN*).

## CHAPTER 11

Writing Requirements That Work

AT THE VERY START OF ITS BIRTHING PROCESS, OUR PRODUCT IS AN abstract idea that lives in the heads of one or a few individuals. And that abstract idea is probably focused on the end benefit of the product—on the *really cool* things it does—rather than the "background" features such as the product's size, color, and battery life. Those features are less fun to think about and generally assumed to be ideal values: the size *is whatever is best*, the color is *one that people like*, the battery life is *infinite*, and so on.

Some months or years later, a *real product* is shipped to customers. It has perhaps hundreds of *real* features. Size, color, and battery life are now real and hopefully they enhance the product rather than hurt it.

> **TIP** Requirements planning is the process of consciously turning our abstract ideas into real product features by way of creating requirements for those features as early as we can in order to minimize surprises down the line.

Requirements are a list of things that some group of people agrees the product must do by the time it is ready to be sold. They typically (but not necessarily) look something like these requirements for the MicroPed activity tracker:

- MicroPed shall have a Bluetooth Smart wireless interface
- MicroPed's step accuracy shall be within 5% of actual on a flat, paved surface

- MicroPed shall operate for one year or longer on a single battery

Requirements are all about setting common expectations for stakeholders. Stakeholders work together at the beginning of a project to agree on the things a product must do to be successful, and these things become requirements set forth in a document. The document serves a couple of specific purposes:

- In principle, anyone can look at the requirements long before a product is built and see the critical things the product will do, as well as get some information on characteristics like size, weight, and reliability. This way, we know what we can tell prospective customers, investors, and others. *(But beware—requirements can change during development.)*

- The folks developing the product can use it as a set of instructions that describe what they should build. At the end of the project, the testing that makes sure the product is OK to sell generally focuses on demonstrating that the requirements were met.

Like most of the tools in our product development arsenal, requirements planning isn't one-size-fits-all. For a couple of entrepreneurs in a garage, the process might be as simple as jotting down a list of a few key items to keep in mind during development. For an aircraft manufacturer, the process might involve dozens (or even hundreds) of full-time staff working for months or years.

Before we dig into the details, let's define some terms.

Requirements Versus Goals Versus Specifications

The nomenclature around requirements planning is both ample and confusing. Many words are used that mean different things to different people. In this chapter, we'll try to steer clear of jargon in favor of concepts. Jargon is important because it gives us a shorthand way to express concepts, but given the malleability of commonly used words in this area, I'll leave it to product development teams to agree on the jargon they want to use.

We do need to label a few basic concepts including requirements, goals, and specifications, which all have to do with describing the functionality of our product. They often get confused with one another—again, probably because there are no hard-and-fast definitions.

Here's how we'll use these descriptors in this chapter:

- *Requirements* are quantifiable things that the product must do.

- *Goals* are general things that we strive for but which are difficult to quantify or difficult to meet. For example, we might have a requirement for at least five hours of battery life, but a goal of seven hours. This helps us to pay attention to the "nice to haves" during the development process.

- *Specifications* are quantifiable descriptions that are outputs from some portion of the development process. For example, the product we develop might turn out to reliably run for six hours on a battery charge, and we'll want to claim that in our advertising, manuals, etc. "Runs for six hours on a charge" now becomes a specification, which describes what the product actually does. The tricky part here is that specifications can become requirements, and requirements can become specifications. For example, if the battery we selected is discontinued, then we'll probably want to select another battery that also supports at least six hours of operation. So in many cases, specifications that we don't want to change become requirements.

Designer/developers like to design/develop stuff, and requirements planning is not something most of us love to do. And as we'll see, no matter how careful we plan our requirements, they'll be somewhat off the mark. So why go through the exercise? Let's take a look at why it's important.

Why Requirements?

As with much in the world of product development, requirements planning is about reducing risks earlier rather than later, when they're more expensive to fix. In fact, in my own experience, a lack of a good requirements planning process is, by far, the greatest cause of grief in the product development process.

> **TIP** I'll say that again because it's so important. In my personal experience, a lack of a good requirements planning process is, by far, the greatest cause of grief in the product development process.

Let's look at a simple but not-uncommon example of disaster caused by missing requirements. Suppose that Marketing has an idea in its head that a new product with embedded software will be initially released in the US, Canada, the UK, Germany, and France. But they don't capture this idea as a *requirement* to the hardware or software developers. What could go wrong? It's just a matter of changing some words on the screens, right?

Here are some of the things that can (and often do!) go wrong when we neglect internationalization issues until (what we thought was) the end of the development process:

- Perhaps the software platform (OS, language) was selected to be "lean and mean" in order to run on a very inexpensive processor, and so it does not have a facility for easily substituting screen text based on language tables. There's no built-in way for an application to use the same layout and graphics for each screen while substituting a different text file based on the user's language. In this case, developers will need to handcraft new screens for each language or develop their own mechanism for swapping in different text strings based on language. In either case, it will significantly increase both development and test efforts. Even the UK and Canadian version might require their own screens due to different spellings (e.g., colour versus color) and other subtle language differences.

- Text translations, particularly German and French, might not fit on screen layouts created to use English: it's not uncommon for these particular languages to require 50% more screen space to express the same ideas, and sometimes even much more for short phrases. The remedy could involve either a total redesign of the screens to have less information on each screen, or a hardware redesign to support a larger LCD. Both are significant.

- Perhaps the product stores some user data on a centralized database over the Internet. Because of different data privacy laws in different countries, the backend database might need re-architecting and redevelopment to ensure, for example, that any important personal data obtained in the EU is stored only in certain countries.

- Data privacy laws aren't the only regulations that vary from country to country. As we reviewed in some more detail in Chapter 10, different countries (or groups of countries) have different requirements around safety and other considerations. Without documentation demonstrating that the product meets EU standards, no EU importer or distributor will touch it. The product might need to be redesigned to meet EU safety standards, and be documented as doing so.

Here are a few more examples of issues that I've seen crop up due to a lack of sufficient requirements early in the project:

1. A modified version of the Linux kernel is developed for use in a military device. Just before the device was to begin field testing, the team realized that Linux's GPL *requires* that these kernel changes be released to the public, which was deemed inappropriate for a device of this type. Legal wrangling and software rewrites ensued, stressing budgets, timelines, and nerves. A requirement that "the licenses used by all software on the project must not include disclosure of source code or binaries to any other party" would have been very helpful here when an OS was selected.

2. A project used single-board computers that had non-replaceable, non-rechargeable batteries to back up their real-time clocks. The entire board needed replacement after 2–3 years when the batteries went dead. A requirement that the product have a real-time clock battery that will last X years without replacement and/or have a battery that is easily replaceable by the user could have avoided this.

3. LCD displays that sometimes mysteriously fail when shipped to certain destinations. It turns out that some LCDs have a minimum storage temperature rating that's higher than temperatures encountered in airline cargo holds. Once the temperature drops below the manufacturer's rating, all bets are off. A storage temperature requirement that takes into account the range of temperatures encountered in cold planes and hot warehouses could have helped here.

In all of these cases, a little more thought up front would have prevented many person-days (or person-months, or person-years) of work in the future. A requirements planning process that consciously decides on product attributes requires some more time up front, but results in far less aggravation later.

As important as good requirements are for a successful project, requirements can also cause harm; let's see how that happens and how we can avoid it.

The Case Against Requirements

While it's possible (and all too common) to not put enough effort into requirements, it's also quite possible to be overly reliant on requirements.

In some cases, a product group will get it into their head that they can do a really stellar and rigorous job of developing perfect requirements at the start for a development process that looks exactly as shown in Figure 11-1.

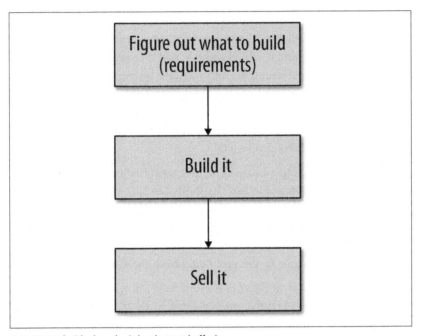

FIGURE 11-1. An ideal product development effort

Before the first line of code is written or the first chip is selected:

- Marketing will work really, really hard at the start to make sure that we're building exactly the product the customer wants to buy.

- Design will spend ample time working with prospective customers on the content, look, and flow of software screens to make sure that they delight the user in getting their tasks done.

- And when requirements are locked and development starts, they only change if The Lord herself asks for a change.

In theory, eliminating any ambiguity before developing the product will make the development process highly predictable:

- Technologists can make accurate estimates of development costs and schedules because they know what's needed — no guessing necessary.

- Work can proceed most efficiently without the cost and schedule hits that come when we need to make product changes because of requirements changes later in development.

- Developers and engineers don't have to work defensively, such as building things that "give us some flexibility in the future because we might decide to do X later on." After all, we *know* we won't have to do X later on.

The only problem is that such a thing can't be done. It's simply impossible to write perfect requirements at the start. Or even to write requirements that are close to perfect. For almost anything with a sophisticated user interface or that is tackling a new problem, generating requirements and blindly building to them will likely result in tragedy. There are four major reasons for this:

1. Customers don't really know what they want until they actually have it.

2. Technologists build what you *ask* them to build, not what you *meant* for them to build.

3. We gain important insights as the project progresses.

4. The world around us keeps changing.

Before we take a closer look at each of these, let me state that these should not be excuses for not writing good requirements at the start of a project. Rather, they are issues to consider that can help us understand why requirements will change as we proceed, and we might not want to get too detailed about some requirements at first (those around features that we know we need to understand better). But as with other planning activities, even if we get some of the details wrong, we'll get much more of them right, and the process itself will greatly increase our odds of success.

CUSTOMERS DON'T REALLY KNOW WHAT THEY WANT UNTIL THEY ACTUALLY HAVE IT

At first glance, it'd seem that users know what they want. Just ask them and they'll tell us. But blindly following user requests often leads to misery ("I know I said that I wanted X, and you did a great job of creating X, but unfortunately...").

It turns out that customers can often tell us what they *think* they want. But for various reasons, that might be different from what they *actually* want. This inaccurate information from customers can be due to anything from users truly not knowing what they want, to human forgetfulness, to the customer misunderstanding our questions, to us misunderstanding their answers.

GETTING MORE-ACCURATE INFORMATION FROM USERS

There are certainly ways to improve the quality of information that we get from prospective users during the requirements phase. For example, people are generally much better at describing past behavior than in predicting future behavior, so we can ask them about experiences with other products: What features did they end up liking and using? What were the problems?

Even better than asking about past behavior, we can observe users in the actual environment they'll use the product in to get a feel for what's really going on. Even better, we can make device models and screen mockups for users to try in their usual environment (or a close replica), and get feedback from the process.

TECHNOLOGISTS BUILD WHAT WE ASK THEM TO BUILD, NOT NECESSARILY WHAT WE MEANT FOR THEM TO BUILD

Fundamentally, requirements are instructions to the technologists. It's often the case, however, that requirements are correct but also unclear or incomplete. In Figure 1-3, we saw the example of Marketing wanting a Lamborghini designed, and specifying four wheels, a motor, etc. The technologists built a VW Beetle that meets the requirements just fine. Marketing got what it asked for but not what it wanted due to incomplete requirements.

Besides generating requirements that don't capture the essence of what we're looking for, requirements can also be inherently ambiguous. For example, consider this requirement:

- WiFi communications shall support WEP, WEP2, WPA, or WPA2 security.

This would likely mean that the chipset should support *all* of these, and use whichever is appropriate for the LAN it's attaching to. However, it could be read as the system only needing to support any *one* of those. So an electrical engineer might pick an older WiFi module that only supports WEP (if such a thing exists) and, technically, it would be what's specified—but not what was desired.

A better way to capture the intent of the requirement might be:

- The system shall support each of the following WiFi security schemes: WEP, WEP2, WPA, and WPA2 security.
- The WiFi security scheme shall be individually settable by the user for each network, in the network setup screen.

WE GAIN IMPORTANT INSIGHTS AS THE PROJECT PROGRESSES

As the project proceeds, new information and ideas bubble up. Opportunities to improve the odds of our product being successful might arise, such as:

- We get insights into functionality from talking with more prospective customers, possibly leading to new requirements.
- Marketing might uncover previously unrecognized markets with needs that are *almost* the same as the original target market. We might want to update requirements to support these other markets.
- We find out that we goofed. We *thought* that we could reuse some software that *almost* does what our new product needs, but the subtle differences we need turn out to be not subtle at all. Some of our requirements can no longer be met without a lot of extra cost and time. So we loosen up or remove those requirements.
- When a group of people spends a good bit of their time thinking about a product every day, there will be many *a-ha!* moments when individuals come up with improvements. Some of these might push changes to requirements: for example, we might determine that showing help *videos* rather than text on a device's screen will improve usability, but we'll need to change requirements to increase screen

size because videos are difficult to watch on the original small screen we specified.

> **TIP** Insights and improvements are a double-edged sword. On the one hand, they can cause requirements to change, which makes our product better and more profitable. On the other hand, they almost inevitably cause delay.

THE WORLD AROUND US KEEPS CHANGING

While we toil away at developing our product, things happen that are beyond our control. Perhaps a supplier of key technology goes out of business or otherwise stops selling components to us. For example, a huge OEM chooses the same 4" transreflective LCD display that we did, and has purchased all production for the next three years. It was *perfect* for outdoor use but neither it nor any similarly sized transreflectives are available to us any more. Our requirements might well have to change to accommodate a different-sized LCD or a backlit LCD. But this backlit LCD will need to be specified as having a very powerful backlight for use in sunlight, which in turn might affect the power requirements.

Or maybe 20% of the way into the development process, a major customer guarantees the purchase of one million units, but the sales folks won the business by cutting the selling price to below what we had expected. We might need to change the requirements to lower the cost of manufactured units (but since we know we'll be selling a lot of units, we hope we'll have a larger budget to do more work on cost reduction).

You'll notice that in some of these cases, requirements were changed or removed. It sounds a little funny—if it's removable, why was it a *requirement* in the first place?

In practice, while some requirements are truly necessary (like a medical device being approvable by the FDA) many requirements are really about getting everyone on the same page. If a feature is required, then everyone on the project knows that it's scheduled to happen. But sometimes it turns out that a requirement can't be reasonably met; in that case, there should be a conscious effort to agree on requirements changes so that all parties are OK with it.

That wraps up our list of reasons why requirements must change somewhat as a project moves forward. Next, let's dig in with some suggestions on writing requirements that help.

Writing Good Requirements

Here are some suggestions on writing requirements that help rather than hurt. Requirements can do both!

CAREFUL: REQUIREMENTS ARE DESIGN CONSTRAINTS

On the one hand, a requirement acts as a goal for technologists to achieve. On the other hand, it also acts as a design constraint because it eliminates other ways of doing things.

For example, I'm fond of using replaceable swappable batteries (such as AAs and AAAs) in devices. They're fairly small, cheap, and pack a nice amount of power. Unlike devices with sealed rechargeable batteries, if my replaceable-battery-powered device runs out of juice, I can simply swap new batteries in to be back in action in moments—no need to find an outlet and wait for a recharge. I can buy a bunch of rechargeable AAs and keep some on hand, or in a pinch go buy some disposable cells in any drugstore or convenience store.

If I were writing requirements for a new portable product, it might be tempting for me to add: "must run off of replaceable AA batteries." But this seemingly simple requirement actually has many design implications, including:

- It sets the minimum size of the product. Obviously, the product will need to be large enough to enclose the batteries.

- The product will need to support battery replacement. Thus the enclosure must be designed with a door that opens and internal features that support the batteries and guide them into place, which adds design time. If it's a door that snaps shut without screws (but with a satisfying click, of course), then there might be limitations on the enclosure materials and molding processes that can be selected.

- It affects the mechanical configuration of the product (how parts are arranged). Batteries will need to be located in an area where they are next to the enclosure so they can be replaced, which might prevent clever arrangements of components to reduce size, improve heat dissipation, etc.

- For a given amount of charge, standard replaceable cells are larger and heavier than some other types of batteries. This might result in a heavier device in order to obtain a desired battery life or shorter battery life to obtain a desired size and/or weight.

- Unlike some other types of batteries, the charge remaining in AA cells cannot be measured accurately while in use. We won't be able to show the user a nice battery gauge with time remaining. At best, they'll have a bit of warning before the battery dies.

In some instances, there is a strong incentive to specify AAs or other battery types that are routinely replaced and widely available. Examples include cameras and other portable products that use a fair bit of power and for which recharging every few hours would be a serious nuisance. But unless we know that the ability to swap batteries is important, it's best to leave battery swapability out as a requirement so the designers can specify a power source that helps us to meet other requirements that are truly critical to our specific application, such as product size, weight, battery life, etc.

> **TIP** When developing requirements, we must be careful to require only those things that are important to us (which includes what's important to our customers), and let the designers work creatively within those constraints to build the best possible product.

REQUIREMENTS SHOULD BE TESTABLE

One of the hallmarks of a good requirement is that it's unambiguous. There should be no disagreement when the requirement is met. Another way to say that is that requirements should be testable. In many, or most, instances we will want to test the product design against our requirements to make sure that it does what we want it to do.

"The product shall be safe" is a typical well-intentioned but poorly written requirement. Who defines safe? How do we test that something is safe? The better way to write this would be along the lines of: "The product shall meet all safety regulations in the places it is marketed and sold." In that way, the burden of defining "safe" moves from us to the government, which makes sense because they're the ones that we need to make happy. And it turns out that most all governments have well-defined standards and tests for product safety.

A subtler example might be around a product that's intended to be carried in a pocket. We could write a requirement that "The product shall fit inside a pocket." However, pockets come in all sorts of shapes and sizes, from little shirt pockets to big pockets on lab coats, so this is an ambiguous goal.

We could take a guess at a specific size that would fit most pockets, say, "The product shall be no larger than 3" x 4" x 0.5." This could still result in a product that is too big or small because it's only a guess; but at least the designers have something specific to shoot for.

Another way to write a suitable size requirement for our device would be to express it in terms of user perception. Something like "90% of users in the target market we define will, after testing the product, agree with the statement that the product readily fits in their pocket." This is a good requirement because, in the end, product goodness or badness is all about how users see the product, not how we see it. A requirement like this also captures other subtleties, like the need for the product to easily slide into and out of a pocket. On the negative side, testing whether we've met this requirement will require bringing in a group of people to try the product and tell us what they think, which is a much more involved effort than whipping out a ruler.

REQUIREMENTS ARE INTERFACE-CENTRIC

As far as the outside world is concerned, a product is what it's perceived as. Effectively, a product is a group of interfaces to the outside world, with "stuff" inside that makes these interfaces work.

It follows that requirements should mainly be focused around the interfaces between the product and the outside world:

- Interfaces between the product and users (i.e., the user interface)

- Interfaces between the product and other products (e.g., USB ports, Internet services)

Requirements that pertain to interfaces tend to be *what* requirements: *what* we want the product to do. By contrast, requirements that pertain to the "stuff" inside the product tend to be *how* requirements: *how* we want the product to do what it should do. Most requirements should be *what* requirements because *how* requirements tend to tell designers and developers how to do their job and that's really their job, not ours. As much as possible, requirements should stick to the *whats* and let the designer/developers figure out the *hows*.

People are complicated but stuff is also complicated

We've seen that it's quite difficult to create perfect requirements in advance for interfaces to people. But it should be easy to write requirements for interfaces between hardware and software because that's just bits, voltages, currents, and physics. Right?

In theory, we can document interfaces between inanimate "stuff" really well, and then send developers off to build it in a way that meets the requirements. After development, we can bring the stuff together and it will all integrate nicely because it all meets the interface requirements.

In reality, as with human interfaces, *stuff interfaces* need to be tested early and often during the development process. If we assume that we'll get it right at the start, we'll be in for some unpleasant surprises.

Some interfaces are easier than others to specify. For example, if our product communicates to a computer via Bluetooth, then the Bluetooth interface is pretty well standardized. But when we move up a level to what gets communicated over Bluetooth, things can become more complex, depending on what we're communicating. The communication of some types of data over Bluetooth is standardized, such as between headset and phone, music player and wireless speaker, and so forth. But if we're passing data that's not supported by a standard Bluetooth profile, then we'll need to define the higher-level data formats and protocols so that senders and receivers can understand one another. In effect, when the sender sends information to the receiver, Bluetooth will ensure that the receiver will get it. But what will the receiver *do* with it? That's up to us.

Other "standard" interfaces vary in their standardization. For example, like Bluetooth, USB is a communications "pipe" that also supports certain higher-level interface definitions, which is the way transmitted information is interpreted and standardized in certain usage scenarios such as keyboards, mice, game controllers, and mass storage. But even if our product's USB communications conform to one of these standard scenarios, USB is a bit of a mess when it comes to supplying and drawing power. There are multiple power standards, and many USB devices bend those standards. It's important to test any product's interfaces that use USB with many other devices early and often throughout the product's life cycle.

TIP The initial requirements for any interfaces that we develop from scratch, between internal subsystems for example, are very likely to be incomplete, ambiguous, and/or just plain wrong. Interface design is a skill, and unless we've designed a very similar interface before and taken it all the way to production, we are likely to make some mistakes. It's important to specify these requirements reasonably well before starting work, but provisions should be made to test the subsystems early and often as development proceeds.

I recall one development project that I was involved with (working at a subcontractor), which was a large and sophisticated effort at one of the largest major electronic product makers. They'd been burned before by subsystems not playing well together due to what they believed was a nonoptimal requirements process that created too much ambiguity. So this time they were going to make darned sure that they got the subsystem interface requirements right. No effort would be spared to make sure these requirements were perfect. Perfect!

After a process that took many months, many people, and many dollars, the requirements were complete. There was no need to waste time testing subsystems with each other until they were complete, of course, because the requirements were so good. We thought we'd bolt them together at the end, and all would work. Or at least be pretty close.

Of course, utter chaos still prevailed when things *were* finally bolted together. Since subsystems were far along in their development process, changes were generally expensive to make. And fixing one issue would break other things. The project eventually came together, but years late and way over budget.

The moral, of course, is that while ignoring requirements at the beginning of a project is folly, it's no better (and perhaps worse) to assume that we can adequately generate perfect requirements at the start. Requirements will change as the product is developed and exposed to the real world so we need to follow a process that exposes our product to the real world early and often.

Now that we have an idea of what makes a good requirement, how do we determine the features and functions that we'll write requirements for? Next, we'll try to answer that question.

Positive Requirements Versus Lurking Requirements

I like to break requirements into two types:

1. *Positive requirements,* which address the key thing(s) our product does. These are the things we'd mention if given 15 seconds to describe our product. For example, a positive requirement for a pedometer might be "the product will create challenges to motivate the user."

2. *Lurking requirements,* which address all the background stuff that isn't central to our product's mission but will cause trouble if we don't address it properly. Examples include size, weight, battery life, regulatory requirements, reliability, and so forth.

 Breaking requirements into these two categories is not any sort of industry standard. It's my own construct — feel free to use it or reject it as you wish.

There's no hard and fast rule as to which requirements fall into which category. Items that are a key to one product's success might be background issues for others. The utility in calling out these two groups of requirements is more of a reminder than anything else: there are some types of requirements that are fun and easy to talk about (positive requirements), and there are some that we must make an effort to address or else our great product will have feet of clay (lurking requirements).

A LURKING REQUIREMENTS CHECKLIST

It's easy to miss some lurking requirements at the start of a project. Below is a checklist of categories of lurking requirements that can be useful to review at the start of a project:

- Countries we'll be selling our product in.
- Inclusion of manuals, labeling, etc.
- Languages for applications, manuals, labeling, etc.
- Regulatory requirements. These typically include safety and electromagnetic compatibility.
- Reliability. This is typically expressed as a *mean time between failures* (MBTF) or other measure. In practice, determining and/or estimating reliability prior to selling units is a nontrivial exercise.
- Availability of parts. For example, all parts are expected to be available for five years after manufacturing begins.

- Brightness, loudness, etc. How bright should LCD screens be? How loud should speakers and alarms be?

- Environmental conditions during use. Max/min temperature, humidity, altitude, drop height, shock resistance, airplane or other travel modes (silent), airport security scanners.

- Environmental conditions during shipping/storage. Again, max/min temperature, humidity, altitude.

- Size/weight/color. Any special requirements not covered in positive requirements.

- Resistance to water and/or dust. These are typically expressed using the *standard ingress protection* (IP) rating. For example, a liquid ingress IP rating of 4 means that our product resists splashing water. A list of IP ratings and associated tests to demonstrate that we meet a given rating can be easily found on the Web (showers, swimming, rainstorms, laundry).

- Usability. Define the users, and some measure of usability. For example "90% of a random sample of Registered Nurses shall be able to successfully complete all of the following tasks, unaided, after reading the manual." Include considerations for users that have disabilities (vision, hearing, etc.) as appropriate.

- Cost of goods sold (COGS). What's the maximum manufactured price at which we can make a buck?

- License restrictions around IP created elsewhere. For example, the need for any software used to be licensable in a way that does not require the release of modified source code.

- Licensing of the device/software and upgrades. Per-use, per-user, or other licensing requirements that might need to be enforced by the device software/hardware.

- Security. Personal data, financial data, password storage, protecting the designs and code in the product from reverse engineering

- Power requirements. 120V AC? 240V AC? Car plug? Etc.

- Hardware/software platform: if our product requires the use of other systems, such as when it includes installable software, we should specify (as possible) the hardware and software that we'll support. Examples are operating systems including versions and patch levels, web browser types and versions, minimum memory and processor requirements for computers, interfaces including revisions (e.g., USB 2.0), smart phone versions, etc.

- Support. Examples might include the need for logs of errors that occur and ways to transmit that information to service personnel.

- Responsiveness. How quickly should the system respond to events, such as a user selecting an option on a screen? How long from turn on until the device is ready for use? Will there be a splash screen or lights to let the user know something's happening?

- Serviceability. Can the device be serviced if something fails, or should it be replaced? If serviceable, which parts should be serviceable? Does it need periodic maintenance?

- Real-time clock issues. For any device with an internal clock that keeps track of date and time, a number of issues come up. How long should the clock run off its battery? Is the battery rechargeable or replaceable? How will the clock be set (user or Internet Network Time Protocol)? Should the device store local time or GMT/Zulu time? How much clock drift is acceptable (e.g., one minute per year)?

- Manuals. Should the product need a manual? If so, should it be printed and/or on the Web?

- Disposal. Should the device be disposed of as normal trash? Or can there be special requirements?

- Packaging. Will the packaging be fancy or functional? What kind of shipping stresses should it protect against?

Communicating Requirements

The "standard" way of writing requirements is to write each requirement as a sentence, along the lines of:

- The product *shall* have a wireless-n network interface which conforms to IEEE 802.11n

- The wireless-n network interface *should* use an off-the-shelf module that is precertified against relevant regulations in all target markets.

- The wireless-n network interface *may* use an external antenna to achieve additional range. If used, the antenna must be flexible and less than 3" long

What's with the *shall, should,* and *may*? They're standard requirements terms with specific meanings:

- *Shall/shall not*: something the product must or must not do.
- *Should*: something that would be good to have, but is not absolutely necessary.
- *Should not*: something we'd prefer not to have, but can live with it.
- *May*: totally optional. May not is redundant with may.

So the above sentences, translated, are:

- Our product *must* support 802.11n.
- The people writing the requirements are suggesting that it would be a good idea to use a wireless module that's precertified for the target markets. Since certification is a pain in the butt and not cheap, this is virtually always a good idea for lower-volume products. But there's some flexibility here, in case doing a circuit from scratch will truly work out better.
- The product can have a small antenna if it helps.

That's the way it's often done, but it certainly doesn't have to be that way. We can use a spreadsheet or database, for example, where the first column holds what we want and the second column holds its degree of necessity, as shown in Table 11-1.

TABLE 11-1. Requirements in table format

#	Feature	Necessity
1	Wireless IEEE 802.11n interface	Mandatory
2	Wireless uses OTS module precertified in all markets	Preferred
3	Wireless external antenna < 3"	Optional

We can even break the mold some more and increase the number of "importance" ratings beyond 3, turning them into priority ratings, say, on a scale from 1–10 where 10 = *Must* and 1 = *Must Not*.

MAKING REQUIREMENTS CLEARER

In general, our job is to make requirements as easy to read and clear as possible. To that end, we can go beyond lines of text for our requirements wherever it's helpful. For example, we can use a mix of pictures, use-case diagrams, state tables, and other artifacts. It's a good idea to tie these all together with a single document or table that points to all of these other items. For example, we can expand Table 11-1 in this way, as shown in Table 11-2.

TABLE 11-2. Referencing other artifacts from within requirements

#	Feature	Importance
1	Wireless IEEE 802.11n interface	Mandatory
2	Wireless uses OTS module precertified in all markets	Preferred
3	Wireless external antenna < 3"	Optional
4	Wireless setup workflow matches that of [previous product X]; see attached use case Exhibit A	Preferred
5	Color screen	Mandatory

We can also add other bits of information to each requirement that will help us down the line:

Rationale

Why do we have this requirement? This will push us to make thoughtful requirements, and can also help readers to understand requirements that can seem odd.

Test Method

A brief description of how we will test that the requirement is met. This pushes us to write only testable requirements and to start thinking about what will be needed for the test process.

So now our requirements table now grows a bit more, as shown in Table 11-3.

TABLE 11-3. Requirements with additional detail

#	Feature	Importance	Rationale	Test Method
1	Wireless IEEE 802.11n interface	Mandatory	Need an industry standard for LAN communications. 802.11n is ubiquitous, gives us sufficient bandwidth, and is more convenient than a wired Ethernet port.	Test results demonstrating conformance to 802.11n standard.
2	Wireless uses OTS module precertified in all markets	Preferred	Not needing our own intentional radiator testing reduces fixed costs by $25k or more; reduces risk of not passing testing and needing redesign; initial product volumes are low, so increased unit cost is still worthwhile	Obtain copies of certifications from module manufacturer. Verify certificate is real.
3	Wireless external antenna, bendable, < 3"	Optional	If this gives us substantial extra signal and keeps us within budget, it will not significantly detract from product appearance.	Measure antenna, and try bending it.
4	Wireless setup workflow matches that of [previous product X]; see attached use case Exhibit A	Preferred	We'd like current users of [previous product] to feel right at home with our new product, and we know that this workflow has been easy for users to learn.	Verification testing.
5	Color screen	Mandatory	Our competitors have color screens; market research found that potential buyers see it as a negative if we don't have one.	Visual inspection.

It's also useful to add an owner to each requirement who is a person or department that's responsible for that requirement being met. If it's a department, a specific person within each department should be assigned as the "point person" for that department's requirements and they can delegate to others as needed.

At the start of this chapter, we discussed that a key purpose of requirements is to set common expectations for stakeholders. Next, let's take a look at how we can develop better requirements by getting better stakeholder involvement.

Great Requirements Come from Great Participation

The best-quality requirements emerge from a process where all stakeholders truly participate. Big bonus points if the process is also enjoyable. If you have fun creating the product, your customers are likely to have fun using it. Getting people into rooms with whiteboards and food works a lot better than simply passing documents around. There's something magical about people ideating face-to-face.

In many cases, requirements are written by a single person and then sent around for review and comment. This rarely works well. The person writing the requirements usually doesn't have all of the knowledge needed to generate good requirements, and they will surely miss items. Reviewers, working alone, tend to scan and look for glaring problems rather than spending quality time thinking through the issues.

Small companies usually have no problems generating positive requirements. After all, being creative is what they're best at. The trickier aspect is that teams are typically smaller and less experienced so it's easier to overlook lurking requirements. Being methodical and using a checklist like the one presented earlier in this chapter can help.

Folks at larger companies tend to be better at execution than at ideation so they might need some prodding to get the creative juices flowing. Larger firms can also have an additional hurdle in that a project might have many stakeholders, sometimes scattered across the globe, which can become unwieldy. What can work well is a process along the following lines:

1. Start by holding one or more a cross-functional meetings with representatives of all major stakeholders (e.g., Engineering, Design, Marketing, Sales, Corporate, Regulatory, Finance, etc.) to flesh out the major *positive* requirements. Some groups might only need representatives present at a subset of meetings. For example, Finance might only attend the kickoff meeting to give guidance on what's feasible from their point of view.

2. Write up the positive requirements that were agreed upon at the meeting, and meet again to review and refine.

3. Have each stakeholder group individually identify each type of lurking requirement that falls under their area of responsibility, and suggest those requirements or create a plan to determine those requirements. For example, Regulatory might be able to write their requirements without doing research because they've been involved with similar products. But Design might write a plan to do some studies to understand how the product will be used before writing requirements on size, weight, etc.

4. Have a cross-functional meeting with representatives of all major stakeholders to review and finalize (for now) the positive and lurking requirements.

We earlier discussed the certainty of requirements changing after stakeholders have agreed on them. While changes are ubiquitous, changing is not a trivial undertaking. Next we'll look at how we can effectively approach this task, and at some automation that can help in the process.

Maintaining Requirements

Most requirements aren't set in stone; they should be updated regularly as we have new information. The update process should ensure that:

- All relevant stakeholders have input.

- All relevant stakeholders are notified of changes so they can adjust to the changes.

- We consider the effect of any change on other requirements. For example, as we saw earlier this chapter, if we change from using lithium-ion rechargeable batteries instead of swappable off-the-shelf batteries, many requirements might have to change.

- We consider the effect of any requirements change on any *tests* that validate that the requirement was met.

One other thing to consider is that as development progresses, "optional" and "preferred" requirements resolve into real features that are mandatory. Our requirements should be updated to reflect this, in part because requirements drive testing and we need to be certain of what we'll be testing.

REQUIREMENTS MANAGEMENT SOFTWARE

A number of software packages exist for managing the requirements process. Examples include IBM Rational DOORS, IBM Rational Requisite-Pro, Borland Caliber, PTC Integrity, Enterprise Architect, and Parasoft Concerto. There are several tens of well-known software products sold today to address this task. Some of these packages primarily target requirements management, while others address requirements as part of addressing the overall product life cycle, a.k.a. Product Life Cycle Management (PLM) or Applications Life Cycle Management (ALM). While it's great to have tools that do everything, not just requirements management, these tools can be very nontrivial to configure in a way that makes them easy to use.

The advantages of these requirements management systems is that they can keep track of all the picky details of the process, such as tracking who's reviewed a requirement and signed off, which product features fulfill which requirement, and so forth.

Perhaps the most important function of requirements management software is to track the relationship between requirements and test procedures. In principle, all requirements should be fully tested before a product is released. In highly regulated industries (e.g., medical devices), full testing of all requirements is mandatory because it demonstrates that the product truly does what we claim it will do.

In some cases, a single requirement might lead to multiple tests to fully verify that it's been met. In other cases, a single test can help verify multiple requirements. The resulting *traceability matrix* showing the relationships between all requirements and all tests can become quite large, sometimes covering hundreds or thousands of requirements and dozens of test procedures. It's possible to construct such a matrix by hand—say, by using a spreadsheet—but living with the matrix over time can be extremely challenging. For example, suppose that customers find a nasty bug in our product, and we decide to change a test procedure so the same problem will get caught in testing if it comes up again. If that test procedure helps to verify multiple requirements, we should also review whether the changed test will still test those other requirements properly.

Keeping track of all of this using a spreadsheet can be very cumbersome. By contrast, a good requirements management package will automate much of the process. When a test procedure changes, it will alert as to which requirements should be reviewed, keep track of who's reviewed them and their conclusions, etc.

Some of the drawbacks of these packages are:

- They are a bit pricey. Plan on spending $3k–10k or more for a "serious" package.

- Learning curves are typically somewhat steep. Plan on at least one person spending a few days coming up to speed, and then helping others.

- Package must be configured for each company's specific needs. This requires time and/or professional consulting help.

- Organizations must commit to using a package regularly throughout the product development life cycle. Otherwise, the information will grow stale and become irrelevant.

Final Thoughts

This has been a long chapter for a subject that's rarely discussed at length —but for a good reason. In my experience, the lack of solid requirements is the biggest source of confusion, disputes, and overruns in product development. Gaining agreement on the details of what we're creating is critical to ensuring that everyone's working toward a shared goal. As Yogi Berra said, "If you don't know where you are going, you'll end up someplace else."

The number of details to be decided for a product that "seemed like it oughta be straightforward" can be surprising and it can be painful to spend time on planning rather than doing, but here's my guarantee: for each hour we spend on requirements planning, we'll save multiple hours on implementation.

This is particularly true for hardware, where creating revisions of circuits and mechanical components can take weeks or months. Sweating the details up front of what we're trying to accomplish can easily avoid an extra round of revisions, shaving months and serious dollars from the project.

I hope this chapter proves helpful to your efforts in creating requirements that are comprehensive enough to guide development, but not so comprehensive as to stifle problem solving. That's not always an easy balance to achieve, but even getting 80% of the way there will make a huge difference in a development effort's harmony and productivity, and in the quality of the result.

Resources

This chapter's covered requirement-ing at a fairly basic level. Various resources exist that get into a lot more detail. These can be quite helpful, although they sometimes (in my opinion) either get too exuberant about the fine details and/or assume that the process can be somewhat more cut-and-dry than it is in practice. Here are a few:

- The Systems Engineering Body of Knowledge (SEBOK) Wiki page on Systems Requirements (*http://sebokwiki.org/wiki/System_Require ments*), which in turn is based on the International Council on Systems Engineering (INCOSE) Systems Engineering Handbook (*http:// bit.ly/1CVpx3P*).

- The Project Management Institute (PMI) Guide to the Project Management Body of Knowledge (PMBOK) (*http://bit.ly/1CVpxkq*)

- *Customer-Centered Products: Creating Successful Products Through Smart Requirements Management,* by Ivy Hooks and Kristin Farry

- A helpful set of slides used in the MIT's Fall 2009 graduate course, Fundamentals of Systems Engineering (*http://bit.ly/1CVpy7W*), available through MIT's wonderful OpenCourseWare.

As mentioned in this chapter, shipping can expose a product to environmental extremes. The Fedex document Packaging Guidelines for Shipping Freight (*http://bit.ly/1CVpAgi*) has useful numbers for minimum temperature and pressure.

If you're shopping for an ALM tool to manage requirements and more, The Gartner Group's 2015 *Magic Quadrant for Application Development Life Cycle Management* can be helpful in seeing what's available, and Gartner's opinions (*http://gtnr.it/1CVpBka*) is also a good resource.

## CHAPTER 12

Meta-Stuff: Project Planning and Infrastructure

"WE *totally* FORGOT TO BUDGET FOR THAT."

"We spent 80% of our budget in 80% of the allotted time. I thought we were doing OK, but now I hear we're only half done?"

"Oh yeah, I saw that was a problem a few months ago and forgot about it. I guess I should have told someone before we got those PCBs fabricated."

"Oops, there's the problem. You were using an old copy of the interface specification when you designed this. The correct specification's pretty different."

It should be pretty obvious that these types of problems can wreak havoc in product development efforts, unnecessarily inflating budgets and schedules. They tend to be larger problems for larger efforts (ones with more people involved), in part because they primarily stem from missed communications: the amount of communications (and opportunities to mess it up) tends to rise exponentially with the number of people in an effort.

In this short chapter, we'll take a quick look at a few different "infrastructure" topics that can greatly influence the success of our development efforts:

1. Project planning (determining the who, what, where, when, and cost of what needs to get done)

2. Project management (ensuring that *project* and *project plan* remain similar to one another)

3. Issue tracking (ensuring that new information is appropriately acted upon)

4. Document control (ensuring that all team members have correct information)

5. Change management (ensuring orderly changes in design/development and manufacturing)

We can never make management of these big-picture issues totally painless but by paying attention to them throughout development, we'll end up with results that are cheaper, better, and faster.

Let's start at the chronological beginning of our efforts, with project planning.

Project Planning

Suppose that we ask a professional musician to improvise a new piece of music on the spot. If the musician has some talent, she might do a fine job, perhaps even great one. Ask two musicians to do the same, together, and a great performance is possible but less likely. If you get three or four musicians together, the odds of a quality performance without prior planning drops to almost nil. And what about a symphony orchestra of even the greatest musicians on Earth playing an improvised piece? Guaranteed cacophony.

Particularly as more players are involved, musicians need a plan for things to come together in a harmonious way. In the music performance world, these plans (of course) are called a score, or *sheet music*. A composer writes the piece with all of the individual parts in mind, and then the individual parts are meted out so each musician can do their part. When everyone does their part together, a wonderful result can emerge.

This observation is no less true of technology projects. As projects become more complex, they tend to require more formal planning; namely, a *project plan*. A simple project with a single experienced participant might not need a project plan, although it usually helps. Creating a skyscraper, which requires the interactions of thousands of people, will obviously require great big project plans. In fact, many people will be employed full-time just to develop the project plans and keep them updated throughout the project. Most projects fall somewhere between these two extremes in size and complexity, and so does their need for project planning.

Even if we're not in that group of people who want to make project planning a career, it always helps to better understand our projects, including:

- Cost and timeline

- Skills needed. For example, who should we hire/assign?

- Dependencies: when do we need what? For example, we don't want to have to wait weeks to test a prototype because we didn't think to order a specialized piece of equipment until it came time to begin testing.

Technology projects are notorious for going far beyond their original estimates for budget and schedule. In my experience, one of the prime drivers of ballooning development efforts is inadequate project planning. Not so much that doing things in a different sequence would have gotten the job done faster and cheaper, though there is some of that. Rather, thorough planning at the beginning of a project helps us remember many tasks that need to be done, which people have a tendency to forget when making rough estimates of time and cost. "That ought to take a month, tops!" often turns into a more-realistic three months when we work with experts to create a comprehensive plan that lists tasks and estimated efforts for each.

The project planning process can be as informal as creating and updating a spreadsheet with estimated hours/days of work for each resource (team member). For projects that involve more than a few people, I think it's best to use specialized project planning applications because these support some useful features that we'll soon introduce. In this chapter, I'll show screen snapshots from one of these specialized applications (Microsoft Project) to illustrate concepts because the features it supports are good to know about. Even if you end up using a spreadsheet, you might be able to program or otherwise create some of these specialized features if you think they'll be helpful. Figure 12-1 shows the initial project plan created for MicroPed's first phase.

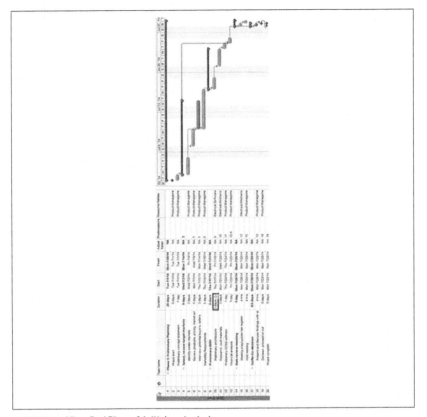

FIGURE 12-1. MicroPed Phase 1 initial project plan

As we'll see, this example is somewhat of a loose plan. Let's walk through it and see how it works, and then look at a more-detailed plan for another part of our project.

The project plan consists of a list of *tasks*. Each task, in turn, can have *subtasks* (seen as indented right under their overarching task). Subtasks can also have subtasks of their own and we can go down a fair number of levels. In our plan, *Phase 1: Preliminary Planning* is the top-level task, and *Risk review meeting* is a subtask that has two subtasks of its own.

Each task has a duration. In the case of tasks comprised of subtasks, the overall duration is automatically calculated, typically from the start of its earliest subtask to the end of its latest. (In some cases, even the duration of tasks without subtasks are calculated, as we'll discuss in a few moments.)

Tasks can have *dependencies* (the *Predecessor* column) that constrain when they can start and/or end. For example, task 13 (*Financial analysis*) is marked as not being able to start until task 4 (*Select, review target markets*) and task 12 (*Preliminary COGS estimate*) are complete. Other types of dependencies can be set. For example, we could set a *finish-finish dependency* if a task can't finish before another task does. We can also assign *resources* to a task (*Resource Names* column), so that everyone using the plan is clear on who's involved with each task.

One useful feature of project planning applications is that they can calculate the estimated start and end dates for each task based on dependencies and durations, along with project's start date that we set. The application will take into account days that we don't work, such as weekends and holidays that we set in the project plan's calendar. This can help prevent some surprises, particularly in the holiday-filled stretch of calendar that lies between Thanksgiving and New Year's Day. As we update our progress (e.g., a task finishes early), the application can change future start and finish date estimates based on our true progress.

The right side of Figure 12-1 is a *Gantt chart* automatically generated from the task information we've entered. Gantt charts can be pretty helpful in visualizing our project and planning changes. They show each task as a bar that begins and ends at the correct date. You'll notice that some bars are red and some are blue; in this chart, red denotes that the task is on the project's *critical path*. A critical path task is defined as one that will definitely affect the project's overall finish date if its start or end dates change. By contrast, changing duration of tasks not on the critical path won't necessarily affect the overall finish date. For example, tasks 6 and 7 in our example start at the same time (since they're both dependent on task 5). But 7 is on the critical path while 6 isn't, so shortening 6 won't end this phase any earlier.

Project managers often spend a lot of time with a project plan's critical path, usually in an effort to shorten the project duration. In our example, generating marketing requirements puts five work days in the critical path. One way to pull in the phase's finish date is to begin the marketing requirements before the target market task is complete—but we shouldn't complete our marketing requirements until we know our markets, so we could still leave a couple of days after markets are identified. We could do this in the project software by setting up a (somewhat fancy) dependency.

Our example project here is small, and most tasks lie on the critical path. In larger projects, which can often contain hundreds of tasks and a lot of parallel efforts, the critical path is often not at all obvious. Project planning applications that determine the critical path for us are incredibly helpful in these cases.

I set the task durations in this example based on "gut feel," but there's a better way to do it, as we'll see next.

EFFORT-DRIVEN PROJECT PLANNING

Suppose that we have one person working full time to complete a task, and we add a second person to help. Depending on the type of task, adding a second person should roughly halve the task duration because most tasks require a certain amount of effort (e.g., person-days or person-hours) to complete and we've now doubled the number of person-hours we can get per day.

Specifying task effort, rather than duration, is known as *effort-driven planning*. Duration is automatically calculated based on our specifying the effort required to complete the task and the resources available. Project planning software makes the mechanics of this process relatively easy; if we add a resource to a task, its duration automatically gets shorter.

Most projects contain a mix of tasks that are inherently effort-based, and somewhere duration is fixed (e.g., vendors will take a certain fixed time to create tooling). The project plan for the MicroPed nRF51822 breakout board, shown in Figure 12-2 and Figure 12-3, demonstrates both types of tasks (see the *Type* column)

#	Task Name	Duration	Start	Finish	Actual Finish	Predecessors	Type	Effort Driven	Work	Cost	Resource Names
27	nRF51822 breakout board	24.25 days	Tue 7/1/14	Mon 8/4/14	NA		Fixed Duration	No	94 hrs	$6,260.00	
28	Schematic	5.5 days	Tue 7/1/14	Tue 7/8/14	NA		Fixed Duration	No	27 hrs	$2,300.00	
29	Schematic Specification	1 day	Tue 7/1/14	Tue 7/1/14	NA		Fixed Duration	Yes	8 hrs	$500.00	Electrical Engineer
30	Select PCB Layout Tech	6 days	Tue 7/1/14	Tue 7/8/14	NA		Fixed Duration	Yes	5 hrs	$500.00	Electrical Engineer[13%]
31	Draft schematic	1 day	Wed 7/2/14	Wed 7/2/14	NA:29		Fixed Units	Yes	8 hrs	$500.00	Electrical Engineer
32	Schematic review	3 days	Thu 7/3/14	Mon 7/7/14	NA:31		Fixed Duration	Yes	2 hrs	$200.00	Electrical Engineer[13%]
33	Schematic review meeting	2 hrs	Tue 7/8/14	Tue 7/8/14	NA:32		Fixed Duration	No	2 hrs	$200.00	Electrical Engineer
34	Schematic updates	0.25 days	Tue 7/8/14	Tue 7/8/14	NA:33		Fixed Units	Yes	2 hrs	$200.00	Electrical Engineer
35	PCB Layout	14 days	Tue 7/8/14	Wed 8/16/14	NA		Fixed Duration	No	27 hrs	$1,930.00	
36	Initial layout	2 days	Tue 7/8/14	Thu 7/10/14	NA:30,34		Fixed Units	No	16 hrs	$1,040.00	Layout Tech
37	Layout review	3 days	Thu 7/10/14	Tue 7/15/14	NA:36		Fixed Duration	Yes	3 hrs	$300.00	Electrical Engineer[13%]
38	Layout review meeting	2 hrs	Tue 7/15/14	Tue 7/15/14	NA:37		Fixed Units	Yes	2 hrs	$200.00	Electrical Engineer
39	Layout updates	0.75 days	Tue 7/15/14	Wed 7/16/14	NA:38		Fixed Units	Yes	6 hrs	$390.00	Layout Tech
40	Board Build	16.5 days	Tue 7/8/14	Wed 7/30/14	NA		Fixed Duration	No	6 hrs	$1,230.00	
41	Order components	0.25 days	Tue 7/8/14	Tue 7/8/14	NA:34		Fixed Work	Yes	2 hrs	$30.00	Electrical Engineer[nRF1822 brea...
42	Order PCBs	0.25 days	Wed 7/16/14	Wed 7/16/14	NA:39		Fixed Units	Yes	2 hrs	$380.00	Layout Tech,nRF51822 breakou...
43	Recieve components	0-days	Tue 7/15/14	Tue 7/15/14	NA:41FS+5 days		Fixed Units	Yes	0 hrs	$0.00	
44	Recieve PCBs	0-days	Wed 7/23/14	Wed 7/23/14	NA:42FS+5 days		Fixed Units	Yes	0 hrs	$0.00	
45	Create PCBA kits and initiate PCBA build order	0.25 days	Wed 7/23/14	Wed 7/23/14	NA:44,43		Fixed Units	Yes	2 hrs	$200.00	Electrical Engineer
46	Build PCBAs	5-days	Thu 7/24/14	Wed 7/30/14	NA:45		Fixed Units	Yes	0 hrs	$300.00	nRF51822 breakout board asse...
47	Board Verification	2.25 days	Thu 7/31/14	Mon 8/4/14	NA		Fixed Duration	Yes	24 hrs	$3,400.00	
48	Board checkout	0.25 days	Thu 7/31/14	Thu 7/31/14	NA:45		Fixed Units	Yes	2 hrs	$200.00	Electrical Engineer
49	Board verification effort - hardware	2 days	Thu 7/31/14	Mon 8/4/14	NA:48		Fixed Units	Yes	16 hrs	$1,600.00	Electrical Engineer
50	Board verification effort - software	2 days	Thu 7/31/14	Mon 8/4/14	NA:48		Fixed Units	Yes	16 hrs	$1,600.00	Embedded Software Devel...
51	nRF51822 breakout boards ready for use	0-days	Mon 8/4/14	Mon 8/4/14	NA:49,50		Fixed Units	Yes	0 hrs	$0.00	

FIGURE 12-2. nRF51822 breakout board project plan task list

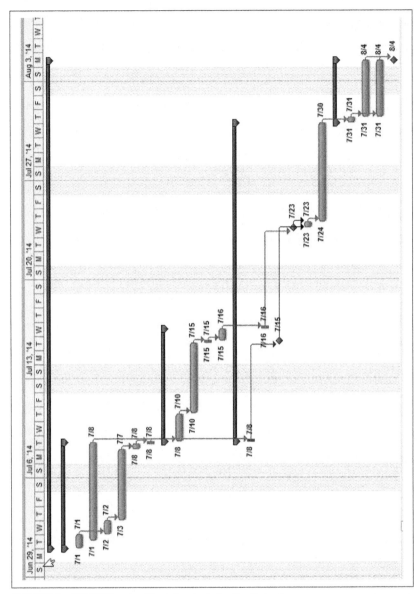

FIGURE 12-3. nRF51822 breakout board project plan Gantt chart

I've also assigned somewhat arbitrary hourly labor rates for the people assigned to tasks, as well as fixed estimates for buying parts and paying for external services (PCB fabrication and PCBA assembly). As can be seen, the software will use this info to calculate costs.

Specifying effort is relatively straightforward (we estimate the number of person-hours or person-days), but specifying resources is a little more interesting. The simplest way to specify a resource is as a generic job title (e.g., Senior Mechanical Engineer). If we have three Senior Mechanical Engineers, we can assign one, two, or all three to a task and the task duration will automatically shorten or lengthen as appropriate. We can also specify fractional efforts, such as that we want 1.5 Senior Mechanical Engineers on a task (e.g., one full-time and one half-time).

If we tell our project planning application that we have three Senior Mechanical Engineers, the application can warn us of times in the project where more than three Senior Mechanical Engineers are scheduled so we can either move things around in the project plan, add extra resources such as contract help, or sweet talk someone into working some overtime.

The application can also arrange tasks for us based on resource availability and other constraints we've added. This is known as *leveling*, and it seeks to prevent overloaded resources. Leveling can be a handy feature, but it can also result in unwelcome surprises. It's important to always review a plan after leveling to make sure nothing's amiss.

We can get even more granular in our effort-driven planning by calling out specific team members as resources instead of generic job titles. This has a number of benefits:

- Of course, no two people are interchangeable. While Deborah, Chris, and Robert might all be Senior Mechanical Engineers, they might have different subspecialties and experiences that make each person particularly suited to tackle different tasks.

- We can configure each team member's individual calendar in the application, which will help keep our project plan estimates accurate. For example, if we schedule a Senior Mechanical Engineer for a task that will take place the last week of April, but the particular engineer we had in mind is Chris and she's on vacation that week, the task will slip. If Chris herself is scheduled for the task and her calendar's been entered into the software, the application will help us to see and mitigate the problem (e.g., perhaps we can move things around so Chris can finish her task before heading out on vacation).

Now that we've walked through some of the mechanics of project planning, let's turn to how we use these mechanics to create a good plan.

First off, planning is guessing. We're guessing at the tasks that need to be done, and at the time each will take. Since our project plans are used to determine cost and timeline, getting the best possible guesses is pretty important. I have a few thoughts to share here:

- Experience matters. People who have been through the process before are much more likely to guess well than those who haven't.

- Get granular, but not too granular. Breaking the project down into bite-sized pieces is helpful as it pushes us to remember all of the little details that add up to significant time. By contrast, if we abstract a group of tasks into a single larger task, there's a tendency to forget about the details and underestimate effort. On the other hand, we don't want to get too crazy and end up managing hundreds of one-hour tasks. In my experience, tasks shorter than half a day or so should be rolled into larger tasks, unless those tasks are specific events that need visibility, such as meetings. The nRF51822 breakout board example earlier is pretty typical of the granularity that I like to work with.

- Don't forget systems engineering and project management activities in the project plan. As a rough guide, I tend to plan on these activities using 15%–20% of the personnel budget. This includes time spent by systems engineers and/or project managers, and also engineers at project meetings such as daily stand-up, sprint planning, and close-out meetings, etc.

- Try to get as many subject matter experts to review the parts of the plan that touch their subjects. Ask them what similar tasks they've needed to do in previous projects, and how long they recall those tasks taking.

- Use historical data where possible. Old project plans are very helpful, particularly if they were updated as work progressed and we can see the real tasks performed and effort expended.

- Be humble. Work hard to create an accurate project plan, but realistically even great project plans will likely be wrong, and most often they'll be optimistic. It's much easier to forget to include a task than to add tasks that are unneeded. Even when highly experienced people develop our project plan, it's realistic to add a 20% contingency factor to the time and cost we arrive at (although management types often chafe at it). If the planners have less experience in general planning or in the specific type of product being developed, it's a good idea to increase the contingency budget and time. In that case, raising them to 50% or more is not unreasonable.

Once our project plan is together and we feel good about it, we'll have an estimate of the project's duration. We can also assign costs to resources—people, materials, and services—and project planning software can generate estimates of total cost as well as how spending will vary over time (e.g., estimated cost for each calendar month), which can be very useful for budgeting.

Estimating duration and budget is only the first use for our project plan. Next, we'll look at how we can use our plans, and other tools and techniques, to actively manage our development effort toward optimal results.

Project Management

Project management is the art and science of keeping projects "on the rails" as they move forward. Much information is available on the science part of this, some of which is called out in this chapter's "Resources" section. Here, we'll just give the briefest of overviews for those who are new to the concept.

We begin detailed development with a project plan, but that project plan (including timing and costs) will be shown to be provably wrong within hours or days of starting out. This is where project managers earn their keep by following a process that's roughly as follows:

1. Checking on actual progress versus the plan.

2. Identifying the gaps between the plan and the reality as known at present (e.g., what do we know now that we didn't before?).

3. Working with the right people to determine the ways in which gaps might be mitigated (stretching durations, adding resources, etc.).

4. Communicating potential mitigations to the right stakeholders and getting agreement on a plan to move forward.

5. Updating the project plan.

6. Communicating this updated plan to (at a minimum) everyone on the team who needs to know it.

This is a more-or-less continuous process throughout development, though it's often broken into discrete blocks of perhaps one week; in other words, the cycle is repeated and an updated project plan is released once a week.

While this description is not inaccurate, it does not begin to do justice to the challenges and importance of good project management. It requires technical chops, an understanding of human psychology, good negotiating and sales skills, tremendous energy, and a long list of acquaintances to draw upon as needed.

Project planning is most challenging and necessary in the largest projects, less of an issue in smaller projects. One interesting debate is around the degree of technical knowledge that a project manager should possess. There's no doubt that serious technical skills are required for good project management. They're needed to help evaluate the progress that's been made and to drive the process of developing mitigations when surprises crop up. In some cases, a nontechnical project manager can rely on technical leads to help as necessary, but in my experience the best results have come when project managers themselves have good technical skills that are respected by technical staff.

As mentioned, one of the keys to project management is acting on new information. Next we'll look at issue tracking, an important part of ensuring that new information is captured and efficiently managed.

Issue Tracking

There's a lot of important information floating around during a development project, and it's easy for important observations, questions, and ideas to be forgotten if there's not a mechanism to capture and address them.

Issue tracking provides a way to capture, consider, and manage any issues that come up during development—bugs, questions, concerns that wake us in the middle of the night, new information, cool ideas for new functions, and so forth. It can serve as a catch-all to ensure that important information of any sort is properly considered and acted upon (or not acted upon if that's determined to be the better course of action).

Figure 12-4 diagrams the top level of a basic issue-tracking scheme. Issues can be entered by anyone (tester, designer/developer, customer-service rep, manager, etc.). On a regular basis, perhaps weekly, a cross-functional team meets to review and classify any new issues. In this case, there are five classifications:

- If the issue is the same as one that's already in the tracking system, the new issue is marked as a duplicate.

- If the issue is not something that should result in further action, it's classified as closed.

- If the issue is a bug, it's classified as such and assigned to the responsible group(s) to be fixed.

- If the issue is a potential new feature, it's assigned to the appropriate group for consideration for the current effort, or perhaps a future effort.

- If there's not enough information for the cross-functional team to make a decision as to whether it's one of the preceding categories, the issue is assigned to the appropriate group for research.

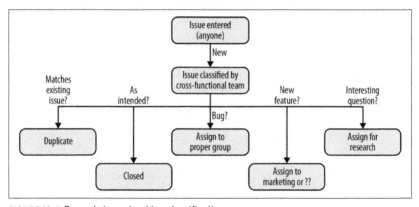

FIGURE 12-4. Example issue-tracking classification

Depending on an issue's classification, there will be more steps to follow (unless the issue has been closed). Figure 12-5 shows what the process might look like for a bug.

Note that these examples are simplistic. Processes in actual use, particularly in larger development efforts, will have more classifications and more steps. For example, there'd be steps to ensure that a bug is reproducible, whether it's significant enough to be worth fixing, how the fix might impact other parts of the system, etc.

One tricky bit about issue tracking is that it needs to be phased in as a development effort progresses. At the beginning of development, for example, it would be silly to track bugs because nothing really works yet —everything's a bug!—but high-level issues such as concerns and questions can be tracked from the start. As the product takes shape, the project team should begin to track lower-level issues as appropriate. As things get close to product release, all anomalies should make it into the system.

A second challenge with issue tracking is that it adds overhead to a project; people need to find time to enter issues, and a team needs to meet regularly to classify issues and so forth. But my own experience is that this is an invaluable exercise that ultimately reduces total effort by getting better information to the right people early on when the cost of addressing issues is relatively low. Another nice benefit is that by formalizing the process and capturing what decisions were made and why, we can reduce the likelihood of having the same discussion over and over again and we can always look back to remind ourselves of what happened.

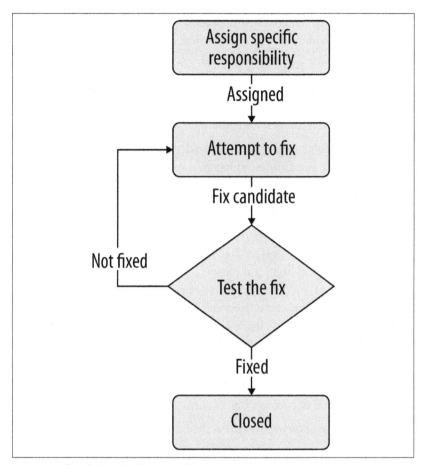

FIGURE 12-5. Bug fix branch of issue-tracking process

Mitigating issues typically involves updating the product, which in turn results in updating source code, schematics, requirements, tests, and other documents. Keeping these documents straight, known as *document control*, so that everyone's (literally) working from the same page, is important. Let's look at this topic next.

DOCUMENT CONTROL

We technologists tend to think of documents as tedious stuff that slows "real" work. While documentation can be tedious, some amount of it is useful and/or necessary. For example, any smart product development effort will result in schematics, source code, and usually mechanical drawings, all of which are documentation. And even in small projects, it's very useful to document certain other things, such as:

- Requirements, so we keep them in mind as we develop.

- Design decisions, so in the future we understand why we did what we did. For example, we don't try to make a design change that was already tried and failed for some nonobvious reason.

- Test procedures (and results) so we don't have to reinvent these as we update our design and need to run tests. Test results also serve to show that tests were performed, which can be helpful, for example, if we ever need to demonstrate that we were careful to make a safe product.

In more-complex projects, all manner of things might get documented for technical and legal reasons. This is particularly true for products in regulated industries such as medical, aerospace, and military, where documentation (objective evidence) of what was done is the only solid way to demonstrate that regulations were followed. Having thousands of pages of documentation is not uncommon for these types of products.

A couple of things that can get tricky as projects get larger are:

- Ensuring that documentation is correct

- Ensuring that everyone on the team has the latest version of the documentation

Document control is the way we achieve these ends. A basic document control process is shown in Figure 12-6.

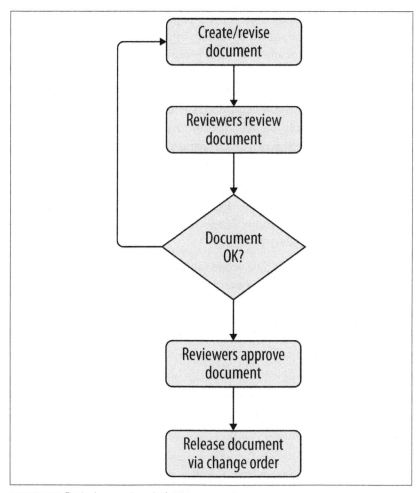

FIGURE 12-6. Basic document control process

The first step, of course, is to create a document. In many cases, a document is assigned a unique ID number at this point to make it easy to refer to in an unambiguous way; for example, SCHEM-003 might be assigned to the third schematic that's been created for a product. The next step is to make sure that the document is agreeable to the appropriate stakeholders, which is accomplished by a review process. If reviewers find any issues in the document that they'd like to see addressed, the document is revised and sent back out for re-review. Once reviewers are OK with the document, they approve it. Approvals are often signed electronically (e.g., via facilities available in Adobe reader or other commercial application) but signing with pen on paper is still common, often followed by scanning the signed document into an electronic copy.

Integral to the document control process is the idea that while many different documents and versions of documents may be floating around, at any one time there is only one set of documents that are "correct." These are known as the *released* documents. In many companies, documents can often only be released by a *change order* (CO) issued in response to a *change request* (CR). Having a CR/CO process slows things down, but it helps in a couple of ways:

- It creates a checkpoint to ensure that the correct process was followed in preparing/approving the document to be released. For example, the person(s) or algorithm that allow a CO can make sure the correct people have reviewed the item.

- COs can include multiple actions that need to occur together when a document is released. For example, if the new document is replacing an older version, the CO should call for the older version to become obsolete. Also, the CO might trigger a notification of the changes to a list of people whose work might be affected by the change(s).

> **TIP** For historical reasons, change requests and change orders are often known as *engineering change requests* (ECRs) and *engineering change orders* (ECOs).

Making sure that users have access to and are using only the released documentation is another aspect of document control. Typically, there is a single spot on the computer network where users can look for all released documents. This could be a folder that actually contains the documents, an internal web page that links to them if they're stored in various places, a software application used for this purpose, or similar. Users should get used to accessing documents from this single spot rather than keeping their own local electronic or paper copies of documents that might become obsolete without their knowledge.

The sophistication and cost of implementing document control can run the gamut, from using networked folders and perhaps a spreadsheet to keep track of what documents (and document numbers) exist, up through using fancy purpose-built applications.

Version control systems (VCSs) used for software code (discussed in Chapter 6) can also work pretty well for document control. I've personally only used Subversion (SVN) for this, but I don't see why other VCSs shouldn't work well either. The downside of using source-code VCSs for document control is that they weren't quite designed for this purpose, so various gotchas will crop up. SVN, for example, doesn't handle access control (read-write versus read-only) on a directory-by-directory basis without some extra effort.

Dedicated document management software applications and online services exist that offer more functionality, such as enforcing workflows (making sure the right people have electronically signed off on a document before allowing it to be released). Microsoft's SharePoint is most commonly used for this purpose, but many others are also available, such as Alfresco, docStar, and others.

At document control's high end lie *product life cycle management* (PLM) and *application lifecycle management* (ALM) applications, such as Oracle's *Agile* and Siemens' *TeamCenter*. As mentioned in Chapter 11, these are general-purpose products and they can be used for much more than document management: for example, they can also track parts lists (BOMs), orders, traceability between requirements and tests, and virtually anything else one can imagine. They're also expensive, and require serious effort to configure and maintain. For complex products and/or large organizations, PLMs can be very helpful: for example, as I write this, my "day job" involves developing a product (a medical device) that has thousands of components, thousands of requirements and specifications, and hundreds of design documents. Keeping track of how all of these bits relate to one another would be almost impossible without a PLM. On the other hand, using a PLM for the MicroPed activity tracker development effort described earlier in this book would add huge overhead complexity with little or no benefit.

Document control is often thought of as subject of its own, and that's how we've looked at it in this section. But document control is just one critical aspect of the larger issue of handling changes in design/development and manufacturing, generically known as *change management*.

Change Management

Change orders are not just for document control: the change request/ change order process is commonly used to change just about anything product-related in product-producing organizations larger than a handful of people. For example, if purchasing wants to change vendors for a 47 µF capacitor used in production, they'll usually need to create a change request asking for this change. Anyone who would be affected by the change (e.g., electronics designer/developers, the purchasing department, manufacturing) would review the request and if they all approve, the change order will issue. This can be a pretty cumbersome and frustrating process to go through just to make a small change, but it also ensures that changes aren't made willy-nilly and result in nasty surprises. An example of a nasty surprise is ordering 47 µF capacitors that cost a penny less but are of a slightly different design that changes other parameters in the device, such as inductance or temperature dependence. Electrical designers/developers should be the ones to determine if the new part is electrically adequate *before it's ordered.*

Final Thoughts

A few friends working together on a bootstrapped project can usually safely skip the "meta" practices discussed in this chapter, aside from doing some minimal project planning. But as products and organizations grow and become more sophisticated, design/development and manufacturing become the sum of many individual efforts, and ensuring that these efforts all work together toward a singular vision instead of becoming a jumble becomes more critical, and more challenging.

Few people enjoy dealing with any of the subjects we've discussed in this chapter. But, like medical care, they exist despite the pain and inconvenience because the alternative is even worse.

The key to making these practices work well is to make them as palatable as possible. Here are a few suggestions:

- Processes and practices should be as lightweight and easy-to-follow as possible. Implement no more than what you're pretty sure will have tangible benefits (no matter what the nice PLM salesperson tells you). Tools should be selected and configured with ease-of-use as a primary goal.

- Work to make processes part of people's regular routines: try to integrate them into activities that should be done anyway. For example, having each software team member mention the task they're working on and percentage completion at daily stand-up meetings tends to be less stressful than weekly visits from a project manager for the purpose of collecting this data.

- Management must account for the time needed to implement these processes. Few things are more frustrating than a schedule getting knocked off course by a process-slowing-things-down issue. Change requests, say for releasing an enclosure design so tooling can be built, can take days to turn into change orders. Either accommodate that time in the project plan or "grease the rails" ahead of issuing the request to speed things up, such as by making sure that approvers won't be on vacation and that they'll have the needed time on their calendars to do a review.

- Create processes that team members respect. Good processes will make sense to team members, particularly if we take the time to explain why they're helpful. Processes that feel like they're imposed by "the suits" or "the quality people" can be a struggle to implement and tend to sap morale. If we can't explain a process in a way that makes team members want to follow it, we should probably reconsider whether we need it at all or whether we should be doing it differently.

Great team members don't automatically turn into an effective team; management and infrastructure are needed. If we motivate rather than coerce, favor a light touch, and make it easy for team members to work well together, a great development effort can come together to produce a wonderful product, coherent but unique, and forged from the skill and creativity of each member.

Resources

Other than the technical parts (i.e., not the psychology) of project management, much of what's covered in this chapter isn't easily learned from books, course, or articles on the web.

The trickiest part of project planning is in creating a reasonably accurate and comprehensive prediction of the tasks to be done and the effort they'll require. This is largely a function of tapping the knowledge of experts who've been successful at development efforts that are similar to what we're contemplating. Software estimation is particularly tricky, and there are a couple of good books I can recommend:

- *The Mythical Man-Month* by Fred Brooks

- *Software Estimation: Demystifying the Black Art* by Scott McConnell

As mentioned in the chapter, software tools can help us structure these tasks in a way that helps predict costs and timelines. I typically use Microsoft Project for this but other offerings are available, including some that are cloud-based. I've heard good things about using Smart-Sheets for project planning, but have not used it yet myself.

The Project Management Institute (*http://www.pmi.org*) (PMI) has done a good job of popularizing and standardizing project management techniques and terminology. PMI's Project Management Book of Knowledge (*http://bit.ly/1OTJp8z*) (PMBOK) Guide is the standard reference here. Another good resource is O'Reilly's *Head-First PMP*. PMI's Project Management Professional (PMP) certification (*http://bit.ly/1OTJtW1*) has become a popular option for project managers.

While reading books and gaining certification for project management are certainly helpful, a bigger part of the challenge is in people skills: how do we properly inform, motivate, reward, beg, and cajole stakeholders to move things forward? These skills tend to come with experience (and bruises), although courses are available, such as from business schools.

In a sense, document management is pretty straightforward: it's about making sure the right people approve documents, and that the right documents are available to the right people. Getting all the details right can be a pain, which is where software tools can help. Microsoft Office and SharePoint (or Microsoft's hosted OneDrive for Business) can be used to implement a reasonable document control system. Other commercial, free, and open source solutions are available, some cloud-based. Alfresco is a popular commercial document management system that's also available as a free "community edition."

Setting up a generalized change management system, in my experience, is where PLM software comes into play. But it's certainly possible to use document management software or even spreadsheets to handle this. The advantage of PLM software is that it can help to automate and enforce the rules around changes. Otherwise, these must be remembered and enforced by team members (and some are better at this than others).

Index

About the Author

Alan Cohen is a software/electronics/systems engineer specializing in medical devices. Since childhood, he's enjoyed working with technology, and (even better!) using it to solve problems. At Cornell, he majored in electrical engineering, minored in neurobiology, and managed to graduate. Since that time he's also done a lot of software engineering, from embedded code to web applications; he's also contributed to or led the development of numerous FDA-regulated products ranging from defibrillators to brain-wave monitors to wearable heart monitors. Alan is currently helping to bring a system to market that kills cancerous tumors by precisely scanning them with a proton beam in three dimensions. Besides writing this book, he has authored articles in several technical publications and a college textbook on computer communications. Alan is also a speaker at technical conferences and holds seven US patents.

Colophon

The cover image is a Steam Engine engraving from iStock. The cover fonts are URW Typewriter and Guardian Sans. The text font is Scala Pro; the heading fonts are URW Typewriter and Benton Sans Condensed; and the code font is Dalton Maag's Ubuntu Mono.

Have it your way.

Get even more for your money.

Join the O'Reilly Community, and register the O'Reilly books you own. It's free, and you'll get:

- $4.99 ebook upgrade offer
- 40% upgrade offer on O'Reilly print books
- Membership discounts on books and events
- Free lifetime updates to ebooks and videos
- Multiple ebook formats, DRM FREE
- Participation in the O'Reilly community
- Newsletters
- Account management
- 100% Satisfaction Guarantee

Signing up is easy:

1. Go to: oreilly.com/go/register
2. Create an O'Reilly login.
3. Provide your address.
4. Register your books.

Note: English-language books only

To order books online:
oreilly.com/store

For questions about products or an order:
orders@oreilly.com

To sign up to get topic-specific email announcements and/or news about upcoming books, conferences, special offers, and new technologies:
elists@oreilly.com

For technical questions about book content:
booktech@oreilly.com

To submit new book proposals to our editors:
proposals@oreilly.com

O'Reilly books are available in multiple DRM-free ebook formats. For more information:
oreilly.com/ebooks

O'REILLY®

CPSIA information can be obtained at www.ICGtesting.com
Printed in the USA
BVOW06s1056140815

413332BV00003B/3/P